# Sources of the Holocaust

*Also by Steve Hochstadt*

Mobility and Modernity: Migration in Germany 1820–1989

# Sources of the Holocaust

Edited by

Steve Hochstadt

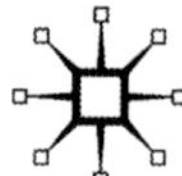



First published 2004 by
PALGRAVE MACMILLAN
Houndmills, Basingstoke, Hampshire RG21 6XS and
175 Fifth Avenue, New York, N. Y. 10010
Companies and representatives throughout the world

PALGRAVE MACMILLAN is the global academic imprint of the Palgrave Macmillan division of St. Martin's Press, LLC and of Palgrave Macmillan Ltd. Macmillan® is a registered trademark in the United States, United Kingdom and other countries. Palgrave is a registered trademark in the European Union and other countries.

ISBN 0–333–96344–X hardback
ISBN 0–333–96345–8 paperback

This book is printed on paper suitable for recycling and made from fully managed and sustained forest sources.

A catalogue record for this book is available from the British Library.

Library of Congress Cataloging-in-Publication Data

Sources of the Holocaust / edited by Steve Hochstadt.
p.cm
Includes bibliographical references abn index.
ISBN 0–333–96344–X (cloth) — ISBN 0–333–96345–8 (pbk.)
1. Holocaust, Jewish (1939–1945)—Germany--Sources. 2. Jews—Persecutions—Germany—Sources. 3. Antisemitism—Germany--History—20th century—Sources. 4. Germany—Politics and government—1933–1945—Sources. 5. World War, 1939–1945—Atrocities—Sources. I. Hochstadt, Steve, 1948–

D804.19.S68 2004
940.53′18—dc22 2003064016

10 9 8 7 6 5 4 3 2 1
13 12 11 10 09 08 07 06 05 04

Transferred to digital printing in 2006.

dedicated to the members of my family who escaped from the Nazis
and to those who did not

Here you stand silently,
but when you turn, do not be silent.

on memorial to murdered Jewish children and Soviet POWs at Bullenhuser Damm, Hamburg

# Contents

*Acknowledgments* xii

**I. Introduction** 1

**II. The Context of Christian Antisemitism** 7

1. Excerpts from the New Testament 9
2. Jewish chronicle of murders in Rhine cities in 1096 during the First Crusade 11
3. Excerpts from Martin Luther, *On the Jews and Their Lies*, 1543 13
4. Papal bull about Jews, 'Cum nimis absurdum' by Pope Paul IV, 14 July 1555 16
5. Excerpts from article 'Jewish Morality' in Vatican newspaper, 10 January 1893 19

**III. The Creation of Monsters in Germany: Jews and Others** 22

6. Bavarian petition opposing equality for Jews, 10 January 1850 23
7. Excerpt from Heinrich von Treitschke, 'Our Views', 1879 26
8. Excerpt from *Permission for the Extermination of Life Unworthy of Life*, 1920 29
9. Court judgment in the murder on 10 August 1932 of a Polish laborer by SA men 32

**IV. The Nazi Attack on Jews and Other Undesirables in the Third Reich, 1933–1938** 36

10. Bavarian state report about the murder of a Jewish businessman, 20 March 1933 37

11. Memoir by Dr Paula Tobias about boycott of 1 April 1933 39
12. Report from underground Social Democratic Party on persecution of German Jews, August 1935 42
13. Nuremberg Law against intermarriage between Jews and German citizens, 15 September 1935 44
14. Form for Jehovah's Witnesses to renounce their religious beliefs, 1936 47
15. Speech by Heinrich Himmler to SS leaders on homosexuality, 18 February 1937 49
16. Children's story from Ernst Hiemer, *The Poisonous Mushroom*, 1938 52

**V. The Physical Assault on Jews in Germany, 1938–1939** 56

17. Memoir by Walter Grab about persecution of Jews in Vienna after the *Anschluss* of March 1938 58
18. Letter urging that Jews be fired from Austrian industry, 29 June 1938 61
19. Letter resisting the confiscation of a Jewish business, 14 July 1938 63
20. Letter confirming possession of Chinese visa, 23 September 1938 65
21. British memorandum on Evian conference, 17 October 1938 67
22. Report of Darmstadt SA on *Kristallnacht*, 11 November 1938 70
23. Letter about finding work in British households for Czech Jewish refugees, 17 November 1938 73
24. Gestapo report from Bielefeld about *Kristallnacht* destruction, 26 November 1938 75
25. Instruction from Foreign Office on eliminating Jews from German life, 25 January 1939 79
26. Instruction from US Secretary of State on preventing refugees to Shanghai, 18 February 1939 83

**VI. The Perfection of Genocide as National Policy, 1939–1943** 85

27. Letter from Reinhard Heydrich planning the 'concentration' of Polish Jews, 21 September 1939 87
28. War diary of Lt. Col. Helmuth Groscurth about massacres of Polish civilians on 7–8 October 1939 90
29. Announcement that Jews in the Lódź region must wear yellow armband, 14 November 1939 93
30. Postwar testimony about the first successful gassing of mentally handicapped on 4 January 1940 95
31. Minutes of conference about deportation of Poles, Jews and Gypsies, 30 January 1940 98

32. Report of meeting of German mayors concerning murder of the handicapped, 3 April 1940 103
33. Memorandum from US State Department on delaying immigration, 26 June 1940 106
34. Table of money saved by murdering the handicapped, 1941 108
35. Report of Einsatzgruppen murders in Soviet Union, 2 October 1941 110
36. German Army orders on the 'Conduct of the Troops in the Eastern Territories', 10 October 1941 112
37. Plan for 'solution of the Jewish question' by mass gassing, 25 October 1941 116
38. Foreign Office memorandum on murder of Jews in Yugoslavia, 25 October 1941 118
39. German Army report on shooting of Jews and Gypsies in Yugoslavia, 27–30 October 1941 121
40. Report on police battalion murder of Jews in Belorussia, 30 October 1941 124
41. Article by Josef Goebbels on Jews in *Das Reich*, 16 November 1941 129
42. Minutes of the Wannsee Conference about the 'final solution', 20 January 1942 132
43. Report on use of trucks to kill Jews with exhaust gas in Soviet Union, 16 May 1942 137
44. Proposal that several million Jews be sterilized for slave labor, 23 June 1942 140
45. Letter from Gestapo ordering deportation of Jews in Schwerin, 6 July 1942 143
46. Report by Gestapo on French-German cooperation on deportation of Jews, 8 July 1942 146
47. Protest of the Bishop of Montauban against deportations in France, 26 August 1942 150
48. Report by Himmler to Hitler on mass murder of 'partisans' in Soviet Union, 29 December 1942 152
49. Gestapo report on deportation of Jews from France, 6 March 1943 154
50. Protest by Bulgarian legislators against deportation of Jews, 17 March 1943 158
51. Order by Himmler to destroy Ukraine, 7 September 1943 161
52. Speech by Himmler to SS Gruppenführer in Posen, 4 October 1943 163
53. Postwar testimony about exhumation and cremation of corpses in 1943–44 166
54. Report by Odilo Globocnik on how death camps were financed, December 1943 170

**VII. 'Arbeit Macht Frei': Work and Death in Concentration Camps and Ghettos** 179

55. Normal murders at Buchenwald in 1941 181
56. Speech by Chaim Rumkowski, Chairman of Lódź Jewish Council, 17 January 1942 183
57. Call for resistance in the Vilna Ghetto, January 1942 186
58. Letter about feeding Soviet POWs working for German industry, 21 February 1942 190
59. Order to Warsaw Jewish Council to organize deportation 'to the East', 22 July 1942 192
60. Diary of Oskar Singer in Lódź Ghetto, 27 July 1942 195
61. Diary of Emanuel Ringelblum in Warsaw Ghetto, 14 December 1942 200
62. Report of SS Concentration Camp Office on mortality of prisoners, 28 December 1942 205
63. SS report on revolt in Warsaw Ghetto, 13 May 1943 208
64. Diary of Hanna Lévy-Hass in Bergen-Belsen, March 1945 211
65. Mauthausen death list, 19 March 1945 214
66. Report of SS doctor on health conditions in Neuengamme, 29 March 1945 218

**VIII. Assembly Lines of Death: Extermination Camps** 222

67. Postwar deposition about the use of gas chambers in Belzec in August 1942 223
68. Memoir by Filip Müller on use of gas chambers at Auschwitz in 1942 227
69. Memoir by Irene Schwarz of Gestapo office work at Birkenau 232
70. Memoir by Shalom Kohn of the revolt in Treblinka on 2 August 1943 235
71. Postwar statement by Arnest Tauber about slave labor at Auschwitz between 1942 and 1944 242
72. Letter by British Foreign Secretary Anthony Eden about bombing Auschwitz, 7 July 1944 246
73. Memoir by Judith Isaacson on selection of women in Auschwitz, July 1944 248
74. List of transports to Birkenau gas chambers during October 1944 253

**IX. The Aftermath** 255

75. London Agreement among Allies about nature of war crimes trial, 8 August 1945 257

76. Summary of evidence from defense witnesses at Nuremberg Trial, August 1946 261
77. West German law to compensate victims of persecution, 29 June 1956 266
78. Statement of Lutherans about Christians and Jews, July 1983 270
79. Speech by Elie Wiesel about President Ronald Reagan's planned visit to Bitburg cemetery, 19 April 1985 273
80. Resolution of the East German Parliament on the Holocaust, 12 April 1990 276

**X. The Holocaust in Contemporary Life** 279

81. Recommendation of Norwegian government to compensate Jews, 26 June 1998 280
82. Article 'In Defense of Hitler' in Egyptian government newspaper, 27 May 2001 285
83. International Tribunal judgement against Radislav Krstić for Srebrenica massacre, 2 August 2001 288
84. Joint resolution of Maine legislature on Holocaust remembrance, 13 March 2002 291

**XI. Conclusion** 294

*Sources* 300

*Bibliography* 307

*Index* 312

# Acknowledgments

An intellectual project encompasses circles of people whose thoughts and labors raise the quality of the final product. Alex Grab of the University of Maine at Orono first suggested this project as a collaboration. When he decided to focus on his research about Napoleon in Italy, I adopted the idea as my own. Other scholars too numerous to mention have inspired, advised, and admonished me as I sought to understand the Holocaust. Several went out of their way to help me. David Kertzer provided his translation of a Vatican document he found. David Hackett and David Wyman sent me copies of documents. Chris Browning offered suggestions of sources I might wish to include. Eric Johnson, a college roommate who likewise turned to German history, has provided both documents and reliable support.

My academic home for 24 years, Bates College and its staff have allowed me to make intellectual labor a life's work. Bates has provided all the support I could have asked for. In particular, I want to thank the interlibrary loan staff at the Ladd Library for bringing a world of books to Lewiston, Maine, and Sylvia Hawks for consistently flawless secretarial work. Francesco Duina, Dolores O'Higgins, and Tom Hayward helped with translations. Administrators can help faculty reach our goals: I thank Donald Harward and Jill Reich for helping to create conditions in which I could complete this book. My colleagues in the History Department form a warm circle within which to do historical work and make friends for life.

The staff at Palgrave Macmillan helped me accomplish the publishing project that I first envisioned many years ago. Terka Acton took seriously my desire to use the format of this book to communicate my understanding of the Holocaust, and Sonya Barker and Brian Morrison ensured that every detail of the text was correct.

I might never have brought myself to teach the Holocaust had it not been for Theodore Zev Weiss of the Holocaust Educational Foundation. Zev has transformed Holocaust education at the college and university level in the United States, and he is now embarked on a similar mission in Europe. I have also received encouragement and financial support from the Dimmer-Bergstrom Fund, the Lucius N. Littauer Foundation, Donald Day and the Memorial Foundation for Jewish Culture, and Bates College.

Teaching the Holocaust has meant that I have met hundreds of students who would not normally take courses in modern European history. Bates students have brought me to learn and relearn terrible facts, to read and speak about the most difficult subjects, to face the Holocaust and decide what I wanted to say about it. A few have helped me directly with this project: I thank Sasha Rickard, Noellyn Davies, Laura McConaghy, Michaela Patterson, and Shelby Graham for their work. The questions, comments, and papers of many hundreds of others have become an integral part of my approach to the Holocaust.

My grandmother Amalia Hochstädt showed me that we can approach an event as enormous as the Holocaust through the narratives of individual lives. Her willingness to tell me her story began my odyssey through the life histories of 100 German-speaking refugees to Shanghai. I learned to see persecution through the eyes of the hunted, who never behaved as the ideology of the master race claimed. The survivors I have met have personalized my understanding of the Holocaust; there were many more than 6 million victims and each story is worth hearing.

My entire academic career has benefitted from a most unusual arrangement. Liz Tobin and I share our job at Bates and the life that we have created around it. For 25 years we have discussed every aspect of intellectual work. I can no longer separate my own inclinations from the lessons I have absorbed from her. Life is better as collaboration.

Steve Hochstadt

The editor and publishers wish to thank the following for permission to use copyright material:

Am Oved Publishers, for the extract from Ber Mark, *The Scrolls of Auschwitz,* trans. Sharon Neemani, p. 215, by permission of Am Oved Publishers;

Augsburg Fortress, for the extracts from Franklin Sherman (ed.), *Luther's Works, Vol. 47*, translated by Martin H. Bertram, pp. 137, 217, 266–75, 292, 305–6, copyright © 1971 Fortress Press, by permission of Augsburg Fortress;

Behrman House Inc., for the material from Lucy S. Dawidowicz (ed.), *A Holocaust Reader*, pp. 334–6, © Behrman House, Inc., reprinted with permission (www.behrmanhouse.com);

Georges Borchardt, Inc., for 'Remarks of Elie Wiesel at the ceremony for Jewish Heritage Week and the presentation of the Congressional Gold Medal, White House, April 19, 1985', by Elie Wiesel, copyright © 1985 by Elie Wiesel, by permission of Georges Borchardt, Inc., Literary Agency;

Humanities Press International, Inc., for the extract from Walter Grab, 'The Jews are Vermin, Except for Grab, My Jewish Classmate', in Jorg Wollenberg (ed.), *The German Public and the Persecution of the Jews* (Amherst, NY: Prometheus Books), pp. 30–3, copyright © 1996 by Humanities Press International, Inc., by permission of Humanities Press International, Inc.;

Ivan R. Dee, Publisher, for the extract from Filip Müller, *Eyewitness Auschwitz: Three Years in the Gas Chambers,* trans. Susanne Flatauer, pp. 35–9, copyright © by Filip Müller, translation copyright © by Routledge & Kegan Paul Ltd, by permission of Ivan R. Dee, Publisher;

Jewish Theological Seminary of America, for the extracts from Kenneth R. Stow (ed.), *Catholic Thought and Papal Jewry Policy, 1555–1593*, 1977, pp. 294–8, by permission of Jewish Theological Seminary of America;

Librairie Arthème Fayard, for the extract from Serge Klarsfeld, *Vichy-Auschwitz: le rôle de Vichy dans la solution finale de la question juive en France – 1942,* p. 364, © Librairie Arthème Fayard, 1983, by permission of Librairie Arthème Fayard;

Lore Shelley, for the extract by Irene Schwarz in Lore Shelley (ed.), *Secretaries of Death: Accounts by Former Prisoners Who Worked in the Gestapo of Auschwitz,* pp. 12–15, by permission of Lore Shelley;

Penguin Putnam Inc. and Penguin Books Ltd, 'Oskar Singer, Sketches', by Oskar Singer, and 'Speech by Chaim Rumkowski, 17 January 1942', by Chaim Rumkowski, from Alan Adelson and Robert Lapides (eds), *Łódź Ghetto: Inside a Community Under Siege*, pp. 206–7, 298–303, copyright © 1989 by The Jewish Heritage Writing Project, by permission of Viking Penguin, a division of Penguin Group (USA) Inc., and Penguin Books Ltd (UK);

Picus Verlag, for extracts from Hans Witek and Hans Safrian (eds), *Und keiner war dabei: Dokumente des alltäglichen Antisemitismus in Wien 1938* (Vienna: Picus Verlag, 1988), pp. 63–4, 108–9, by permission of Picus Verlag;

Princeton University Press and Weidenfeld & Nicholson, for the extract from Tzvetan Todorov, *The Fragility of Goodness: Why Bulgaria's Jews Survived the Holocaust* (Princeton, NJ: Princeton University Press, 2001), pp. 78–80, by permission of Princeton University Press and Weidenfeld & Nicholson;

Sabine Groenewold Verlage, for the extract from Hanna Lévy-Hass, *Vielleicht war das alles erst der Anfang*, edited by Eike Geisel, pp. 54–6, © 1979 Rotbuch Verlag,

Berlin, © Rotbuch/Sabine Groenewold Verlage, Hamburg, by permission of Sabine Groenewold Verlage;

United States Holocaust Memorial Museum, for the extract from Alexander Donat (ed.), *The Death Camp Treblinka: A Documentary*, pp. 224–30, by permission of the United States Holocaust Memorial Museum, Washington, DC, USA;

University of California Press, for the extracts from Robert Chazan, *European Jewry and the First Crusade*, pp. 225, 232–4, copyright © 1987 The Regents of the University of California, by permission of the University of California Press;

University of Illinois Press, for the extract from Judith Magyar Isaacson, *Seed of Sarah: Memoirs of a Survivor*, Second edition, pp. 83–6, copyright © 1990 by Board of Trustees of the University of Illinois, by permission of the University of Illinois Press;

*Vierteljahrshefte für Zeitgeschichte*, for Paul Kluke, 'Der Fall Potempa' *Vierteljahrshefte für Zeitgeschichte*, Vol. 5 (1957), pp. 286–97 and Kurt Gerstein, 'Augenzeugenbericht zu den Massenvergasungen', *Vierteljahrshefte für Zeitgeschichte*, Vol. 1 (1953), pp. 187–93, by permission of *Vierteljahrshefte für Zeitgeschichte*.

Every effort has been made to trace the copyright holders but if any have been inadvertently overlooked the publishers will be pleased to make the necessary arrangement at the first opportunity.

Section I

# Introduction

Why read documents from the Holocaust? What do these details matter now? Contemporary society has become so numbed to violence by its repetition and its constant portrayal, that the Holocaust is sometimes seen as just another historical nightmare, to be acknowledged but also avoided.

For many years two justifications for more public attention to the Holocaust have been strongly voiced. Fighting the lies of deniers and preventing further genocide were powerful reasons to investigate, write, and read, to unearth new information and to examine what is already known. Neither of these reasons retains its former potency. While deniers continue to be loud and active, especially through new electronic media, they have not succeeded in convincing more than a few ideologues, motivated by the same hatreds as the Nazis themselves. In the person of David Irving, as persuasive and knowledgeable as any denier, they have been decisively repudiated in court by the exposure of their claims as deliberately spurious. Irving was unmasked by the prolific historian Richard Evans, who assembled a vast array of documents to demonstrate Irving's lies in a British courtroom.[1]

'Never again' as a wish for humanity and for Jews continues to encourage teaching the Holocaust to young people. I, too, believe that education can hinder genocide and that confrontation with the Holocaust as history is part of a humane education. But the example of the Holocaust has not prevented late 20th-century governments around the world from displaying a repeated willingness to kill their own citizens and their neighbors. Learning about genocide seems inadequate to prevent further killings.

I put forward a third reason to know the Holocaust: as one of the most extraordinary events of human history, we must examine the Holocaust as part of the study of human society, our examination of ourselves. More people may have died in other government-sponsored programs of negative social engineering. Yet the Holocaust stands out, and maybe will always stand out, for its central characteristics: the gradual development of an ideology which justified killing all Jews; the variety of other social groups also targeted for death; the deliberate invention and fastidious organization of efficient procedures of mass murder; and the willingness of its perpetrators to engage in serial killings. Because Germany was such an exemplary modern society, developed an outstanding educational system, and produced an extraordinary culture, its descent into a national program of violence has shaken our faith in the inevitability of progress. The participation of so many people in murder and the capacity of so many more to watch it happen disclose crucial aspects of human society and the modern personality.

No single method of inquiry can adequately understand the place of the Holocaust in modern life. Nearly every discipline has been affected by the knowledge about the Holocaust provided by eyewitnesses and historians, and each uses its chosen tools and attitudes to respond. For example, psychologists have made repeated attempts to investigate the elements of the modern personality which might have contributed to the willingness of individuals to inflict so much suffering on strangers.[2]

Historians respond by emphasizing documents, in the broadest sense, as the source of further knowledge and the basis for all understanding. Historical interpretations are judged by their relationship to documentary evidence. Historians work at two sometimes antithetical tasks: constructing interpretations which best fit the known documents and finding more documents which have not been analyzed.

There are already more Holocaust documents available than any person could read in a lifetime. Yad Vashem in Jerusalem estimates that it possesses 55 million pages of unpublished documents; major archives, such as the US Holocaust Memorial Museum, keep growing, and unknown documents are discovered every year.[3] Vast collections of documents are available, which helped me to choose this small sample. I publish here only a small portion of what I have seen, a collection designed to provoke further reading.

The importance of documents can be illustrated by a central question which has divided historians: who ordered the Holocaust and when was that order given? For decades Adolf Hitler was the focus of these questions. Few of history's dictators have been so proud of the idea that their will alone ruled vast territories. In *Mein Kampf*, written while he was in prison in 1923–1924, Hitler declared that absolute dictatorship was Germanic destiny; he insisted that he was the long-awaited savior of Aryan racial superiority.[4] Yet historians have searched in vain since the end of World War II for a document in which Hitler explicitly orders genocide.

A Hitler order would shed crucial light into the murky world of Nazi decision-making. It appears, however, that no such order will be found, since Hitler preferred to conceal his actions behind bombastic speech-making and vague oral commands to his subordinates, who then fought each other for authority. In that absence, two schools of interpretation have developed, based partially on differing claims about when and by whom the decision for the Holocaust was initiated.[5] So-called functionalists argue that the steady intensification of persecution, including murder, led to genocide without a previously decisive intention. Intentionalists counter that Hitler's announced desire to get rid of the Jewish race, supported by many willing helpers, was the critical motor of genocidal actions. Both sides in this argument deploy interpretations of documents to support their contentions.

Because I believe that familiarity with original sources should inform every judgment about the Holocaust, I have prepared this collection for a wide general audience. Some well known documents, like the Nuremberg Law for the Protection of German Blood and German Honor (document 13), appear here because they speak to the reader of significant moments. Other sources came to official notice after the war in preparation for the Nuremberg trials, but have remained unfamiliar, such as Viktor Brack's proposal to sterilize millions of Jews (document 44). Some have recently been discovered or translated by historians, such as the Bulgarian protest against deportations (document 50). Read together, these sources should complete the most direct portrayal of the Holocaust that is feasible in one volume.

Some possible themes are not represented in this collection by specific documents. It would take many volumes to convey the richness of the Jewish life in Europe which was wiped out, but I have chosen not to do that here. The appeal of National Socialism to ordinary Germans or the development of Adolf Hitler's peculiar fanaticisms are not addressed. Hitler himself remains in the background in this book. The reader seeking more information about him has no shortage of choices. Many historians and many others have clearly explained his personal role in announcing, creating, and leading the Holocaust, although some intriguing elements of his personal life remain uncertain.[6] I wish to draw attention to many other participants, from Heinrich Himmler to Viktor Brack and Odilo Globocnik, whose roles were also crucial.

Half of the documents in this volume come out of the Holocaust itself, the intensely and intently murderous period from 1939 through 1945. That selection could be multiplied many times, but still would not touch on all the issues, events, or persons that historians think are significant. The central and longest section, the 28 documents in Section VI about killing people, mostly Jews, displays the themes which governed my choices. I wished to draw attention to the sheer breadth of the event we call the Holocaust. Killing and decisions about killing were carried out in every corner of the continent, and I include documents from France and Bulgaria, Yugoslavia and Ukraine. Eastern Europe is at the center, and the United States appears only once, at the periphery, where it remained until 1945. The geography of the Holocaust varied across regions and borders, city and countryside, time and culture. I chose here to stress the unifying forces and experiences which characterized the killing period.

The other half of the sources in this collection are sprinkled through the last two thousand years. I became a historian because I shared this discipline's fundamental belief that any phenomenon, however large or small, is embedded in its own history. Although concentrated in a brief period, the Holocaust looms in modern history as a central event, not because historians study it, but because its presence is felt in so many places. Those who practice history seek antecedents and causes in human society, sometimes arguing that events can be connected over the centuries. The first three sections of documents present three overlapping contexts within which the Holocaust developed: the long history of Christian antisemitism, the development among Germans of a vicious and public hatred for Jews during the 19th century, and the rapid escalation of attacks on political and biological enemies by the Nazi state after 1933.

As the Holocaust recedes in time, it has seemed to increase in significance. In most countries of Europe and North America, but also in many countries throughout the world, more attention is paid to the Holocaust than at any time since 1945. Modern society continues to generate voluntary organizations which link the Holocaust to their unique concerns. The final two sections present a few hints about the role played by knowledge of the Holocaust in contemporary political life.

How should one read these documents? Although I have shortened many of these documents, I have not tried to present only the key words or paragraphs. The combination of banal details and discussions of genocide is a characteristic of Nazi communications which I have preserved here. Reading documents requires careful attention to words and tone, to the interests of the writer, to the intended audience. A document's meaning often is revealed only by relating it to other documents, by wondering at the choice of language, by seeing what was not said. If we are to reconstruct the behavior and ideas of complex human actors from a few words on paper, then we must work hard at their reading.

The language of Nazi documents, especially about Jews, is peculiarly dichotomous. Public propaganda in Germany was vivid and vicious, as in documents 16 and 41. Official state plans, such as documents 27 and 42, used a very different language in addressing mass murder: bloodless vocabulary, passive voice, formulaic constructions, euphemistic descriptions. The deliberate Nazi invention of a new German dialect to obscure the reality of their deeds makes the reading of their documents especially difficult. In his manual on the interpretation of Holocaust documents, the dean of Holocaust studies, Raul Hilberg, pays particular attention to Nazi style.[7] This manner of discussing killing is one clue to what the Nazis thought about what they were doing.

I have chosen to do my own translations from the German originals where possible. I have found that existing translations frequently display arbitrary distortions of the original texts: not merely unsuitable words chosen to represent the original, but also omissions of phrases, changes in sentence structure, alterations of word order. Some translations were done in great haste, such as the Army translations of captured documents in preparation for the Nuremberg trials. Others may have introduced these changes for aesthetic reasons. I believe that such changes ultimately distort the meaning of the text and the intent of the author. My efforts at providing more accurate translations are meant to display as much as possible the precise linguistic choices, grammatical structures, even tone and cadence of the original sources. Few of these writers were accomplished prose stylists, but they all had a style of their own, influenced by their situation and intent. I have tried to minimize the inevitable loss of translation, to allow the writing styles of these authors to help the reader understand their purposes and attitudes. I have reproduced their efforts to use format, spacing, underlining, and capitalization to convey their messages.

I have placed short commentaries after each document, which taken together provide an outline of the Holocaust. The reader should first confront the documents as they are and seek the meanings they contain. The commentaries are designed to offer context and information rather than prescriptions for reading. I hope that the commentaries will bring the reader back to the document again, for a second or third reading. Many of these documents continued to yield insight for me long after I had become intimately familiar with their contents. Historians understand the labor of interpretation as extending over years, involving both conscious inquiry and subconscious rumination. Every careful reader can participate in this human drive to understand and explain.

My commentaries reflect my own historically produced idiosyncracies. My family's connection to the Holocaust was in open view as I grew up, in the form of Chinese sculptures, notably sitting Buddhas, that my Viennese grandparents brought back from their exile in Shanghai after the war. I was aware and proud of my father's ability to speak flawless English after his arrival as a refugee in the United States. I also avoided facing the Holocaust. Only as an adult did I realize how much the Holocaust meant in their lives and in mine. By that time my thought process had been disciplined by the study and teaching of history. So that is how I have approached the Holocaust, channeling sadness and anger into an effort to deepen and spread knowledge. This effort alleviates some of the pain of knowing and some of the frustration at the difficulty of changing human culture.

There are many groups of victims here. Jews are the most prominent; they are accompanied by Gypsies, homosexuals, the handicapped, Jehovah's Witnesses, Orthodox Russians, and Catholic Poles. The killers made careful distinctions among the objects of their violence, but killed them with the same methods in the same places. I hope that this approach makes visible the differences in their treatment, while highlighting the broad ideology which envisioned mass murder as the correct method for dealing with all of these groups. In this book, the Holocaust encompasses the killing of many millions of unarmed men, women, and children, in which Jews were the most significant target.

Even after decades of study, I am still shocked at the humanly constructed ideas expressed in these sources. I cannot imagine coming to the end of this book without more questions, which can only be answered by seeing more documents. There are so many gaps in the coverage and hints about what is missing. This book is not meant to be the last word on any subject or to prove anything. I have tried to illustrate and exemplify, not demonstrate or debate. This book is most useful as part of a broader program of reading memoirs, watching videotaped interviews, talking with survivors, and absorbing historical scholarship. I hope that it meets our need to learn more about how and why men in Germany wanted to kill and then killed so many men and women, war veterans and children, pregnant women and infants, and kept on killing until they were forced to stop.

## Notes

1 Richard Evans, *Lying about Hitler: History, Holocaust, and the David Irving Trial* (New York: Basic Books, 2001).

2 The psychologist Stanley Milgram made an extremely disturbing film about his experiments, in which he duped volunteers into thinking they were delivering potentially fatal shocks to other volunteers: Stanley Milgram, *Obedience* (University Park, PA: Pennsylvania State University, 1969).

3 For example, in 1997, documents were found that showed that banks in Brazil and the Federal Reserve Bank of New York had taken possession of assets stolen from Holocaust victims: *The Holocaust Chronicle* (Lincolnwood, IL: Publications International, Ltd.: 2001), p. 694.

4 In an accessible paperback version, Adolf Hitler, *Mein Kampf*, trans. Ralph Manheim (Boston, MA: Houghton Mifflin, 1971), for example on p. 443.

5 An example of how the selection of a particular date for the decision is connected to a broader interpretation of Nazi policy is given by Eberhard Jäckel in 'The Holocaust: Where We Are, Where We Need to Go', in Michael Berenbaum and Abraham J. Peck (eds), *The Holocaust and History: The Known, the Unknown, the Disputed, and the Reexamined* (Bloomingon, IN: Indiana University Press, 1998), p. 23–9.

6 A combination of a fascination with evil and the impulse to sell may be the reason that unlikely arguments about Hitler attract so much attention: Hitler was partly Jewish, Hitler was gay, Hitler was a sexual pervert. Less exciting, but much more useful is the best recent biography by Ian Kershaw in two volumes, *Hitler 1889–1936: Hubris* and *Hitler 1936–1945: Nemesis* (New York: W.W. Norton, 1999 and 2000).

7 Raul Hilberg, *Sources of Holocaust Research: An Analysis* (Chicago: Ivan R. Dee, 2001). The particular use of the German language by Nazis was addressed by Victor Klemperer, the Jewish philologist who survived in Dresden, in a 1957 book, now available in English as *The Language of the Third Reich: LTI – Lingua Tertii Imperii: A Philologist's Notebook*, trans. Martin Brady (London: Continuum, 2002). Very useful to me for translation was Robert Michael and Karin Doerr, *Nazi-Deutsch / Nazi-German: An English Lexicon of the Language of the Third Reich* (Westport, CN: Greenwood Press, 2002).

Section II

# The Context of Christian Antisemitism

Within the long history of Western Christianity, antisemitism has played a significant but changing role in relations between Christians and Jews. I have chosen a handful of documents which recognize the influence of certain forms of antisemitism on the history of Jews in Europe. Antisemitism is only one facet of the Christian tradition of doctrine and practice. A few documents cannot tell the history of even this single element, but they can illustrate key points in the development of Christian attitudes toward Jews during nearly 2000 years of coexistence in Europe.

The relationship between Jews and Christians evolved in the Near East, where monotheistic religions struggled under persecution and isolation. Despite their common position as targets of the hostility of political rulers, Christians and Jews increasingly diverged, as they competed for the minds of those around them and sometimes struggled against each other for political opportunities. The brilliance and humanity of their religious worldviews shared the wealth of the Old Testament. But the ideas and claims of the New Testament, revered as the word of God by Christians and ignored as profoundly mistaken by Jews, divided them bitterly.

Parts of the New Testament reflect the antagonism from the Christian side. Because Christianity came to dominate European society, while Judaism remained a dispersed minority, Christian attitudes and ideas about Jews were spread vigorously across Europe into every human settlement. Christians of all classes, educational attainments, religious beliefs, and political ideologies accepted some form of these strongly negative images of Jews.

The presence of these ideas in the text of the New Testament does not alone demonstrate that Christianity inevitably incorporates antisemitism. There are many ideas contained in both the Old and New Testaments which have since been repudiated by the Judeo-Christian tradition. Not every attitude expressed in these holy works was adopted as a cultural assumption. Antisemitism persisted as the core of Christian understanding of Jews because it was preached and understood as correct Christian doctrine on the highest authority.

Jews and Christians nevertheless inhabited the Mediterranean world for 1000 years without significant physical conflict. As Christianity spread from Southern Europe to the edges of the continent, Jews were tolerated as a minority from Spain and England to Poland and Greece. At the moment of the Crusades, when European Christians were excited about the prospect of regaining the Holy Land and defeating religious rivals, toleration turned to mass violence. Since then violence against Jews has repeatedly surfaced, sometimes localized, occasionally spread across large regions. A Russian word, *pogrom*, meaning destruction, was incorporated into Yiddish. Until the 20$^{th}$ century, this word sufficed to name these threats to the security of Jewish life in Europe.

# 1. Excerpts from the New Testament

The Gospel According to St. Matthew 27.20–22, 24–26:

But the chief priests and elders persuaded the multitude that they should ask Barabbas, and destroy Jesus. The governor answered and said unto them, Whether of the twain will ye that I release unto you? They said, Barabbas. Pilate saith unto them, What shall I do then with Jesus which is called Christ? They all say unto him, Let him be crucified. And the governor said, Why, what evil hath he done? But they cried out the more, saying, Let him be crucified....

When Pilate saw that he could prevail nothing, but that rather a tumult was made, he took water, and washed his hands before the multitude, saying, I am innocent of the blood of this just person; see ye to it. Then answered all the people, and said, His blood be on us, and on our children. Then released he Barabbas unto them: and when he had scourged Jesus, he delivered him to be crucified.

The Gospel According to St. John 8.42–47:

Jesus said unto them [the Jews], If God were your Father, ye would love me: for I proceeded forth and came from God; neither came I of myself, but he sent me. Why do ye not understand my speech? even because ye cannot hear my word. Ye are of your father the devil, and the lusts of your father ye will do. He was a murderer from the beginning, and abode not in the truth, because there is no truth in him. When he speaketh a lie, he speaketh of his own: for he is a liar and the father of it. And because I tell you the truth, ye believe me not. Which of you convinceth me of sin? And if I say the truth, why do ye not believe me? He that is of God heareth God's words: ye therefore hear them not, because ye are not of God.

The Revelation of St. John the Divine 2.9, 3.7, 3.9:

[Jesus instructs John to write to the angel of the church in Smyrna]
I know thy works, and tribulation, and poverty (but thou art rich) and I know the blasphemy of them which say they are Jews, and are not, but are the synagogue of Satan....

And to the angel of the church in Philadelphia write ...
Behold, I will make them of the synagogue of Satan, which say they are Jews, and are not, but do lie; behold, I will make them to come and worship before thy feet, and to know that I have loved thee.

---

These passages from the New Testament present a portrait of Jews expounded as holy text. The passage from the Gospel According to St. Matthew occurs in the first pages of the New Testament. Jewish leaders are portrayed as demanding the death of Jesus and mocking him on the cross. In the Gospel According to St. John, Jesus argues that Jews who do not believe in him are not proper children of Abraham. Later, in John 18.35, Pilate, the Roman governor of the Holy Land, says that 'Thine own nation' delivered Jesus to him for death, and in John 19, Jews are again depicted as urging the death of Jesus by crucifixion.

These quotations express several of the key antisemitic ideas of Christian theology. The sole responsibility of the Jews for the death of Jesus is emphasized, while the idea that Jews would be tainted for all time by this murder of the son of God is attributed to the Jews themselves. Jesus himself claims that Jews are the spawn of Satan, one of the staples of Christian teachings for nearly 2000 years.

Jewish rejection of Jesus as the Messiah prophesied in the Torah denied the basis of the new Christian doctrines. John Chrysostom, one of the leading Christian proselytizers of the fourth and fifth centuries, recognized the theological incompatibility of his beliefs with Judaism and drew the most dire conclusions: 'If the Jewish rites are holy and venerable, our way of life must be false. But if our way is true, as indeed it is, theirs is fraudulent.' He argued that since God hates Jews, Christians who love God must also hate Jews.

A particular conception of Jews was developed by early Christian leaders, written into the New Testament, and preached broadly. Official church councils developed rules which punished Christians for normal social interactions with their Jewish neighbors. By the time that the Emperor Constantine legalized Christianity in the Roman Empire in 313, he could call Judaism an 'abominable sect' and forbid any of his citizens to marry a Jew or attend Jewish services.

# 2. Jewish chronicle of murders in Rhine cities in 1096 during the First Crusade

I shall begin the account of the former persecution. May the Lord protect us and all Israel from persecution.

It came to pass in the year one thousand twenty-eight after the destruction of the Temple that this evil befell Israel. There first arose the princes and nobles and common folk in France, who took counsel and set plans to ascend and to rise up like eagles and to do battle and to clear a way for journeying to Jerusalem, the Holy City, and for reaching the sepulcher of the Crucified, a trampled corpse who cannot profit and cannot save for he is worthless. They said to one another: "Behold we travel to a distant land to do battle with the kings of that land. We take our souls in our hands in order to kill and to subjugate all those kingdoms that do not believe in the Crucified. How much more so the Jews, who killed and crucified him." They taunted us from every direction. They took counsel, ordering that either we turn to their abominable faith or they would destroy us from infant to suckling. They – both princes and common folk – placed an evil sign upon their garments, a cross, and helmets upon their heads....

It came to pass that, when the saintly ones, the pious of the Almighty, the holy community in Mainz, heard that some of the community of Speyer had been killed and the community of Worms twice, then their spirit collapsed and their hearts melted and turned to water. They cried out to the Lord and said: "Ah Lord God of Israel! Are you wiping out the remnant of Israel? Where are all your wondrous deeds about which our ancestors told us, saying: 'Truly the Lord brought you up from Egypt.' But now you have abandoned us, delivering us into the hands of the gentiles for destruction." Then all the leaders of Israel gathered from the community and came to the archbishop and his ministers and servants and said to them: "What are we to do with regard to the report which we have heard concerning our brethren in Speyer and Worms who have been killed?" They said to them: "Heed our advice and bring all your moneys into our treasury and into the treasury of the archbishop. Then you and your wives and your children and all your retinue bring into the courtyard of the archbishop. Thus will you be able to be saved from the crusaders." They contrived and gave this counsel in order to surrender us and to gather us up and to seize us like fish enmeshed in a fatal net. In addition, the archbishop gathered his ministers and servants – exalted ministers, nobles and grandees – in order to assist us and to save us from the crusaders. For at the outset it was his desire to save us, but ultimately he failed....

It came to pass on the new moon of Sivan that the wicked Emicho – may his bones be ground up on iron millstones – came with a large army outside the city, with crusaders and common folk. For he also said: "It is my desire to go on the crusade." He was our chief persecutor. He had no mercy on the elderly, on young men and young women, on infants and sucklings, nor on the ill. He made the people of the Lord like dust to be trampled. Their young men he put to the sword and their pregnant women he ripped open. They camped outside the city for two days....

---

In 1096, bands of Crusaders on their way to Jerusalem slaughtered the Jewish communities of Worms, Mainz and Cologne, massacring perhaps several thousand people. A number of separate groups, espousing the radical crusading ideology described in the above account, attacked Jews in Spain, Eastern France, the Rhineland, Prague, and finally around Jerusalem. Count Emicho of Leinengen led the attacks in the Rhineland. Both religious and secular rulers tried to restrain these armies and protect Jews in their territories, but not always with success. During the Second Crusade in 1146, Jewish communities in the Rhine cities were attacked again. The Jewish chronicler also expresses here extremely disdainful attitudes toward Christianity and Christ. Jews, however, did not advocate violence against their Christian neighbors.

This was the first significant outburst of popular violence of Christians against Jews. Although widespread violence did not occur again until the 14th century, Christian attitudes toward the Jews who lived among them became more extreme in the later Middle Ages. A set of legends about Jews seeking to kill Christians developed and spread across Europe. Jews were depicted as kidnapping and murdering Christian children for religious rites, as secretly trying to kill Christ again by stabbing the Host, as poisoning wells, and as generally being in league with the Devil.

The protection against physical persecution offered by religious and lay leaders also diminished after the Crusades, as they recognized that popular antisemitism pressured them to take stronger actions against Jews. Between 1290 and 1492, Jews were politically expelled from the kingdoms of England and France, from many of the smaller German states and cities, and finally from Spain. Although Jews were later allowed to return to all of these countries, their migratory search for secure permanent residence eventually led to the development in Eastern Europe of the world's largest concentration of Jews.

## 3. Excerpts from Martin Luther, *On the Jews and Their Lies*, 1543

I had made up my mind to write no more either about the Jews or against them. But since I learned that these miserable and accursed people do not cease to lure to themselves even us, that is, the Christians, I have published this little book, so that I might be found among those who opposed such poisonous activities of the Jews and who warned the Christians to be on their guard against them....

... dear Christian, be advised and do not doubt that next to the devil, you have no more bitter, venomous, and vehement foe than a real Jew, who earnestly seeks to be a Jew.... Therefore the history books often accuse them of contaminating wells, of kidnapping and piercing children, as for example at Trent, Weissensee, etc....

... they hold us Christians captive in our own country. They let us work in the sweat of our brow to earn money and property while they sit behind the stove, idle away the time, fart, and roast pears. They stuff themselves, guzzle, and live in luxury and ease from our hard-earned goods. With their accursed usury they hold us and our property captive. Moreover, they mock and deride us because we work and let them play the role of lazy squires at our expense and in our land. Thus they are our masters and we are their servants, with our property, our sweat, and our labor. And by way of reward and thanks they curse our Lord and us! Should the devil not laugh and dance if he can enjoy such a fine paradise at the expense of us Christians? He devours what is ours through his saints, the Jews, and repays us by insulting us, in addition to mocking and cursing both God and man....

So we are even at fault in not avenging all this innocent blood of our Lord and of the Christians which they shed for three hundred years after the destruction of Jerusalem, and the blood of the children they have shed since then (which still shines forth from their eyes and their skin). We are at fault in not slaying them. Rather we allow them to live freely in our midst despite all their murdering, cursing, blaspheming, lying, and defaming; we protect and shield their synagogues, houses, life, and property. In this way we make them lazy and secure and encourage them to fleece us boldly of our money and goods, as well as to mock and deride us, with a view to finally overcoming us, killing us all for such a great sin, and robbing us of all our property...

What shall we Christians do with this rejected and condemned people, the Jews? ... I shall give you my sincere advice:

First, to set fire to their synagogues or schools and to bury and cover with dirt whatever will not burn, so that no man will ever again see a stone or cinder of them....

Second, I advise that their houses be razed and destroyed. For they pursue in them the same aims as in their synagogues. Instead they might be lodged under a roof or in a barn, like the gypsies....

Third, I advise that all their prayer books and Talmudic writings, in which such idolatry, lies, cursing, and blasphemy are taught, be taken from them.

Fourth, I advise that their rabbis be forbidden to teach henceforth on pain of loss of life and limb....

Fifth, I advise that safe-conduct on the highways be abolished completely for the Jews. For they have no business in the countryside, since they are not lords, officials, tradesmen, or the like. Let them stay at home....

Sixth, I advise that usury be prohibited to them, and that all cash and treasure of silver and gold be taken from them and put aside for safekeeping....

Seventh, I recommend putting a flail, an ax, a hoe, a spade, a distaff, or a spindle into the hands of young, strong Jews and Jewesses and letting them earn their bread in the sweat of their brow, as was imposed on the children of Adam....

When you lay eyes on or think of a Jew you must say to yourself: Alas, that mouth which I there behold has cursed and execrated and maligned every Saturday my dear Lord Jesus Christ, who has redeemed me with his precious blood; in addition, it prayed and pleaded before God that I, my wife and children, and all Christians might be stabbed to death and perish miserably. And he himself would gladly do this if he were able, in order to appropriate our goods. Perhaps he has spat on the ground many times this very day over the name of Jesus, as is their custom, so that the spittle still clings to his mouth and beard, if he had a chance to spit....

I wish and I ask that our rulers who have Jewish subjects exercise a sharp mercy toward these wretched people, as suggested above, to see whether this might not help (though it is doubtful). They must act like a good physician who, when gangrene has set in, proceeds without mercy to cut, saw, and burn flesh, veins, bone, and marrow. Such a procedure must also be followed in this instance. Burn down their synagogues, forbid all that I enumerated earlier, force them to work, and deal harshly with them, as Moses did in the wilderness, slaying three thousand lest the whole people perish.... If this does not help we must drive them out like mad dogs, so that we do not become partakers of their abominable blasphemy and all their other vices and thus merit God's wrath and be damned with them. I have done my duty. Now let everyone see to his. I am exonerated....

My essay, I hope will furnish a Christian (who in any case has no desire to become a Jew) with enough material not only to defend himself against the blind, venomous Jews, but also to become the foe of the Jews' malice, lying, and cursing, and to understand not only that their belief is false but that they are surely possessed by all devils. May Christ, our dear Lord, convert them mercifully and preserve us steadfastly and immovably in the knowledge of him, which is eternal life. Amen.

---

So ends the longest treatise that Luther wrote about Jews. These short excerpts from the book *On the Jews and Their Lies* (1543) offer a clear synopsis of his attitudes toward Jews. While he had at times written about Jews with much more tolerance, hoping to convince them to convert to his reformed version of Christianity, his earliest lectures offered much the same view of Jews as displayed here. In a letter to his wife, also in 1543, he claimed that he contracted an illness because of the Jews in a town he travelled through.

Luther summarizes the common medieval religious and social prejudices about Jews which were generally accepted by Christians and promoted by the official teachings of the Catholic Church. Luther adds socioeconomic resentments to the conventional religious prejudices, foreshadowing the changed antisemitism of the modern age. Jews are rich and lazy, while Germans do honest work. Luther also attacks Catholics and Moslems as infidels, unbelievers, and generally evil people, but only Jews are singled out as the murderers of Christians. That powerful charge, that Jews kill Christians, is repeated four times in these passages, and serves as the justification for Luther's call to eliminate the Jews entirely, through a combination of conversion, expulsion, and murder.

The medieval folklore about Jews which Luther accepted and promulgated was made visible and concrete on an outside corner of Luther's church in Wittenberg by a carving of small human figures suckling on a pig, symbolizing beliefs about the *Judensau*, the Jewpig, dirty, foul-smelling, less than human. Although many of Luther's Protestant contemporaries were dismayed by his violent attack on Jews, a number of princes took his counsel and revoked existing rights of Jews in their territories.

These and other passages from Luther's book on the Jews were liberally cited in Nazi educational and propaganda materials in the 1930s, to show that the great figures of German intellectual and religious history shared the Nazi viewpoint about Jews.

# 4. Papal bull about Jews, 'Cum nimis absurdum' by Pope Paul IV, 14 July 1555

Laws and Ordinances to be observed by Jews
living in the Ecclesiastical State

Bishop Paul, the servant of the servants of God,
for the future and memory of this matter

Since it is exceedingly absurd and improper that Jews, whose own guilt has consigned them to perpetual servitude, under the pretext that Christian piety receives them and tolerates their presence, should be so ungrateful to Christians, that instead of gratitude they return arrogance to them, and they seek to exchange the servitude they owe to Christians for dominion over them; we, to whose notice it has lately come that these same Jews, in our dear city and in some other cities, holdings, and territories of the Holy Roman Church, have erupted into insolence, so that they presume not only to dwell side by side with Christians and near their churches, with no distinction of attire intervening, but also to erect homes in the better known sections and streets of the cities, holdings and territories where they dwell, and to buy and possess fixed property, and to have nurses, housemaids, and other hired Christian servants, and to perpetrate sundry other things in ignominy and contempt of the Christian name, considering that the Roman Church tolerates these same Jews as testimony of the true Christian faith and to the end that they, led by the piety and kindness of the Apostolic See, should at length recognize their errors, and make all haste to arrive at the true light of the Catholic faith, and thereby to agree that, as long as they persist in their errors, they should recognize through experience that they have been made slaves while Christians have been made free through Jesus Christ, God and our Lord, and that it is iniquitous that the children of the free woman should serve the children of the maid-servant –

1. Desiring to make sound provisions as best we can, with the help of God, in the above manner, we sanction by this our perpetually valid constitution that, among other things, in all future times in this city, as in all other cities, holdings, and territories belonging to the Roman church, all Jews should live solely in one and the same location, or if that is not possible, in two or three or as many as are necessary, which are to be contiguous and

separated completely from the dwellings of Christians. These places are to be designated by us in our city and by our magistrates in the other cities, holdings, and territories. And they should have one entry alone, and so too one exit.

2. And in the individual cities, holdings, and territories where they dwell, they should have one synagogue alone in its customary location, and they may construct no new synagogue. Nor may they possess any real property. Accordingly, they must demolish and destroy all their synagogues except for this one alone. The real property which they now possess, they must sell to Christians within a period of time designated by the local magistrates.

3. And so that they be identified everywhere as Jews, men and women are respectively required and bound to wear in full view a hat or some obvious marking, both to be blue in color, in such a way that they may not be concealed or hidden....

4. [And they shall not] have nurses or serving women or any other Christians serving them, of whatever sex. Nor shall they have their children wet-nursed or reared by Christian women.

5. Nor may they themselves or anyone in their employ labor in public on Sundays or other feast days declared by the Church....

7. Nor should they be so presumptuous as to entertain or dine with Christians or to develop close relations and friendships with them....

9. Additionally, these Jews may carry on no business as purveyors of grain, barley, or other items necessary for human sustenance, but must be limited to dealing only in second-hand clothing ...

10. As for those among them who are physicians, even if they are summoned and requested, they may not come forth and attend to the care of Christians....

Given at Rome at St. Mark's, in the year of the Incarnation of the Lord one thousand five hundred fifty-five, on the day before the Ides of July, in the first year of our pontificate.

---

The Papal bull 'Cum nimis absurdum' of 1555, expressed by Pope Paul IV in angry words much like those of Luther a decade earlier, established the official policy of the Roman Catholic Church toward Jews for the next three centuries. While none of these restrictions were unprecedented, enforced together they represented a significant new level of persecution of Jews in northern Italy. Based on the model of the ghetto first established in Venice in 1516, Rome's Jews are confined to 'one and the same location', separate from all

Christians. This separation was also to be enforced visually, symbolized by the blue marking to be worn at all times.[1]

The theological justification for this persecution is contained in the first paragraph: 'to the end that they ... should at length recognize their errors'. But the expansion beyond religion into economics is also clear, both in the theological justification and the new restrictions. For the insolence of living well, Jews were severely constrained to second-class urban trades. The policies of Paul IV and other 16th-century Popes were designed to force the mass conversion of Jews, as prophesied in the New Testament. This bull was lenient compared to the pronouncements of other early modern Popes. Paul IV's predecessor had the Talmud burned in 1553. In 1566 Pius V extended the provisions of 'Cum nimis absurdum' to Jews who lived outside Papal territories, demanding that secular rulers enforce them. The Papal order expelling Jews from Bologna in 1569 included the destruction of the Jewish cemetery. Gregory XIII in 1584 prescribed that Jews hear Christian preaching in their synagogues every week. Clement VIII in 1593 expelled Jews from all places of residence in Papal territories except Rome, Ancona, and Avignon.

In Rome, the Jewish ghetto was established on a tiny plot of land, on the banks of the Tiber River but lying a few feet below the water level, and thus subject to frequent flooding. Every night all Jews were locked inside the ghetto walls. As late as the 19th century, popes continued to enforce the physical confinement of Italian Jews. The ghetto was dissolved only when the Vatican was forced to give up its temporal power by the entry of Italian soldiers into Rome in 1870 and the proclamation of the city as the new capital of Italy. The Papacy continued to view Jews as the eternal enemies of Christians, now able to do evil without restriction.

## Note

1 This document is translated and highlighted in Kenneth R. Stow, *Catholic Thought and Papal Jewry Policy 1555–1593* (New York: Jewish Theological Seminary of America, 1977), whose discussion of Papal policy on pp. 3–59 I have relied upon here.

## 5. Excerpts from article 'Jewish Morality' in Vatican newspaper, 10 January 1893

... once freedom of religion had been granted and citizenship given to the Jews, they knew well how to take advantage of the new situation, and from our equals they became our masters. Indeed, politics is today controlled by the Stock Exchange, and this is in the hands of the Jews; Freemasonry runs the government, and this too is controlled by the Jews; public opinion is shaped by the press, and this too is in large part inspired and subsidized by the Jews....

We do not write with any intention of sparking or fomenting any antisemitism in our country. Rather we seek to sound an alarm for Italians so that they defend themselves against those who, in order to impoverish them, dominate them, and make them their slaves, interfere with their faith, corrupt their morals and suck their blood....

All our wealth belongs to the Jews; because they alone are men, and have however the right to own, while we are not people, but things. Thus the Talmud and the doctors claim as legitimate the Jews' usury, fraud, thefts and robbery against the Christians....

Well, should we be surprised if he has already become owner of our things? Travel across Italy, and you will see that the majority of our valuables, where the Church was stripped, are now in the hands of the Jews. Ask, when in Venice, Florence, Padua, Turin, or in other Italian cities, in whose hands have fallen so many ducal and princely palaces and so many lordly villas; and they will answer you, in the hands of Jacob, Moses, and Salomon, all Jewish people. Find your way into secret things, and investigate the origins of several downturns and bankruptcies of great Italian houses, and you will discover therein the Jewish hand....

Journalism, in fact, which is propaganda's main tool, is perhaps two-thirds in the hands of Jews, and horribly harasses sacred persons and things. Secular schools, where atheism is taught and practiced, or if nothing else the poison of anti-Christian doctrines is spread, are in many cities, especially in Austria, led by Jews. The *loggia*, or the Masonic congregation, where war is waged against Christianity, and whence comes a stream of deputies, ministers, prefects, of public employees, is also at the service of the synagogue. Jews make up the majority of the supreme Council that heads the Masonic body; it is Jewish hatred that is thrown against the Church of Jesus

Christ; the program of the masonry is Jewish, which is — to rebuild the salomonic temple on Christian ruins, or to speak beyond metaphors, — to dechristianize the world; Jewish are the names of the various masonic positions and leadership posts, Jewish are the passwords, Jewish are the symbols, the rituals and all that which concerns masonry....

Maimonides, one of their highest doctors, teaches them that "Any Jew, who does not kill a non-Jew, when he could, violates a negative precept." (Sepher Mitzvot, fol.85, c. 2,3.) To save oneself from the hands of the Jews, it is not sufficient to be an innocuous, nay beneficial, person; because the Abhoda-Zarah declares that the *best among the Goyim, or Christians, deserves death*....

"The Jew that kills a Christian offers God a pleasing sacrifice." "After the destruction of the temple there shall be no other sacrifice than the extermination of Christians." "The highest spot in paradise is reserved for he who kills Christians" nothing more, nothing less. What a wonderful ethic!...

And after this, will the Jews have the courage to label as lie the accusation that Christians rightly move against them of direct hostility based upon a dogma, system, moral and religious duty? Will they be correct in complaining if Christian governments such as France, Spain, Portugal, Germany, Italy, have often pushed them outside their States; if recently Russia expelled them from the empire; and if against them, in many parts of Europe, the anti-semitic fire, which threatens to devour them, has been kindled? Will they kindly tell us, dear Jews, if it will be unreasonable to presume in them a bad disposition against us and a desire and intention to hurt us, while they develop a law of hatred, of persecution and extermination of Christians with a promise of, even, paradise? Then, one of two things: either they send their Talmud to hell with all of its comments, which are insults to common sense and an affront to natural law itself; or resign themselves to be perpetually in the gloom and abomination of all other nations, especially Christian.

---

This article by Father Saverio Rondina appeared in *Civiltà cattolica*, a biweekly periodical founded by Jesuits in 1850 and supervised by the Pope. The worldwide network of Catholic newspapers cited it as the voice of the Papacy. David I. Kertzer employed this article and many others to describe Papal policy at the turn of the century. The editors said in 1900 that this journal was 'created by the Holy See and placed at its exclusive service for the defense of the Sacred doctrine and the rights of the Church'.[1]

In the early 1880s, one of the journal's founders, Father Guiseppe Oreglia, wrote a series of 36 articles on the Jews, endlessly repeating the central themes of Catholic antisemitism. Rondina's article of 1893 was part of a second wave of pieces in *Civiltà cattolica* about Jews. It exemplifies the content and style of late 19$^{th}$- and early 20$^{th}$-century official Catholic publications about the increased Jewish threat to Christian society since the emancipation of Italian Jews in the middle of the 19$^{th}$ century. Deliberate misrepresentations of Jewish religious texts combine with familiar social claims about Jewish domination of economic life. Rondina refers approvingly to the wider antisemitic movement in European politics at the end of the 19$^{th}$ century. At this time the 40,000 Jews in Italy represented a fraction of 1% of the total population.

The protestation that the author does not wish to foment antisemitism is immediately followed by the assertion that Jews suck the blood of Christians. This claim had already been made more literally in one of Father Oreglia's articles in 1882, which explained the meaning of the label 'kosher for Passover' on matzoh: it indicated the presence of a Christian child's blood. Father Rondina followed the article quoted here with another devoted to explaining that Jews continued to commit ritual murder and describing in detail how Christian children were killed. Catholic newspapers like *Civiltà cattolica* continued to spread this legend all over Europe well into the 20$^{th}$ century.

By this time the theological understanding about Jews derived from Biblical sources was increasingly replaced, at the highest levels of the Catholic hierarchy, with socioeconomic complaints. Jews were dangerous, not because their ancestors had killed Christ, but because they now rob, cheat, and kill Christians in the name of modern secular progress.

## Note

1 Quoted from the fiftieth anniversary issue of *Civiltà Cattolica*, as cited by Kertzer, *The Popes Against the Jews: The Vatican's Role in the Rise of Modern Anti-Semitism* (New York: Alfred A. Knopf, 2001), p. 311, note 4. Much of the specific material about Papal attitudes toward Jews here comes from Kertzer's careful and persuasive study of the role of Catholic leaders in promoting antisemitism right up to the Holocaust.

Section III

# The Creation of Monsters in Germany: Jews and Others

In Germany during the $19^{th}$ century, enormous social energy was poured into emphasizing the most monstrous aspects within the web of Christian antisemitic beliefs. A few documents illustrate the strength and character of attitudes toward Jews which became increasingly prominent in Germany.

Not all Germans shared these beliefs or agreed with these proposals. Historians would like to know how many people advocated or accepted antisemitism, but our sources offer only partial glimpses into the thoughts of a limited number of literate people. Those Germans found that angry expressions of hatred for Jews did nothing to impede their reputations. Richard Wagner's nasty diatribes against Jews certainly helped make the composer beloved by the nationalist right. These documents are revealing precisely because the broad social acceptance of such vicious attacks allowed Germans to be direct and clear about their vision of Jews in Germany. The voices who argued publicly against the political, religious, and cultural advocacy of antisemitism are not represented here. Isolated and unorganized, they were drowned out by 1900.

Jews were not the only social targets of hatred in Germany in the late $19^{th}$ and early $20^{th}$ centuries. Poles and other Slavs were described in negative terms, especially as expansionist Germans looked eastward for possible territorial acquisitions. Scientific thinking about human society became increasingly dominated by biological categories based on racial categorization. Political and religious prejudices were transformed into racist hierarchies with pseudo-scientific justifications. Life and death became racialized and ending lives an acceptable instrument of national policy. The new science of eugenics for improving the human race is exemplified here by the arguments of two German professors about eliminating the handicapped.

# 6. Bavarian petition opposing equality for Jews, 10 January 1850

### High Chamber of Councillors!

Painfully and with great displeasure, we have learned of the disgrace threatening the entire Christian population of the country, in that the Jews, an alien nation by origin and religion, by customs and mores, are to receive civic and political rights completely equal to those of the Bavarian people.

Until now we had thought it impossible that a majority of the Chamber of Deputies would agree to such a decision, even if the Jews made every effort to achieve their emancipation.

More than any other region, the people of Lower Franconia surely had the most legitimate reason to expect, instead of having the Hebrews granted greater, indeed completely equal rights, exactly the opposite, namely, energetic protection again the excessive abuses that these people have already notoriously made of the rights granted to them earlier. We expect protection and more effective laws against Jewish swindling, against their fraud and usury, against the systematic exploitation of townspeople and countrymen, who, quite commonly, after an initially small debt to the Jews, soon find themselves so ensnared that they can no longer avoid ruin. But, instead of such expected protection against the Jews, the Christian people are, conversely, to be totally delivered to Jewish oppression and exploitation through the grant of completely equal rights to that nation. After so many families have already been reduced to beggary by them, so many bloody tears extracted because of them, we are to see them henceforth even as our judges, are to open to them all ministerial and government offices, are to allow Jewish rent officials to harass the people and to play into the hands of their fellow tribesmen, and we, the Christians, are to bow before their ilk! They are to be allowed to meddle in all of our communal affairs, indeed even have a say in our church and endowment matters! Such rights are to be granted to an alien people that is hostile to Christians everywhere, that to this day harbors the same hate toward our religion with which it once nailed the Savior to the Cross!

With indignation we have learned that 91 members of the Chamber of Deputies have voted in favor of it; but we still have a High Chamber of Councillors and it is to that body that we hereby direct the trustful and fervent plea that it

reject the entire Emancipation law and pressure the government to submit a different, wholly new bill by which the rights of the Christian people will be fully safeguarded, namely that
1. no Jew be allowed to settle or to marry in a community unless two-thirds of all community members have given their voluntary consent in open communal assembly;
2. no Jew be admitted to a judicial or revenue office, lest we have to humble ourselves before the Jews, swear the Christian oath before the Jews, and be exposed to quite novel financial speculations; also, lest our courts be peopled by Jewish trainees and secretaries, which would play into the hands of their nation in the most outrageous way;
3. that no Jew be admitted to ministerial or higher administration positions, or, in general, such offices as require some trust, lest the people be betrayed and sold out;
4. that no Jew be given a voice in matters of Christian Church administration, endowments, etc.;
5. that the Jews be prohibited, entirely and under threat of severe penalty, from engaging in haggling and peddling, because, in addition to the shameful importunity of such trading, these not only encourage fraud but draw the countryman into the claws of the Jews, from which he can seldom extricate himself.

With the most humble plea that the High Chamber give due attention to this remonstration and reject a law that so grievously infringes on the rights of the Christian population, we remain most respectfully the most obedient servants

of the High Chamber of Councillors

Hilders, 10 January 1850

[83 signatures of Hilders' citizens]

In witness of the above signatures, and unanimously joining the request expressed in this declaration, the following sign

Hilders, 10 January 1850

The Administration of the Market Community
Hohmann, Mayor
Handyert, Community Treasurer
Hohmann, Catholic Parish Priest
[5 other signatures]

---

In December 1849, the lower house of the Bavarian parliament voted to emancipate Jews in Bavaria, mandating full equality of Christians and Jews. This vote unleashed a storm of popular protest. The Bavarian population was immediately aroused by the issue of Jewish emancipation to undertake an unprecedented petition campaign that involved thousands of ordinary citizens and their local leaders. Over 1700 Bavarian communities sent petitions to the Bavarian parliament protesting this action, in the hopes that the upper house would oppose this bill, which it did in February 1850. At this time Jews made up about 1% of the Bavarian population. James F. Harris used these petitions to describe the nature and extent of popular antisemitism in Germany, at a moment when discrimination against Jews was publicly challenged.[1]

Religious accusations are cited as justification for opposing equality. Some Bavarian petitions explicitly cited the passage from Matthew 27.25 noted earlier: 'His blood be on us and on our children!' Jews are also feared as economic and political competitors, dishonest exploiters of Christians, a threat to Christian livelihood. Jews are perceived as an 'alien nation', a 'tribe' which works together against the interests of good Bavarian citizens. This petition, like many others, not only demands that the emancipation be rejected, but that existing discriminatory laws be strengthened.

German Jews received full legal equality in the laws of the newly unified German Empire in 1871. Discrimination in practice continued, especially in the judiciary, the upper reaches of the bureaucracy, the military, and the universities. On a much larger scale than Bavaria, national emancipation unleashed a wave of public antisemitism.

## Note

1 Harris, *The People Speak! Anti-Semitism and Emancipation in Nineteenth-Century Bavaria* (Ann Arbor, MI: University of Michigan Press, 1994).

# 7. Excerpt from Heinrich von Treitschke, 'Our Views', 1879

... The number of Jews in Western Europe is so small, that they cannot have any noticeable influence upon the national culture; but over our eastern border year after year, a horde of assiduous pants-selling youths burst out of the inexhaustible Polish cradle, whose children and grandchildren some day will rule Germany's stock exchanges and newspapers; this immigration grows visibly, and the question becomes more and more serious, how we can merge this alien people with ours. The Israelites of the West and the South belong mostly to the Spanish branch of Jews, which looks back on a comparatively proud history and which always adjusted fairly easily to the Western way of life; in fact, they have become in their great majority good French, English, Italians – as far as this can be justly expected from a people with such pure blood and such distinct peculiarity. We Germans, however, have to deal with that Polish branch of Jews, in whom the scars of many centuries of Christian tyranny have been imprinted; according to experience, they are much more alien compared to the European, and especially to the German being.

What we demand from our Israelite fellow citizens is simple: they should become Germans, feel themselves simply and justly as Germans – without prejudice to their faith and their sacred old memories, which all of us find honorable; for we do not want an era of German-Jewish mixed culture to follow thousands of years of German civilization. It would be a sin to forget that very many Jews, baptized and unbaptized, Felix Mendelssohn, Veit, Riesser among others – not to mention ones now living – were German men in the best sense, men in whom we revere the noble and fine traits of the German spirit. It remains just as undeniable that numerous and powerful groups of our Jews definitely do not cherish the good will to become simply Germans. It is painful enough to talk about these things; even conciliatory words are easily misunderstood here. I think, however, many of my Jewish friends will agree with me, with deep regret, when I maintain that recently a dangerous spirit of arrogance has arisen in Jewish circles, and that the influence of Jewry upon our national life, which in former times was often beneficial, has recently been harmful in many ways.... There is no German commercial city which does not count many honest, respectable Jewish firms; but it is incontestable that the Semites have a great part of the falsehood and deceit, of the bold greed of business excesses, a heavy guilt for that contemptible materialism of our age, which regards all work only as business and threatens to suffocate the old comfortable joy in work of our people; in thousands of German villages sits the Jew, who buys out his neighbors through usury. Among the leading men of art and science, the number of Jews is not large; much greater is the bustling horde of Semitic talent of the third rank....

Most dangerous, however, is the unjust preponderance of the Jews in the daily press – a fateful consequence of our old narrow-minded laws, which prohibited the entry of the Israelites into the most learned professions. For ten years public opinion in many German cities was "made" mostly by Jewish pens.... What Jewish journalists achieve in abuse and mockery against Christianity is plainly outrageous, and such blasphemies are offered to our people in our language as the newest achievements of "German" Enlightenment! Hardly was the emancipation obtained, when one insisted boldly on their "certificate"; one demanded literal parity in all and everything, and did not want to see that we Germans are, after all, a Christian people and the Jews are only a minority among us; we have experienced that the removal of Christian pictures and even the introduction of the Sabbath celebration in mixed schools was demanded.

If we consider all this – and how much more could be said! – then the noisy agitation of the moment appears only as a brutal and spiteful, but natural reaction of the Germanic national consciousness against an alien element which has taken too much space in our life. It has at least the one involuntary merit of having freed us from the ban of an unspoken falsehood. It is already a gain that an evil, which each sensed but nobody wanted to touch, is now openly discussed. Let us not deceive ourselves: the movement is very deep and strong.... Up to the best educated circles, among men who would reject with horror any thought of Christian fanaticism or national arrogance, it sounds today, as from one mouth: the Jews are our misfortune!

---

Heinrich von Treitschke was one of the most famous German historians of the 19th century. He edited the *Prussian Yearbooks*, a prestigious academic journal, in which he published a series of articles in 1879 and 1880 about Jews in Germany. His characterizations of Jews as arrogant, dishonest, and blasphemous helped make antisemitism acceptable in intellectual circles. As Treitschke's words show, antisemitism was not only connected to criticisms of secular modern democratic culture, but Jews were specifically blamed for its evils. Treitschke held their Polish origin responsible for German Jews' alien and oriental nature, leading to a justified Christian antisemitism.

Treitschke interspersed his harsh criticisms of Jews in Germany with a few kind words praising individual Jews who expressed the 'German spirit'. This relative restraint was abandoned by the rising vehemence of public antisemitism, which used the newly democratized German electoral system to promote itself as a political ideology. In the same year as Treitschke wrote these articles, Wilhelm Marr introduced the word 'antisemite' into political language by founding the League of Antisemites. Simultaneously, the Emperor's court preacher, Adolf Stoecker, changed the direction of his Christian Social Workers' Party with a speech entitled 'Our Demands on Modern Jewry', blaming assimilated Jews for deliberately promoting social discord. A couple of years later, Karl Lueger began to use antisemitism as a primary appeal in Austrian politics. All used fraudulent claims about Jewish hatred for Christians to promote Christian hatred of Jews.

While Marr faded from view, Stoecker remained a major force in German right-wing politics past 1900. Lueger served as Mayor of Vienna from 1897 to his death in 1910. Treitschke's lectures influenced a generation of students in Berlin. By the early 20th century, university students were among the most vehement promoters of antisemitism in Germany and Austria.

# 8. Excerpt from *Permission for the Extermination of Life Unworthy of Life*, 1920

from Professor Dr. Karl Binding, "Legal Argument"

Are there human lives, which have so completely forfeited the quality of a legally protected entity, that their continuation, for the living person as well as for the society, has permanently lost all value?

One need only ask this question and an anxious feeling rises in each person, who has gotten used to calculating the worth of the individual life for the living person and for the collectivity. One perceives with pain how wastefully we handle the most valuable life, filled with the strongest will and the greatest vitality, and how much completely uselessly squandered labor, patience, and wealth we use, only in order to preserve life unworthy of life, until nature – often so unsympathetically late – robs it of the last possibility of continuation.

One imagines simultaneously a battlefield covered with thousands of dead youth, or a mine, in which explosive gas has buried hundreds of industrious workers, and then one compares our institutions for idiots with their care for their living inmates – and one is shaken to the core by this glaring dissonance between the sacrifice of the most valuable good of humanity in great number on the one side and the greatest care of not only absolutely worthless, but even negatively valued existences on the other side.

That there are living humans, whose death would be a deliverance for themselves and at the same time a liberation from a burden for the society and the state, the carrying of which, outside of the sole value of being a model of the greatest selflessness, has not the smallest use, cannot be doubted in any way....

Again, I find, either from the legal, social, ethical, or religious standpoint, absolutely no reason not to permit the killing of these people, who embody the terrible countertype of a true human and awaken horror in nearly everyone.

from Professor Dr. Alfred Hoche, "Medical Remarks"

I set up a survey of all relevant German institutions to provide me with useable material. It turns out that the average expense per person and year for the care of idiots has reached 1300 M. If we add up the number of idiots in institutional care who are present at the moment in Germany, we arrive at approximately a total of 20 – 30,000. If we assume for the individual case an average lifespan of 50 years, it is easy to measure what enormous capital in the form of food, clothes, and heat are removed from the national wealth for an unproductive purpose....

The question, whether the necessary expense for this category of dead-weight existences can be justified in all directions, was not urgent in past times of prosperity; now things are different, and we must occupy ourselves with it seriously. Our situation is like that of the participant on a difficult expedition, in which the largest possible capacity for achievement of all is the indispensable precondition for the success of the undertaking, and in which there is no place for half-, quarter-, and eighth-strength.

---

Karl Binding was a jurist, Alfred Hoche a psychiatrist. Their book excerpted here focuses entirely on the justifications for killing of the mentally handicapped, 'life unworthy of life'. It fits into the broader Western concern in the early 20$^{th}$ century with the quality of humans and the cold application of science to making humans better.

Their work illustrates the slippery logic of denying the right of life to people with genetic handicaps. Binding begins with a defense of suicide as the right of the sovereign individual, then moves to helping those who wish to die avoid a painful death, and ends by advocating this 'help' even if the sick person does not give permission. Hoche, the psychiatrist, argues that doctors can decide 'with 100% certainty' who should be killed because they are 'brain dead'. Yet at the end of Hoche's excerpt, he has shifted from dismissing 'worthless' lives to an argument that even those of 'half-strength' have no place in modern Germany. The language used to refer to the targets of their arguments is telling: ballast existences, human shells, defectives. The emphasis by both Binding and Hoche on the economic costs of caring for people who are not productive is later echoed in Nazi discussions of their euphemistically termed 'euthanasia' policy.

The eugenics movement led to many aggressive state actions in Western nations: sterilization of the handicapped or criminals; restrictive immigration laws; and willingness to perform medical experiments secretly on institutionalized people. Sterilization laws were passed in some US states after 1900.

Governments broadened the targets of such actions beyond those considered 'brain dead' to various kinds of people considered less worthy: blacks, Jews, the poor, Southern Europeans, Asians. In 1922 the German Society for Racial Hygiene, the major eugenics organization, urged the sterilization of people with genetic illnesses. As in many areas, the Nazis adopted the most radical policies, sterilizing about 200,000 people between 1933 and 1937.[1]

## Note

1 Saul Friedländer, *Nazi Germany and the Jews: Volume 1: The Years of Persecution, 1933–1939* (New York: HarperCollins, 1997), p. 40. This book provides an excellent description of the mounting state pressure against Jews leading up to the Holocaust.

# 9. Court judgment in the murder on 10 August 1932 of a Polish laborer by SA men

G. K. Sg. 1/32

In the Name of the People!

In the criminal case against

1.) the electrician Reinhold Kottisch from Mikultschütz, born on 19 November 1906 in Eichenau, Polish Upper Silesia,
2.) the miner Rufin Wolnitza from Mikultschütz, born on 10 May 1907, in same,
3.) the miner August Gräupner from Rokittnitz, born on 16 August 1899 in Schwarzwald-Kolonie, Polish Upper Silesia,
4.) the timekeeper Helmuth Josef Müller from Friedrichswille, born on 12 May 1898 in Sterkrade,
5.) the miner Hypolit Hadamik from Rokittnitz, born on 16 July 1903 in Langendorf, County Gleiwitz OS,
6.) the miner Karl Czaja from Rokittnitz, born on 18 October 1894 in Ruda (Polish Upper Silesia),
7.) the former police watch master Ludwig Nowak from Broslawitz, born on 20 August 1891 in Stollarzowitz,
8.) the innkeeper Georg Hoppe from Tworog, born on 17 September 1889 in Kotzin, Poland,
9.) the innkeeper Paul Lachmann from Potempa, born on 20 December 1893 in Erdmannsheim, County Lublinitz, Polish Upper Silesia,

for political murder, political bodily injury, incitement and abetting....

Grounds.

... Having arrived in front of the house of the witness Mrs. Pietzuch, Gräupner directed that Wolnitza and Dutzki remain outside as guards, Wolnitza took his post in the courtyard, Dutzki on the street. Kottisch now opened the unlocked house door and entered the house. Gräupner, Müller, Prescher and Golombek followed him. Golombek remained in the background, in order not to be recognized. Since Kottisch, who was not familiar with the surroundings, went straight through the hall, it was said to him by Golombek that he should go through the door on the right. At that moment Golombek handed Kottisch an electric flashlight. The door to the right was also not locked. In the room into which the intruders now arrived, 2 beds were located against the wall across from the door. In the bed to the left slept the witness Marie Pietzuch, in the bed to the right slept the witness Alfons Pietzuch and his brother Konrad. The witness Mrs. Pietzuch, who had already been awakened by the noise of the steps in the hall, sat up in bed and asked what the intruders wanted. She was told by someone who held a pistol at her that she should be quiet or she would be shot. Simultaneously the accused Kottisch and one of the others stepped to the bed of the brothers Pietzuch and held their pistols at them. Kottisch shined the electric flashlight at the two lying in bed. It was shouted: "Hands up, out you damned Communists." Golombek, who had remained at the door, shouted: "The big one should be beaten!" Konrad Pietzuch was then pulled out of bed. As protection, Konrad Pietzuch held the covers in front of him. Gräupner then jumped in. Konrad Pietzuch was now beaten in an inhumane manner. Lying in bed, Alfons Pietzuch also received a powerful blow with a hard object, apparently a billiard cue or a rubber truncheon, on the left temple, so that he had a strongly bleeding wound and became unconscious for a time. When he came to again, he heard the cracking of many blows. The witness Alfons Pietzuch was not able to provide a precise description of the events, since as a result of the powerful blow that he had received, he was still dazed. Marie Pietzuch is also not able to do this ... In addition the flashlight fell from the accused Kottisch, so that the room temporarily remained dark. In particular Marie and Alfons Pietzuch do not know, if Konrad Pietzuch fell to the floor. Konrad Pietzuch was able, despite the serious wounds which he had suffered, to flee into the next room. From that room he then called: "Alfons, Alfons." Meanwhile one of the intruders stepped to the bed of Alfons Pietzuch and asked him if he had a weapon. To his negative answer, was shouted: "Out you damned, on the wall! You are also going to get it, you will also be shot." Alfons Pietzuch had to stand at the wall with his face towards the door. After a time, the witness Alfons Pietzuch was told to get back into bed; the intruders went back to the entrance door. From the door called Golombek to Kottisch: "Shoot, shoot!" Kottisch stepped to the door, pushed it open, shone the flashlight into the room and took a shot at Konrad Pietzuch. By the light of the flashlight he saw how Konrad Pietzuch fell over. Now the accused Müller shouted: "Out of the room! Let's go, SA!" The perpetrators then left the apartment and the house of the widow Pietzuch. After their departure, Alfons Pietzuch heard the death-rattle of his brother in the other room. He went out to be sure that the perpetrators had actually left. Meanwhile the witness Marie Pietzuch woke her daughter-in-law, living in the same house, who looking at the clock said it was 2 o'clock. Both went into the room where they found Konrad Pietzuch already dead....

The expert witness, medical examiner and public health officer Dr. Weimann found during the autopsy of Konrad Pietzuch a total of 29 wounds on the murdered man. The wounds were located nearly entirely on the upper body, only 2 on the right leg. All wounds were caused by great force. On the right and left sides of the neck there were traces of strangulation. In particular, on the neck there were extensive skin abrasions, hemorrhages in the neck, lacerations of tissue, and a complete rupture of the right large carotid artery. Furthermore the expert witness found a bullet wound through the right upper arm, with shattering of the upper arm bone. The cause of death, according to the opinion of the expert witness, was the penetration of blood into the air passages, so that in this way aspiration of the blood occurred. The expert witness assumed it as certain that Konrad Pietzuch, lying on the floor, was kicked with full force, so that the heel of the shoe was pressed into the neck. The kick in the neck thus brought on death. Against that, all other wounds were not to be regarded as causes of death....

For punishment, the accused Kottisch, Wolnitza, Gräupner and Müller, on account of political murder by § 1 Number 1 of the Terror Decree, were sentenced to death, as well as the accused Lachmann on account of incitement.... For the accused Hoppe on account of abetting to dangerous bodily injury from political motives, a prison sentence of 2 years was determined.... Against the accused Lachmann stands the fact that the crime occurred at his instigation and that he did not shrink from using the still young accused Kottisch, Wolnitza, Gräupner and Müller for his personal ends.... For him, the deprivation of civic rights was determined (§ 32 St.G.B.).

Furthermore, the weapons seized in this matter, besides ammunition, both rubber truncheons and the billiard cue, are to be confiscated (§ 40 St.G.B.).

The costs of the case, insofar as convictions have occurred, are to be imposed on the accused, otherwise on the treasury (§§ 465, 467 St.P.O.).

signed Himml Hoffmann

as well as the Court Official Dr. Stahl, away on leave.

The correctness of the transcript attested:<br>
Beuthen O./S., 12 September 1932.<br>
Murawski<br>
Justice Department Inspector<br>
as Clerk of the Court.

This case of political murder caused a sensation in Germany in the final months of 1932. A carload of uniformed SA-men drove around the village of Potempa on the Silesian border with Poland, armed with pistols and other weapons, looking for someone to kill. They found Konrad Pietzuch, an unemployed Polish laborer, whom they trampled to death before the eyes of his mother and brother.

The murder was part of a terror campaign organized by the armed and uniformed *Sturmabteilung* in Eastern Germany before and after the parliamentary elections of July 1932, when the Nazis became the largest party in the Reichstag. In June more than 80 people died in nearly 500 violent incidents in the state of Prussia alone. During the first two weeks of August, bombings, shootings and arson by the SA spread through the provinces of East Prussia and Silesia. According to the public prosecutor, Pietzuch's murder was one of 30 incidents that night, planned at local SA headquarters. While this campaign was concentrated on leftists, the SA also constantly attacked Jews. 1000 SA men had taken part in a modern pogrom in Berlin on Jewish New Year 1931.

Nazi leaders were open about their support of political violence. After this verdict had been delivered, Hermann Göring telegraphed the murderers that they had only been defending their 'lives and honor' and sent their families money; SA chief Ernst Röhm visited them in prison. Most important, Adolf Hitler sent a telegram which declared his 'unbounded loyalty' to these men, and promised to work for their freedom. The German political right demanded clemency. Within two weeks, the Prussian ministry commuted the sentences to life imprisonment.[1]

Four months after the verdict, Hitler was made Chancellor of Germany on 30 January 1933. In March Pietzuch's murderers were set free. By then, SA terror had become the legal instrument of the new German government.

## Note

1 Richard Bessel, *Political Violence and the Rise of Nazism: The Storm Troopers in Eastern Germany 1925–1934* (New Haven, CT: Yale University Press, 1984), pp. 88–91; Bessel, 'The Potempa Murder', *Central European History*, 10 (1977), pp. 251–2.

Section IV

# The Nazi Attack on Jews and Other Undesirables in the Third Reich, 1933–1938

The Holocaust did not begin immediately when the Nazis took power in Germany in 1933. During its first five years, the Nazi government disposed of all political rivals, militarized the state and economy, prepared for wars of aggression, and employed a variety of strategies to eliminate Jews from German life. Jews were only one target of the Nazis in power. Socialists and Jehovah's Witnesses were persecuted, arrested, and killed as political challengers; homosexuals, Gypsies, and the handicapped were attacked as racial inferiors and threats to the purity of Aryan blood. The documents in this section show some of these strategies and trace the rapid isolation of various social groups from their German neighbors. The lack of public opposition to the persecution of certain German citizens allowed the Nazis to continually escalate their attacks on these groups.

The documents of this period are relatively open in their expression of Nazi hatred for these social groups. Words retain their obvious meanings. The persecution through boycotts, denial of citizenship, restrictions on employment, and local harassment was public, for all to observe. Although violence was not yet the main tactic, murders of individual Jews by uniformed state officials occurred in the first months after Hitler was sworn in as Chancellor, and were reported relatively freely. Thus these documents from 1933 to 1938 display for our view the nature of persecution of Jews and others by the Nazis, as they were consolidating their power in Germany.

# 10. Bavarian state report about the murder of a Jewish businessman, 20 March 1933

No. 352. Regensburg, 20 March 1933

Half-Monthly Report
of the District President
of Niederbayern and Oberpfalz.

I. General Political Situation.

The political revolution took place mainly without great disturbances. Wide circles of the population hope now for a unification of all forces ready for construction. Generally welcomed were the sharp measures against the Communists and other troublemakers. The result of house searches would doubtlessly have been much better, if the preceding announcement on the radio had not created the possibility of removing materials.

In the ranks of the supporters of the KPD and SPD it has become quiet. Occasionally voluntary dissolution of local groups of the KPD and the Reichsbanner is reported.

The cooperation of the authorities with the leaders of the SA takes place smoothly, once some misunderstandings have been cleared away....

An incident occurred in the night from the 4th to the 5th of this month at the rectory in Landau a.d. Isar between members of the SA and the Bayernwacht, who inexpediently were lodged in a room in the rectory. Both parties accused each other of tearing down posters. When the city priest rose up against them, and threatened shooting in case of a forcible entry of the SA-men into the rectory, this led to cursing and threats against the priest. It did not come to violence. Then when the priest described the incident in the Sunday service and presented it as if an attack on him and the rectory had occurred, a considerable agitation spread in the population of Landau, against which the local authorities successfully intervened through explanation of the actual occurrence. In the local press, comments about these proceedings continued for a long time.

On the 15th of this month, about 6 AM, several men in dark uniform appeared in a motor vehicle in front of the apartment of the Israelite businessman Otto Selz in Straubing. Selz was taken out of the apartment in night clothes and carried off in the vehicle. About 9:30 Selz was found shot in a woods near Weng, district Landshut. The vehicle is supposed to have come from the direction Munich-Landshut and to have driven back again on the same route. It was occupied by 6 uniformed men and carried the sign: II A. The license number could not be determined. Several country people say they noticed on some passengers of the vehicle the red armband with the swastika. The local police informed the Landshut District Attorney and the Munich Police Headquarters....

signed Dr. Wirschinger.

---

Official violence against Jews and other enemies of the Nazis began immediately after the seizure of power on 30 January 1933. During March, the SA, the Nazis' paramilitary formations, committed vicious public acts against Jews in Berlin and other large cities. Although the total number of victims was small, the lives of all German Jews were thereby threatened.

This report depicts some of the conflicts that arose as the Nazis began to sweep away all competitors for power. In Bavaria, conservative Catholics were represented by the Bavarian People's Party (BVP), whose voluntary militia was called the Bayernwacht. The evening incident at the rectory concerned political posters for the Reichstag election the next day, 5 March, in which the Nazis and the BVP were bitter opponents. The Nazi victory was followed by the replacement of the Bavarian Minister President by a Nazi.

The process of creating a party dictatorship backed by terrorist police forces was just beginning here. This report describes rural Bavarians willing to observe carefully, report on, and even oppose the armed forces of the Nazi Party. The political controversy and the alleged attack on the local Catholic priest by the SA caused considerable outcry in the local population and press. There was little popular reaction of any kind to the murder of a local Jewish businessman, which was seen, discussed, and reported to proper authorities. The effects of this murder and other similar attacks rippled through the entire Jewish community, however, and nearly 40,000 Jews emigrated from Germany in 1933, about 7% of the total Jewish population. To hasten this process by removing Jewish influence from economic life, the Nazi government declared that on 1 April 1933, all good Germans should boycott Jewish businesses.

# 11. Memoir by Dr Paula Tobias about boycott of 1 April 1933

... at the day of the boycott on April 1st. there had been all day two Brownshirts with rifles in front of our house.

It may be of interest for you to know how this day on the whole worked out in our special situation. We did not know it was coming, and after as usual at 6.30 a.m. I had opened the gate and helped our boy to come out with his bicycle, from across the road there came two young fellows in full array and told me in the most embarrassed manner that they were supposed to stand in front of our property and not to leave any patient in. When I replied that, after all, command was command and that there probably was nothing we or they could do about it, they were greatly relieved and moved towards their place in front of the gate. The population learned the news immediately and did not bother with coming. But some of them watched what was going on, and when for a couple of hours in the afternoon nobody was to be found to function as sentry, they sneaked in. The poor fellows who had been standing there had been considerably annoyed by passers-by and besides they used every excuse possible not to be ordered for this duty. The farmers flatly refused to have their boys go and found a lot of emergency-work for them to do. One of them told his offspring it would be a far more useful job for the nation, to cart the dung out of the stables than to stand there with a shotgun and ridicule themselves.

In the morning our chauffeur and I went to our nearby vegetable-garden. We had planned the day before to plant our potatoes and so we did, though my husband told me it would be very foolish for me to go and plant potatoes for others. I reassured him that we ourselves would eat them in fall, and that was what we did. Some hours later I persuaded him, as long as we would not have to work, to go out for a nice long walk in the woods, which we otherwise never could afford on a weekday. The Party-doctor who was stationed in the nearby inn to attend to the patients, did not have anything to do either, because suddenly nobody needed a doctor. People who had come in from the country, just went home again after they had found out about the situation. Our chauffeur walked around like a gobbler, bawled at the sentries and told them how to stand and hold their guns as long as they were standing at a veteran-officer's house. With the exception of one notorious rowdy none of the young fellows — they were relieved every two hours — said an undecent word or did anything objectionable, every one was glad, when his time was up. When our boy came home from school, they chattered with him and cracked some jokes.

It did not work that way everywhere. In Holzminden for example there had been bloody riots with plenty of arrests and shattered windows....

Elisabeth P. was another extremely capable and successful educator.... She had to leave already on April 1st. 1933. Previous to that time she had been ill and I had asked her to come for a final examination before she would leave and to bring a specimen of her urine. So she came the morning of the boycott. In one hand she had her bottle with the urine, in the other a big bouquet of beautiful tulips. After the preliminary encounter with the sentinel, she argued that if not as a patient, she certainly might go in as a friend on a farewell-call. She set the bottle in front of them on the pavement with such a bang that it cracked and then marched in between them with her flowers. When she was in the house, she was so stunned with herself and the events, that she was not to do anything but to drop her head on the table and cry. And she certainly was not an overly sentimental person.

---

Paula Tobias and her husband were doctors in Bevern, a town of about 1800 people in central Germany. In 1935 they emigrated to San Francisco. Tobias died in 1971. This excerpt from her memoir is reproduced as Tobias typed it, with errors in English spelling and punctuation unchanged.

As Tobias mentions, the Saturday 1 April boycott was experienced in quite different ways in different communities. In large cities with well-organized SA troops, like Berlin, the effect of armed guards was very threatening. In Bevern, Tobias and her husband were perceived more sympathetically than the uniformed young men who stood at her gate. The population quickly adjusted to the boycott, but did not see the need to stop visiting their regular doctors because of Nazi antisemitic ideology. Even the SA guards were embarrassed by the requirement to express antisemitism against known neighbors. The persecution of Jews in rural areas was generally less harsh at first than actions against the majority of German Jews who lived in big cities.

This armed and uniformed attack on Jewish businesses and professions, just two months after the Nazis took power in Germany, was the first major Nazi effort to dislodge Jews from the German economy. Although the government succeeded in organizing its forces of intimidation, the German population was not especially supportive. In a variety of cities, customers patronized Jewish businesses anyway. The lack of popular enthusiasm and mounting international criticism led the government to end the boycott after one day. At the same time, the Nazis were developing their apparatus of persecution: on 1 April, Heinrich Himmler was appointed head of the Bavarian police and he officially inaugurated Dachau as the first concentration camp.

This memoir is one of about 200 autobiographies written in response to a prize competition organized by three Harvard professors in 1939–1940, which requested the submission of manuscripts describing 'My Life in Germany before and after 30 January 1933'. These lengthy documents (the organizers asked for a minimum of 20,000 words) are a little-used resource for the experiences of Jewish refugees during the period of persecution leading up to the Holocaust. They represent one of the largest deposits of memoirs for the period up to 1939, valuable both for their rich detail on the precise nature of persecution and the refugees' reaction to it. Mainly written by classically educated members of the Jewish middle class, about 30% of the memoirs were by women.[1]

## Note

1 The competition and the entries are described by Detlef Garz in his edition of one of these memoirs: Käthe Vordtriede, *'Es gibt Zeiten, in denen men welkt': Mein Leben in Deutschland vor und nach 1933* (Lengwil, Switzerland: Libelle Verlag, 1999), pp. 243–6. This source was brought to my attention by Wiebke Lohfeld, author of *Im Dazwischen: Porträt der jüdischen und deutschen Ärztin Paula Tobias (1886–1970)* (Opladen: Leske und Budrich, 2003), from which the further information about Tobias originates.

# 12. Report of underground Social Democratic Party on persecution of German Jews, August 1935

Germany-Report
of the Sopade

2nd Year, No. 8 August 1935

... II. The Terror Against the Jews

We reported in the previous month within the scope of a comprehensive overview of the terror in the Third Reich also about the terror against the Jews. We supplement this overview with the following, based on newly arrived reports from the last month.

The published announcements in the press show with what methods one has driven the Jews into a modern ghetto:

Bergzabern, Edenkoben, Schotten, Höheinöd, Breunigweiler and other places forbid entry to Jews and prohibit the sale of real estate to Jews.

Bad Tölz, Bad Reichenhall, Garmisch-Partenkirchen and the Bavarian highlands no longer allow Jews entry to the spa facilities.

In Apolda, Berka, Blankenstein, Sulza, Allstadt and Weimar (1 movie theater), entry to the cinema is forbidden to Jews.

Magdeburg forbids Jews use of the libraries; the street cars carry signs on the doors: "Jews unwelcome!"

The restaurants in Stralsund, Putbus and other places prohibit entry to Jews; all businesspeople in Frankenthal (Pfalz) refuse to sell to Jews; 500 businesses, restaurants and cafés of the district Alsfeld and the restaurants of the whole Harz region maintain signs: "Jews unwelcome"; the barbers of Stralsund no longer serve Jews.

The cattle markets in Oldenburg, Fulda and numerous other places have become free of Jews; at the yearly fairs in Görlitz and Schriesheim, Jews are unwelcome.

In countless communities the bathing facilities are forbidden to Jews, and "race defilers" are arrested, beaten up, led around the town, and dragged off to concentration camps.

Visit to the Externstein – forbidden, visit to events of all kinds in Schriesheim – forbidden ... it is a chain of tricks, prohibitions, defamations, which find their completion in the instructions to Aryans to avoid association with Jews.

In Mainz-Bischofsheim, use of community fields is terminated for those who associate with Jews; businesspeople from Nidda, Auerbach and other places who have dealings with Jews have their city contracts withdrawn.

Berlin-Steglitz, Hirschberg and other places forbid public employees, teachers and welfare recipients from buying from Jews; Adelshofen takes disciplinary action against administrators, city councillors and public employees who buy from Jews; Finsterwalde and Langenselbold threaten welfare recipients with withdrawal of support. Coburg also prohibits city officials, employees and workers from social association with Jews; Braunschweig draws up lists of peasants who trade with Jews earlier or today, while in Alzey the names of 4 people who play cards with Jews were publicly denounced....

---

The Social Democratic Party of Germany, the most important political party in the Weimar Republic, was effectively destroyed as a political force by Nazi repression in 1933. Leaders were arrested and beaten, while others fled the country. Workers' organizations were disbanded.

Each month from April 1934 through April 1940, the exiled SPD published a lengthy report based on information from a network of sympathizers in Germany. These reports are excellent sources for details about politics, culture, economics, youth, religion, and daily life in Nazi Germany. They invariably emphasized all the weaknesses of Nazi policy and tended to exaggerate popular rejection of Nazi initiatives. Only occasionally was the persecution of Jews discussed: in 1935 three of the monthly reports had sections on antisemitic actions, centered around outbreaks of public violence against Jews beginning in July, leading up to the Nazi Party Congress in Nuremberg in September.

This report shows that within two years of taking power, what the author calls a 'modern ghetto' had been established by the combination of central directives and local action. Local activists were encouraged by the propaganda of the Nazi leadership and the passivity of the population. The towns and cities mentioned here were located in all regions of Germany. The ability of Jews in city and village to make a living was thus already in question by 1935. Jews were increasingly segregated from other Germans in all aspects of daily life. These myriad local restrictions were displayed for all to see, but also effectively isolated the German population from seeing the effects on their Jewish fellow citizens.

# 13. Nuremberg Law against intermarriage between Jews and German citizens, 15 September 1935

## Law for the Protection of German Blood and German Honor

15 September 1935

Inspired by the knowledge that purity of the German blood is the prerequisite for the continued existence of the German people, and animated by the inexorable will to secure the German nation for all time, the Reichstag has unanimously adopted the following law, which is hereby promulgated:

§ 1

1) Marriages between Jews and subjects of the state of German or related blood are forbidden. Marriages nevertheless concluded are invalid, even if concluded abroad to circumvent this law.

2) Only the State Prosecutor can bring annulment proceedings.

§ 2

Extramarital intercourse between Jews and subjects of the state of German or related blood is forbidden.

§ 3

Jews may not employ female subjects of the state of German or related blood under 45 years old in their households.

§ 4

1) Jews are forbidden to fly the Reich and the National flags and to display the Reich colors.

2) They are, on the other hand, permitted to display the Jewish colors. The exercise of this right stands under state protection.

§ 5

1) Whoever violates the prohibition of §1 will be punished with the penitentiary.

2) A man who violates the prohibition of § 2 will be punished with jail or the penitentiary.

3) Whoever violates the provisions of § § 3 or 4 will be punished with jail up to one year and with a fine, or with one of these penalties.

§ 6

The Reich Minister of the Interior, in coordination with the Deputy of the Führer and the Reich Minister of Justice, issues the legal and administrative regulations which are required for implementation and completion of this law.

§ 7

The Law takes effect on the day following promulgation, § 3 however first on 1 January 1936.

Nuremberg, 15 September 1935,
at the Reich Party Congress of Freedom

**The Führer and Reich Chancellor**
Adolf Hitler
The Reich Minister of the Interior
Frick
The Reich Minister of Justice
Dr. Gürtner
The Deputy of the Führer
R. Hess
Reich Minister without Portfolio

---

After two years of unpredictable outbursts of violence and persecution, the Nazi state took a major step toward separating Jews from other Germans by passing three Nuremberg Laws in September 1935. These laws displayed the ideological obsession with blood purity as the expression of racial exclusion. The Reich Citizenship Law protected the body politic by allowing only those 'of German blood' to be citizens. This Law for the Protection of German Blood and German Honor addressed the human body, forbidding sex between Jews and Germans and invalidating mixed marriages. The traditional fear about young Christian women working for Jewish families, mentioned by Pope Paul IV in 1555, appears here again. The Reich Flag Law made the swastika flag the national symbol, which Jews were forbidden to display. By the end of 1935, Jews lost their right to vote; civil servants who were World War I veterans were dismissed; and Jewish state employees, like professors, teachers, lawyers, and physicians, were fired.

Despite the unprecedented nature of the official discrimination proclaimed in the Nuremberg Laws, many Jews still hoped they could carry on their lives in Germany. The Reich Representation of Jews in Germany, founded in 1933, issued a statement which hoped that these laws, although they were 'the heaviest of blows', could still 'create a basis on which a tolerable relationship becomes possible between the German and the Jewish people'.[1]

'Purity of the German blood' excluded more people than just Jews. The Law for the Protection of the Hereditary Health of the German People, published one month later, was directed at excluding others of 'alien' blood. These were soon defined as Gypsies and blacks, who also were forbidden to marry Germans.

## Note

1 The full statement by the Reichsvertretung is translated in Yitzhak Arad, Yisrael Gutman, and Abraham Margaliot (eds), *Documents on the Holocaust: Selected Sources on the Destruction of the Jews of Germany and Austria, Poland, and the Soviet Union* (Jerusalem: Yad Vashem, 1981), pp. 84–6. This hope among some German Jews, that each escalation in government persecution represented the final step, was no more unreasonable than the muted responses outside Germany to Nazi antisemitism. At no point until mass murder actually began was the Holocaust an obvious outcome.

## 14. Form for Jehovah's Witnesses to renounce their religious beliefs, 1936

Concentration camp ________________________
Department II

# Declaration

I, ____________________________________________________________
born on ____________________________ in ____________________________
herewith make the following declaration:

1. I have recognized that the International Bible Students Association is spreading erroneous teachings and under the cloak of religious activity follows subversive purposes.
2. I therefore turned away from this organization entirely and also made myself mentally free from this sect.
3. I herewith give assurance that I will never again take any part in the activity of the International Bible Students Association. Any persons approaching me with the teaching of the Bible Students, or who in any manner reveal their connections with them, I will denounce immediately. All literature from the Bible Students that should be sent to my address I will deliver at once to the nearest police station.
4. I will in the future respect the laws of the State, especially in the event of war, will defend my fatherland with weapon in hand, and fully join the community of the people.
5. I have been notified that I can expect renewed arrest if I should act against the Declaration given today.

____________________________, Dated ____________________________
Signature ____________________________

KL/47/4.43 5000

The Jehovah's Witnesses were a small proselytizing Christian group, which had existed in Germany since early in the 20th century under the name International Bible Students Association. They had often attracted the hostile attention of the state, because of the political implications of their religious beliefs: Witnesses refused to offer allegiance to a secular state, refused to serve in the military or work for any military purposes.

For the Nazis, Jehovah's Witnesses were ideological but not racial enemies. If they abjured their subversive religious doctrine, they would no longer be dangerous. They were a significant target of early Nazi persecution: of perhaps 25,000 to 30,000 Witnesses in Germany, about 10,000 were arrested after the Nazis came to power, with 2000 put in concentration camps. In jails and camps, various versions of this Declaration were used after 1936 to try to entice Witnesses to proclaim loyalty and obedience to the Nazi state. If they signed, they would be allowed to leave. This version became the official form in December 1938 on the order of Himmler.

Extraordinary measures were employed by the SS to obtain signatures. Witnesses were special targets for SS torture, especially after September 1939, when their refusal to serve in the war made them particularly hated by the regime. It is estimated that 1200 Witnesses died in the camps. One Witness, August Dickmann, was executed by SS in Sachsenhausen on 15 September 1939 in front of the other Witness inmates. They were then threatened with death if they did not sign. Each one was given this form. None signed.

# 15. Speech by Heinrich Himmler to SS leaders on homosexuality, 18 February 1937

... We have in Germany according to the latest censuses about 67 to 68 million people, which means around 34 million men, if I take round numbers. Then there are about 20 million sexually capable men (that is, men over 16 years)....

If I assume one to two million homosexuals, that means that about 7-8-10% of the men in Germany are homosexual. That means, if that continues, that our people will go to pieces from this plague. A people will not endure in the long run, if its sexual budget and balance is disturbed in this way....

I want to develop with you a few ideas about this question of homosexuality. There are people among the homosexuals who take the viewpoint: what I do concerns nobody else, that is my private matter. All things which concern the sexual area are not, however, the private matter of the individual, but rather they mean the life and death of the people, they mean world power and Swissification. A people which has very many children has the prospect of world power and world domination. A people of good race, which has very few children, owns a sure ticket to the grave, for insignificance in 50 and 100 years, for burial in two hundred and five hundred years....

We must realize that if we continue to have this depravity in Germany, without being able to fight it, then that is the end of Germany, the end of the Germanic world. Unfortunately, we no longer have it as easy as our ancestors. For them, these few were individual cases of abnormality. The homosexual, whom one named Urning, was sunk in a swamp. The professors who find these bodies in the moor are certainly not aware that they have in ninety of one hundred cases a homosexual in front of them, who had been sunk in a swamp with clothes and all. That was not a punishment, but was simply the extinguishing of this anomalous life. It had to be removed, as we pull out stinging nettles, throw them in a pile and burn them. There was no feeling of revenge, but the person had to be removed.

So it was for our ancestors. For us that is unfortunately, I must say, no longer possible. Within the scope of the SS I would like to explain the following very clearly. I stress explicitly that I know exactly what I am saying. This is of course not meant for leadership meetings, but you can discuss it conversationally with one or the other:

We still have in the SS today one case per month of homosexuality. In the whole SS about eight to ten cases will appear in a year. I have now decided the following: these people will of course in each case be publicly demoted and expelled and handed over to the court. After serving the penalty set by the court, they will be brought on my order to a concentration camp and will be shot in the concentration camp trying to escape.... Thereby I hope that I can get this type of person out of the SS to the last one, in order to keep the good blood, that we have in the SS and this growing recovery of the blood that we are cultivating for Germany.

The question for all of Germany is still not thereby solved. One should not be fooled about the following. If I bring the homosexual before the court and have him locked up, the case is not settled, but the homosexual comes out of prison exactly as homosexual as he went in. Thus the whole question is not cleared up....

---

Himmler delivered this speech to SS-Gruppenführer (Major Generals) at the SS training academy in Bad Tölz, a spa in the Bavarian Alps. As he often did, Himmler pretended to broad and exact knowledge about homosexuality in Germany, but neither his statistics nor his history are to be trusted. The usefulness of this speech lies in the demonstration of Himmler's thinking about homosexuality. The multiplication of the pure Germanic race leads inevitably to world domination, and thus protection of racial purity is the state's highest priority. Individual lives must be emotionlessly extinguished for the health of the *Volk*.

Although Himmler is explicit about how homosexuals in the SS should be treated, he leaves the larger question of homosexuality in Germany without an explicit solution. The persecution of Germany's homosexual men, however, began immediately upon the seizure of power in 1933. After the assassination of Ernst Röhm and other leaders of the SA on 28 June 1934, homosexuality was attacked more vigorously. The Gestapo notified police departments across the country to compile lists of homosexuals, which were used in the first large wave of arrests of homosexuals that fall. On the anniversary of Röhm's murder in 1935, new laws against homosexuality widened the scope of persecution.

Thousands of German men were sent to concentration camps within the Reich for homosexuality. There they were marked with a pink triangle, and sank with the Jewish prisoners to the bottom of the camp hierarchy. After the war began, 'the extinguishing of anomalous life' became state policy. The number who died will never be exactly ascertained, but probably around 10,000 were put into the camps, and most were killed or died there.[1]

The Nazis did not understand the causes of homosexuality and thus had no clear policy for its elimination. There would be no 'final solution' for homosexuals, since homosexuality appeared in every generation of German youth. In some camps, SS doctors tried to 'cure' homosexuals by forcing them to have sex with female prisoners. Homosexuals in occupied Europe were generally not pursued, possibly in the hope that they would contribute to the further degeneration of the captive population.

## Note

1 A thorough and well documented study is Richard Plant, *The Pink Triangle: The Nazi War Against Homosexuals* (New York: Henry Holt and Co., 1986).

# 16. Children's story from Ernst Hiemer, *The Poisonous Mushroom*, 1938

How Inge Fared at a Jewish Doctor

Inge is sick. For several days she has had a light fever and headache. Inge does not want to go to the doctor.

"Ach, because of such a little thing to run to the doctor?" she says over and over again, when her mother urges and warns. One day, however, mother becomes annoyed.

"March! You go now over to Doctor Bernstein and let yourself be examined!" So ordered the mother.

"Why to Doctor Bernstein? He is a Jew! And no German girl goes to a Jew," answered Inge.

Mother laughed.

"Ach, stop talking nonsense! The Jewish doctors are fine. But you in your BDM chatter obvious foolish nonsense! What do you girls know about it?"

Inge protested.

"Mother, you can say what you want, but you may not insult the BDM. And you must notice one thing: we BDM girls know more about the Jewish question than many of our parents. Our group leader gives a short lecture nearly every week about the Jews. Just the other day she said: 'A German may not go to a Jewish doctor! And especially not a German girl! The Jews only want to corrupt the German people. So many girls who sought cures with a Jewish doctor found there disease and disgrace.' Yes, Mother, that's what our group leader said. And she is right!"

The mother became nervous.

"Ach, you always want to be smarter than your elders. What you say is not true at all. Look, Inge, I know Doctor Bernstein very well. He is quite a proficient doctor!"

"But he is a Jew! And the Jews are our mortal enemies!" answered Inge.

Now the mother became seriously angry.

"Now it's enough, you fresh child! You go right away over to Doctor Bernstein! And if you refuse, then you'll get it from me!"

Thus the mother shouted and threatened with her hand.

Inge did not want to be disobedient and went. She went over to the Jewish Doctor Bernstein!

Inge sits in the anteroom of the Jewish doctor. She must wait a long time. She looks through the magazines, which lie on the table. But she is much too restless to be able to read even a few sentences. Over and over again she thinks about the conversation with her mother. And over and over again the warnings of her BDM group leader come to mind: "A German may not go to a Jewish doctor! And especially not a German girl! The Jews only want to corrupt the German people. So many girls who sought cures with a Jewish doctor found there disease and disgrace!"

As Inge stepped into the waiting room, she had a remarkable experience. Out of the office of the doctor she heard crying. She heard the voice of a girl:

"Doctor! Doctor! Leave me alone!"

Then she heard the scornful laughter of a man. Then it suddenly became very quiet. Inge listened breathlessly.

"What could all that mean?", she asked herself, and her heart pounded in her throat. And again she thought about the warnings of her BDM leader.

Inge had waited an hour already. Again she grabbed the magazines and tried to read. Then the door opens. Inge looks up. The Jew appears. A cry escapes from Inge's mouth. In fright she lets the magazine fall. Terrified she jumps up. Her eyes stare into the face of the Jewish doctor. And this face is the face of the devil. In the middle of this devil's face sits a huge bent nose. Behind glasses glitter two criminal eyes. And a sneer plays on the bulging lips. A sneer that says: "Now I have you at last, little German girl!"

And then the Jew comes toward her. His fleshy fingers grab at her. Now however Inge has composed herself. Before the Jew can grasp her, she hits the Jewish doctor in his fat face with her hand. Then a leap to the door. Breathless Inge runs down the steps. Breathless she rushes out of the Jewish house.

She arrives home crying. The mother is startled when she sees her child.

"My God, Inge! What happened?"

It takes a long time before the child can speak even a word. Then however Inge tells of her experience at the Jewish doctor. Appalled, the mother listens. And as Inge ends her story, the mother sinks her head in shame.

"Inge, I should not have sent you to a Jewish doctor. After you left, I already reproached myself. I had no peace. I wanted most of all to call you back. I suspected suddenly that you had been right. I suspected that something would happen to you. But now everything is okay. Thank God!"

The mother groaned and had difficulty to hide her tears.

Gradually Inge calmed down. Now she smiled again. "Mother, you have been so good to me. I thank you for that. But now you must promise me one thing: about the BDM ..."

The mother interrupts her child.

"I already know what you want to say, Inge. I promise you. I gradually realize that one can even learn something from you children."

Inge nods.

"You are right, Mother. We BDM girls, we know already what we want, even when you don't understand us completely. Mother, you have taught me many sayings. Today I want to tell you a saying, that you must pay attention to."

And slowly and meaningfully Inge said:

The Jewish doctor in Germany
Was sent to us by the devil.
And like a devil he corrupts
The German woman, the German honor.

The German people will not be healthy
If it does not soon find the way
To German medicine, German sense,
To German doctors henceforth.

---

This children's book typifies the work of Julius Streicher and his colleagues at *Der Stürmer*, the newspaper which spread the most extreme form of antisemitic propaganda throughout Germany. Streicher founded *Der Stürmer* in 1923, and by the late 1930s half a million copies were printed every week. Every issue headlined the saying of Heinrich von Treitschke, 'The Jews Are Our Misfortune'. Ernst Hiemer was one of the editors from the early 1930s.

Hiemer's *Der Giftpilz* is a collection of 17 short stories, like this one. Each story presents a crude lesson about the evil nature of Jews in their interactions with good Germans. As in the pages of *Der Stürmer*, Jews have no redeeming qualities. One of the stories claims that the Talmud, one of Judaism's holiest books, says that Jews are allowed to cheat Christians, that Jews are forbidden to lend money to Christians without charging excessive interest, and that Jews may rob, lie to and kill Christians. Each story is accompanied by a colorful drawing by Fips, the pseudonym for Philip Rupprecht, who drew the semi-pornographic cartoons of Jews in *Der Stürmer*. His caricatures ridicule mainly male Jews as fat and ugly, with incredibly large hooked noses, protruding teeth, big ears, and flat feet. Each story ends in a brief rhyme, including the verse, 'The world will only be healed, when we free it from Jews'. Streicher is pictured on the final page saying, 'The Jew is our misfortune'. At least 50,000 of these books were sold in 1938.

In late 1930s antisemitism explicitly entered all forms of educational material: school texts in math, biology, and geography, the handbook for Hitler Youth,[1] publications by social scientists in journals and academic series, and state-sanctioned popular readings for the young purveyed the racial ideology of the Nazis about Jews. In this story, Inge repeats the antisemitic lessons of the BDM, the League of German Girls. The broader ideological isolation of other social groups was also taught as truth. A middle school math text of 1936 asked students to draw a graph comparing the yearly costs to the state of taking care of the mentally ill with the cost of educating healthy school children.[2]

The publication of *Der Giftpilz* coincided with an escalation of persecution of Jews in Germany in 1938. The main synagogue in Munich was destroyed by official order on 9 June, and Streicher arranged the demolition of the synagogue in Nuremberg in August, as thousands watched. Those who had spent years creating the Jew as monster now attacked him with state organized violence.

Hiemer continued to write for *Der Stürmer* during the war, penning such articles as 'The Holy Hate' in 1943. In 1946 he testified at Nuremberg about Streicher, minimizing his own responsibilities at *Der Stürmer*. Streicher was found guilty and hanged on 16 October 1946. Hiemer received no penalty.

## Notes

1 Fritz Brennecke, *Vom deutschen Volk und seinem Lebensraum: Handbuch für die Schulungsarbeit in der HJ* (Munich: Zentralverlag der NSDAP, 1937); available in translation as *The Nazi Primer: Official Handbook for Schooling the Hitler Youth*, translated by Harwood L. Childs (New York: Harper and Brothers, 1938).

2 R. Dorner, *Mathematische Aufgaben aus der Volks-, Gelände- und Wehrkunde, 1. Teil* (Frankfurt am Main: 1936), p. 2, as cited in Johannes Tuchel (ed.), *'Kein Recht auf Leben': Beiträge und Dokumente zur Entrechtung und Vernichtung 'lebensunwerten Lebens' im Nationalsozialismus* (Berlin: Wissenschaftlicher Autoren-Verlag, 1984), p. 47.

Section V

# The Physical Assault on Jews in Germany, 1938–1939

Words in documents lose their ability to convey the real meaning of historical events when those events become violent. Until 1938 a major mode of attack on Jews and other racial inferiors was through the power of language. Jews were constantly confronted with signs of their persecution, ranging from the crudely lettered 'Don't Buy from Jews' placards of the SA on 1 April 1933, to the officially printed 'Not for Jews' signs which proliferated in public places, to 'Jews Not Welcome' affixed to sites of service, entertainment, and transport. The Nuremberg Laws were proudly published for all to read. Less open forms of persecution also affected the entire German Jewish community: loss of jobs in the public sector, government-sponsored humiliations, and occasional threats of violence. Other despised groups were attacked more physically in 1933 to 1937. First socialists and communists, then Jehovah's Witnesses and homosexuals were arrested and often brutalized in the system of concentration camps scattered across Germany. Jews were threatened in every way, but violence was only rarely directed towards them.

Beginning with the *Anschluss*, the forcible incorporation of Austria into the newly expanded Greater German Reich in March 1938, Nazi policy against Jews turned much more strongly toward violence. In a surprisingly rapid series of steps, physical assault on Jewish persons and their property became the primary method of persecution. As policy changed, so did the nature of the words in those documents which accompanied the new policies. The transparency of earlier Nazi documents became clouded, because these papers were designed not only to explain but also to cover up what the Nazis were doing. The clearest example was the attempt to pass off the organized assault on Jewish synagogues and property during the so-called *Kristallnacht* as a spontaneous popular uprising.[1] Even the crude humiliation which Walter Grab describes in the first document was accompanied by a false claim about the source of the disgusting mess he was supposed to clean up. This cover up is evidence that Nazis at all levels agreed that what they were doing was wrong, even in the eyes of the broad German population. Shame has entered the picture.

These documents cannot be read in the same way as the more direct writings from before 1938. Words are no longer used primarily to communicate, but also to obscure. Information is being protected. The combination of documents produced by the Nazis and those on behalf of victims shows the importance of 1938 as a major step from persecution to the Holocaust. The two documents from the diplomatic offices of the British and American governments (documents 21 and 26) show how little effect German state-sponsored violence against Jews had on official Western consciousness.

## Note

1 I use the label *Kristallnacht* (Night of Broken Glass) in this book, although that word is a Nazi euphemism which can obscure the real violence done to Jews on that night. The documents here which come out of that nationwide assault on Jews show precisely what the word meant.

# 17. Memoir by Walter Grab about persecution of Jews in Vienna after the *Anschluss* of March 1938

On the afternoon of 25 April 1938, after six weeks of Nazi domination in Austria, I was on the way home. Near our apartment a Jewish gymnasium was located in the cellar of Liechtensteinstrasse 20. When I was a child of 7 or 8 years, I had often done gymnastics there. As I got near this building, I was stopped by Nazis, who made a chain and carried armbands with swastikas. One shouted at me, "Are you a Jew?" When I said yes, he pushed me to the building, where the gymnasium was, and ordered me to go down the stairs. In this large cellar, perhaps 30 meters long, where Jewish children did their exercises and where much gymnastics apparatus was located, there were also rooms where the boys and girls changed clothes. In this anteroom of the gymnasium I saw about 20 or 25 Jews, whom the Nazis had seized before me and had pushed together into a corner. A Nazi pushed me there, too. The large gymnasium and also this anteroom were, by your leave, perfectly covered with shit. The floor and also the walls were completely covered with excrement. It stank atrociously. By my estimation, a whole regiment of SA or SS or some other Nazis must have relieved themselves there, and in fact very shortly before one began to seize the Jews; the excrement was still very fresh and damp. Besides the Jews, 15 or 20 Nazis were standing in the changing room. Behind me still other Jews were pushed down the stairs, so that we were 35 or 40 at the end – only men. For the Nazis this was great fun, they amused themselves tremendously, because they could now take it out on these helpless and confused Jews, whom they had chased into the gymnasium befouled with excrement. They laughed and screamed 10 or 15 minutes and ridiculed us, because we were afraid. Finally one stepped forward and said, "You Jews have left us your gymnasium this filthy. Jewish gymnasiums are so dirty. One sees again, how filthy Jews are. And now you have to lick it up." What does one say, when one is at the mercy of these barbarians, who look as if they had a human face? Nothing. We stood there speechless. We were at their mercy and thought anything was possible. But they had only made a joke. They thought it up to humiliate and degrade the Jews. This was not a commanded action, like the Jewish pogrom of November 9, when the Jewish businesses were plundered and the apartments demolished. No, this was a true mob prank. I am not sure, whether such "pranks" happened in other cities, but in Vienna they happened. We were entirely at the mercy of these Nazis. And they amused themselves tremendously at how we fearfully pressed together. How could one lick up this Nazi excrement?

And then one shouted: "Now get going! To work!" Some Jews actually tried to scrape the excrement together by hand and throw it into the toilet bowl. But that was impossible. At best one could only smear the excrement. It was not possible to clean the anteroom and the gym this way. The Nazis laughed and jeered at us, but eventually brought a scoop, a broom, a bucket, and a couple of rags, and we turned the water faucet on. But one would have needed a fire hose to clean up. I took a rag in my hand, had a frantic fear of being killed by the Nazis in this cellar, and tried to crawl behind the other Jews and throw the excrement into the toilet. The whole thing lasted 15 or 20 minutes, during which we tried to follow the orders of the Nazis. There was not much success. And while I squat and bend over, in order to make myself in my fear as inconspicuous as possible, I raise my eyes and I meet exactly the gaze of one of these laughing Nazis, who are standing around with their swastika armbands on brown shirts. And I recognized him immediately. He was a school comrade from the Volksschule. I had in fact left the Volksschule already in 1929, and meanwhile nine years had passed; but I knew right away that this Nazi was a boy with whom I was in the same class in the first four years of elementary school. In fact he sat next to me one time, we played together in the school yard. His name was Lichtenegger. That I will never forget.

And this former school comrade Lichtenegger sees me, and recognizes me just as I recognized him. This recognition was uncomfortable and painful for him. I noticed that in this split second; I felt that he did not want to humiliate me, the Jew whom he knew, but rather the anonymous Jew, the Jewish bogeyman of Nazi racial madness. "The Jew" is the vermin that one must step on, eradicate, but the school comrade Grab, he had known him as a fellow human, he did not mean him. These were his thoughts, that I understood in a second, as our gazes met. And I got myself up, threw the rag away, and went to Lichtenegger, while the other Jews tried to clean up the filth. In my broadest Viennese I said, "Hey, listen, Lichtenegger, you know me, let me out of here." He cast down his eyes, ripped a piece from a newspaper, which was lying around for wrapping up the excrement, and wrote on it: "The Jew can leave." Apparently he had some little authority, was some sort of lower officer of these Nazis. After he wordlessly gave me the notice, I went to the steps, said to the Nazi who guarded them, "Lichtenegger said I can leave," and held the scrap of paper out. Then I ran up, showed the note to the Nazi at the door, and hurried home as fast as my legs could carry me. It was not more than an hour from the moment when I was halted on the street to my flight out of the gymnasium.

I believe that this little episode throws a characteristic light on the contradiction between the antisemitic racial madness and the confrontation of Nazis with actual Jews.

---

The *Anschluss* of Austria into the Third Reich on 13 March 1938 was the signal for a spontaneous outpouring of popular violence against Jews by Austrians. During this entire week, Austrian SA troops, Nazi party members, and unaffiliated antisemites took the opportunity to attack and rob their Jewish neighbors. Jews all over Austria were assaulted in the streets and in their homes, beyond anything seen yet in Germany. Three thousand Viennese Jews were arrested in the next few weeks, and Jewish property was stolen, destroyed, or confiscated by the state and by individual citizens. Walter Grab wrote this description of his own experience long afterwards for a book of essays on public involvement in persecution. He called the outbreak of violence against Jews in Austria 'an eruption of the mob'.

Like many Austrian Jews, Grab reacted to these sudden attacks by fleeing. Through his mother's relatives in Jerusalem, he received permission to study at the University of Jerusalem, and left in July. While about one-third of German Jews had fled between 1933 and 1938, that proportion of Austrian Jews escaped in just the 8 months between March and November 1938.

Grab became a professor of history at the University of Tel Aviv, where he founded an institute for the study of German history. He died in 2001.

# 18. Letter urging that Jews be fired from Austrian industry, 29 June 1938

League of Austrian Manufacturers,
Association for the Region of the City of Vienna,
Viennese Association of Manufacturers
Vienna III, Schwarzenbergplatz 4 (House of Industry)

Strictly Confidential! Vienna, 29 June 1938

To Business Managers!

The following persons should be terminated on 30 June 1938 and removed as quickly as possible from the enterprises:
a) Jews according to Par. 5 of the First Decree of the Reich Citizenship Law of 14 November 1935 or
b) Mischlinge according to Par. 5 of the First Decree of the Reich Citizenship Law of 14 November 1935 or
c) Persons who are married to Jews or
d) Persons whose behavior during the Forbidden Time was such that their remaining in a National Socialist work force seems untenable.

Furthermore, pension and maintenance payments to such persons should be stopped.

All information about a period of notice and any payments which need to be made, as well as about stoppage of pension and maintenance payments, will be delivered by our Association orally. Simultaneously we note the Austrian Decree on Settlement of Legal Claims, G.Bl.153/38.

The police (State Secretary Dr. Kaltenbrunner) are to be notified of such terminations of the above named people.

Furthermore, after the successful accomplishment of the matter, a written report on the measures taken with information about the individual people is to be made to our Association.

The cases mentioned in point d) should be handled in agreement with the Nazi company cell, together with a detailed written report to our Association, for the purpose of further informing the State Commissary for Private Business. The State Commissar will then make the decision in this cases.

Heil Hitler!

The Provisional Director: The Manager:

Hans Freiherr von Posanner m.p. Dr. Richard Friesz m.p.

---

After the violent attacks on Jewish families and businesses during the *Anschluss*, came a series of official efforts to remove all Jewish influence over the Austrian economy. The German laws which forced Jews out of civil service were extended to Austria, and Jews were also pushed out of education and the professions. This letter broadens this effort to the private sector in Vienna, as leaders of private industry, with excited haste, take action well beyond the requirements of law, extending their actions to the spouses of Jews and abrogating legal agreements about pensions. The firing of all Jews is combined with revenge against those workers who opposed the Nazis during the 'Forbidden Time', when the Nazi Party was outlawed in Austria after June 1933. Although these new rules appear to be surrounded with legal mechanisms, there are several signs here that the industrialists are anxious to avoid too much public notice of their actions.

Ernst Kaltenbrunner was appointed as minister of state security after the *Anschluss*. He worked with boyhood friend Adolf Eichmann to force the emigration of Austrian Jews. After Reinhard Heydrich's death in 1942, Himmler named Kaltenbrunner as head of the Reich Security Main Office. He was tried at Nuremberg and executed in October 1946.

# 19. Letter resisting the confiscation of a Jewish business, 14 July 1938

14 July 1938

To the Property Transfer Office

On the 5th of this month, 2 women appeared in my millinery and hat store, Vienna XX., Jägerstrasse 23, and explained that they had been sent by the Party, in order to negotiate with me about the takeover of my business, including the connecting apartment. Since I had never expressed the intention of selling my business, which offers me a modest income, I had to refuse the two women. To my suggestion that so many other businesses in all other districts, and some at livelier locations, were for sale, they replied that they were only interested in a business in the XX. District, because only here did they have "acquaintances" in the Party. Two days later, I received a summons from the Economic Office of the N.S.D.A.P. Brigittaplatz, which I obeyed. I was requested to sign papers, by which I committed myself to agree to the sale of the business and also to transfer the apartment to the buyers. I had to refuse the officials my signature. I have been in Vienna since the year 1899, am registered here and honestly and legally acquired the business in the year 1912. It provides a modest living for me and my family. I have neither wealth nor any other source of income! I was allowed to leave with the remark that I absolutely must return with my business license and sign the sale contract!

Since in this case a forced aryanization is neither of national or economic importance, nor for protection of Aryan employees or other interests, I request most politely a dismissal of this demand.

We have always fulfilled our duties, promptly paid all social and public fees, and are of good reputation. My husband fought at the front with Feldjäger Baon 27 (Commander Ferari) and was captured by the Russians on the Galician front.

I request most politely a favorable disposition of this matter and sign myself with great respect

Ella Czecher

In this particular case, Ella Czecher had twice resisted demands that she accept the confiscation of her property. Here she offers resistance a third time by requesting that the main office in charge of the aryanization process in Vienna allow her to keep her property. Czecher stresses those facts which she feels are relevant: her lengthy residence in Vienna, her husband's patriotism and wartime service, and her honesty in business. She apparently did not realize that such protestations were irrelevant to the Nazis, who saw all Jewish participation in the economy as inevitably dishonest. The social rules and legal system which Ella Czecher had believed in since she arrived in Vienna nearly 40 years before were no longer in force.

The two women who demanded Czecher's store, referring to friends in the Nazi Party, were seeking to enrich themselves at the expense of Jews by relying on connections in the Party. In the new marketplace of Jewish property, the demands of Austrians seeking personal advantage suddenly rose to meet the supply. What Czecher had not yet been told was that the purchase price, which would be set absurdly low by the authorities, would not be paid to her, but rather put into a special account, over which she would have no control. She could hope to see little if any of this money.

The official process of stealing Jewish property in the name of the state was bewilderingly rapid in Austria. Even before the Property Transfer Office (*Vermögensverkehrsstelle*) was created for this purpose, in the two months after the *Anschluss*, one-fifth of the 33,000 Jewish businesses in Vienna had already been taken over. By the end of 1938 over half of the 70,000 apartments owned by Jews had been aryanized. Private and public greed cooperated to dispossess Austria's Jews of commercial and private real estate, bank accounts, home furnishings, and personal possessions.

# 20. Letter confirming possession of Chinese visa, 23 September 1938

CHINESE GENERAL CONSULATE
VIENNA

Vienna, 23 September 1938.

To Herr Dr. Paul L a g s t e i n ,

V i e n n a .

The Chinese General Consulate confirms, that in your German passport No. 23,405 on 23 September 1938 a Chinese entry visa was entered, which is valid for one year.

The Chinese General Consulate:
by instruction

[signature illegible]

---

Paul Lagstein was born in 1904 and earned a PhD in chemistry at the University of Vienna. He, three siblings, and his brother-in-law procured Chinese entry visas in September 1938 from Feng Shan Ho, the Chinese Consul General in Vienna. Paul's younger sister Ady was given 5 ship tickets from Southampton to Shanghai by her sympathetic boss, a Swiss citizen working in Vienna. None of these documents were meant to be used for actual travel to China: they were simply a means to get out of Austria. With these papers in hand, the Lagstein family left Vienna shortly after *Kristallnacht*, and went to Yugoslavia, Italy, and finally to Paris. Ady was able to get to the US, but the others remained in France where they were repeatedly arrested and interned. They were eventually hidden in Nice by a local family until war's end. Paul Lagstein died in Nice at age 89.[1]

Dr Feng Shan Ho was a Chinese diplomat with a doctorate from the University of Munich, who was posted at the Chinese legation in Vienna. In May 1938 he became the Consul General. After the *Anschluss*, and the accompanying outbreaks of antisemitic persecution, Ho began issuing Chinese visas to any Jews who asked to aid their escape from Germany. The Gestapo demanded proof of emigration before allowing Jews to leave the Reich, and some countries, like Italy, required proof of an end destination before allowing refugees to enter. By the time that the Lagsteins arrived at the Chinese Consulate in September, visa applicants already formed long lines. After *Kristallnacht*, the desperation of German and Austrian Jews deepened. Ho defied the orders of his superiors not to issue any more visas, eventually stamping thousands of passports, whose holders managed to escape to Latin America, Palestine, the Philippines, Cuba, and Shanghai. In May 1940 Consul General Ho was transferred out of Vienna. Although he rarely mentioned his humanitarian work, Ho was honored by Yad Vashem in 2000 as one of the 'Righteous Among the Nations'.

Ho was one of a number of foreign diplomats in Europe who used their offices to help Jews escape the Holocaust. In Kovno, Lithuania, the Japanese Consul Chiune Sugihara and the Dutch Consul Jan Zwartendijk issued visas to Jews fleeing the Nazi occupation of Poland in 1940. These visas were legally meaningless, but they were recognized by various nations, such as the Soviet Union, who allowed their holders to travel through. About 2200 refugees crossed the Soviet Union on the Trans-Siberian Railroad and reached Japan. Half were able to travel further to the US, Canada, and Palestine, while the remainder ended up in Shanghai.

This help was desperately needed, because the normal destinations for emigration were closing their doors during the later 1930s. Unannounced policies of the US State Department prevented even the restricted quota of immigrants from Germany being reached between 1933 and 1938. While American consulates were harassing potential refugees with demands that they fill out endless forms, the US government made a show of concern by calling an international conference on refugees in July at the Evian-les-Bains spa in France.

## Note

1 This information comes from Serge Bluds, the nephew of Paul Lagstein and son of Ady Lagstein Bluds.

# 21. British memorandum on Evian conference, 17 October 1938

MEMORANDUM.

On March 24th the United States Government asked a number of Governments, including His Majesty's Government in the United Kingdom, whether they would co-operate in setting up a special Committee for the purpose of facilitating the emigration of refugees from Germany.

On July 6th the representatives of thirty-two Governments met at Evian in response to the United States Government's invitation.

The Inter-Governmental Committee adopted two unanimous resolutions. The more important drew attention to the consequences for other countries of what was termed the "involuntary emigration" of large numbers of people, and stressed the necessity of "a long-range programme, whereby assistance to involuntary emigrants, actual and potential, may be co-ordinated within the framework of existing migration laws and practices of Governments". The Committee further considered that "if countries of refuge or settlement are to co-operate in finding an orderly solution of the problem they should have the collaboration of the country of origin" and the Committee was therefore persuaded that the country of origin "will make its contribution by enabling involuntary emigrants to take with them their property and possessions and emigrate in an orderly manner".

The Committee made a number of recommendations to Governments, of which the following are relevant:–

"(a) The persons coming within the scope of the activity of the Inter-Governmental Committee shall be: (1) persons who have not already left their country of origin (Germany including Austria) but who must emigrate on account of their political opinions, religious beliefs or racial origin; and (2) persons as defined in (1) who have already left their country of origin and who have not yet established themselves permanently elsewhere."

"(b) An Inter-Governmental Committee should be set up in London 'to continue and develop the work of the Evian meeting'. This Committee should appoint a director of authority (1) 'to undertake negotiations to improve the present conditions of exodus and to replace them by conditions of orderly emigration'; and (2) 'to approach the Governments of the countries of refuge and settlement with a view to developing opportunities of permanent settlement'."

The Inter-Governmental Committee met in London on August 6th. It is composed of representatives of all the countries represented at Evian with the exception of Switzerland and one or two of the countries of South and Central America. It appointed Lord Winterton as Chairman, and the representatives of the United States, France, the Netherlands and Brazil as Vice-Chairmen. It appointed Mr. George Rublee, an American citizen, as its Director.

The Committee arranged for an exchange of information as to the opportunities of settlement in the various countries, and the Director has been making enquiries with a view to obtaining information in regard to the openings for immigration.

He has not yet been able to begin the other part of his work, namely discussions with the German Government in regard to the conditions in which emigrants are able to depart. The attitude of the countries of immigration is likely to be influenced by the outcome of these discussions, and, until it is known, those countries cannot give a definite indication of the number of refugees they are able to accept. The Director and his assistant, Mr. Pell, desire to begin consultations with the competent German authorities as soon as possible.

Inasmuch as the Inter-Governmental Committee is seeking a solution of the problem of involuntary emigration along strictly practical lines, it would seem reasonable to anticipate that the German Government will assist the other Governments upon which this problem has been forced by relaxing the pressure upon people who desire to leave sufficiently to permit the arrangement of orderly emigration and by permitting them to take with them a reasonable percentage of their property. The German Government, in forcing these persons to leave its territory without funds and without property, cannot be unmindful of the fact that it is thereby imposing great burdens on its friendly neighbours and on other nations throughout the world who, for humanitarian considerations, are doing what they can to alleviate the lot of these people. All other countries represented in the Inter-Governmental Committee are thereby given new and serious problems to solve.

It is on these grounds desirable that the Director should visit Berlin at an early date with a view to discussing the various aspects of the emigration problem with the competent German authorities.

British Embassy,<br>
Berlin.<br>
17th October, 1938.

---

This memorandum from the British Embassy in Berlin was directed at the German Foreign Office three months after the July conference of 32 nations at Evian. President Franklin Roosevelt had called this conference as a means of relieving the pressure on the United States and other Western nations to accept large numbers of Jewish refugees from the Third Reich. The conference invitation stated that no nation would be expected to increase the number of emigrants it accepted. This memo shows how British diplomats saw emigration as a problem for themselves rather than for the Jews. It reflects and repeats much of the wording of the final decisions of the Evian Conference.

The hope expressed here that the Nazi government would worry about either the welfare of Jews, who were being forced by the threat of concentration camps to leave, or the 'great burdens on its friendly neighbours' demonstrates the unwillingness of the Western democracies to understand the plight of Jews under Nazi rule. The violence against Austrian Jews illustrated by Walter Grab's essay had been publicized in the world press. Over one thousand Jews had been arrested and sent to concentration camps in the summer of 1938. During the summer, the great synagogues in Munich and Nuremberg were destroyed. Aryanization had robbed Jews throughout Germany of their property. All of these events were well-known.

The German Foreign Office rejected the suggestion of this memo that the Director of the Inter-Governmental Committee visit Berlin, stating that the Germans had no intention of allowing Jews to emigrate with some of their property, and noting that the Committee was 'sterile'.

# 22. Report of Darmstadt SA on *Kristallnacht*, 11 November 1938

SA. of the NSDAP
Brigade 50 (Starkenburg)
Division F, Ref. No. 4309

Darmstadt, 11 November 1938
Moosbergstrasse 2
Tel. 7042 and 7043
Postal Checking Account: Frankfurt a.M. 234-38
Bank Account: City Savings Bank 155

To
SA Group Kurpfalz
Mannheim .

The following order reached me at 3 o'clock on 10 November 1938:

> "On the order of the Gruppenführer, immediately all the Jewish synagogues within the 50th Brigade are to be blown up or set on fire. Neighboring houses occupied by Aryan population may not be damaged. The action is to be carried out in civilian clothes. Rioting and plundering are to be prevented. Report of execution to Brigade Leader or office by 8.30."

The Standartenführer were immediately alerted by me and exactly instructed, and the execution began at once.

I hereby report, the following were destroyed in the area of

Standarte 115

| | | | |
|---|---|---|---|
| 1.) Synagogue in Darmstadt, Bleichstrasse | | | destroyed by fire |
| 2.) | " | " " Fuchsstrasse | " " " |
| 3.) | " | " O./.Ramstadt demolished | interior and furnishings |
| 4.) | " | " Gräfenhausen | " " |
| 5.) | " | " Griesheim | " " |
| 6.) | " | " Pfungstadt | " " |
| 7.) | " | " Eberstadt | destroyed by fire |

Standarte 145

| | |
|---|---|
| 1.) Synagogue in Bensheim | destroyed by fire |
| 2.) " " Lorsch in Hessen | " " " |
| 2.) " " Heppenheim | " " " and explosion |
| 3.) " " Birken | destroyed by fire |
| 4.) Prayer House in Alsbach | " " " |
| 5.) Meeting Room in Alsbach | " " " |
| 6.) Synagogue in Rimbach | furnishings completely destroyed |

Standarte 168

| | |
|---|---|
| 1.) Synagogue in Seligenstadt | destroyed by fire |
| 2.) " in Offenbach | " " " |
| 3.) " in Klein-Krotzenburg | " " " |
| 4.) " in Steinheim on Main | " " " |
| 5.) " in Mühlheim on Main | " " " |
| 6.) " in Sprendlingen | " " " |
| 7.) " in Langen | " " " |
| 8.) " in Egelsbach | " " " |

Standarte 186

| | |
|---|---|
| 1.) Synagogue in Beerfelden | destroyed by explosion |
| 2.) " in Michelstadt | furnishings demolished |
| 3.) " in Koenig | " " |
| 4.) " in Höchst in O. | " " |
| 5.) " in Gross-Umstadt | " " |
| 6.) " in Dieburg | " " |
| 7.) " in Babenhausen | " " |
| 8.) " in Gross-Bieberau | destroyed by fire |
| 9.) " in Fränk. Crumbach | furnishings destroyed |
| 10.) " in Reichelsheim | " " |

Standarte 221

| | |
|---|---|
| 1.) Synagogue and Chapel in Gr. Gerau | destroyed by fire |
| 2.) " in Rüsselsheim | torn down a. furnishings destroyed |
| 3.) " in Dornheim | furnishings destroyed |
| 4.) " in Wolfskehlen | " " |

The Führer of Brigade 50 (Starkenburg)
[signature illegible]
Brigadeführer

This is one of many reports by local SA groups across Germany and Austria of their actions on 9–10 November. The order to destroy all synagogues was passed from the Gruppenführer in Mannheim to the Brigadeführer in Darmstadt, who sent off his Standartenführer to accomplish the task in the early morning of 10 November. The area covered was about 700 square miles just south of Frankfurt. It was expected that the entire process would be finished within 6 hours. By 9 o'clock that morning, Brigadeführer Lucke telephoned Mannheim to report that most of the work had been accomplished.

In addition to the destruction of over 250 synagogues in Germany and Austria, about 7500 Jewish businesses were attacked, and uncounted residences were vandalized and looted. In one night, the physical presence of Jewish life in German communities was visibly smashed through coordinated action by agents of the state. Nearly 30,000 Jewish men were arrested and sent to concentration camps in Dachau, Buchenwald, and Sachsenhausen. Almost 100 Jews were murdered and many more committed suicide. The shattered shop windows gave this highly organized attack its official German name, *Reichskristallnacht.*

It is difficult to imagine what this modern pogrom meant to German Jews. Samuel Monaker, the American Consul General in Stuttgart, described the people who appeared at his office the next day:

> Jews from all sections of Germany thronged into the office until it was overflowing with humanity, begging for an immediate visa or some kind of letter in regard to immigration which might influence the police not to arrest or molest them. Women over sixty years of age pleaded on behalf of husbands imprisoned in some unknown place. American mothers of German sons invoked the sympathy of the Consulate. Jewish fathers and mothers with children in their arms were afraid to return to their homes without some document denoting their intention to immigrate at an early date. Men in whose homes old, rusty revolvers had been found during the last few days cried aloud that they did not dare ever again to return to their places of residence or business. In fact, it was a mass of seething, panic-stricken humanity.[1]

## Note

1 Letter of Monaker to Hugh R. Wilson, American Ambassador in Berlin, 12 November 1938, reprinted in John Mendelsohn, (ed.), *The Holocaust: Selected Documents in Eighteen Volumes, Vol. 3, The Crystal Night Pogrom* (New York: Garland Publishing, Inc., 1982), pp. 182–9.

# 23. Letter about finding work in British households for Czech Jewish refugees, 17 November 1938

GERMAN JEWISH AID COMMITTEE
(COUNCIL FOR GERMAN JEWRY)

TELEPHONES:
EUSTON 4091
(PRIVATE BRANCH EXCHANGE)

CABLES:
REFUGEES, KINCROSS, LONDON

WOBURN HOUSE,
UPPER WOBURN PLACE,
LONDON, W.C. 1.

All communications should be addressed to the Secretary and not to individuals.

*In reply kindly quote reference*: RLS/DOM

17 November 1938.

Mrs. Schmolkova,
Prague,
Tachymova 3.

Very esteemed Mrs. Schmolkova,

We received your address from the "British Committee for Refugees from Czechoslovakia" and request you to have the persons listed on the accompanying questionnaire summoned to you, and to send us for each an exact personal description (particulars, fitness for household positions, special circumstances), 3 passport photos, biography, copies of testimonials, if possible health certificate, and an exactly filled out questionnaire according to the enclosed sample.

We will take the liberty in the near future to regularly send you such applications and would be very thankful to you if you would handle these as quickly as possible. On our end, we will exert ourselves to accommodate the applicants in household positions here and to provide them with the necessary permits.

With many thanks in advance for your efforts,

Yours respectfully,

*Formerly*
Jewish Refugees Committee

[signatures] Levitt / Schwarz
DOMESTIC EMPLOYMENT SECTION

---

In halting German, activist English Jews sought to find appropriate female refugees, who could squeeze through the loopholes in British immigration laws. One week after *Kristallnacht*, the search for refuge by Jews in the Third Reich had suddenly reached a crisis. Mrs. Schmolkova was the chair of the central committee for all organizations of German-speaking refugees in Czechoslovakia. She was also on the executive board of WIZO, the Women's International Zionist Organization. Thus she knew both that Jewish organizations in England were trying to find positions for young women as household servants and how difficult it was to find such places. Schmolkova replied that she was willing to insure that the tasks asked of her would be accomplished.

For German and Austrian refugees who had fled across the border in the wake of the escalating persecution in 1938, providing the papers demanded in England was difficult. A visa requirement had been reinstated in England after the *Anschluss* to slow the immigration of refugees without resources. Those who succeeded left their families behind in order to become the servants of the British upper and middle classes. The so-called *Kindertransport* brought about 10,000 young children to England in 1939, who also had to leave their parents behind, since the English would not accept complete families. After war began in 1939, many refugees were interned in 1940 on the Isle of Man as enemy aliens.[1]

At this moment, Czech Jews could still offer assistance to German and Austrian Jews who fled across the border, but themselves were becoming increasingly desperate. In September 1938, British Prime Minister Neville Chamberlain had brokered the agreement in Munich which gave Hitler the green light to invade and annex the Sudetenland. Just a few months later, in March 1939, German troops occupied Bohemia and Moravia, and Slovak fascists created an independent Slovakia allied with the Nazis.

## Note

1 An excellent overview of British immigration policy is provided by Louise London, *Whitehall and the Jews, 1933-1948: British Immigration Policy, Jewish Refugees, and the Holocaust* (Cambridge: Cambridge University Press, 2000).

# 24. Gestapo report from Bielefeld about *Kristallnacht* destruction, 26 November 1938

Copy.

State Police
II B 2 – 3861/38

Bielefeld, 26 November 1938.

To
the Secret State Police
Office of the Secret State Police
in Berlin

Regarding: Protest action against Jews on 10 November 38.
Reference: None.

In the police district Bielefeld, 37 synagogues were destroyed on the occasion of the protest action against Jews. Of these 19 synagogues were destroyed by fire and 18 synagogues in other ways. The damages amount to about 450,000 RM.

Of businesses and commercial spaces, a total of 102 were destroyed. Of these, 5 were destroyed by fire and 97 in other ways. The damages amount to about 420,000 RM. Through the destruction of the commercial enterprises, a total of 32 employees were put out of work, of whom up to now 3 could again be put to work. In the very near future, the remainder can be accommodated elsewhere.

Of private houses, a total of 110 were destroyed or damaged. Of these, 7 houses were fully burned down. The remaining houses are more or less badly damaged. The repair of the damaged houses is possible in every case. The damages total about 200,000 RM.

Of apartm ent furnishings, 47 were totally destroyed. 57 apartments were more or less damaged. The total damages of the destroyed apartments come to about 250,000 RM.

During the action two people lost their lives:

a) the Jew David Schlesinger, born on 20 November 1880 in Albaxen, resident in Albaxen, No. 10. Schlesinger jumped out of a jeep of the SA after his arrest and incurred a skull fracture, as a result of which he died;

b) the Jewess Miss Julie Hirschfeld, born on 29 September 1856 in Horn i/L., resident in Horn i/L., Nordstr. 11. Hirschfeld is near-sighted and for this reason fell down the stairs. As a result she died in the hospital in Detmold.

5 people received injuries during the action, and indeed the Jew Paul Stern broke some ribs in Herzebrock. He is now in the hospital in Herzebrock. The other 4 people were lightly injured. Physical abuses did not occur.

In 21 places during the action, thefts in Jewish businesses or apartments occurred. Goods and other material assets with a value of about 60,000 RM were stolen. In addition about 3,000 RM in cash were taken. Up to now a small portion of the stolen items were recovered. The investigations continue.

Of weapons, in the action 13 automatic pistols, 10 revolvers, 14 hunting rifles, 7 small caliber rifles, and 6 bird rifles, as well as 100 rounds of ammunition to the listed weapons, were confiscated. Of hand weapons, 32 sabers and bayonets and 26 daggers and knives were confiscated. In addition a small number of personal military arms were confiscated.

In 17 synagogues archival material was secured and handed over to the SD for evaluation.

Of cash and bank accounts about 9,000 RM were secured. Their return could not yet be accomplished due to the absence of the owners.

The synagogues and other buildings and commercial spaces were without exception insured. How high the insured values were, individually and in total, can at the moment not be given, since the policy owners mostly were arrested.

In general one cannot speak of an emergency for the Jewish families in which male family members were arrested. Individual cases have, however, become known, where the families are in a real emergency and must rely on public welfare.

Among the 406 Jews delivered from here to the concentration camp Buchenwald, 4 deaths thus far are to be noted. Upon application from here, about 45 Jews so far have been released from the camp Buchenwald.

All Jews have the firm intention to emigrate. All Jews who have commercial enterprises want to aryanize or liquidate.

The action of 10 November 1938 has quite unfavorably affected the mood of the population in general.

The destruction of the synagogues was in fact disapproved of only from ecclesiastical circles, from both the Protestant and the Catholic sides. Similarly, the smashing of the windows of Jewish businesses and private residences did not generally cause offense. Openly criticized, on the other hand, in all circles of the population, especially among the workers, was the destruction of material assets, for which especially the workers have no understanding. Comparisons are constantly being made between the austerity measures and collections of trash and the like as part of the Four Year Plan, and the wanton destruction of assets.

Because the execution of the action lay in the hands of the Party, which is of course generally known among the population, the reputation of the movement was also damaged, since in many places youth were used for the execution of the action. Thus it was observed in a host of cases that school children took part in the smashing of windows and even in laying fires and destroying furnishings and the like.

In this connection it should be remarked that the method of reporting about the course of the action through the press generally has caused offense. Since, as already noted, the population in almost no case took part in the action, the continual assertion of the press that it was a spontaneous revolt of the people has a downright ridiculous effect, given the fact that the action was organized from above, since the overall uniform execution of the action was unmistakable.

On the other hand, the laws on atonement promulgated by General Field Marshall Göring have met with approval throughout the population. Similarly few voices have been raised against the arrest of the Jews.

signed vom Felde

---

This report about the destruction of 9–10 November by the head of police in Bielefeld is especially useful for the critical remarks he offers about how this action was regarded among the local population. Even after 5 years of Nazi rule, the report makes clear that many Germans still felt capable of expressing approval or disapproval of government actions, mocking the official press, and distinguishing among policies they liked or did not like. Vom Felde's comments are echoed in other local reports: on 22 November Mayor Budde of Bielefeld reported to the Gestapo that most people could not understand the destruction of valuable property and that they did not believe the reporting about spontaneous action of the people; on 23 November the mayor wrote to the District President in Minden of his opinion that the destruction was against the law and therefore probably not desired by Hitler.[1] In fact, the actions in Bielefeld area were done mainly by the SS. In general the official reports of various parts of government, both civilian and police, in November and December were critical of the destructiveness and the false reporting, but do claim that the population welcomed sharper measures against Jews in the economy.

On the other hand, comments about how Jews received injuries during their arrest are not credible. The 58-year-old David Schlesinger is claimed to have jumped out of an SA jeep, and the 82-year-old Julie Hirschfeld fell down the stairs. The passive voice is used to describe other Jews receiving injuries, as well as the deaths of 4 within two weeks of being sent to Buchenwald.

The efforts of the Nazi leaders to disguise their well-planned and nationally coordinated attack on the Jews of the Third Reich failed. But the public protests against this *'Protestaktion'* were so quiet that it was clear that the German population would not offer significant resistance to the forcible removal of all Jewish influence in Germany, as long as this was accomplished without destroying valuable property.

## Note

1 See discussion and reprinted documents in Joachim Meynert and Friedhelm Schäffer, *Die Juden in der Stadt Bielefeld während der Zeit des Nationalsozialismus*, Bielefelder Beiträge zur Stadt- und Regionalgeschichte, Vol. 3 (Bielefeld: 1983), pp. 70–8, 163–8. The District President of Niederbayern and Oberpfalz in Bavaria offered the same evaluation of public rejection of the destruction of property in his monthly report of 8 December 1938: Martin Broszat, Elke Fröhlich, and Falk Wiesemann (eds), *Bayern in der NS-Zeit: Soziale Lage und politisches Verhalten der Bevölkerung im Spiegel vertraulicher Berichte* (Munich: R. Oldenbourg Verlag, 1977), pp. 473–4.

# 25. Instruction from Foreign Office on eliminating Jews from German life, 25 January 1939

Foreign Office
W I 110

Berlin, 25 January 1939

To all Missions and Professional Consulates

Since the seizure of power, the National Socialist Government has already eliminated the Jews living in Germany from the political life of the nation; in 1938 it has also created the legal basis for the dejudaization of our economic life.

The legislation and decrees in this area enacted in 1938 had as their goal:

1. to ascertain the influence of Jewry through exact surveys of the number of Jewish enterprises and the amount of Jewish property, and to prevent the Jews from increasing their property within the German economy, and

2. to confiscate property in Jewish hands.

These measures were initiated by the internal order of 4 January 1938, which for the first time, defined the concept of "Jewish enterprises". The concept was legally determined by the Third Decree to the Reich Citizenship Law of 14 June 1938. According to it, an enterprise is considered to be Jewish, if the proprietor is a Jew (Art. 5 of the First Decree to the RGB of 14 November 1935). The enterprise ... is considered to be Jewish if one or more personally responsible partners are Jewish. An enterprise of a juridical person is considered to be Jewish if one or more of the persons legally representing it, or one or more of the members of the board of directors are Jews, or if Jews have a controlling interest through capital stock or voting rights. Beyond this, an enterprise is considered to be Jewish if the influence of Jews is predominant.

At the same time, the creation of a public register for Jewish enterprises was ordered. The Reich Minister of Economics was empowered to order the firms in this register to bear a special characterization. Both the creation of the register and the threat of public characterization are intended to cause the Jews to dispose of their enterprises voluntarily in a speedier way. Both measures have not been put into effect.

The decree of 26 April 1938 concerning the registration of the property of Jews provides that all property in the hands of Jews must be reported, in case the total amount exceeds 5,000 Reichsmark in any individual case.

Accordingly, and in conjunction with the Implementation Decree of 18 June 1938, the following persons were liable to register:
1. Jews of German nationality and stateless Jews, and their German and foreign property, irrespective of whether they have their residence in Germany or abroad.
2. Jews of foreign nationality residing in Germany, and their German property.

The German property of foreign Jews residing abroad could not be included.

Pursuant to this decree, the following total worth was registered in the Reich after the target date of 27 April 1938:

| | | |
|---|---|---|
| a) from 135,750 Jews of German nationality | RM | 7,050,000,000 |
| b) from 9,567 foreign Jews | | 415,000.000 |
| c) from 2,269 stateless Jews | | 73,500.000 |
| Total: | RM | 7,538,500,000 |

Not contained in this list are registered properties of non-Jewish spouses of Jews. These spouses were liable to register, in order to prevent transfers of property, but it was not planned to extract from them any levies, etc. This was also not done on the occasion of the reprisal levy.

On 6 July 1938, the law amending the Trade and Industry Code became effective, according to which Jews and Jewish enterprises are banned from carrying on the following trades after 31 December 1938:

a) Security guard
b) Information services
c) Real estate trade
d) Brokerage agencies for real estate contracts and loans
e) House and real estate administration
f) Marriage agencies (except between Jews)
g) Visitors guides
h) Itinerant trades
I) Peddling
k) Commercial travelling (as long as Trade and Industry Code licenses are required).

Through these measures, in conjunction with a decree against the camouflaging of Jewish property, an expansion of the economic activity of the Jews was prevented in the first place and their elimination from economic life initiated.

The second group of measures, which created the legal basis for an accelerated and forced aryanization of the economy, was initiated by the decree of 12 November 1938 "For the Elimination of Jews from German Economic Life".

According to it, from 1 January 1939, Jews are forbidden to be active in retail trade, in crafts and in market trade; Jews may be neither enterprise leaders according to the law organizing national labor nor leading employees in economic enterprises; Jews must cease to be members of co-operative societies. Though this decree makes no distinction between Jews of German and foreign nationality, the Reich Minister of Economics on 30 December 1938 directed the competent state agencies to provisionally refrain from foreclosures of retail businesses and craft workshops, if the Jewish owner is a foreign national. An inventory of these businesses has been ordered, after which the Reich Minister of Economics will give further instructions from case to case.

When the decree of 12 November 1938 was issued, about 9,000 retail enterprises (excepting the bookselling and innkeeping trade) were in Jewish hands....

Jews are forbidden to acquire, to pawn or to sell privately items of gold, platinum or silver, as well as precious stones and pearls. Such items may only be acquired by the public buying centers set up by the Reich. The same applies to other jewelry and objects of art as long as the price for any object is in excess of RM 1,000. Foreigners are generally exempted from this provision.

Furthermore there is an obligation for Jews of German nationality and stateless Jews to deposit their securities. Access to securities in a Jewish deposit is subject to the approval of the Reich Ministry for Economics. This measure aims at the protection of the German securities market.

According to Art. 15 (2) of the Decree, the Jewish seller can be ordered to accept, instead of the payment fixed in the selling agreement, German Reich bonds. The Reich Minister for Economics has not yet made use of this power.

It may be assumed that as a result of the legislation enacted so far, especially the Decree on the Utilization of Jewish Property, the dejudaization of our economic life will be completed during 1939.

In view of the frequently incorrect descriptions of these measures in foreign countries, it seemed appropriate to advise the foreign missions on the matter for their information and for guiding their utterances. The following should be added: the measures have given rise to numerous representations, amongst them protests of foreign governments on behalf of Jews of foreign nationality. Some of them demanded a general assurance that their nationals in Germany would not be subjected to any discriminatory treatment on the grounds of race or religion. These demands were never met. On the other hand, the promise was given that individual cases would be examined in the light of current treaties with the country in question.

By instruction
[signature] Wiehl

---

This memorandum provides a useful description of the series of acts through which the Nazi state pursued the 'elimination of Jews from German economic life'. Step by step the government gathered information about what Jews owned, took control over properties, restricted Jews from more and more kinds of work, and forced Jews to turn over possessions at a fraction of their worth. The triumphant tone of this communication shows the active participation of German diplomats in the national plunder of Jews. The sum which the Nazis imagined they could take from Jews was enormous: the 7.5 billion Marks listed in this document would have nearly covered the entire foreign debt of Germany in 1939.[1]

At exactly the same time as Western diplomats at Evian made their acceptance of Jewish refugees dependent on the German government allowing them to leave with considerable resources, the Germans were openly taking everything they could, even from foreign Jews. From the beginning, the plundering of Jews was a central principle of Nazi policy.

### Note

1 According to Arthur Schweitzer, *Big Business in the Third Reich* (Bloomington, IN: Indiana University Press, 1977), p. 338, that debt was 9.5 billion Marks.

# 26. Instruction from US Secretary of State on preventing refugees to Shanghai, 18 February 1939

TELEGRAM SENT

## Department of State

Washington,
February 18, 1939

AMEMBASSY
BERLIN (GERMANY)

Your 127, February 17, 1 p.m.

The American Consul General at Shanghai reported early in January on the serious situation created there by the arrival of large numbers of destitute German refugees, principally on German and Italian vessels. We have taken the matter up with the President's Advisory Committee and the Intergovernmental Committee in order that appropriate steps might be taken to discourage refugees from going to Shanghai. It is suggested that, in your discretion and after you have learned the German reaction to the British demarche, you mention informally to the German authorities the desirability of discouraging the travel of Jews to Shanghai on German vessels.

[signature] Hull

Eu:TCA:NNB FE A-M

---

One of the most painful and controversial issues for the Western democracies was their unwillingness to alter restrictive immigration policies and to allow increased numbers of German and Austrian Jews to escape Nazi persecution after 1933. Those who defend American and British policies point to domestic political obstacles to accepting more Jewish refugees, such as the continuing economic effects of the Depression and the anti-immigration sentiment in the US Congress and British Parliament. Yet even the legally defined quota of

German refugees was not filled during the first 5 years of Nazi rule: from 1933 to 1937, only about 20% of the quota places allotted to immigrants to the US from Germany were used. In response to the escalation of persecution after the *Anschluss*, President Roosevelt opened the German-Austrian quota to full use, and perhaps 85,000 refugees entered the US from March 1938 through September 1939. Desperate German and Austrian Jews sought refuge anywhere in the world, including Shanghai.

This telegram shows the priorities and behavior at the top of the US State Department. Three months after *Kristallnacht*, thousands of Jewish refugees had already arrived in Shanghai, creating considerable consternation among the Western businessmen who effectively ruled Shanghai's municipal government. Their complaints travelled from their Consuls in Shanghai back to Western governments. Secretary of State Cordell Hull immediately took broad action to close this unique escape route for Jews trapped in Nazi Germany.

British reaction was similar. 'Your 127' refers to a telegram sent to Hull from Berlin the day before, reporting that the British Embassy in Berlin had received instructions to take steps 'to prevent further Jewish emigration to Shanghai'. The telegram noted that 'the British were "discouraging" the travel of Jews to Shanghai on British ships.' This was all prompted by a meeting of the Consular Corps in Shanghai, which asked that further Jewish emigration be prevented; perhaps this meeting encouraged the American Consul General to make the report that Hull refers to.

Hull's action here was not called for by isolationist Congressmen nor could it be defended as protecting American jobs from immigrant competitors. This telegram simply put the economic interests of a few American citizens living in Shanghai at a higher priority than the lives of Jews in Germany.

In early 1939 the Nazis were still committed to a policy of expelling Jews from the Reich, and these 'informal' efforts at persuasion had little effect. But such signals from the West about their lack of concern for the welfare of Jews, even after the pogrom of November 1938, helped to convince the Nazis that they could do as they wished with their 'Jewish problem'.

Section VI

# The Perfection of Genocide as National Policy, 1939–1943

This section is designed to outline the evolving Nazi policy of genocide; this is the Holocaust. The makers of these documents realized the enormity and the inhumanity of what they were planning and doing, so they developed a coded and obscure language to use in their communications. Secrecy, camouflage, euphemism, omission, and deception pervade these documents. Not only were the intended victims to be deceived, but also participants at lower levels, Germans at home, and the rest of the world. The Nazis attempted to carry out unprecedented genocides and to cover them up at the same time. Their documents here must be read with great care.

The nature of the operations described here presents another obstacle for the reader. We simply cannot imagine shooting 30,000 Ukrainians into a trench outside Kiev, herding thousands of Poles into gas chambers day after day, deporting trainloads of children from France to their deaths. So the reader must expend extraordinary effort to get beyond the words, to abandon our assumptions about what is possible for humans to do to each other, and to listen to what is said, however outlandish it appears.

The Nazi leadership, a much larger group than the few names that are familiar to most people, invented industrial genocide in the midst of their war on Europe. This section shows their changing plans and procedures, as they worked hard to perfect their methods. Genocide was a national policy, because the circles of significant participants went beyond those directly connected to the central state to include important segments of society. Doctors, mayors, lawyers, industrial managers, and social scientists worked with soldiers, police, diplomats, and bureaucrats; active perpetrators permeated all areas of the national political structure.

A few documents here depart from the bloodless language which typifies the majority. The German writers who were critical of the murders of Polish civilians or of men and women in Sluzk in the Soviet Union (documents 28 and 40) used vivid language to describe what they saw. The one victim whose voice is reproduced in this section, Gol Szloma (document 53), is the most direct. The subsequent two sections include many more documents from victims, whose words were chosen with entirely different purposes. In this section, language serves mainly to protect the writers from confrontation with their own deeds.

# 27. Letter from Reinhard Heydrich planning the 'concentration' of Polish Jews, 21 September 1939

The Chief of the Security Police
PP (II) – 288/39 secret

Berlin, 21 Sept. 1939

Express Letter

-.-.-.-.-.-.-.-.-.-.-.-

To: Chiefs of all Einsatzgruppen of the Security Police
Regarding: Jewish Question in Occupied Territory

I refer to the discussion which took place today in Berlin and point out once more, that the planned overall measures (that is, the final objective) are to be kept strictly secret.

Distinction is to be made between

1.) the final objective (which requires longer periods) and
2.) the phases of the fulfilment of this final objective, (which will be immediately accomplished.)

The planned measures require the most thorough preparation in technical, as well as economic respects.

It is obvious that the approaching tasks cannot be determined from here in all details. The following instructions and principles serve at the same time the purpose of encouraging the chiefs of the Einsatzgruppen towards practical reflections.

I.

As first prerequisite for the final objective ranks above all the concentration of the Jews from the countryside into the larger cities.

This is to be carried out with speed.

Distinction is thereby to be made:

1.) between the regions Danzig and West Prussia, Posen, East Upper Silesia and
2.) the remaining occupied regions.

If possible, the region mentioned under number 1) should be made free from Jews, or at least the goal should be to create only a few cities of concentration.

In the regions mentioned under number 2) the fewest possible concentration points should be established, so that later measures will be facilitated. In this connection, attention must be paid that only such cities are established as concentration points which either are railroad junctions or at least lie on railroad lines.

A fundamental principle is that Jewish communities with fewer than 500 people are to be dissolved and conveyed to the nearest concentration city....

II.

Jewish Councils of Elders

1.) In each Jewish community a Jewish Council of Elders is to be set up, which as far as possible is to be composed of the remaining significant personalities and rabbis. Up to 24 male Jews (according to the size of the Jewish community) will belong to the Council of Elders.

It is to be made literally completely responsible for the exact and punctual implementation of all orders, issued or to be issued.

2.) In cases of sabotage of such orders, the sharpest measures are to be announced to the Councils.

3.) The Jewish Councils will undertake an emergency census of Jews – if possible categorized by sex (age groups), a) up to 16 years, b) from 16 to 20 years, and c) over 20, and by the most significant occupational groups – in their local areas, and report the results without delay.

4.) The Councils of Elders are to be notified of deadlines for moving out, possible destinations, and finally the streets for departure. They are then to be made personally responsible for the departure of Jews from the countryside.

The justification for the concentration of Jews in the cities is that Jews have decisively participated in guerrilla attacks and plundering actions.

5.) The Councils of Elders in the cities of concentration are to be made responsible for the appropriate accommodation of the Jews arriving from the countryside.

The concentration of Jews in cities will probably require arrangements in these cities, on the grounds of general police security, that Jews are completely forbidden in certain city districts, that they – always in consideration of economic necessities – cannot, for example, leave the ghetto, after a certain evening hour may not go out, etc.

6.) The Councils of Elders are also to be made responsible for the adequate provisioning of the Jews during transport to the cities.

There are no objections, if the outmigrating Jews take along their movable possessions, as far as technically possible.

7.) Jews who do not obey the order to move to the cities are, in justified cases, to be allowed a short extension. They are to be notified of the strictest punishment, if they also should not comply with this extension....

signed H e y d r i c h

---

This letter was written three weeks after the invasion of Poland, even before Warsaw had finally capitulated. Reinhard Heydrich, second in command to Himmler and head of the SS Security Service, issued these instructions about ghettoization as the first phase of Nazi 'planned overall measures'. The frequent reference to the final objective (*Endziel*), the location of concentration cities on railroad lines, and the order for a census of Jews all point toward the still secret later stages of this plan. The dissolution of Jewish communities of under 500 meant the immediate uprooting of thousands of rural and small town Jews, and their concentration in city ghettos, mainly Warsaw and Lódź.

The geographical distinction between Western and Central Poland represented the German desire to remove all Jews from those areas which were to be incorporated into the Greater Reich. The newly formed General Gouvernement in Central Poland was envisioned as the collecting point for Polish Jews.

Heydrich outlines the creation of Jewish councils which would act as a conveyer belt of Nazi orders, taking responsibility for implementing the ghettoization. He uses the spurious justification, which was repeated endlessly on the Eastern Front throughout the war, that anti-Jewish measures were simply responses to Jewish attacks on the German forces. In November 1939 a more detailed order about the creation of Jewish Councils was issued by Hans Frank, the Governor-General for Occupied Polish Territories.

# 28. War diary of Lt. Col. Helmuth Groscurth about massacres of Polish civilians on 7–8 October 1939

Excerpts from Report of Medical Transport – Sect. 3, Comp. 581.

-----------------------------------------------------------------

Report!

To the Commander-in-Chief of the Wehrmacht and Führer of the German People Adolf Hitler!
Through official military channels! I report: On Sunday, 8.Oct. about 13:00 the NCO Kleegraf, Priv. Kluge, and Priv. Roschinski reported to me in the presence of all Comp. officers. (5 names of doctors follow.)

On Sunday 8 October about 9:30, with about 150 Wehrmacht comrades, they were eyewitnesses to the official execution of 20–30 Poles at the Jewish cemetery in Schwetz. The execution was carried out by a detail composed of a member of the Schutzstaffel, two men in the old blue Schupo uniform and a man in civilian clothes. In charge was a Sturmbannführer of the SS. At the execution about 5–6 children aged from 2–8 years were shot. The above named are prepared to swear to their statements.

signed Dr. Möller
Major (medical) of Res. and Comp.F.

... Questioning of Priv. Kluge before various witnesses follows:
On Saturday 7 October 39, during a walk through the city, I heard in conversations with comrades, that in the morning at the Jewish cemetery in Schw. a large number of Poles had been shot; and that on Sunday morning another shooting would take place. Discussion about the coming shooting was common among the soldiers in Schw. Therefore I proceeded on Sunday morning with most of my comrades to the Jewish cemetery, where we waited in vain at first up to 9:00. We were about to proceed again to our quarters, when a large bus loaded with women and children drove into the cemetery. We went back again to the cemetery. We saw then how a group of a women and three children, the children aged from about three to 8 years, were led from the bus to a shovelled out grave of

about 8 meters width and 8 meters length. The woman had to climb into this grave and took her youngest child on her arm. Both other children were passed to her by two men of the execution Kommando. The woman had to lay on her stomach flat in the grave, that is with the face to the earth, her three children lined up on the left in the same way. – Then 4 men similarly climbed into the grave, pointed their guns so that the muzzle was about 30 cm. from the back of the neck, and shot in this way the woman with her three children. I was then ordered by the Sturmbannführer in charge to help with the shovelling. I followed this order and could thus see from close up each time, that the next groups of women and children were shot in the same way. In all 9–10 groups of women and children, each time in fours in the same mass grave.
About 200 soldiers of the Wehrmacht watched the execution from a distance of about 30 m.
Somewhat later a second bus with men arrived at the cemetery, among them yet another woman. These men had to climb into the grave, in which the fresh corpses lay barely covered with sand, lay themselves on their stomachs, where they were then disposed of by shots to the neck from the 4 men of the Kommando.
In all on this morning about 28 women, 25 men and 10 children aged 3–8 years were shot.

signed Dr. Möller
Major (medical) of the Res. and Comp.F. signed P. Kluge Priv.

---

The document cited here, the war diary of Lt. Col. Groscurth of the General Staff, is a long way from the murders described in it. This diary entry was compiled from reports by Dr Wilhelm Möller, a reserve major in a medical transport unit. It identifies a sequence of people who witnessed or were immediately informed about massacres of Polish civilians five weeks after the German invasion of Poland.

On the weekend of 7 and 8 October 1939, a detail headed by an SS officer and a member of the so-called 'Ethnic German Self-Defense' murdered about 90 men, women, and children in Schwetz, about 60 km inside Poland. Dr Möller heard of these events and immediately arranged to have three witnesses report to the doctors in his medical transport company about the massacres. That same day he wrote the report to Hitler himself, noting the murder of 20 to 30 Poles, in the apparent belief that Hitler might not be aware of such atrocities. As part of his further investigation into the incidents, later in October Dr Möller took lengthy statements from Kluge (quoted here),

Roschinski, and Kleegraf; they corroborated in detail each other's reports and raised the probable number killed to over 90. These reports were sent to the headquarters of the High Command of the Army, where they were edited by a Captain Seeliger in November.

Groscurth had the version translated here inserted into his war diary, because he was compiling evidence of Nazi atrocities in Poland. Groscurth was a leader of a conspiratorial opposition to Hitler and the Nazi party leadership which had developed within the military. They collected files about war crimes to eventually win over the German public. Despite years of plotting, the opposition was unsuccessful. Groscurth became head of the General Staff of the German units near Stalingrad in 1942, was captured by the Soviet Army, and died of typhus in a POW camp in 1943.

The mass murders of the Holocaust began in the immediate aftermath of the invasion of Poland. Thousands of Poles, Jewish and Catholic, were executed in September and October.[1] While the shooters were mainly SS, police, and 'Self-Defense' militia, regular Army soldiers observed or knew of such executions. Reports like Dr Möller's acquainted a chain of Army leaders and top Nazis in Berlin with the details of mass murders as they occurred. At no time was genocide a secret restricted to the actual perpetrators.

## Note

1 Martin Gilbert, in *Atlas of the Holocaust* (Oxford and New York: Pergamon Press, 1988), p. 33, estimates that over 16,000 Polish civilians were killed in the first six weeks after 1 September.

## 29. Announcement that Jews in the Łódź region must wear yellow armband, 14 November 1939

# Decree

of 14 November 1939

Substantial abuses caused by Jews in the public life of the administrative area of the District President at Kalisch induce me to order the following for the administrative area of the District President at Kalisch:

§1

As special emblem Jews will carry, regardless of age and gender, on the right upper arm directly under the armpit, a 10 cm. wide armband in Jewish yellow color.

§2

In the administrative area of the District President at Kalisch, Jews may not leave their residence between the hours of 5 PM and 8 AM without my special permission.

§3

Violations against this decree will be punished by death. In the case of extenuating circumstances, a fine in unlimited amount or prison, alone or in combination with each other, can be imposed.

§4

This decree, except the decision in §1, is in force immediately, §1 from 18 November 1939.

Lodz, 14 November 1939.

The District President at Kalisch

**Uebelhoer**

The public marking of Jews with a badge of identification began in Poland almost immediately after the German invasion. From September through November, local German civilian and military authorities published a variety of orders placing severe restrictions on the daily life of Polish Jews. The first requirement for a special badge was issued for the town of Włocławek on October 24. This order by Friedrich Uebelhoer adds a very restrictive curfew, allowing Jews to be outside their homes for only 9 hours per day.

During the first months of occupation, civilian, military and SS leaders competed for authority over Polish Jews. By November local initiatives were superseded by more centralized regulations. Hans Frank extended the practice of marking Jews to the entire General Gouvernement on 23 November, with the added stipulation that the Star of David appear on the armbands. In December a curfew between 9 pm and 5 am was extended to all Jews in the General Gouvernement, with the penalty of hard labor for violations.

The area under Uebelhoer's authority included the city of Łódź, whose Jewish population of over 200,000 made it one of the largest Jewish centers in Europe. Uebelhoer asserted considerable authority over the ghetto which was soon established in Łódź. In a memo of 10 December 1939, Uebelhoer wrote that it was clear that the Łódź ghetto was 'only a transitional measure. ... the final aim must be to burn out entirely this pestilent abscess.'[1]

## Note

1 Cited in *Łódź Ghetto: Inside a Community under Siege*, compiled and edited by Alan Adelson and Robert Lapides (New York: Viking Penguin, 1989), pp. 23–6.

## 30. Postwar testimony about the first successful gassing of mentally handicapped on 4 January 1940

... At the beginning of the first euthanasia experiment in the Brandenburg asylum near Berlin, I was ordered there by Brack. It was in the first half of January 1940 when I travelled to the asylum. Structures of the asylum were fixed up especially for this purpose. A room, similar to a shower room and covered with tiles, approximately 3 by 5 meters and 3 meters high. There were benches around the room and about 10 cm above the floor, a water pipe about 1" in diameter ran along the wall. There were small holes in this pipe, from which the carbon monoxide gas poured out. The gas cylinders stood outside this room and were already connected to the pipe. The installation of this facility had been carried out by a workman from the SS Main Building Office in Berlin.... In the entrance door, which was constructed like an air raid shelter door, was a rectangular peephole through which the behavior of the delinquents could be observed. The first gassing was carried out by Dr. Widmann personally. He turned the gas tap and regulated the amount of gas. At the same time, he instructed the asylum doctor, Dr. Eberl, and Dr. Baumhart, who later took over the extermination in Grafeneck and Hadamar. Prominent personalities who were there, as far as I can remember: the doctors already mentioned: Dr. Eberl, Dr. Baumhart, Dr. Widmann, ... Prof. Dr. Brandt, the Führer's personal physician, a Detective Wirth, at that time head of the homicide branch of the Stuttgart police department and later head of the Hardtheim asylum near Linz. For this first gassing about 18 to 20 people were led into this "shower room" by the nursing staff. These men had to undress in an anteroom, so that they were completely naked. The doors were shut behind them. These people went quietly into the room and showed no signs of excitement. Dr. Widmann operated the gas, through the peephole I could see that after about a minute the people collapsed or lay on the benches. There were no scenes or disorder. After a further 5 minutes the room was ventilated. Specially assigned SS people carried the dead on special stretchers out of the room and brought them to the crematorium ovens. When I say special stretchers, I mean stretchers specially constructed for this purpose. They could be placed directly in front of the ovens and the corpses could be conveyed into the oven mechanically by means of a device, without the people carrying them coming into contact with the corpse. These ovens and the stretchers were also constructed in Brack's department. Who was responsible for this, I can't say. The second attempt and the further extermination procedures were then carried out by Dr. Eberl alone and on his own responsibility. Following this successful test, Victor Brack, who naturally was also present and whom I forgot to mention, said a few words. He expressed satisfaction with this test and emphasized once again that this action should only be carried out by doctors, according to the motto, the syringe belongs in the hand of the doctor. Subsequently, Prof. Dr. Brandt spoke and also stressed that doctors alone should carry out these gassings. With that, the start in Brandenburg was considered a success, and the matter continued further under Dr. Eberl.

---

Industrialized mass murder, one of the most significant inventions of the Nazis, began with this experiment described by Dr August Becker on about 20 mentally handicapped asylum patients near the capital of Germany. By this time the killing of the handicapped was already underway, organized out of Hitler's personal Chancellery, directed by Karl Brandt, Hitler's doctor, and Viktor Brack. Thousands of children had been individually killed by doctors through lethal injection in this 'euthanasia' program. To hide these actions from the Catholic Church, from which objections were expected, Brack camouflaged the entire program under the code name T4, with separate departments to locate potential victims, transport them to the killing facilities, and handle the finances.

Brack approached Arthur Nebe, head of the Reich Criminal Police, about how to kill large numbers at one time. Nebe sent him to Dr Albert Widmann, head of the chemical section of the Criminal Technical Institute in Berlin, who experimented with explosions of dynamite, morphine suppositories, and ampoules of hydrocyanic acid as efficient methods of killing. The importance of this trial gassing is underlined by the presence of Dr Brandt and Christian Wirth, who later was commandant of the extermination camp at Belzec (document 67). The success of this venture convinced everyone involved that gas was an ideal method. Within a couple of months, Dr Becker had transferred canisters of gas from the BASF chemical factories in Ludwigshafen to killing facilities at Brandenburg, Grafeneck in Southwest Germany, and Hartheim in Austria.

Many of the innovations mentioned here, such as collective cremation and specially constructed doors with peepholes, would be used after 1941 in the extermination camps. Meanwhile Dr Widmann continued to perfect killing methods. In September 1941 he carried out gassing experiments using auto exhaust in a psychiatric hospital in Mogilev, in the Soviet Union, killing at least 20 patients. This led to construction of mobile gas vans, which were used after December 1941 behind the Eastern Front and in Serbia.

In this testimony, Becker consistently minimizes his involvement. One of his questioners wrote in a 'Note on the Interrogation of Dr Becker' that same day that Becker 'admitted only that which was energetically presented to him and proved with concrete witness statements ... he admitted only after long and insistent reproaches to have carried out with his own hands gassings of people.'[1] Becker said that he participated in gassing only to make it proceed more smoothly, thereby sparing the victims pain and distress. In a later interrogation, he said he never heard of Treblinka, Sobibor, or Belzec.

## Note

1 'Vermerk zu Vernehmung des Dr Becker', 5 April 1960, Bundesarchiv Ludwigsburg, B 162 ARZ 6000018a/Vol. 1.

# 31. Minutes of conference about deportation of Poles, Jews and Gypsies, 30 January 1940

Copy.

- IV D 4–III ES

Berlin, 30 January 1940.

Subject: Conference on 30 January 1940.

N o t e.

1./ SS-Gruppenführer Heydrich reported that today's meeting was convened by order of the Reichsführer-SS, in order to develop a uniform policy among all participating offices for carrying out the resettlement measures ordered by the Führer. The evacuations already accomplished included around 87,000 Poles and Jews from the Warthegau, in order to create space for the Baltic Germans who are to be settled there. An unplanned, so-called illegal emigration took place besides.

On the basis of the statements of Reichsminister SS-Gruppenführer Seyss-Inquart and SS-Obergruppenführer Krüger, SS-Gruppenführer Heydrich states that no fundamental objections were raised against the evacuations toward the General Gouvernement by the competent offices of the General Governor. The complaints thus far were directed merely against the fact that the previous evacuations did not hold to the originally planned numbers, but went beyond them. With the establishment of the Office IV D 4 for the purpose of central direction of the evacuation measures, the asserted objections fall away.

It seems most urgent, in order to make room for Baltic Germans, to deport 40,000 Jews and Poles from the Warthegau into the Gouvernement. The order of the Reichsführer-SS serves as the guiding principle for the selection, according to which no racial German may be deported, without concern for their antecedents.

After this movement, a further improvised removal is to be undertaken, for the benefit of the Volhynia Germans, who are coming to the eastern provinces for settlement. Under the assumption that the Volhynia

German families have on average 6 to 7 children, a number of about 20,000 households results, who are to be accommodated. The number of Poles to be removed for this is provisionally assumed to be about 120,000 ....

While the people to be deported for the benefit of the Volhynia Germans are nearly exclusively rural population, those to be deported for the benefit of the Baltic Germans are nearly exclusively urban population.

SS-Gruppenführer Koppe reports that the evacuation, which takes place for the benefit of the Volhynia Germans, must be put into action so that the agricultural operation is not interrupted. The Volhynia Germans should be brought to the selected settlement places with trucks and exchanged against the previous Polish owners. The Poles will be gathered in camps and there be subjected to a selection. The part which is not useful for the eastern provinces and the Old Reich is designated for deportation to the General Gouvernement. Only after this selection will the exact numbers who come into question for absorption in the General Gouvernement be certain. Moreover in the Warthegau 4–5000 Poles and Jews are already collected in camps, who were unlodged for the benefit of the Baltic Germans, although their deportation was not yet possible.

SS-Obergruppenführer Krüger mentions that 60,000 refugees from Russia are to be expected in the General Gouvernement, who also must be accommodated in the General Gouvernement.

2./ SS-Gruppenführer Heydrich announces the following fundamental orders issued by the Reichsführer-SS:

Neither ethnic Germans nor those of Germanic extraction may be deported, also no Kashubes, Masurs, and similar peoples; the latter on the grounds that these groups have been friendly to Germans and are racially mixed with the German people. The Reichsführer-SS does not wish, however, that thereby a Kashube or Masur question develops. During the deportation it should simply be stated that the German provinces are being cleared of the alien population. Thus the possibility is left open for a later time, based on a racial investigation, to deport also completely inferior Kashubes, etc.

In regard to the general Polish question, it is ordered that a racial selection for use of agricultural laborers is not now to be done. If good and bad Poles are to be distinguished from the mass, confusion could develop among the German population.... Altogether according to the most recent determination, 800,000 to 1,000,000 Poles come into Germany for labor, in addition to the prisoners of war....

3./ After the two mass movements
a) of 40,000 Poles and Jews for the benefit of the Baltic Germans and
b) of about 120,000 Poles for the benefit of the Volhynia Germans, the deportation of all Jews of the new eastern provinces and 30,000 Gypsies out of Germany into the General Gouvernement should take place as the last mass movement. After it was determined that the removal of 120,000 Poles would begin around March 1940, the evacuation of Jews and Gypsies must be pushed back until the end of the above-named actions...

SS-Obergruppenführer Krüger reported that practice areas in the Gouvernement for the Army, Air Force and SS troops of fairly considerable size must be prepared, which are required for a resettlement inside the Gouvernement of about 100,000 to 120,000 people. It is thus desirable, in order to avoid a double resettlement, to take this into consideration for the removals in the direction of the General Gouvernement. SS-Gruppenführer Heydrich remarked that the building of the Wall and other plans in the East will surely provide opportunity to gather several 100,000 Jews in forced labor camps, whose families then could be distributed among the Jewish families already in the Gouvernement, which would solve this problem. SS-Obergruppenführer Krüger remarked also that ethnic Germans (mainly peasant elements) should be resettled out of the General Gouvernement and come into the Reich. Moreover, remarked SS-Brigadeführer Greifelt, the solution of this question is scheduled for the long term by the Reichsführer-SS....

Middle of February 1940, 1000 Jews from Stettin, whose apartments are urgently needed on grounds of war economy, should be removed and simultaneously deported into the General Gouvernement.

SS-Gruppenführer Seyss-Inquart recapitulated the numbers, that the General Gouvernement has to absorb in the immediate future, which are

40,000 Jews and Poles,
120,000 Poles and all the Jews from the new eastern provinces and 30,000 Gypsies from the Old Reich and Austria. He referred to the transport difficulties which could thereby arise for the Reich Railways and finally to the poor nutritional situation in the General Gouvernement, which will not improve before the next harvest. Thus it is necessary that the Reich continues to provide subsidies....

Finally SS-Gruppenführer Heydrich called attention to the fact that it is especially important that the persons to be evacuated, especially the urban population, be made known to the appropriate Trustee Office, so that the securing of valuables can take place.

After this meeting, which lasted from 11:30 to 1:15, the officials representing the inspectors of the new eastern provinces and the commanders of the Security Police and the SD in the General Gouvernement met together with III ES and IV D 4 to discuss detailed questions.

-----

---

The imperialist dream of colonizing the vast lands beyond the Eastern border had inspired German military and civilian leaders since before World War I. Many Germans perceived themselves as a 'Volk ohne Raum', a people without space, whose destiny lay in territories held by primitive Slavs. As soon as military victory in Poland allowed these racist dreams to appear capable of realization, the Nazis set out to move millions. Descendants of German settlers across Eastern Europe were gathered as replacements for the inferior peoples who occupied Poland. By 1941 these plans had grown into the so-called General Plan East, which envisaged the deportation of 31 million people beyond the Ural Mountains over a 30-year period.

The leadership of this program was lodged in the SS: Heinrich Himmler was simultaneously Reichsführer-SS and Reich Commissioner for the Strengthening of Germanism. In a secret memorandum dated 28 November 1940, Himmler gave Hitler his opinion on the 'Treatment of Foreign People in the East':

> For the non-German population of the East there should be no higher school than elementary school. The goal of this elementary school should be only: simple counting up to 500, writing the name, the teaching that it is a god-given law to be obedient to the German and to be honest, diligent, and well behaved. I don't believe reading is necessary.[1]

Although murder was not mentioned at this meeting, the scheme to Germanize former Polish territories was integrally connected with the murder of millions of Poles, Jewish and Catholic. Evacuation soon became a euphemism for annihilation. Among the 40 SS officers participating in this 'resettlement' conference were some of the leaders in carrying out the Holocaust who appear in later documents in this section, including Odilo Globocnik, Adolf Eichmann, and Theodor Dannecker. The commanders of two of the four Einsatzgruppen who murdered over 1 million Jews in the Soviet Union attended. The Holocaust was simultaneously a program of eliminating hated enemies and making room for valued Germanic relatives.

Germanic settlers from the Baltic states of Latvia, Lithuania, and Estonia, and from Volhynia in the Ukraine were brought to Western Poland with the promise of the farms evacuated by Polish peasants. They received the clothes and other property from Jewish victims of the gas chambers. After the war, these German speakers were expelled from Poland and ended up in West Germany.

## Note

1 Translated from Nuremberg Document NO-1880, National Archives, Record Group 238, p. 3.

# 32. Report of meeting of German mayors concerning murder of the handicapped, 3 April 1940

Secret Reich Matter
For the secret files of the administration
Only Chief Inspector Hopfe to be informed.

On 3 April 1940, a secret meeting of the German *Gemeindetag* took place in Berlin. It was chaired by Herr Reichsleiter Fiehler; an old party comrade, Brack, spoke about patients in city mental institutions. He explained:

In the many mental institutions in the Reich there are an endless number of incurably ill patients of all kinds, who are completely useless to humanity; in fact, they are nothing but a burden, their care creates endless expense, and there is no possibility that these people will ever become healthy or useful members of human society. They vegetate like animals, and are antisocial people unworthy of living, but otherwise their internal organs are absolutely healthy and they could live on for many decades. They only take nourishment away from other, healthy people, and often need two to three times as much care. Other people must be protected from these people.

If, however, we must already make preparations for maintenance of healthy people, then it is all the more necessary first to eliminate these beings, even if only to better maintain curable patients in mental hospitals.

The space that would thus become free is needed for all sorts of things important to the war effort: military hospitals, regular hospitals, and auxiliary hospitals.

Thus those seriously ill, that is, incurable patients who are involved must be

packed into very primitive special asylums,

and in these specially created asylums, nothing must be done to maintain these seriously ill patients; on the contrary, everything must be done in order to have them die as quickly as possible.

In order to carry out this operation, a

commission of physicians has been appointed

to sift through all the asylums involved and decide which patients should be sent to such asylums.

A High Commission superior to this commission will make final decisions in special cases.

The entire problem is very difficult, and it is necessary to act very cautiously, for the public must learn nothing of it. It is difficult above all because of the church, which is absolutely opposed to cremating the dead; a dispute now with the Pope is completely undesirable. It is also dangerous because of the Americans, who could enter the war against us for such a reason.

One can keep the entire problem secret from the population; that is not such a big problem.

Much more difficult is the question of the asylums themselves. It would be best if those involved were to be placed in very bad barracks, where they could contract pneumonia; in other words, accelerate their death rather than artificially maintaining them.

Those who die in this way would have to be cremated to prevent epidemics, not in city crematoriums, but in the asylums' own ovens. When doing this, it is necessary to consider the dispute with the church, namely with the Catholic church, and to avoid any tensions. Nor must it be forgotten that most of the relatives would still be against cremation.

In practice, the entire operation would have to proceed more or less as follows: those patients involved are sifted through by the commission, and then evacuated to other institutions, so that cremation of the corpses can proceed in these asylums.

The best way to deal with the relatives of the patients involved is for the asylum to inform the relatives of the dead, with the notation that [cremation] of the patient has already occurred to prevent epidemics, and the urn with the mortal remains is available to the family and will be sent at no cost; however, if there is no place to store the urn in their hometown or its surroundings, the urn will be sent to the nearest cemetery office free of charge for temporary storage, where the urn will be available at any time to the relatives as soon as they would like it.

When such urns are sent to the cemetery offices, the cemetery office must keep no files on them. And no cost lists for expenses that may arise, so that no traces of the operation can be found. The storage of such urns should occur simply and without any extravagance, primitively and functionally. All such urns should be stored in one place, so their purpose can be recognized at any time, for the name of the patient, dates of birth and death, and home community are on the urn, so that if the relatives want the urn it can be found immediately. Relatives should not be brought to the site of the urns; instead, the urns should be picked up by the cemetery administrator.

The practical procedure at the cemetery should occur as follows:

One fine day, a package will arrive at the cemetery with more or less the accompanying letter:

Enclosed please find an urn for the deceased person involved, name, dates of birth and death, name of home community. We request storage of the enclosed urn.

The cemetery administration will bring this urn to a predetermined site, at which all urns sent later in the same way will be stored, and there the urns remain. That takes care of the entire ceremony.

Few expenses can arise for the communities, as the cost of cremation will be paid by the Reich. Otherwise, the operation relieves the communities to a great extent, as future costs of care are eliminated in each individual case.

Questions should be addressed to Herr Deputy Dr. Schlüter at the *Gemeindetag* in Berlin.

---

The *Gemeindetag* was the official conference of German mayors of large cities. This meeting with Viktor Brack was held in Berlin, with the agenda not announced before the meeting. These notes were taken down by the mayor of Plauen, Wörner, who indicates they are to be communicated to Hopfe, his cemetery inspector. Political leaders of all major German cities, some of whom like Schlüter had been elected before the Nazis seized power, were thus well-informed about the plans to kill thousands of handicapped Germans. The justification for this policy is precisely the argument made by Binding and Hoche in 1920. The need to hide this operation from the public, the likely opposition of the Catholic Church, and the fallacious letters to be sent to relatives of the victims were all openly discussed with these German civilian leaders. They returned home prepared to carry out their part in the killing program. In April 1941, a similar meeting of judges and state attorneys was held, in which Brack explained the program, including the need to hide it from the public.

Despite the apparent candor, key points of T4 were not discussed with the mayors. Brack implies that the incurably ill victims were about to die anyway. No mention was made of the method of killing. Brack is unwilling here to tell the mayors that healthy victims are being deliberately killed. Instead he pretends that they will die an artificially accelerated but natural death.

# 33. Memorandum from US State Department on delaying immigration, 26 June 1940

A–L

June 26, 1940.

A–B – Mr. Berle
PA/D– Mr. Dunn

Attached is a memorandum from Mr. Warren. I discussed the matter with him on the basis of this memorandum. There are two possibilities and I will discuss each category briefly.

Nonimmigrants

Their entry into the United States can be made to depend upon prior authorization by the Department. This would mean that the consuls would be divested of discretion and that all requests for nonimmigrant visas (temporary visitor and transit visas) be passed upon here. It is quite feasible and can be done instantly. It will permit the Department to effectively control the immigration of persons in this category and private instructions can be given the Visa Division as to nationalities which should be admitted as well as to individuals who are to be excluded.

This must be done for universal application and could not be done as regards Germany, for instance, or Russia, for instance, or any other one government because it would first, invite retaliation and second, would probably be a violation of some of our treaty arrangements. The retaliation clause is in connection with Germany because it could mean the closing of our offices in almost all of Europe.

Immigrants

We can delay and effectively stop for a temporary period of indefinite length the number of immigrants into the United States. We could do this by simply advising our consuls to put every obstacle in the way and to require additional evidence and to resort to various administrative advices which would postpone and postpone and postpone the granting of the visas. However, this could only be temporary. In order to make it more definite it would have to be done by suspension of the rules under the law by the issuance of a proclamation of emergency – which I take it we are not yet ready to proclaim.

Summing up

We can effectively control nonimmigrants by prohibiting the issuance of visas unless the consent of the Department is obtained in advance, for universal application.

We can temporarily prevent the number of immigrants from certain localities such as Cuba, Mexico and other places of origin of German intending immigrants by simply raising administrative obstacles.

The Department will be prepared to take these two steps immediately upon the decision but emphasis must be placed on the fact that discrimination must not be practiced and with the additional thought that in case a suspension of the regulations should be proclaimed under the need of an emergency, it would be universally applicable and would affect refugees from England.

The Canadian situation and travel across that border we can handle through an exception to the general rule and so advise our consuls in Canada.

---

Even after the beginning of war in Europe, it was still possible for Jews to leave Germany. The major obstacle to emigration for those whose lives were now clearly threatened was what David Wyman has called 'paper walls' erected by the United States government. The tactics outlined here were used to frustrate visa applicants in Germany and elsewhere in Europe. While publicly expressing fears that enemy aliens would enter the United States as refugees, State Department policy focused on preventing anyone in difficult economic circumstances, meaning almost any German Jew. These restrictions were not made known in Europe, so that hopeful emigrants continued to assemble documents, buy ship tickets, get medical exams, only to be continually delayed by local American consulates.

This memo from Breckinridge Long, Assistant Secretary of State, was addressed to Assistant Secretary of State Adolf A. Berle, Jr. and James C. Dunn, adviser to the State Department on political relations, and referred to Avra Warren, who was in charge of the Visa Division. These men consistently attempted to restrict immigration of European refugees to the United States. This memo began a period of much more restrictive procedures after the brief liberalization since 1938.[1]

## Note

1 A thorough discussion of the changing American immigration policies is provided in two books by David S. Wyman: *Paper Walls: America and the Refugee Crisis 1938–1941* (Amherst, MA: University of Massachusetts Press, 1968), and *The Abandonment of the Jews: America and the Holocaust, 1941–1945* (New York: Pantheon Books, 1984).

# 34. Table of money saved by murdering the handicapped, 1941

Based upon the estimated monthly average cost per day of RM 0.56, the actual amount already saved up to 1 September 1941 can be computed. This savings, without taking into account the date of death determined by us, is –

RM 8,969,116.80

| Month | Year | Number of Disinfected | Reichsmark |
|---|---|---|---|
| January | 1940 | 95 | 30,324.00 |
| February | 1940 | 339 | 102,513.60 |
| March | 1940 | 995 | 284,172.00 |
| April | 1940 | 887 | 238,425.60 |
| May | 1940 | 2726 | 686,952.00 |
| June | 1940 | 3723 | 876,355.20 |
| July | 1940 | 5356 | 1,169,750.40 |
| August | 1940 | 5791 | 1,167,465.60 |
| September | 1940 | 4883 | 902,378.40 |
| October | 1940 | 4139 | 695,352.00 |
| November | 1940 | 3711 | 561,103.20 |
| December | 1940 | 2579 | 346,617.60 |
| January | 1941 | 2692 | 361,804.80 |
| February | 1941 | 4023 | 405,518.40 |
| March | 1941 | 3794 | 318,696.00 |
| April | 1941 | 3369 | 226,396.80 |
| May | 1941 | 5815 | 293,076.00 |
| June | 1941 | 5754 | 193,334.40 |
| July | 1941 | 6481 | 108,880.80 |
| August | 1941 | 3121 | – |
| Total: | | 70,273 | 8,969,116.80 |

---

From the beginning of the discussion in the early 20th century about 'useless eaters' or 'burdensome existences', the possible social savings as a result of getting rid of the institutionalized handicapped were always at the forefront. Dr Eduard Brandt, an 'expert' in the T4 program, prepared this table as part of a statistical brochure in 1941 about how many people had been killed in the program since the first gassing in January 1940 and the resulting estimated savings. Even in this document for purely internal consumption, the fiction of 'disinfection' is used, although the brief heading notes the 'date of death'. Using a crude arithmetic formula, Brandt calculated that the murder of 70,000 patients by September 1941 had already saved the Reich nearly 9 million Reichsmarks. Elsewhere in the brochure, using a different calculation, he foresaw savings over 10 years of nearly 900 million Reichsmarks.

The victims listed in this table were killed in gas chambers in 6 locations in Germany and Austria, including Hartheim in Southeastern Austria, where this document was found. The figure of 70,273 deaths is probably an undercount, since it refers only to people who were killed by gas. Many others, including children, lost their lives by injection, starvation and other methods of murder. At this point in 1941 the T4 program was officially ended by Hitler's order, due to protests especially by Catholic Church leaders, but the killing of patients and concentration camp inmates in hospital gas chambers continued until the end of the war.

Relatives were told by form letter that the patient had been transferred to one of these killing centers, had arrived in good health, but that visits and even further questions were not allowed.[1]

## Note

1 Examples of these form letters are reprinted in Elisabeth Klamper (ed.), *Dokumentationsarchiv des Österreichischen Widerstandes, Vienna*, Archives of the Holocaust, Vol. 19 (New York: Garland Publishing, Inc., 1991), p. 79–80.

# 35. Report of Einsatzgruppen murders in Soviet Union, 2 October 1941

The Chief of the Security Police
and the SD.
- IV A 1 - B.No. 1/B 41 - Grs. -

Berlin, 2 Oct. 1941.

Secret Reich Matter!

48 Copies.
36th Copy.

Operational Report USSR. No. 101 .
= = = = = = = = = = = = = = = = = = = = = =

I. Reports of the Einsatzgruppen and -commandos.

From the Einsatzgruppen A and B there are no reports.

Einsatzgruppe C.
Location K i e v .

The Sonderkommando 4a in cooperation with Headquarters and two commandos of Police Regiments South executed 33,771 Jews on 29 and 30 September '41 in Kiev.

Einsatzgruppe D.
Location N i k o l a e v .

The freeing of the region from Jews and communist elements by the commandos was continued. Especially in the report period, the cities of Nikolaev and Kherson were made free of Jews, and functionaries still present were handled appropriately. From 16 September to 30 September, 22,467 Jews and Communists were executed. Total number 35,782....

This report was issued by the Reich Security Main Office, Himmler's headquarters in Berlin, as a composite of reports from the four Einsatzgruppen who were assigned to cover the entire front from the Baltic Sea to the Black Sea. Copies were distributed throughout the military and political leadership of the Nazi state. While these reports, including the one excerpted here, detailed a variety of military operations and described the political and economic situation, the murder of Jews and other Soviet citizens was their major subject.

This report laconically notes perhaps the biggest single execution in history, the shooting of nearly 34,000 Jews from Kiev in 2 days at Babi Yar. Kiev had one of the largest Jewish populations in the Soviet Union, numbering about 175,000 before the war began. Shortly after the occupation of Kiev by German troops, the Einsatzgruppen began to organize the murder of Kiev's Jews. German authorities ordered Jews to assemble on 29 September for resettlement. Those who complied were taken outside of the city to Babi Yar and methodically shot by units under the direction of Paul Blobel.

In September 1941 the Einsatzgruppen killed over 190,000 people, 4 times as many as any other month of the war. Other German military units joined in the mass murders throughout the Eastern Front: documents 39 and 40 describe simultaneous massacres later in October by a regular Army unit in Yugoslavia and a police battalion in Belorussia. The killing of hundreds in Poland, of thousands of handicapped in Germany, had expanded towards the killing of millions across Eastern Europe.

# 36. German Army orders on the 'Conduct of the Troops in the Eastern Territories', 10 October 1941

Army High Command 6 | Army H.Q., 10 October 1941.
Div. Ia–Az. 7

Subject: Conduct of the Troops in the Eastern Territories.

Regarding the conduct of troops towards the Bolshevistic system, vague conceptions are still prevalent in many cases.

The most essential aim of the war against the Jewish-Bolshevistic system is the complete destruction of their means of power and the extermination of Asiatic influence in the European area.

Hereby tasks develop for the troops, which go beyond conventional one-sided soldiering. The soldier in the Eastern territories is not merely a fighter according to the rules of the art of war, but also bearer of a ruthless national idea and the avenger of all the bestialities, which have been inflicted upon German and racially related people.

Therefore the soldier must have full understanding for the necessity of a severe, but just revenge against Jewish subhumanity. This has the further purpose to nip in the bud revolts in the rear of the army, which from experience have always been plotted by Jews.

The struggle against the enemy behind the front line is still not being taken seriously enough. Treacherous, cruel partisans and degenerate women are still being made prisoners-of-war, and partly uniformed or plainclothed snipers and vagabonds are still treated like proper soldiers, and sent to prisoner-of-war camps. In fact, captured Russian officers explain mockingly that Soviet agents move openly on the streets and often eat at German field kitchens. Such behavior of the troops can only be explained by complete thoughtlessness. So it is now time for the commanders to call forth an understanding of the present struggle.

The feeding of local residents and prisoners-of-war, who are not working for the Armed Forces, from army kitchens is an equally misunderstood humanitarian act, as is the giving away of cigarettes and bread. Things which the people at home lack under great sacrifices, things brought by the Command to the front with great difficulty, should not be given to the enemy by the soldier, not even if they originate from booty. It is an important part of our supply.

When retreating the Soviets have often set buildings on fire. The troops have an interest in extinguishing of fires only as far as it is necessary to preserve sufficient accommodation for troops. Otherwise the disappearance of symbols of the former Bolshevistic rule, even in the form of buildings, is part of the war of extermination. Neither historic nor artistic considerations play a role in the Eastern territories. For the preservation of raw materials and productive facilities important for the war economy, the command issues the necessary directives.

The complete disarming of the population in the rear of the fighting troops is imperative considering the long vulnerable lines of communications. Where possible, captured weapons and ammunition should be stored and guarded. Should this be impossible because of the battle situation, then weapons and ammunition are to be rendered useless. If individual partisans are found using firearms in the rear of the army, drastic measures are to be taken. These measures are to be extended to the male population who were in a position to hinder or report the attacks. The indifference of numerous allegedly anti-Soviet elements, which originates from a wait-and-see attitude, must give way to a clear decision for active collaboration against Bolshevism. If not, no one can complain about being judged and treated as a member of the Soviet system. The fear of the German counter-measures must be stronger than the threats of the wandering Bolshevistic remnants.

Far from all political considerations of the future, the soldier has to fulfil two tasks:

1.) complete annihilation of the false Bolshevistic doctrine, the Soviet State and its armed forces,
2. the pitiless extermination of foreign treachery and cruelty and thus the protection of the lives of German military personnel in Russia.

This is the only way to fulfil our historic task to liberate the German people once and for all from the Asiatic-Jewish danger.

Commander-in-Chief:
signed v. Reichenau
General Field Marshal

---

The mass murder of European Jews began almost immediately after the German invasion of the Soviet Union on 22 June 1941. The Holocaust and the war on the Eastern Front were intimately connected. Although most of the shooting of Soviet Jews was carried out by SS Einsatzgruppen, the Wehrmacht was a full participant in the mass murder of civilians. Regular German soldiers were inundated with propaganda about the special nature of the war and the need to support the ideological as well as the military battle.[1]

The order from Field Marshal Walter von Reichenau, the Commander of the 6th Army in the Ukraine, illustrates the Army's efforts to convince soldiers of their special tasks. Although it was intended only for von Reichenau's own troops, Hitler's endorsement of the wording led to its promulgation throughout the Eastern Front, stamped 'Secret'. Quartermaster General Eduard Wagner of the High Command of the Army sent it out with approval. The Commander of the Army Group South, Field Marshal Gerd von Rundstedt, distributed copies to infantry, air force, engineering, transportation, and signal units, accompanied by a note expressing his full agreement. Von Reichenau's order was typed and retyped as it circulated across the Eastern Front in October 1941.[2]

Not every commander agreed with von Reichenau's extreme recommendations. General Erich von Manstein, commander of the 11th Army in the Crimea, wrote an order on the same subject one month later, in which he ordered soldiers to seek cooperation with 'non-Bolshevists' and to respect Moslem religious customs. But his attitude toward Jews was identical to von Reichenau's: 'The soldier must appreciate the necessity for harsh punishment of Jewry.'[3]

The German army leadership was constantly worried about the tendency of soldiers to follow conventional rules of European warfare in their treatment of civilians and prisoners of war. Even before the Soviet invasion, the High Command of the Wehrmacht (OKW) issued an order which demanded the 'relentless liquidation of guerrillas', using 'the most extreme methods'. Soldiers were expressly exempted from any prosecution for offenses against civilians, based on the claim that Bolshevik influence had caused all the sufferings of the German people since World War I. In September 1941, the High Command sent out orders about Soviet POWs, which stated that 'the Bolshevik soldier has lost any claim to treatment as an honorable soldier according to the Geneva Convention.'[4]

## Notes

1 The works of Omer Bartov analyse the indoctrination of the German army on the Eastern Front with antisemitic propaganda: see *Hitler's Army: Soldiers, Nazis and War in the Third Reich* (New York and Oxford: Oxford University Press, 1991).

2 Among the Nuremberg documents in the National Archives are two different typed versions of the order, D-411 including the cover letter from Wagner, and NOKW-309 with von Rundstedt's cover.

3 Nuremberg document PS-4064 in *Trial of the Major War Criminals before the International Military Tribunal, Nuremberg, 14 November 1945 – 1 October 1946*, Vol. 34 (Nuremberg: 1949), pp. 129–32.

4 OKW Order for the Exercise of Military Jurisdiction and Procedures in Area 'Barbarossa', and Special Military Measures, issued by the Chief of the OKW, Keitel on 13 May 1941, translated in Matthew Cooper, *The Phantom War: The German Struggle against Soviet Partisans 1941–1944* (London: Macdonald & Jane's Publishers, 1979), pp. 167–8; directive of OKW on treatment of Soviet POWs of 8 September 1941 is Nuremberg document PS-1519, reprinted in *Trial of the Major War Criminals*, Vol. 27 (Nuremberg, 1948), pp. 275–6.

# 37. Plan for 'solution of the Jewish question' by mass gassing, 25 October 1941

Draft

Reich Minister
for the Occupied Eastern Territories

Berlin, 25 October 1941.

Official in Charge AGR. Dr. Wetzel

Secret!

Re: Solution of the Jewish Question

1. To the
Reich Commissar for the East

Re: Your report of 4 October 1941 regarding solution of the Jewish question.

With reference to my letter of 18 Oct. 1941, I inform you that Oberdienstleiter Brack of the Chancellery of the Führer has declared himself ready to cooperate in the production of the necessary shelters as well as the gassing devices. At present, the devices in question are not available in sufficient number, they must first be manufactured. Since in Brack's opinion the manufacture of the devices in the Reich causes much greater difficulties than on the spot, Brack considers it most expedient, if he immediately sends his people, especially his chemist Dr. Kallmeyer, to Riga, who will arrange for everything else there. Oberdienstleiter Brack points out that the procedure in question is not safe, so that special protective measures are needed. Under these circumstances, I request you to address yourself through your Higher SS- and Police Leader to Oberdienstleiter Brack in the Chancellery of the Führer, and request the dispatch of the chemist Dr. Kallmeyer as well as additional workers. I might point out that Sturmbannführer Eichmann, the official in charge of Jewish Questions in the Reich Security Main Office, is in agreement with this procedure. According to information from Sturmbannführer Eichmann, camps for Jews will be created in Riga and Minsk, to which Jews also from the Old Reich territory will come. Jews are now being evacuated out of the Old Reich, who are supposed to come to Litzmannstadt, but also to other camps, in order then later to be used, insofar as capable of work, in work details in the East.

As matters stand, there are no objections if those Jews who are not capable of work are disposed of with Brack's remedy. In this way, the occurrences which resulted from the shooting of Jews in Vilna, according to a report I have before me, and considering the fact that the shootings were undertaken publicly, can hardly be excused, will no longer be possible. On the other hand, those capable of work will be transported to the East for work. That among the Jews capable of work, men and women are to be kept separate, ought to be self-evident.

I request that you inform me of your further measures.

---

This draft letter by Dr Erhard Wetzel, a judge and expert on Jewish affairs, outlines the communication among the crucial organizers of genocide: Viktor Brack from the Führer's personal Chancellery; Adolf Eichmann, the Jewish expert in Himmler's Reich Security Main Office; Hinrich Lohse, the Reich Commissar for the Ostland (the Baltic states and Belorussia); and Wetzel's boss, Alfred Rosenberg, Reich Minister for the Eastern Occupied Territories. The Einsatzgruppen had already shot about 300,000 Jews over the past 4 months, including nearly 10,000 just outside Vilna. Although the use of mass shootings in the Soviet Union continued through 1942, this method was too personal and inefficient for dealing with millions of European Jews. Brack's remedy, developed in the process of killing the handicapped inside Germany, raised no objections.

The plan described here changed significantly in the next few months. By early 1942 death camps using the gassing devices which had been tested on the handicapped were being constructed in Poland, not further east in Riga and Minsk. German companies constructed the equipment used in the gas chambers. The first murder using hydrocyanic acid, with the trade name Zyklon B, had just taken place at Auschwitz, killing several hundred Soviet POWs. This chemical, supplied by the German firms Degesch and Testa, eventually replaced carbon monoxide as the primary killing agent. The Holocaust was always a work in progress.

# 38. Foreign Office memorandum on murder of Jews in Yugoslavia, 25 October 1941

Secret

Berlin, 25 October 1941.
D III 535 g.

Memorandum on the Outcome of My Official Trip to Belgrade

The purpose of the trip was to investigate on the spot whether the problem of the 8,000 Jewish agitators whose deportation was demanded by the Legation could be solved on the spot.

The first discussion with Minister Benzler and State Councillor Turner at the office of the Military Commander of Serbia indicated that more than 2,000 of these Jews had already been shot in reprisal for attacks on German soldiers. By order of the Military Commander, 100 Serbs are to be shot for every German soldier killed. In execution of this order, first of all the active communist leaders of Serbian nationality—about 50 in number—were shot, and then regularly Jews as communist agitators.

In the course of the conversation it developed that from the very start it was not a matter of 8,000 Jews, but only of about 4,000, of whom, moreover, only 3,500 can be shot. The Gestapo needs the other 500 in order to maintain sanitary and security services in the ghetto to be established.

In the first conversation it could not be clarified how the difference between 8,000 and 4,000 Jews arose. The investigations which I conducted in this matter indicated that State Councillor Turner had cited the figure of 8,000 to Minister Benzler, consisting of 1,500 from Smederevo, 600 from the Banat (a remainder from 2,000), 1,200 from Šabac and 4,700 from Belgrade.

In this compilation a mistake was made in that the Jews from Smederevo and the Banat were counted double, and were contained once more in the Belgrade figure of 4,700; furthermore, a portion of the Belgrade Jews had in the meantime decamped for the area of insurrection.

In the first conversation State Councillor Turner in bitter words expressed his disappointment that the first calls for help had not been immediately answered. The situation had been very precarious, and only as a result of the arrival of the German divisions had it been somewhat improved. I explained the reasons why the Jews could neither be deported to

Romania nor to the General Gouvernement nor to the East. State Councillor Turner could not appreciate these reasons. He continues as before to demand the expulsion of the remaining Jews from Serbia.

Detailed negotiations with the specialist on the Jewish question, Sturmbannführer Weimann of Turner's office, the chief of the Gestapo office, Standartenführer Fuchs and the members of his staff concerned with the Jewish question, led to the following:

1. The male Jews will be shot by the end of this week; in this way, the problem brought up in the report by the Legation is settled.

2. The remainder consisting of about 20,000 Jews (women, children, and old people) as well as about 1,500 Gypsies, of whom the males will likewise be shot, are to be assembled in the so-called Gypsy quarter of the city of Belgrade as a ghetto. The food for the winter could be assured in scanty amounts.

In a final discussion at State Councillor Turner's office the latter was willing to accept such a solution in principle. However, in his opinion the Gypsy quarter of the city of Belgrade is an absolute breeding ground of epidemics, and must be burned down for hygienic reasons. It could be considered only as an interim station.

Therefore the Jews and Gypsies who are not shot in reprisal at first are to be assembled in the Gypsy quarter and then transported at night to the Serbian island of Mitrovica. There two separate camps will be established. In the one the Jews and Gypsies are to be kept, and in the other 50,000 Serbian hostages.

Then, as soon as the technical possibility exists within the framework of the total solution of the Jewish question, the Jews will be deported by water to the reception camps in the East.

Rademacher

---

The 1941 campaign in the East began with the April invasion of Yugoslavia and Greece; Yugoslavia surrendered in only 2 weeks. When German troops were withdrawn to help in the June invasion of the Soviet Union, a resistance developed in Serbia. The Army's response took the form of reprisal executions. General Franz Böhme was military commander of Serbia; State Councillor and SS-Gruppenführer Harald Turner was head of his administrative staff. On 10 October Böhme ordered his units to arrest all suspected Communists and all Jews, and to execute 100 hostages for every German soldier killed. In Serbia, the German Army, rather than SS Einsatzgruppen, performed the killing operations.

Franz Rademacher submitted this memo to his boss in the Foreign Office, Martin Luther, who was liaison with Eichmann in the SS on Jewish affairs. The killing of Serbian Jews was arranged in Rademacher's negotiations with local civilian diplomats, Gestapo officers, and military personnel. Rademacher labels Jews as 'communist agitators' in order to justify their murder. Even that specious justification was not needed to explain the killing of Gypsies. At this point, women, children, and older people were treated differently, but the 'total solution' in the East looms in the immediate future. Until then, Jews and Gypsies were killed as described in the following report.

# 39. German Army report on shootings of Jews and Gypsies in Yugoslavia, 27–30 October 1941

## Secret

First Lieutenant Walther
Commander 9./I.R.433.

Local Headquarters, 1 November 1941.

Report on the Shooting of
===================
Jews and Gypsies
============

By agreement with the office of the SS, I picked up the selected Jews and Gypsies from the prisoner camp Belgrade. The trucks of the 599$^{th}$ Headquarters, which were at my disposal, proved to be unsuitable for two reasons:

1. They are driven by civilians. Thus secrecy is not guaranteed.
2. They were all without cover or canopy, so that the population of the city saw whom we had on the vehicles and where we then drove. In front of the camp, wives of the Jews had gathered, who wailed and cried, as we drove away. The place where the shooting was carried out is very favorable. It lies north of Pancevo directly on the route Pancevo – Jabuka, on which an embankment is located, which is so high, that a man can only get up with effort. Across from this embankment is swampland, behind it a river. At high water, (as on 29 October) the water reaches nearly to the embankment. An escape of the prisoners can thus be prevented with a few men. Similarly favorable is the sandy ground there, which makes the digging of the pits easier and thus also shortens the work time.

After arrival about 1 1/2–2 kilometers from the selected place, the prisoners climbed out, reached it by marching, while the trucks with the civilian drivers were immediately sent back, in order to give them as few reasons as possible for suspicion. Then I closed the road to all traffic on grounds of security and secrecy.

The place of execution was secured by 3 light machine guns and 12 riflemen:

1. Against attempts at escape by the prisoners.
2. For self-protection against any attacks by Serbian bands.

The excavation of the pits took most of the time, while the shooting itself went very quickly (100 men 40 minutes).

Pieces of luggage and valuables had been collected earlier and taken in my trucks, in order to hand them over to the NSV.

The shooting of the Jews is simpler than that of the Gypsies. One must admit that the Jews go to their death very calmly, – they stand very quietly, – while the Gypsies wail, cry and continually move, when they already stand at the shooting site. Some even jumped into the pit before the volley and tried to pretend they were dead.

At the beginning my soldiers were not affected. On the second day, however, it was already noticeable that one or the other did not have the nerves to carry out a shooting over a longer time. My personal impression is that during the shooting one has no moral scruples. These appear, however, after several days if one reflects about it quietly in the evening.

[signature] Walther
First Lieutenant.

---

Walther's report demonstrates the careful planning and methodical routine of mass shootings carried out by the German Army all over Eastern Europe. The original order to kill was issued by General Franz Böhme, the Commanding General in Serbia; 2200 Jews were to be shot as 'atonement' for the 22 German soldiers who had died in a skirmish with partisans. Although the specific order to execute prisoners from the concentration camp at Belgrade was given only one day before the shootings began, the army units were clearly well-prepared with plans for a simulated work detail, site preparation and security, and even photography at 5.30 the next morning. Besides the shooters themselves, the Army provided vehicles from headquarters.

This execution of 449 civilians at an early stage in the Holocaust has all the characteristics which became typical of such actions. Some effort was expended to delude the victims into thinking that their conditions were going to improve, as a means of preventing resistance. Medical doctors took an active role in murder. Confiscation of valuables was organized for the benefit of the security forces. Detailed reports represented the satisfaction of the local leaders in a job well done.

Walther observes here many reactions to the shooting of men, women, and children, done day after day. He describes with surprise the behavior of Jews, which he sees as honorable and worthy of respect, behavior he would naturally expect in much higher quantity and quality from Aryans, without any evidence that this was so. Gypsies grovel for their lives. His men also behave in two ways. Most can carry out a shooting as their daily experience. The minority without sufficient nerve cannot. Walther's subject shifts in his final sentences to include himself among those who recognize moral scruples. After leading the killing of 600 Jews and Gypsies, Walther asked to be relieved from such executions. One step removed from the actual shooting, Harald Turner at Böhme's headquarters could write to a friend that 'the Jewish question solves itself most quickly in this way.'[1]

These shootings took two full days to accomplish in the manner of formal military executions. By December 1941, over 20,000 civilians had been shot in Serbia by the Army, including nearly every male Jew in Serbia. Clearly, however, these methods could not be utilized to murder millions. By the spring of 1942, a specially equipped truck sent from Berlin was used to gas the remaining Jewish women and children.

## Note

1 Guenter Lewy, *The Nazi Persecution of the Gypsies* (New York: Oxford University Press, 2000), pp. 128–32.

# 40. Report on police battalion murder of Jews in Belorussia, 30 October 1941

Copy / T
of a copy

The Commissioner of the
Territory of Sluzk

Sluzk, 30 October 1941

To the
Commissioner General
in Minsk.

**Secret !**

Re: Action against Jews.

Referring to the report made by phone on 27 October 1941, I now inform you in writing of the following:

On 27 October at about 8 o'clock in the morning, a first lieutenant of the police battalion No. 11 from Kauen (Lithuania) appeared and introduced himself as the adjutant of the battalion commander of the security police. The first lieutenant explained that the police battalion had received the assignment to undertake here in the town of Sluzk the liquidation of all Jews in two days. The battalion commander with his battalion in strength of four companies, including two companies of Lithuanian partisans, was on the march and the action must begin immediately. I replied to the first lieutenant that I had to discuss the action in any case first with the commander. About half an hour later the police battalion arrived in Sluzk. As requested, immediately after arrival the discussion with the battalion commander took place. I first explained to the commander that it would not be possible to carry out the action without previous preparation, because everybody had been sent to work and it would lead to terrible confusion. It was at the least his duty to inform me a day ahead of time. Then I requested him to postpone the action one day. He rejected this, however, with the remark that he had to carry out this action everywhere in all towns, and that only two days were available for Sluzk. In those two days, the town of Sluzk had to be free of Jews without fail. I immediately raised the sharpest protest against it, pointing out that a liquidation of Jews must not take place in an arbitrary manner. A large part of the Jews still present in the town were artisans and families of artisans. These Jewish artisans were not simply expendable, because they were indispensable for maintaining the economy. I further pointed out that White Ruthenian artisans are so-to-speak non-existent, that therefore all vital enterprises would have to be shut down with one blow, if all Jews were liquidated. At the end of our discussion, I mentioned that all artisans and specialists, if they were indispensable, had identification papers in hand, and that these should not be pulled out of the enterprises. It was further agreed that all Jews still present in the town should first be brought into the ghetto for purposes of classification, especially with regard to the families of artisans, which I did not want to have liquidated either. Two of my officials should be charged with the classification. The commander contradicted my viewpoint in no way, so I had faith that the action would be carried out accordingly. A few hours after the beginning of the action, however, the greatest difficulties already developed. I observed that the commander had not held to our agreement at all. All Jews without exception were pulled out of the enterprises and shops, and taken away in spite of our agreement. Some of the Jews were, in fact, moved by way of the ghetto, where many were processed and segregated by me, but a large part was loaded directly on trucks and liquidated without further delay outside of the town. Shortly after noon complaints already came from all sides that the enterprises could not function any more, because all Jewish artisans had been removed. Since the commander had travelled on to Baranowitschi, after searching a long time, I got in touch with the deputy commander, a captain, with the demand to stop the action immediately, because my instructions had been disregarded and the damage done so far with respect to the economy could no longer be repaired. The captain was greatly surprised at my view and stated that he had received orders from the commander to clear the whole town of Jews without exception, as they had done in other towns. This cleansing had to take place for political reasons, and economic reasons had not played a role anywhere. Due to my energetic intervention, however, he did halt the action toward evening.

As for the rest of the conduct of the action, I must stress to my deepest regret that it bordered on sadism. The town itself offered a horrifying picture during the action. With indescribable brutality on the part of both the German police officers and particularly the Lithuanian partisans, the Jewish people, but also among them White Ruthenians, were pulled out of their dwellings and herded together. Everywhere in the town shots sounded and in different streets corpses of murdered Jews piled up. The White Ruthenians were in greatest distress to free themselves from the encirclement. Regardless of the fact that the Jewish people, including also artisans, were brutally mistreated right before the eyes of the White Ruthenian people, the White Ruthenians themselves were also worked over with rubber clubs and rifle butts. One could not speak any more of an action against Jews, rather it looked more like a revolution. I myself with all my officials have been in the middle without interruption all day long in order to save what could be saved. In several instances I literally had to drive out with drawn pistol the German police officials, as well as the Lithuanian partisans, from the enterprises. My own police were employed in the same task, but often had to leave the streets on account of the wild shooting in order not to be shot themselves. The whole picture was altogether more than ghastly....

I was not present at the shooting outside of town. Therefore I can say nothing about the brutality. But it should suffice, if I point out that persons who were shot worked themselves out of their graves a long time after they had been covered.

Regarding the economic damage, I note that the tannery has been affected worst of all. 26 experts worked there. Among them, 15 of the best specialists have been shot. Four more jumped from the truck during the transport and escaped, while 7 were not apprehended because they fled. The plant barely continues to operate today. Five wheelwrights worked in the wheelwright shop. Among them, four wheelwrights were shot, and the shop must be maintained now with one wheelwright. Additional artisans, such as carpenters, blacksmiths, etc., are lacking. It is still impossible for me to obtain a precise overview. As I mentioned already at the beginning, the families of artisans should also be spared. But now it seems that in almost all families some persons are missing. Reports come in from all over, from which it is clear that in one family the artisan himself, in another family the wife, and in the next family children are missing. Thus almost all families have been torn apart. Whether under these circumstances the remaining artisans show any interest in their work and produce accordingly seems very doubtful, particularly as even today they are running around with faces beaten bloody from the brutality. The White Ruthenian people, who had full confidence in us, are dumbfounded. Though they are intimidated and don't dare to utter their free opinion, one hears the opinion that this day was no glorious page for Germany and that this day will remain unforgotten. I am of the opinion that much has been destroyed through this action, which we have achieved during the past months, and that it will take a long time until we shall regain the lost confidence of the population.

In conclusion I find myself obliged to point out that the police battalion looted in an unheard of manner during the action, and not only in Jewish houses, but also in the houses of the White Ruthenians. Everything useful, such as boots, leather, cloth, gold and other valuables, they took away. According to statements of members of the Wehrmacht, watches were openly torn off the arms of Jews on the street, and rings were pulled off the fingers in the most brutal manner. A major in the finance department reported that a Jewish girl was ordered by the police to obtain 5,000 rubles immediately, then her father would be released. This girl is said to have actually gone everywhere in order to obtain the money.

Also within the ghetto, the individual barracks, which had been nailed up by the civil administration and were filled with Jewish goods, have been broken open and robbed by the police. Even from the barracks in which the unit was quartered, window frames and doors have been torn out and used for campfires. Although I had a discussion with the adjutant of the commander on Tuesday morning concerning the looting, and was promised in the course of the discussion that none of the policemen would enter the town any more, I was forced some hours later to arrest two fully armed Lithuanian partisans, because they were found looting. During the night from Tuesday to Wednesday, the battalion left the town in the direction of Baranowitschi. The people were openly only too glad, when this report circulated in the town.

So much for the report. I shall shortly come to Minsk, in order to discuss the affair personally. At the present time, I am not in a position to continue with the action against the Jews. First, order has to be established again. I hope to be able to restore order as soon as possible and, despite the difficulties, also to revive the economy. I beg you to grant me only one request: "Spare me in the future by all means from this police battalion!"

signed: Carl

---

Carl, Nazi Party member and the Commissioner of the Sluzk region, south of Minsk, sent this letter to Wilhelm Kube, the Commissioner General of White Ruthenia. The matter was then passed upwards from Kube to Hinrich Lohse, the Reich Commissioner for the Baltic region. Eventually documentation reached Rosenberg and Heydrich.

Carl's report demonstrates the conflicts between the civil administration put into place behind the Eastern Front and the troops under Himmler's command who were ordered to seek out and murder Jews. Both civil administration and

Wehrmacht officials were concerned with maintaining the local economy and exploiting it for their purposes. The sudden elimination of Jews, who could be a significant proportion of the population, created havoc in the economy, as Carl details. Yet the Einsatzgruppen and police battalions under Himmler's authority saw their 'political' objectives as primary. The savagery of their tasks expressed itself in behavior which was rarely reported so explicitly.

The police units which Carl witnessed in Sluzk came from the Order Police under SS leadership which helped the Einsatzgruppen kill Jews after the invasion of the Soviet Union. The Germans in the Order Police have been described by Christopher Browning as 'ordinary men', often middle-aged reservists who were not Nazi Party members. The reserve police battalion Browning studied, made up of 500 men, were responsible for the deaths of over 80,000 Jews in 1942–43.[1]

Carl's language here provides useful insight into widespread attitudes among Nazi authorities in the East about the Holocaust. Although Carl vociferously objects to a variety of police practices, nowhere does he reject the fundamental idea of murdering Jews. He wishes to see the shooting of men, women and children carried out in an orderly fashion, without the 'brutality' that he decries. He does not wish to alienate the local population who might be eventually won over to support for Germany. Looting is unworthy of German armed forces. When order could be finally restored, Carl was willing to finish the *Judenaktion*.

## Note

1 Christopher R. Browning, *Ordinary Men: Reserve Police Battalion 101 and the Final Solution in Poland* (New York: HarperCollins, 1992).

# 41. Article by Josef Goebbels on Jews in *Das Reich*, 16 November 1941

The Jews Are To Blame!
By Reich Minister Dr. Goebbels

The historic guilt of world Jewry for the outbreak and expansion of this war is so amply proven, that no more words are to be lost over it. The Jews wanted their war, and now they have it. But what also turns out to be true for them is the prophecy which the Führer pronounced on 30 January 1939 in the German Reichstag, that if international finance Jewry should succeed once more in plunging the nations into a world war, the result would not be the Bolshevization of the earth and thus the victory of Jewry, but the destruction of the Jewish race in Europe.

We are experiencing the accomplishment of this prophecy, and a fate for Jewry comes true which is hard, but more than deserved. Pity or even regret is entirely out of place here. World Jewry, in plotting this war, estimated the forces at its disposal entirely falsely, and is now suffering a gradual process of destruction, which it had planned for us, and which it would apply without hesitation, if it possessed the power to do so. They perish in line with their own law: "An eye for an eye, a tooth for a tooth!"

In this historic conflict, every Jew is our enemy, no matter whether he vegetates in a Polish ghetto, or leads his parasitical existence in Berlin or Hamburg, or blows the war trumpet in New York or Washington. By reason of their birth and race, all Jews belong to an international conspiracy against National Socialist Germany. They wish for its defeat and destruction, and do whatever is in their power to help bring it about. That they find in the Reich itself only limited possibilities toward this end is not due to their being loyal here, but solely to the fact that we took those measures against them which seemed appropriate to us.

One of those measures is the introduction of the yellow Jewish star, which every Jew has to wear visibly. That way we want to mark him externally, above all so that at the slightest attempt to violate the German national community, he can immediately be recognized as a Jew. It is an extraordinarily humane order, so to say, a prophylactic health measure, which should prevent the Jew from creeping unrecognized into our ranks, to sow disunion.

When the Jews, a few weeks ago, appeared in the streets of Berlin adorned with their Jewish star, the first impression among the citizens of the capital was one of general amazement. Only a very few knew that there were still so many Jews in Berlin. Everyone discovered, in his district or his neighborhood, some harmless contemporary, who had, it was true, attracted attention by occasional griping and complaining, but whom no one had taken as a Jew. He had obviously camouflaged himself, practiced mimicry, adapted in protective coloring to the milieu in which he lived, and waited for his moment. Who among us had any idea that the enemy stood right next to him, that he was a silent or cleverly prompting listener to conversations in the street, in the subway, or in the line standing in front of the tobacco shop? There are Jews who can hardly be recognized any more by their looks. They have assimilated themselves in this respect, too, as much as possible. They are the most dangerous ones....

Therefore let it be said once more, completely unnecessarily:

1. The Jews are our ruin. They plotted and brought about this war. They want with it to destroy the German Reich and our people. This plan must be defeated.

2. There is no difference between Jew and Jew. Every Jew is a sworn enemy of the German people. If he does not display his hostility against us, it is merely out of cowardice and slyness, but not because he does not carry it in his heart.

3. Every German soldier who falls in this war is the Jews' responsibility. They have him on their conscience, and they must therefore pay for it.

4. If one wears a Jewish star, so he is marked as the people's enemy. Whoever still maintains private relations with him belongs to him, and must be considered and treated the same as a Jew. He deserves the contempt of the entire people, which he has deserted in its gravest hour to put himself on the side of those who hate it.

5. The Jews enjoy the protection of the enemy nations. No further proof is needed of their destructive role among our people.

6. The Jews are the messengers of the enemy in our midst. Whoever joins them is going over to the enemy in time of war.

7. The Jews have no right to pretend to have rights equal to ours. Wherever they want to open their mouths, in the streets, in lines in front of the stores, or on public transportation, they are to be silenced, not only because they are wrong on principle, but because they are Jews and have no voice in the community.

8. If Jews pull a sentimental act for you, know that it is a speculation on your forgetfulness; show them immediately that you see through them and punish them with contempt.

9. A decent enemy, after his defeat, deserves our generosity. But the Jew is no decent enemy, he only pretends to be.

10. The Jews are to blame for the war. They suffer no wrong through the treatment we bestow upon them. They have more than deserved it....

---

How much could an average German know about the Holocaust? Without speaking directly of murder, Josef Goebbels, the Nazi Propaganda Minister, makes very clear here what is planned for European Jews. *Das Reich* was a weekly newspaper from 1940 to 1945, which began with half a million copies and by 1944 was printed in 1.5 million copies. It was the most internationally recognized and respected Nazi Party newspaper. Most military officers read it. Goebbels' lead articles were read twice weekly over the radio, Friday evenings and Sunday mornings.

He opens by referring to Hitler's speech on the sixth anniversary of becoming Chancellor, in which he threatened the 'annihilation of the Jewish race in Europe' should a war begin. Goebbels liked this 'prophecy': one week after German Jews were forced to wear the yellow star on 1 September 1941, the Propaganda Ministry printed it in the broadsheet *Weekly Maxims*. In a later article in *Das Reich* of 9 May 1943, Goebbels again referred to Hitler's 1939 speech, saying that no prophecy of his had turned out to be so true, that the war would bring the 'extinction' of the Jewish race. He calls Jews the 'embodiment of general world destruction', arguing that they planned the total destruction of the German *Volk*. He speaks of the Jews' deserved 'death sentence'.[1] Goebbels argued in all of his many public utterances that every Jew is to blame for every German death, that no Jew anywhere should be considered innocent. As the official and ubiquitous voice of the Nazi Party and German government, Goebbels' pronouncements on the fate of the Jews were unmistakable.

## Note

1 Hans-Heinrich Wilhelm, 'Wie geheim war die "Endlösung"?' in Wolfgang Benz (ed.), *Miscellanea: Festschrift für Helmut Krausnick zum 75. Geburtstag* (Stuttgart: Deutsche Verlags-Anstalt, 1980), pp. 131–48.

# 42. Minutes of the Wannsee Conference about the 'final solution', 20 January 1942

Secret Reich Matter
30 Copies
16th copy

Minutes of discussion ...

II. At the beginning, the Chief of the Security Police and the SD, SS-Obergruppenführer Heydrich, explained that the Reich Marshal had appointed him deputy for the preparation of the final solution of the European Jewish question, and pointed out that this discussion had been called for the purpose of clarifying fundamental questions. The Reich Marshal wishes to be sent a plan about organizational, technical and material concerns relating to the final solution of the European Jewish question, necessitating an initial common treatment by all central authorities immediately concerned with these questions, in order to bring their activities into line.

Leadership of the preparation of the final solution of the Jewish question lies centrally with the Reichsführer-SS and the Chief of the German Police (Chief of the Security Police and the SD), without regard to geographical borders.

The Chief of the Security Police and the SD then gave a short survey of the struggle which has been carried on against this enemy. The essential points were:

a) the expulsion of the Jews from every particular sphere of life of the German people,

b) the expulsion of the Jews from the territory of the German people.

To carry out these efforts, the strengthening and planning of accelerated emigration of Jews from the Reich was begun as the only preliminary solution.

By order of the Reich Marshal, a Central Reich Office for Jewish Emigration was set up in January 1939, entrusted to the direction of the Chief of the Security Police and SD. Its most important tasks were

a) to take all necessary steps to <u>prepare</u> for an increased emigration of the Jews,

b) to <u>direct</u> the stream of emigration,

c) to accelerate the procedure of emigration in each <u>individual case.</u>

The goal was, in legal ways, to clear the German territory of Jews.

All the offices realized the drawbacks of such enforced emigration. For the time being these had to be accepted, given the lack of other possible solutions.

The emigration efforts were not only a German problem, but also a problem with which the authorities of the destination countries had to deal. Financial difficulties, such as the increase by various foreign governments in the money which had to be presented at the time of the landing, lack of shipping space, increasing restrictions on immigration, extraordinarily increased the difficulties of emigration. In spite of these difficulties, 537,000 Jews were induced to emigrate from the seizure of power to the deadline 31 October 1941. Of these

| | |
|---|---|
| from 30 January 1933 from Germany | approx. 360,000 |
| from 15 March 1938 from Austria | approx. 147,000 |
| from 15 March 1939 from the Protectorate of Bohemia and Moravia | approx. 30,000. |

The financing of the emigration was accomplished by the Jews or Jewish political organizations themselves. In order to avoid impoverished Jews staying behind, the principle was followed that the wealthy Jews had to finance the evacuation of the poor Jews; here an emigration fee, graduated by wealth, was imposed, which was used for the financial obligations in connection with the emigration of poor Jews....

In the meantime the Reichsführer-SS and Chief of the German Police, due to the dangers of emigration during war-time and consideration of the possibilities in the East, had prohibited emigration of Jews.

III. Instead of emigration, another possible solution, with the appropriate previous agreement of the Führer, has arisen, the evacuation of the Jews to the East.

Such actions are, however, to be regarded only as provisional possibilities, but practical experience is already being collected, which is of great importance in relation to the coming final solution of the Jewish question.

Approximately 11 million Jews will be involved in the final solution of the European Jewish question, who are distributed among the individual countries as follows:

| | Country | | Number |
|---|---|---|---|
| A. | Old Reich | | 131,800 |
| | Austria | | 43,700 |
| | Eastern territories | | 420,000 |
| | General Gouvernement | | 2,284,000 |
| | Bialystok | | 400,000 |
| | Protectorate Bohemia and Moravia | | 74,200 |
| | Estonia | -free of Jews- | |
| | Latvia | | 3,500 |
| | Lithuania | | 34,000 |
| | Belgium | | 43,000 |
| | Denmark | | 5,600 |
| | France / Occupied Territory | | 165,000 |
| | Unoccupied Territory | | 700,000 |
| | Greece | | 69,600 |
| | Netherlands | | 160,800 |
| | Norway | | 1,300 |
| B. | Bulgaria | | 48,000 |
| | England | | 330,000 |
| | Finland | | 2,300 |
| | Ireland | | 4,000 |
| | Italy incl. Sardinia | | 58,000 |
| | Albania | | 200 |
| | Croatia | | 40,000 |
| | Portugal | | 3,000 |
| | Romania incl. Bessarabia | | 342,000 |
| | Sweden | | 8,000 |
| | Switzerland | | 18,000 |
| | Serbia | | 10,000 |
| | Slovakia | | 88,000 |
| | Spain | | 6,000 |
| | Turkey (European part) | | 55,500 |
| | Hungary | | 742,800 |
| | USSR | | 5,000,000 |
| | Ukraine | 2,994,684 | |
| | Belorussia | | |
| | excluding Bialystok | 446,484 | |
| | Total: | over | 11,000,000 |

... Under proper guidance, in the course of the final solution the Jews will be appropriately allocated for labor in the East. In large labor columns, with separation of the sexes, able-bodied Jews will be taken to these districts for work on roads, in the course of which undoubtedly a large part will be eliminated by natural causes.

The possible final remnant will, since it must undoubtedly consist of the toughest part, have to be treated accordingly, as it is the product of a natural selection, which would upon liberation act as a bud cell of new Jewish reconstruction. (See historical experience.)

In the course of the practical execution of the final solution, Europe will be cleaned up from the West to the East. Germany, including the Protectorate of Bohemia and Moravia, will have to be handled first due to reasons of housing and other social-political necessities.

The evacuated Jews will first be sent, group by group, into so-called transit-ghettos from which they will be transported further to the East....

The beginning of the individual large evacuation actions will mainly be dependent on the military situation. Regarding the handling of the final solution in the European territories occupied and influenced by us, it was suggested that the competent officials of the Foreign Office working on these questions confer with the responsible experts from the Security Police and the SD....

Regarding the question of the effect produced by the evacuation of the Jews on the economic life, Under Secretary of State Neumann declared that the Jews assigned to work in plants of importance for the war could not be evacuated as long as no replacement was available.

SS-Obergruppenführer Heydrich pointed out that, according to the directives approved by him governing the carrying out of the evacuation program in operation at the time, these Jews would not be evacuated.

Under Secretary of State Dr. Bühler stated that it would be welcomed by the General Gouvernement if the implementation of the final solution of this question could <u>start in the General Gouvernement</u>, because the transportation problem there would not play a large role and the progress of this action would not be hampered by considerations of labor supply. Jews must be removed as quickly as possible from the territory of the General Gouvernement, because especially there the Jews represented an immense danger as a carrier of epidemics, and on the other hand were continually disorganizing the economic system of the country through black market operations. Moreover out of the two and a half million Jews to be affected, the majority were <u>unfit for work</u>....

In conclusion the various methods of solution were considered, in which Gauleiter Dr. Meyer and also Under Secretary Dr. Bühler took the standpoint that certain preparatory work is to be done immediately in the territories in question, but an unsettling of the population must be avoided.

With the request to participants from the Chiefs of Security Police and the SD that they lend him appropriate assistance in the carrying out of the tasks involved in the solution, the conference was adjourned.

---

This extraordinary conference in a Berlin villa did not make any significant decisions on the fate of European Jews, except to ratify the control of the Reich Security Main Office over their lives. The crucial decisions had already been made and the Holocaust was well under way by this time. Heydrich told the representatives of various government agencies what would happen and called upon them for support, taking only 90 minutes; Eichmann took notes and wrote this summary. It displays the scope of the genocide that the SS was planning and the full participation of Party and government in this national policy.

While Himmler's deputy Heydrich asserted SS control over the entire process, other agencies eagerly collaborated. One month before the Wannsee meeting, the Foreign Office had prepared its own 'Wishes and Ideas' about Jews. They included the deportation to the East of all Jews living in Germany, Croatia, Slovakia, Romania, Serbia, Bulgaria, and Hungary.[1] Martin Luther carried these proposals to Wannsee.

The phrase 'evacuation of the Jews to the East' was a commonly used euphemism for deportation and mass murder in death camps. In his trial in Israel in 1961, Eichmann stated that this discussion explicitly referred to mass murder. Heydrich referred to the practical experience which had been gained through Einsatzgruppen shootings and gassing experiments at Chelmno and Auschwitz. While some details were debated, such as what to do with skilled Jewish workers, there was no serious objection raised at Wannsee about the whole genocidal project.

## Note

1 This memo from the Foreign Office is part of Nuremberg document NG-2586, along with Eichmann's minutes of the Wannsee Conference itself.

# 43. Report on use of trucks to kill Jews with exhaust gas in Soviet Union, 16 May 1942

Army Post Number 32 704 Kiev, 16 May 42.
B.Nr. 40/42 –

**Secret Reich Matter!**

To
SS-Obersturmbannführer R a u f f

in B e r l i n
Prinz-Albrecht-Str. 8

The overhaul of the trucks of Groups D and C is completed. While the trucks of the first series could be utilized in weather conditions that are not very good, the trucks of the second series (Saurer) get stuck in the rain. If, for example, it has rained for only a half hour, the truck cannot be used, because it slides away. It is only usable in completely dry weather. The question arises whether one can use the truck only at the place of execution. First the truck has to be brought to this place, which is possible only in good weather. The place of execution, however, mainly lies 10–15 kilometers off travelled roads and is thus by its location already hard to reach, in damp or wet weather not at all. If one drives or has driven those to be executed to this place, then they notice immediately what is going on and become uneasy, which should be avoided if possible. The only way is to load them in at the collection place and then drive out.

I have had the trucks of Group D disguised as caravans by having window shutters put on, one on each side of the small trucks and two on each side of the large trucks, as one often sees on peasant houses in the countryside. The trucks became so well-known, that not only the authorities, but also the civilian population named the trucks "death trucks", as soon as one of these vehicles appeared. In my opinion, even camouflaged, they cannot be permanently kept a secret.

The Saurer trucks, which I transported from Simferopol to Taganrog, had brake damage on the way. At the Sonderkommando in Mariupol it was determined that the collar of the combined oil-air-pressure-brakes was broken in several places. By persuasion and bribery at the home motor pool, it was possible to get a form made, from which two collars were cast. When I arrived some days later at Stalino and Gorlovka, the drivers of the trucks complained about the same problems....

Because of the uneven land and the indescribable conditions of the roads, the seals and rivets come loose over time. I was asked, whether in such cases the trucks should be transported to Berlin for repairs. Transport to Berlin would be much too expensive and would require too much fuel. In order to save this expense, I gave the order to solder the smaller holes, and if that could no longer be done, to inform Berlin by radio immediately, that truck number ... is no longer in service. In addition, I ordered that during the gassing all men be kept as far as possible away from the trucks, so that their health won't be harmed by leaking gases. I would like to take this opportunity to note that various Kommandos allow their own men to unload after the gassing. I pointed out to the commanders of these S.K.'s the tremendous psychic and physical injury this work can do to the men, if not immediately, then later. The men complained to me about headaches which appear after each unloading. Despite this, there is reluctance to change this arrangement, because of fear that prisoners brought in for such work would use an opportune moment to flee. In order to protect the men from such injuries, I request that appropriate orders be given.

The gassing is without exception not properly done. In order to finish the action as fast as possible, the drivers fully open the throttle. With this method those to be executed suffer death by suffocation and not, as planned, by being put to sleep. My instructions have shown that by proper use of the pedal, death comes more quickly and the prisoners fall asleep peacefully. The distorted faces and excretions, which have been seen previously, can no longer be noticed.

My continuing travel to Group B takes place today, where further reports can reach me.

[signature] Dr. Becker
SS-Untersturmführer

---

Dr August Becker has moved from transporting gas canisters for murdering the handicapped in Germany (document 30) to inspecting mobile gassing vans in the Ukraine, continuing to coordinate German industry and the SS in the refinement of the killing process. His letter is unusual because it does not camouflage murder in euphemistic language. Other communications between Nazi administrators in Berlin and military authorities at the front used terms like 'special handling'.

Walther Rauff was responsible for technical matters in the Reich Security Main Office. He received other communications at this time about the procedures for murdering Jews in gas vans. Willy Just in the transport department wrote Rauff on 5 June 1942 about various technical problems with the vans, including the maximum 'load', connecting hoses, drainage holes, and lighting. Rauff exchanged communications with Einsatzkommando leaders in Riga and Belgrade about orders for repairs or for more vans.[1]

These communications indicate how far the knowledge about the use of these gas vans spread beyond those immediately involved in the killings: the manufacturers at Saurer and Diamond; workers in the transport department of the Wehrmacht; civilians in occupied territories. The Holocaust was not a well-kept secret.

## Note

1 An excerpt from Just's letter is translated in J. Noakes and G. Pridham (eds), *Nazism: A History in Documents and Eyewitness Accounts, 1919–1945*, Vol. 2 (New York; Schocken Books, 1990), pp. 1202–3. Other communications on this matter are part of Nuremberg document PS-501 in *Trial of the Major War Criminals*, Vol. 26, pp. 105–10.

# 44. Proposal that several million Jews be sterilized for slave labor, 23 June 1942

VIKTOR BRACK
SS-Oberführer

Berlin, 23 June 1942
W 8, Voßstr. 4

**Secret Reich Matter**

To the
Reichsführer-SS and Chief of
German Police
Heinrich H i m m l e r

Berlin SW 11
Prinz Albrecht Str. 8

Very Esteemed Reichsführer!

I put a portion of my men at the disposal of Brigadeführer Globocnik for the completion of his special task quite a long time ago, at the instruction of Reichsleiter Bouhler. On the basis of a renewed request from him, I have now given him further personnel. On this occasion, Brigadeführer Globocnik took the view that the whole Jewish action is to be carried out as fast as possible, so that one is not stuck right in the middle one day, when some difficulties force a halt in the action. You yourself, Reichsführer, have already expressed the opinion to me, that one must work as fast as possible, due to reasons of concealment. Both views, which in principle produce the same result, from my own experience are more than justified; despite this, I would like to request your permission to express the following considerations in this connection:

Among about 10 million European Jews are included in my opinion at least 2–3 million quite able-bodied men and women. Considering the extraordinary difficulties which the question of workers causes us, I support the viewpoint to extract and maintain these 2–3 million in any case. Of course, that would work only if one simultaneously makes them sterile. I already reported to you about one year ago, that my subordinates had completed work on the necessary experiments for this purpose. I would like to remind you of these facts again. A sterilization, as it is normally conducted on those with hereditary diseases, is out of the question in this case, since it is time-consuming and expensive. An x-ray castration, however, is not only relatively inexpensive, but also can be conducted on many thousands in the shortest time. I also believe that at the moment it has become insignificant, whether the victims after some weeks or months realize through the effects that they are castrated.

Should you, Reichsführer, in the interest of preserving labor material, decide to choose this path, Reichsleiter Bouhler is ready to put at your disposal the doctors and other personnel necessary for completion of this work. He has authorized me to say to you that I should then order in the quickest way the required apparatus.

Heil Hitler!
Your
[signature] Viktor Brack

---

Viktor Brack, formerly in charge of the T4 "euthanasia" killings, calmly proposes to kill only 7–8 million Jews, thus 'preserving labor material' in order to deal with the wartime shortage of workers. Brack has arranged for the men who gained experience in killing the handicapped to be transferred to Odilo Globocnik, whose special task was the construction and performance of the extermination camps at Sobibor, Treblinka, and Belzec, the so-called *Aktion Reinhardt* camps. Almost 100 people from the T4 project eventually worked in these camps, including Christian Wirth, commandant of Belzec, and Franz Stangl, commandant of Sobibor and Treblinka.[1] The importance of Hitler's personal Chancellery, run by Reichsleiter Philipp Bouhler, in supplying ideas and personnel to Himmler's SS operation is underlined by Brack's central place in the bureaucratic system of the Holocaust.

The conflict between the need for labor during war and the desire to eliminate all European Jews as quickly as possible continued to cause disagreement among the Nazi leadership. Brack's interest in preserving 'labor material', at least temporarily, led him to claim that the apparatus for x-ray sterilizations of several million people was already available. Such an inexpensive and effective process for sterilization had not yet been developed. Considerable experimentation on concentration camp prisoners was directed to this end.

Brack was hanged in Landsberg Prison on 2 June 1948, along with Dr Karl Brandt, after conviction for war crimes. Bouhler committed suicide when caught by American troops. Globocnik appears in other documents below.

## Note

1 Henry Friedlander, 'The T4 Killers: Berlin, Lublin, San Sabba', in Berenbaum and Peck, *The Holocaust and History*, p. 249.

# 45. Letter from Gestapo ordering deportation of Jews in Schwerin, 6 July 1942

Copy.

Secret State Police
– State Police Precinct Schwerin –

Schwerin (Meckl.) 6 July 1942.
Weinbergstrasse 1

B.Nr. II B 2 – 326/42 g.

To
the Police Presidents
in Rostock.

Regarding: Evacuation of Jews to the East.
Previous: None.
Enclosures:

On 11 July 1942, 91 Jews from the districts of the State Police Precinct Schwerin should be evacuated to the East. For the evacuation, those Jews are to be considered, who are listed at the end of this directive for the individual local police authorities. From these Jews the attached property declarations are to be filled out immediately in one copy and sent to me by special delivery by Thursday, 9 July 1942. Before the filling out, it is to be pointed out to the Jews that the instruction provided (take notice) is to be observed carefully. For each person (children and wives also) a separate form is to be filled out. For minors or wives, the legal representative (father) must ordinarily undertake the filling out. This is also applicable, if there is no property or income for the minors or wives. All documents referring to or representing property or regulating property by law (ex. contracts and evidence) are to be enclosed, if available.

It is to be pointed out to the Jews that they must fill out the property declarations most carefully. They are to be explicitly notified that they can count on no leniency, if they do not sufficiently observe this obligation but rather that they can count on strict police measures if it should be determined that the filled out property declarations do not correspond to the true facts.

<u>The Jews may take per person:</u>
1 suitcase or backpack with equipment, namely:
1 pair sturdy work boots,
2 " socks,
2 shirts,
2 underwear,
1 work outfit,
2 wool blankets,
2 sets of bedding (covers and sheets),
1 bowl,
1 cup,
1 spoon and
1 sweater.

Provisions for three days march.
In addition, 50 RM per person.

<u>Not allowed to be taken:</u>
Securities, foreign currency, savings account books, etc.
Valuables of any kind (gold, silver, platinum (with exception of the wedding ring), livestock.

The food ration cards are to be taken away and given to the local economic offices.

Before leaving their apartment, the Jews are to be searched for weapons, ammunition, explosives, poison, foreign currency, jewelry, etc.

The apartments of the Jews after leaving are to be locked and sealed by the local police authorities, so that no unauthorized person can enter the apartment. Before closing the apartments, it is especially to be seen to that gas taps, water pipes and lights are turned off according to instructions.

It is to be pointed out to the Jews before their removal that bringing objects is useless, since these will be taken away in the transit camp in Ludwigslust.

The travel costs from their places of residence to Ludwigslust are to be paid by the Jews themselves.

The Jews are to be entered in the registers of the registry office as destination unknown.

The local police authorities are responsible for carrying out the action.

The transport leaves on Friday, 10 July '42, 7:01 AM, from Rostock....

As transport leader for the transport from Rostock to Ludwigslust the Criminal Assistant Schütt has been appointed. He remains after his arrival in

Ludwigslust until the departure of the transport train on 11 July '42 – from Ludwigslust at 13:39 – in Ludwigslust.

By instruction:
signed Lange.

---

In this Gestapo order, as elsewhere, 'evacuation to the East' serves as a euphemism for mass murder: the train leaving Ludwigslust goes to Auschwitz. This instruction was followed by a list of 24 names of Jews living in Rostock, complete with dates and places of birth. Most were older people; none were between 17 and 29. Young adults were still being used as coerced labor. The necessities which each could carry ended up in a warehouse in Auschwitz, called Canada by the prisoners, since it contained unattainable riches.

For the Gestapo, the most important element of procedure in this deportation appears to be the exact completion of the property declarations. Jews unknowingly on their way to the gas chambers were threatened with 'strict police measures' if they did not list every piece of property they owned. Except for the most limited provision of clothing and a wedding ring, the deported Jews had to leave everything behind to be confiscated. Jews paid for their trip to Ludwigslust and provided their own food.

Haste was one of the deliberate elements of the deportation strategy. The local police were notified by this letter on 6 July that these 24 Jews from Rostock had to carefully fill out property declarations and hand them in by 9 July and board a train at 7:01 AM on 10 July. The impossible schedule left little opportunity to prepare resistance of any sort. This procedure for German Jews was, however, much gentler than that used in the deportation of Polish Jews.

# 46. Report by Gestapo on French-German cooperation on deportation of Jews, 8 July 1942

IV J SA 24 Paris, 8 July 1942

Re: Further Jewish Transports from France –
First Meeting of the Action Committee.

1.) Note:
Participants:
A) SS-Hauptsturmführer Dannecker,
SS-Unterscharführer Heinrichsohn
B) Darquier de Pellepoix,
Mr. Leguay, Representative of the Chief of Police,
Director François, Chief of Prison Camp,
Director Hennequin, Chief of Traffic Police,
Director Tulard, Chief of Jewish Card File of the Prefecture of Paris,
Director Garnier, Representative of the Prefects of the Seine,
Director Schweblin, Anti-Jewish Police,
Mr. Gallien, Cabinet Chief of Darquier,
Mr. Guidot, Staff Officer of the Traffic Police.

In introductory words, Darquier indicated that the occupation authorities have declared themselves ready to take the Jews from the French state, and that the meeting is being held to discuss the technical realization of the deportation.

Then the actual discussion began and SS-Hauptsturmführer Dannecker established:

1.) Whether all men present were fully authorized representatives of their agencies, so that today's decisions would be binding and no further questions or changes would take place. All men declared themselves to be authorized with full powers.

In the course of further discussion

2.) the number of Jews in question in Greater Paris was discussed.

Accordingly there are in Paris around 28,000 Jews according to the special directions (stateless etc.) to be arrested. In addition come the

Russian Jews (white and red), so that after the subtraction of the sick, unable to be transported, and too old Jews, one can reckon with a number of 22,000 Jews for Paris.

Next the point

3.) <u>of the actual arrest procedures was addressed.</u>

Through the inspectors of the prefects, the anti-Jewish police, and female assistants, the file cards in question will be found and sorted by arrondissement.

Then Director Hennequin (Municipal Police) will receive these cards and distribute them to the police commissars of the arrondissements. They will make the arrests according to the cards and give back the cards of the Jews who were not found.

By Friday, 10 July 42, the card-sorting will be done, and early on Monday (13 July 42) the action can take place simultaneously in all arrondissements.

The Jews will then be gathered in the individual districts and subsequently transported to the main collection place (Vél d'hiver). The transportation to the individual camps will be taken over by the French themselves.

Age limits of "16–50 years" were determined.

Remaining children will also be collected at a common place and subsequently taken charge of by the Union of Jews in France, and brought to children's homes.

All Jews within the age limits will be arrested who are able to be transported. (Not those in mixed marriages!)

In the Départements Seine et Oise and Seine et Marne the action will be carried out with the Paris Police following the one in Paris.

In this connection

4.) <u>the capacity of the individual prison camps was addressed.</u>

Hauptsturmführer Dannecker ascertained the following numbers.

| | | | | | | |
|---|---|---|---|---|---|---|
| Drancy | : | 6000 Jews (women and men) | | | | |
| Compiègne | : | 6000 | " | " | " | " |
| Pithiviers | : | 5000 | " | " | " | " |
| Beaune-la-Rolande: | | 5000 | " | " | " | " |

5.) <u>Actual Deportation of Jews to the East.</u>

It was established that from each camp one transport a week would start. One came to this solution, because each transport needs a careful preparation. (search of the Jews, provisions, lists, etc.).

Thus each week four trains with 1000 Jews each will leave the occupied territory in the direction of the East.

The guarding of the trains will be provided by the French police, who will be overseen by a German military police unit of a lieutenant and eight men.

6.) Provisions and supplies of the Jews.
Each Jew is to be supplied as follows:
a) 1 pair sturdy work boots, 2 pairs socks, 2 shirts, 2 underwear, 1 work outfit, 2 wool blankets, 2 sets of bedding (covers and sheets), 1 bowl, 1 cup, 1 canteen, 1 spoon and 1 sweater, further the most necessary toilet articles.
b) Each Jew must carry provisions for 3 days of marching.
Only one piece of luggage (1 suitcase or backpack) may be taken.
c) Further, provisions for a total of 14 days (bread, flour, potatoes, beans, etc. in sacks) is to be put in a separate freight car.

The representative of the Prefecture of the Seine saw here no problems....

[signature] Dannecker
SS-Hauptsturmführer

---

In early July 1942, German and French officials together planned the largest round-up of Jews in France during the war. Theodor Dannecker was chief of the Gestapo's Jewish Office in Paris; Louis Darquier de Pellepoix was his French counterpart, directing the French bureau of Jewish affairs. Their common goal was to accelerate the deportation of Jews from France to Auschwitz.

After the German conquest of France in June 1940, the country was split into halves: the German Army occupied Northern France and a new authoritarian government under Marshal Philippe Pétain declared itself ruler of unoccupied Southern France, with a capital in Vichy. In October, the new Vichy government promulgated its first *Statut des Juifs*, which removed Jews from all public employments, and authorized local prefects to arrest any foreign Jews. German officials prepared a card file of all Jews in France.

Foreign male Jews in France began to be arrested and put into internment camps in May 1941, with the full cooperation of Vichy officials. Between March and July, 1942, about 6000 of them were deported to Auschwitz. Dannecker accompanied the first train all the way to Auschwitz. It is estimated that about 5% survived. In June, German authorities decreed that Jews must wear the yellow star.

Now in July, the next phase was being planned. Men and women were to be arrested, but the fate of children was still uncertain, so they would be 'collected' and given over to the General Union of Israelites of France. What Jews could carry with them was expressed in precisely the same words as the deportation instruction above from Schwerin (document 45), with the addition of a canteen.

At 4 a.m. on July 16, 4500 French police carrying nearly 28,000 cards identifying their victims fanned out across Paris. They arrested 12,884 Jews, mostly women and children. All the adults were sent to Auschwitz within 3 weeks, while Dannecker sought permission from Berlin to deport the 3500 children under 14 who remained. Once it arrived by telegram, the children were packed into cattle cars and sent on the 3-day trip to Auschwitz. None are known to have survived.

# 47. Protest of the Bishop of Montauban against deportations in France, 26 August 1942

letter of his eminence, Mgr. Théas, Bishop of Montauban,
about respect for the human person
To be read on Sunday, 30 August 1942, without commentary in all masses
in all churches and chapels of the diocese

My very dear brothers,

Truly painful scenes, sometimes brutal, take place in France, without France being responsible for them.

In Paris, by tens of thousands, Jews are being treated with the most barbaric savagery. And here in our region, one sees a heart-rending spectacle: families are dislocated, men and women are treated like a base herd of animals and sent towards an unknown destination, with the prospect of more serious dangers.

I pronounce indignant protest of the Christian conscience, and I declare that all people, Aryans and non-Aryans, are brothers, because they were created by God; that all people, whatever their race or their religion, have a right to respect from individuals and from the state.

Now, the present antisemitic measures mean a contempt for human dignity, a violation of the holiest rights of the person and the family.

May God console and strengthen those who are unjustly persecuted. May He give the world true and lasting peace, founded on justice and charity.

signed: Pierre Marie,
Bishop of Montauban

---

Until the deportations of Jews from Paris began in the summer of 1942, no Catholic bishop in France had publicly protested Vichy antisemitic persecution. Public opinion also remained indifferent at best to actions against Jews.

This letter was written on the day that massive arrests of Jews began in the unoccupied zone of France ruled by the Vichy government. Bishop Pierre-Marie Théas followed Archbishop Jules-Gérard Saliège of Toulouse in delivering a pastoral letter condemning the persecution of Jews. He asked

Marie-Rose Gineste, who was active in Catholic social work, to deliver copies of this letter to all the churches in his diocese, to be read on Sunday, 30 August 1942. Afraid of Vichy censorship through the post office, Gineste used a bicycle to carry copies of the letter over the next several days. It apparently was read publicly in every church in dozens of communities, with one exception, where the priest supported the Vichy government. The messages of Saliège and Théas were reproduced widely in pamphlets produced by Resistance and Catholic publications, and read over the BBC.[1]

Other bishops followed these examples in September, but not all of the pastoral letters were as forthright as that of Théas, some referring to Jews as a problem for the state. These interventions by Catholic leaders caused a significant increase in public sympathy for Jews, including foreign Jews. Public support for Jews helped to convince Vichy officials to delay Nazi efforts to deport French Jews, but foreign Jews continued to be sacrificed.

## Note

1 Susan Zuccotti, *The Holocaust, the French and the Jews* (New York: Basic Books, 1993), pp. 146–9. Both Bishop Théas and Gineste have been honored with the title of Righteous Among the Nations by Yad Vashem, and Gineste donated her bicycle to Yad Vashem.

# 48. Report by Himmler to Hitler on mass murder of 'partisans' in Soviet Union, 29 December 1942

The Reichsführer-SS

Field Command Post
29 December 1942

Re: Report to the Führer about
the Struggle against Partisan Gangs
Report Nr. 51
Russia-South, Ukraine, Bialystok.
Successes in the Struggle against Partisan Gangs from 1 Sept. to 1 Dec.1942

1.) Bandits

a) confirmed deaths after battles (x)

| August: | September: | October: | November: | total: |
|---|---|---|---|---|
| 227 | 381 | 427 | 302 | 1337 |

b) prisoners executed immediately

| | | | | |
|---|---|---|---|---|
| 125 | 282 | 87 | 243 | 737 |

c) prisoners executed after lengthy thorough interrogation

| | | | | |
|---|---|---|---|---|
| 2100 | 1400 | 1596 | 2731 | 7828 |

2.) Partisan helpers and suspects:

a) captured

| | | | | |
|---|---|---|---|---|
| 1343 | 3078 | 8337 | 3795 | 16553 |

b) executed

| | | | | |
|---|---|---|---|---|
| 1198 | 3020 | 6333 | 3706 | 14257 |

c) Jews executed

| | | | | |
|---|---|---|---|---|
| 31246 | 165282 | 95735 | 70948 | 363211 |

3.) Deserters a. G. of German propaganda:

| | | | | |
|---|---|---|---|---|
| 21 | 14 | 42 | 63 | 140 |

(x) Since the Russians drag away or bury their casualties immediately, the numbers of deaths even according to reports by prisoners are to be estimated as significantly higher.

This report was prepared in Himmler's field command headquarters on a special machine with large type (called the Führer-typewriter) and was given to Hitler by his personal adjutant on 31 December 1942.[1] It illustrates many aspects of the genocide on the Eastern Front. Soviet resisters are defined as bandits operating in gangs outside of the rules of war. Thus all prisoners were executed. Even those merely suspected of aiding the partisans are executed. Success is understood only in terms of deaths. While a series of minor skirmishes left a few thousand dead, hundreds of thousands of Jewish civilians were murdered. Some 25 Jews were killed for every non-Jewish 'suspect'. Then the totals were carefully tabulated and sent to Berlin, so that these records of success would be preserved. Although Himmler places the mass murder of Jews under the rubric of guerrilla warfare, he did not here use euphemistic language to cover killing.

In April 1943, Hitler was sent another report about 'The Final Solution of the Jewish Question' prepared by Richard Korherr, a statistician employed by Himmler. In that more formal research report, even the euphemism of 'special treatment' was replaced by the phrase 'transport of Jews'. Korherr estimated that 4 million Jews had died since the beginning of the war.[2]

Hitler was fully informed about the facts of the Holocaust as it was occurring, and Himmler assumed Hitler would approve of the numbers he was submitting.

## Notes

1 Gerald Fleming, *Hitler and the Final Solution* (Berkeley, CA: University of California Press, 1984), pp. 3, 129.

2 This report came in a shorter and longer form, Nuremberg documents NO-5193 and NO-5194.

# 49. Gestapo report on deportation of Jews from France, 6 March 1943

IV B – BdS
Rö/Ne.

Paris, 6 March 1943

Regarding: Current Status of the Jewish Question in France

1. Note:

I. Numerical Status

Expelled through 6 March 1943 49,000. According to estimates (Jewish censuses have never taken place in France except for registration requirement of military command in previously occupied region) at present in previously occupied region still 70,000 Jews, in newly occupied region 200,000 Jews.

Up to the end of March 1943 Italians take back out of France Jews of Italian citizenship (in both regions together about 1000 Jews)

Hungary took back to Hungary end of Feb. '43, 70 Jews Hung. cit., shows itself uninterested in the rest (1500).

Turkey wants to take back to Turkey immediately 631 Jews Turk. cit., similarly declares itself uninterested in the rest (about 3000).

Switzerland took back end of Jan. 190 Jews to Switzerland.

Deported in the meantime Jews of the following cit. from the previously occupied region:

| 1. stateless | 7. Lithuanians | 13. former Poles |
|---|---|---|
| 2. Belgians | 8. Luxemburger | 14. " Germans |
| 3. Dutch | 9. Bulgarians | 15. " Austrians |
| 4. Norwegians | 10. Romanians | 16. " Saarl. |
| 5. Estonians | 11. Greeks | 17. " Czecho-slovaks |
| 6. Latvians | 12. Russians (White or Soviet) | 18. " Yugoslavs |

as well as about 3000 French criminal Jews

Unoccupied region furnished thus far for transport around 12,000 Jews.

II. Plan.

a) Collection of all Jews from the provinces (previously occupied region) to Paris and evacuation from Paris to the East.

b) Demand to the French government:

surrender of Jews of the above listed nationalities able to be expelled for the purpose of transport,

enactment of a law for deprivation of French citizenship for Jews naturalized after 1927 or 1933.

Surrender of those Jews thereby made stateless for the purpose of transport

c) Mass transport from April 1943 (weekly 8,000 to 10,000 Jews. Transport materials no problem.).

d) Prerequisite for carrying out of the program is that the French government be <u>forced</u> to make its police forces available. (Given the attitude of the Marshal and several cabinet members only compulsion can be considered.)

III. Attitude of the Italians on the Jewish question:

a) Prevailing attitude in the region of France occupied by Italy must in any case be given up, if Jewish problem is to be solved.

Following especially flagrant cases:

1) End of December 1942 / beginning of Jan. 1943, Italian civil and military officials prevent making the border and coastal areas in the region of France they occupy free of Jews, as well as the internment of particular categories of Jews.

2) Beginning of Jan. 1943, It. officials prevent the stamp "Jew" on identity and ration cards of Jews in the region they occupy, not only for Jews of Italian cit., but also for all other foreign and stateless Jews, with the exception of French Jews.

3) The High Command of the IV Italian Army notified the Commander in Chief of the West on 16 February that the internment of dangerous Jewish elements was in process and the other Jews would be forcibly gathered in certain communities. Measures should begin on 20 February. Nothing has happened.

4) On 19 February, the For. Min. notifies the German Embassy in Paris that, according to report of the German Embassy in Rome, the Italian government, in the interest of the security of the occupation troops, had interned all Jews in the French region occupied by Italy in the interior. Is not true, nothing done.

5) Middle of February '43 the French police want to intern 200 to 300 Jews in the area of Lyon, to carry out a reprisal measure ordered by us. The Italian general stationed in Grenoble demands of the French police officials the retraction of the internment order (Italian Jews were not be arrested according to the internment order.)
6) In the carrying out of the same reprisal measure, the French police in the middle of February in Annecy arrest foreign Jews through the rural police and brings them to the police barracks. Italian military demands immediate release of the Jews, which is refused. Thereupon the barracks are surrounded by armed Italian soldiers.
7) French police arrest 100 foreign Jews (no Italians!) in the region of Grenoble in the middle of February, in order to surrender them to us. Italians enter a protest and prevent the delivery of these Jews on the grounds that the arrested Jews count as "blocked".
The actions of the Italians have been communicated in a series of reports by the RSHA.
For. Off. is informed by RSHA (Eichmann) about the behavior of the Italians, Reich Foreign Minister Ribbentrop wanted to bring up the attitude of the It. on the Jewish question in negotiations with the Duce. Results of the negotiations are not yet known.

signed: Röthke

---

This report by Heinz Röthke displays the differing attitudes and behaviors of German, Vichy French, and Italian authorities toward Jews. Röthke, who replaced Dannecker as chief of the Gestapo's Jewish Office in France, believed his highest priority was to deport Jews to their deaths. He was outraged by any obstacles to his work, and was willing to use force against Vichy officials who were not cooperative. Like Dannecker, he hoped for weekly transports of thousands of Jews to Eastern European death camps. In order to achieve this ambitious goal, French Jews, who had thus far been protected by Vichy, would have to be added to the trainloads of foreign Jews who had been rounded up.

Röthke indicates that Vichy leaders, including Pétain, were no longer as cooperative as they had been in 1942. The protests of Catholic leaders in summer and fall 1942, and increasing public hostility to German occupiers and anyone who collaborated with them, affected the willingness of Pétain and his Prime Minister, Pierre Laval, to continue support for deportations. Defeat at Stalingrad and Allied landings in North Africa made ultimate German military victory less likely. Laval equivocated on the German demand that Vichy denaturalize all Jews who had recently become French citizens, but finally notified Röthke in August 1943 that Vichy would not meet this demand.

Vichy leaders allowed German forces to continue to arrest and deport Jews, both foreign and French, throughout 1943, but remained unwilling to allow French police to aid in arresting French Jews. Even that effort at resistance was abandoned in 1944, when French and German forces cooperated to identify, arrest, and deport any Jew they could find. As Allied troops were liberating Paris in August 1944, a final train departed from Clermont-Ferrand for Auschwitz. Nearly 80,000 Jews were deported from France. Because of the efforts of Vichy leaders to protect French Jews, the great majority of these victims were foreign Jews who had sought refuge in France.[1]

No such cooperation was provided by the Italians. Italian military and government leaders directly intervened to prevent deportations from all areas they controlled. To Röthke's surprise, Italian authorities made no distinctions based on birthplace or citizenship. In Southern France, Croatia and Greece, occupying Italian forces protected Jews from their German ally. Once the Allies landed in Sicily and Italy surrendered, German forces occupied Northern Italy and began deporting Jews from all areas formerly controlled by Italy, including from Rome.[2]

## Notes

1 Zuccotti, *The Holocaust, the French, and the Jews*, chs 10–11.

2 Best on this subject is another book by Zuccotti, *The Italians and the Holocaust: Persecution, Rescue, and Survival* (New York: Basic Books, 1987).

# 50. Protest by Bulgarian legislators against deportation of Jews, 17 March 1943

17 March 1943

Esteemed Mr. Prime Minister,

The great sense of historical responsibility we share with the government in these critical times, our steadfast loyalty to the regime and to its policy, as well as our desire to do all we can to ensure its success, give us the courage to address you, hoping that you will recognize the sincerity and goodwill of our action.

Recent actions taken by the authorities make clear their intentions to take new measures against persons of Jewish origin. What is the precise nature of these steps? On what basis are they being taken, and what is their motivation and scope? Explanations from responsible circles are missing. In a conversation with certain deputies, the Minister of Internal Affairs confirmed that no exceptional measures against the Jews from the old territory were being contemplated. After that conversation such measures were actually cancelled.

Taking all this into consideration and in view of new rumors, we have taken it upon ourselves to appeal to you directly, for if such measures are carried out, it will have to be on the orders of the Council of Ministers. Our sole request is that before any measures whatsoever are undertaken, the real interests of the state and nation, and the good name and moral standing of the Bulgarian people, be taken into account.

We could never oppose measures taken by the government to ensure the country's security, for we recognize that anyone who at this decisive moment in our history would obstruct the sovereign will of the government and the people, directly or indirectly, must be deprived of the power to do so....

The right of the state to remove all obstacles that might stand in the way of its policy cannot be contested, so long as its actions do not go beyond what is truly necessary or fall into excesses that qualify as needless cruelty. Yet how else is one to describe measures taken against women, children, and the aged, people who are guilty of no crime whatsoever?

It is impossible for us to accept that plans have been made to deport these people, even though ill-minded rumors attribute this intention to the Bulgarian government. Such measures are unacceptable, not only because these people — who are still Bulgarian citizens — cannot be expelled from their own country, but also because this course of action would be disastrous, with grave consequences for our country. Our nation's reputation would be stained for ever, its moral and political standing for ever compromised, and thus the arguments that Bulgaria might one day need to rely upon in its dealings with foreign powers would lose all their force....

The small number of Jews in Bulgaria, the strength of our own state, with so many legal means at its disposal, make the elimination of any dangerous elements easy, whatever their origin. For this reason, we are deeply convinced that the use of exceptional and cruel measures, measures that may expose the government and the entire nation to accusations of mass murder, are unwarranted and excessive. The consequences of this policy would be particularly grave for the government, but they would weigh upon the Bulgarian people as well. These consequences can be easily foreseen, and for this reason the policy is inadmissible. We cannot share any responsibility for it whatsoever.

Good government requires basic legal principles, just as life requires air to breathe.

The honor of Bulgaria is not just a matter of sentiment, it is also and above all a matter of policy. It is of immense political capital and no one has the right to jeopardize it without good reasons approved by the whole nation.

We beg you, Mr. Prime Minister, to accept our deep esteem.

[signatures of forty-two deputies]

---

This letter was composed by Dimitâr Peshev, vice-chairman of the Bulgarian National Assembly, signed by deputies of the majority party, and sent to the chairman of the Assembly. The Bulgarian government had begun to implement anti-Jewish policy already in 1940, following similar measures in Romania, Hungary, and France. Only in Bulgaria, however, did racial legislation provoke widespread protests from professional, political, and religious organizations. After officially allying with Nazi Germany in March 1941, Bulgaria occupied Northern Greece and Southern Yugoslavia.

On 21 January 1943 SS-Hauptsturmführer Theodor Dannecker, formerly supervisor of deportations from France, arrived in Sofia to demand the deportation of the Bulgarian Jews. Beginning on 3 March, Jews in territories occupied by Bulgaria were arrested. Despite a number of protests, 11,343 Jews were deported within 3 weeks from the occupied lands to Auschwitz and

Treblinka. Much greater protests greeted the attempts to arrest the 48,000 Jews of Bulgaria. A delegation from the town of Kyustendil, near Sofia, met with Peshev, also from Kyustendil. In his memoirs, Peshev wrote, 'To have remained silent would have been a breach of conscience, it would have been contrary to my sense of responsibility both as a deputy and as a human being.'[1] Peshev carried their protest to the Minister of Internal Affairs Gabrovski, and forced him to order the release of those arrested. Then he circulated the protest letter among the deputies of his party. Once he had gathered signatures of about one-third of his party's deputies, he made the letter public. This was only one among many protests, including one by Cyril, the Orthodox Metropolitan of Plovdiv, who sent a telegram to King Boris. It is clear from Peshev's letter that Bulgarian leaders understood that deportation to Poland meant death.

The Bulgarian leaders were aware that the tide of war had turned against the Germans with their surrender at Stalingrad in February 1943. Peshev's letter, framed in formal and supportive language, alludes to possible future 'dealings with foreign powers' who might be concerned about Bulgaria's actions. Peshev was stripped of his position as vice-chairman of the legislature, but those who had cooperated with Dannecker were blocked by the determination of King Boris that no Bulgarian Jews would be deported. The public protests, especially the work of Peshev in organizing a protest of government policy from within the ruling party, had convinced the King to intervene against any further cooperation in the Holocaust, despite his own antisemitic sentiments. No Jews were deported from within Bulgaria.

Dimitâr Peshev was the only European legislator who used his nation's political process to raise a public protest against the deportation of Jews. His actions and the ultimate decision not to deport the Bulgarian Jews must be seen in the context of the widespread popular rejection of the initial efforts of the Bulgarian government to cooperate in the Nazi Holocaust. Among all the nations occupied by or allied with the Germans, only in Italy, Bulgaria, and Denmark did leading figures create a national policy to obstruct the Holocaust.

Dannecker was captured by the American Army and committed suicide in December 1945.

## Note

1 Quoted in Tsvetan Todorov, *The Fragility of Goodness: Why Bulgaria's Jews Survived the Holocaust*, trans. Arthur Denner (Princeton, NJ: Princeton University Press, 2001), p. 163.

# 51. Order by Himmler to destroy Ukraine, 7 September 1943

The Reichsführer-SS — Field Command Post, 7 September 1943
Diary No. 1741/43 Sec. R. M.
RF/Bn

**Secret Reich Matter!**

To the
Higher SS and Police Leader of the Ukraine
Kiev

7 Copies
7th Copy

Dear Prützmann!

General of the Infantry Stapf has special orders regarding the Donetz region. Get in touch with him immediately. I order you to cooperate with full force. It must be achieved in the retreat from regions of the Ukraine, that no person, no animal, no grain, no train track remains; that no house is left standing, no mine is available that is not impaired for years, no well is available that is not poisoned. The enemy must truly find a totally burned and destroyed landscape. Discuss these things immediately with Stapf and do your very best.

Heil Hitler!
Your
signed H. Himmler

2.) Chief of Order Police
3.) Chief of Security Police and SD
4.) SS-Obergruppenführer Berger
5.) Chief of Anti-Partisan Units

copies sent for your information.

by order of [signature illegible]
SS-Obersturmbannführer

This order went to the SS-Gruppenführer Hans-Adolf Prützmann, one of four Higher SS and Police Leaders on the Eastern Front. These four SS generals had played a major role in the work of the Einsatzgruppen. Now Himmler wanted Prützmann to cooperate with the Army in destroying the Ukraine. The German military had been pushed back from its furthest advance in late 1942 and early 1943, before the mud season stopped normal military movement. The battle of Stalingrad that winter had marked the end of German success in the epic struggle with the Soviet military. In January 1943 a corridor was finally opened by Soviet troops to Leningrad. By the spring of 1943 the battle lines were about the same as one year before. In July 1943 the vast tank battle at Kursk demonstrated the superiority of Soviet mechanized forces. At the moment of this order in September 1943, the German armies were in full retreat.

The carefully determined genocidal brutality and willful destructiveness at the highest levels of the Nazi regime are illustrated in Himmler's orders. The deliberate devastation of the Western Soviet Union by the German military was a major cause of the reciprocally brutal occupation policies of Soviet troops in Eastern Germany after 1945.

It is difficult to fathom the extent of the destruction in the Soviet Union. The following quotation from a Soviet publication on the 70th anniversary of the October Revolution offers a chilling overview:

> The German-fascist invaders completely or partially destroyed and burned 1,710 towns and settlements and more than 70,000 villages and hamlets; burned and destroyed more than 6 million buildings and rendered homeless about 25 million people; destroyed 31,580 industrial enterprises ... destroyed 65 thousand kilometers of railway lines and 4,100 stations ... slaughtered, seized or drove back to Germany 7 million horses, 17 million cattle and oxen, 20 million pigs, 27 million sheep and goats. In addition they destroyed and looted 40 thousand hospitals and other medical establishments, 84 thousand schools, colleges, and research institutes, and 43 thousand public libraries.[1]

Even allowing for exaggeration, these losses, concentrated in the Ukraine and Belorussia, were staggering. Although it is not yet possible to offer reliable estimates of the loss of life in the Soviet Union, it is probable that over 15 million Soviet civilians died as a result of the German invasion.

## Note

1 From *Narodnoe khozyiastvo SSR za 70 let*, as cited in John Barber and Mark Harrison, *The Soviet Home Front 1941–1945: A Social and Economic History of the USSR in World War II* (London: Longman, 1991), p. 42.

# 52. Speech by Himmler to SS-Gruppenführer in Posen, 4 October 1943

... Psychology of the Slavs

Now back to the Slavs! I believe it is necessary that we speak our minds about this. Whether it was Peter the Great or the last tsars, whether it is Mr. Lenin or Mr. Stalin, they know their people, they know exactly that the concepts "loyalty", "not betray someone", "not conspire" do not belong to the vocabulary of the Russians. Whatever you have heard about a Russian, it is all true. It is true, that some of these Russians are devoutly pious and devoutly believe in the mother of God from Khazan or somewhere else, absolutely true. It is true that the Volga boatmen sing wonderfully, it is true that the Russian today in modern times is a good improviser and good technician. It is true that he is mainly even nice to children. It is true that he can work very diligently. It is just as true that he is bone-lazy. It is just as true that he is an unscrupulous beast, who can torture and torment other people, as a devil could not imagine. It is just as true that the Russian, high or low, tends to the most perverse things, to devouring his comrades and to keeping the liver of his neighbor in his bread sack. All of that is contained in the spectrum of emotions and values of this Slavic person...

The Russians know themselves very well and have developed a very practical system, whether it was the tsars with the Okhrana or Mr. Lenin and Mr. Stalin with the GPU or the NKVD....

A basic rule for the SS-man must hold absolutely: honest, decent, loyal and comradely must we be to members of our own blood and to nobody else. What happens to the Russians, what happens to the Czechs, is all totally the same to me. Whatever good blood of our kind exists in these people, we should take by stealing the children, if necessary, and raising them ourselves. Whether other peoples live in comfort or whether they perish of hunger, that interests me only insofar as we use them as slaves for our culture, otherwise it doesn't interest me. If while building a tank ditch 10,000 Russian women die from weakness or not, that interests me only insofar as the tank ditch is built for Germany. We Germans, who alone in the world have a decent attitude toward animals, will also assume a decent attitude toward these human animals, but it is a crime against our own blood to worry about them and to bring them ideals, so that our children and grandchildren have more difficulties with them....

## The Jewish Evacuation

I also want to mention quite frankly in front of you a very difficult topic. Among ourselves it should be expressed once very candidly, even though we will never speak publicly about it. Exactly as little as we hesitated on 30 June 1934 to do our duty and to put comrades who had lapsed against the wall and shoot them, exactly so little have we yet spoken about it and will ever speak about it. It was due to that inner tact, which is thank God for us a matter of course, that we never discussed it among ourselves, never spoke of it. Everyone has shuddered, but everyone was still sure that he would do it again the next time, if it were ordered and if it were necessary.

I mean now the Jewish evacuation, the extermination of the Jewish people. It is one of those things that one says lightly. – "The Jewish people will be exterminated," says every Party member, "entirely clear, it's in our program, elimination of the Jews, extermination, we'll do it." And then they all come along, the worthy 80 million Germans, and each has his decent Jew. It is clear, the others are swine, but this is a fine Jew. None of those who talk like this have witnessed it, none have seen it through. Most of you know what it means when 100 corpses lie together, when 500 lie there or when 1000 lie there. To have stuck this out and – with the exception of human weaknesses – still remained decent, that has made us hard. This is a never written and never to be written page of glory in our history, since we know how difficult we would have made it for ourselves if today in every city – with bombing attacks, with the burdens and deprivations of the war – we still had the Jews as saboteurs, agitators and instigators. We would probably now be in the same place as in 1916/17, when the Jews still sat within the German people.

We have taken from them the riches that they had. I have given the strict order, which SS-Obergruppenführer Pohl has carried out, that these riches should of course be handed over completely to the Reich. We have taken none of it for ourselves. Individuals who have lapsed will be punished according to an order given by me at the beginning, which warns: whoever takes only one Mark from it is a dead man. A number of SS-men – it is not many – have failed and will be dead men, without mercy. We had the moral right, we had the duty to our people, to kill this people, who wanted to kill us. We do not have the right, however, to enrich ourselves with one fur, with one watch, with one Mark, or with one cigarette, or with anything else. At the end, because we have exterminated a germ, we don't want to get sick and die of the germ. I will never accept that even a spot of decay develops here or spreads. Where they arise, we will burn them out together. All in all, however, we can say that we fulfilled this hardest task out of love to our people. And we have suffered no inner damage, in our souls, in our character....

We see the future because we know it. Therefore we do our duty more fanatically than ever, more faithfully than ever, more bravely, more obediently, and more decently than ever. We want to be worthy to have been the Führer Adolf Hitler's first SS-men in the long history of the German people which stands before us.

Now we honor the Führer, our Führer Adolf Hitler, who created the Germanic Reich and who will lead us into the Germanic future.

To our Führer Adolf Hitler

Sieg Heil!
Sieg Heil!
Sieg Heil!

---

At the SS leadership meeting in Posen, Heinrich Himmler gave a very long speech about the war, the SS and the future. The typed transcript is 116 pages. Himmler constantly repeated a few themes: hardness is good; SS men are decent and honorable, which means they have acted in the interests of the German people as defined by the Nazis, without regard for any normal human moral standards of behavior; everything they have done thus far has been correct; they will win the war, because what matters is only the will to win and the determination to keep fighting. As shown here, Himmler advocated utter disdain for all other peoples, who are not as brave, honorable, and worthy as Germans. Slavs are lazy, perverse, and potentially dangerous, and should be killed. Jews are the mortal enemy of Germans, who have the moral right to kill them. These were the official ideas of the German state.

Two days later Himmler gave another speech in Posen to the Nazi Party *Gauleiter* (district leaders) in which he explicitly argued that it was necessary to kill Jewish women and children, too, to avoid leaving another generation to grow up to avenge their men.

# 53. Postwar testimony about exhumation and cremation of corpses in 1943–44

AFFIDAVIT
of SZLOMA Gol.

I, Szloma Gol, declare as follows:

1. I am a Jew and lived in Vilna in Lithuania. During the German occupation, I lived in the Vilna ghetto.

2. The administration of the ghetto in Vilna was conducted by the SA. The City Commissar of Vilna was an SA leader named Hinkst. The Rural Commissar of Vilna was an SA leader named Wolf. The expert for Jewish questions was an SA leader named Murer.

3. In December 1943, 80 Jews from the ghetto, among them four women, myself and my friend Josef Belic, were chosen by an SA Sturmführer, whose name I have forgotten, and by whose command had to live in a wide pit at some distance from the city. This pit had been dug out in order to serve as an underground gasoline reservoir. The pit was circular, 60 meters across and 4 meters deep. While we lived in this pit, it was partly covered with boards, two living rooms were partitioned off with boards, and the same with a kitchen and a toilet. We lived 6 months in this pit before we escaped. The pit was guarded by SA men, about whom I want to provide details below.

4. One morning the Sturmführer appeared at the edge of this pit, accompanied by 14 or 15 SA men, and said to us: "Your brothers, sisters and friends are here nearby, handle them carefully, and if you have accomplished your work, we will send you to Germany, where you will be employed according to your trades." We did not know what was meant by this.

5. After that, SA men threw chains into the pit and the Sturmführer ordered the Jewish foremen (we were a work team) to put the chains on us. The chains were laid around my ankles and also around the body. They

weighed 2 kilograms each and we were only able to take small steps with them. We carried these chains constantly for 6 months. The SA said to us that each one who takes off the chains would be hanged. The four women who worked in the kitchen were not chained.

6. After these events we were led to work. We marched in chains 5–600 meters.

7. Our work consisted of opening mass graves and carrying out the corpses, in order to burn them. I was employed digging out these corpses. My friend Belic was employed with sawing and preparing wood.

8. We dug out 80,000 corpses in total. I know this because two Jews who lived with us in the pit were employed by the Germans in counting these corpses. That was the only task of these two. The corpses consisted of a mixture of Jews, Polish priests, and Russian prisoners-of-war. Among those whom I dug out was my own brother. I found his identity cards on him. He was dead for 2 years, when I dug him out; I know this, because he belonged to a mass of Jews who came from the Vilna ghetto and were shot in September 1941.

9. The burning of the corpses proceeded absolutely methodically. Running parallel, 7 meter long pits were dug out, boards were laid across them; a layer of corpses were laid on them, oil poured over the corpses, then branches spread over them and over these branches blocks of wood. Altogether 14 such layers of corpses and fuel were erected on top of each other into a funeral pyre. Each pyre was built like a pyramid with a wooden chimney which stuck out of the top. Gasoline and oil was poured in from this chimney and fire bombs were laid around the pyre. This whole work was carried out by us Jews. When the pyre was ready, the Sturmführer himself or his helper, named Legel (who also belonged to the SA), personally lit it with a burning rag, which was attached to the end of a stick.

10. This work, which consisted of opening the graves and building the pyres, was watched over by about 80 guards. Over 50 of these were SA men in brown uniforms armed with pistols and daggers and automatic weapons. (The weapons were constantly ready to fire and pointed at us.) The remaining 30 guards consisted partly of Lithuanians and partly of SD and SS. In the course of this work the Lithuanian guards were themselves shot, probably so that they could not blab about what had been done. The commander of the whole place was the SA leader Murer (the expert for Jewish questions), but he watched the work only from time to time. The

SA leader Legel was in command on the spot. During the night our pit was guarded by 10 or 12 of these guards.

11. The guards (especially the SA men) hit and stabbed us. I still have scars on both legs and on my neck. Once I was knocked down unconscious on a row of corpses and could not get up, but my fellow workers pulled me away from the layer of corpses. Then I was sick. We were allowed two days of sickness; on the third day we were brought out of the pit to the hospital – that meant to be shot.

12. Of the 76 persons from the pit, eleven were shot during the work. 43 of us dug with bare hands a tunnel out of our pit, broke our chains, and escaped into the woods. We had been warned by a Czech SS man, who said to us, they would shoot us soon, and they would then also shoot him, and bring us all to the pyre, "flee if you can, but not if I am on guard."

I declare that the above statement is correct:

[signature] Gol Szloma

Sworn before me
Nuremberg, 10 August 1946

[signature] A. G. Wurmser
Major RE.
British Army.

---

Nearly from the beginning of the Holocaust, the organizers tried to hide what they were doing. The placement of the death camps in Poland was one method of keeping the German population from direct contact with mass murder. In 1942, Paul Blobel, one of the leaders of the Einsatzgruppen which killed over 30,000 Jews from Kiev, was selected as commander of a new group with the task of hiding the traces of mass murder on the Eastern Front. He conducted experiments at Chelmno to find the ideal method of digging up corpses and burning them. As the tide of war began to turn against the German armies, this work became even more necessary to hide Nazi crimes from the world.[1] The speech by Himmler in Posen excerpted above alludes to the effort to keep the Holocaust a secret.

This testimony by Gol Szloma describes how these methods were carried out in 1943 and 1944. The bodies included the major groups of Holocaust victims in the East, Jews and Soviet citizens, as well as the Polish priests killed as part of the effort to wipe out the entire Polish cultural leadership. Even this work had to be statistically reported. The shooting of local auxiliary guards was a standard practice.

Blobel was tried at Nuremberg in 1947–1948 as one of the 24 defendants in USA vs. Otto Ohlendorf, also called the Einsatzgruppen Case, since all defendants were SS men, mainly commanding officers, in the Einsatzgruppen behind the lines on the Eastern Front. Blobel's defense against the charge that he was responsible for killing 60,000 civilians consisted of a mixture of justifications and explanations: his unit had killed only about 10,000; his victims were all partisans or suspicious people; his behavior was caused by the economic effects of the Depression after 1929; killing 116 Jews as retaliation for the death of one German soldier was justified. Blobel and 13 other defendants were sentenced to death, although some later had their sentences reduced. Blobel and Ohlendorf were hanged on 8 June 1951.

## Note

1 Leni Yahil, *The Holocaust: The Fate of European Jewry, 1932–1945*, trans. Ina Friedman and Haya Galai (New York: Oxford University Press, 1990), pp. 449–50. Blobel wrote an affidavit on his task of 'covering the traces of executions of the Einsatzgruppen in the East' for his trial at Nuremberg, in which he admits overseeing this effort between June 1942 and summer 1944, but offers only the sketchiest details of his actions: Nuremberg document NO-3947, reprinted and translated in Mendelsohn (ed.), *The Holocaust: Selected Documents in Eighteen Volumes*, Vol. 10, *The Einsatzgruppen or Murder Commandos*, (New York: Garland Publishing, 1982), pp. 136–41.

# 54. Report by Odilo Globocnik on how death camps were financed, December 1943

Report

on the Administrative Handling of the Aktion Reinhardt.

I. All of the assets accruing from this action were centrally registered in an administration that I established, accordingly classified and recorded. The registration covered the entire General Gouvernement. Personnel were from the SS Economic and Administrative Main Office.
The utilization and liquidation of the assets were conducted according to the directions of the Reichsführer-SS. Summarized in the course of the action in instructions of 26 September 1942 and 9 December 1943, and entrusted to the SS Economic and Administrative Main Office for handling with Reich authorities.
The assets I gathered were continuously handed over to the SS Economic and Administrative Main Office against acknowledgment, and they forwarded the assets to the Reichsbank, the Reich Finance Ministry, textile enterprises, etc.
On the order of the Reichsführer-SS, necessities for the support of ethnic Germans could be taken; for the purposes of the SS itself, the Reichsführer-SS has forbidden any use.
The unusual feature of the accounting is that a fixed requirement for proceeds did not exist, since the collection of the assets ensued as a result of orders, and only the decency and integrity, as well as the supervision of the SS-men employed in this task, could guarantee a complete delivery. Certainly, whatever was registered and collected, and taken in by the Aktion Reinhardt, was accounted for and delivered with the greatest exactitude and without error.
A preliminary examination up to 1 April 1943 by SS-Obersturmbannführer Vogt from the SS Economic and Administrative Main Office has already taken place and revealed the most complete organization. A preliminary examination must still be conducted for the rest.
On the basis of an agreement with the Reich Finance Ministry, this preliminary examination is final and the records and documents will be destroyed in accordance with secrecy rules without consideration of the Reich Auditing Office.

II. The assets which have been accounted for were composed of:

1.) Sums in Reichsmarks and Zloty.
From these receipts, the entire expenses, transport charges, fees, etc., from the action were covered. By far the largest portion was made available to the SS economic administrator in the General Gouvernement, and the amounts credited in Reichsmarks to the Aktion Reinhardt by the SS Economic and Administrative Main Office and then handed over to the Reichsbank.
A smaller portion was used as credit for various economic enterprises for reasons of foreign exchange, and then similarly credited by the SS Economic and Administrative Main Office.
In addition excessive prices for the procurement of urgently needed materials were covered. All of these procedures occurred with the permission of the SS Economic and Administrative Main Office. A further amount was continuously made available to the concentration camp, for construction, for expanding the enterprises, and for procuring appropriate agricultural machines. These expenses were exactly accounted for, I constantly confirmed the purchases, and these documents will similarly be part of the final accounting. The accounts were kept by the administrative head of the concentration camp, separate from my administration, since the camp administration was by order of the SS Economic and Administrative Main Office independent of the SS Garrison Administration in Lublin. For these expenditures, a compensation to Reinhardt must come from the department which eventually takes over the operation.
2.) Foreign currencies in notes or coins were collected, sorted, and also handed over to the Reichsbank through the SS Economic and Administrative Main Office.
3.) Precious stones, jewelry, watches, and similar items were sorted according to their value and delivered to the SS Economic and Administrative Main Office. According to its instructions, watches made of base metals were delivered to the troops, repaired glasses made available to the disabled, and worthless utensils mainly given to military offices to cover their immediate needs. The corresponding receipts are available.
4.) Textiles, pieces of clothing, underwear, feather beds, and rags were collected and sorted by quality. The sorted items had to be searched for hidden valuables and finally disinfected.
Over 1,900 boxcars were then according to instructions of the SS Economic and Administrative Main Office made available to offices designated by the Reich Economic Ministry. From these supplies not

only were foreign workers clothed, but a large part was used for respinning. No case of sickness has become known, although the pieces of clothing often originated from those ill mainly with spotted fever, thus the disinfection is sufficient.
The best pieces of clothing were sorted out and used to provision ethnic Germans by order of the Reichsführer-SS. Shoes were also sorted by usefulness and given to ethnic Germans, used in the concentration camps for prisoners, or torn up and put on wooden shoes for clothing prisoners.

5.) Particular valuables of a special nature, such as stamps, coins, and the like were sorted and delivered to the SS Economic and Administrative Main Office, worthless things were destroyed.
6.) Other items which accrued, such as soap, detergent, dishes, and the like were used in the camps for Jews, glass, old iron implements, etc. brought to the Utilization Offices for reprocessing.
7.) Food brought on the transports was used for the provisioning of the camps for Jews.
8.) Valuable fixtures and household effects were repaired and mainly handed over for use by ethnic German settlers. But German government offices and military offices were also allowed to have fixtures in exchange for receipt.
Less valuable goods were either destroyed or used as bonuses for the population for good harvests, etc.
Out of objects which were no longer useful, it was endeavored to remove pieces, such as locks, hinges and the like, and to use them again.
The records of the items loaned out were handed over monthly to the Higher SS- and Police Leader East.

According to the Reichsführer-SS Order of 22 September, the total accrual was closed, utilized and transmitted, so that hardly anything is still on hand. On hand remain installations which were necessary for the carrying out of the action, such as barracks, camp frames, vehicles, and the like, which were bought with the accrued means. These have been collected, and the decision must still be made about what use they might serve.
The total value of the accrued objects according to the accompanying table is about 180,000,000 Reichsmarks. In this connection minimum values were assumed, so that the total value probably reaches twice as much, leaving out the value of collected items in defective condition, like textiles, from which over 1,900 boxcars were delivered to German industry.

[signature] Globocnik
SS-Gruppenführer
and Major-General of the Police

Precious Metals:

| | | | | | | | | |
|---|---|---|---|---|---|---|---|---|
| 236 | pieces | gold ingots | = 2,909.68 | kg | @ RM | 2,800.— | = | RM 8,147,104.— |
| 2143 | " | silver ingots | = 18,733.69 | " | " " | 40.— | = | " 749,347.60 |
| | | platinum | 15.44 | " | " " | 5,000.— | = | " 77,200.— |
| | | | | | | | | RM 8,973,651.60 |

Foreign Currencies in Notes:

| | | | | | |
|---|---|---|---|---|---|
| USA Dollars | 1,081,521.40 | @ RM | 2.50 | RM | 2,703,803.50 |
| Engl. Pounds | 15,646.11 | " | 9.30 | " | 145,512.80 |
| Palest. Pounds | 4,922.50 | " | 9.30 | " | 45,779.25 |
| Canad. Dollars | 8,966.25 | " | 2.50 | " | 22,415.62 |
| Roubles | 2,454,278.35 | " | —.10 | " | 245,427.84 |
| French Frs. | 1,468,486.35 | " | —.05 | " | 73,424.31 |
| Swiss Frs. | 119,302.33 | " | 5.80 | " | 691,953.51 |
| Lira | 6,465.08 | " | —.10 | " | 646.50 |
| Prot. Kr. | 1,745,601.50 | " | —.10 | " | 174,560.15 |
| Turk. Pounds | 39.50 | " | 1.90 | " | 75.05 |
| Belga | 12,449.25 | " | —.40 | " | 4,979.70 |
| Lei | 55,975.54 | " | —.02 | " | 1,119.51 |
| South Afr. £ | 119.$^1/_2$ | " | 4.40 | " | 525.80 |
| Dutch Guilders | 133,986.95 | " | 1.33 | " | 178,202.64 |
| Leva | 5,995,421.— | " | —.01 | " | 59,954.21 |
| Austral. £ | 55.— | " | 2.50 | " | 137.50 |
| Dinar | 435,641.— | " | —.05 | " | 21,782.05 |
| Karbowanets | 164,169.— | " | —.10 | " | 16,416.90 |
| Pengo | 28,392.50 | " | —.60 | " | 17,035.50 |
| Slov. Crowns | 103,538.35 | " | —.10 | " | 10,353.84 |
| Drachmas | 4,875,419.70 | " | —.02 | " | 97,508.29 |
| Swed. Krona | 4,377.— | " | —.60 | " | 2,626.20 |
| Norw. Krone | 775.— | " | —.60 | " | 465.— |
| Argent. Pesos | 977.55 | " | 1.— | " | 977.55 |
| Pesetas | 1,471.— | " | 2.40 | " | 3,530.40 |
| Finn. Marks | 1,140.— | " | —.05 | " | 57.— |
| Dan. Krone | 1,270.— | " | —.52 | " | 660.40 |
| Brasil. Milreis | 63.— | " | —.09 | " | 5.67 |
| Egypt Pounds | 20.— | " | 4.40 | " | 88.— |
| Litas | 175.— | " | —.10 | " | 17.50 |
| Yen (Jap.) | 4.— | " | —.50 | " | 2.— |
| Lats | 20.— | " | —.10 | " | 2.— |
| Paraguay Pesos | 12.— | " | —.60 | " | 7.20 |
| Cuban Pesos | 57.— | " | —.60 | " | 28.20 |
| Uruguay Pesos | 1.— | " | —.60 | " | —.60 |

| | | | | | |
|---|---|---|---|---|---|
| Bolivians Pesos | 4.50 | " | —.60 | " | 2.70 |
| Mexic. Pesos | 3.— | " | —.50 | " | 1.50 |
| Alb. Frs. | 195.44 | " | —.10 | " | 19.54 |
| Rhodesian Pounds | 8.— | " | 4.— | " | 32.— |
| New Zealand Pounds | —,10,— | " | 4.— | " | 2.— |
| Alger. Frs. | 30.— | " | —.10 | " | 3.— |
| Lux. Fr. | 40.— | " | —.50 | " | 20.— |
| Java Guilders | 10.— | " | 1.30 | " | 13.— |
| Danz. Gulden | 1,038.— | " | 1.— | " | 1,038.— |
| Columbian Pesos | 1.— | " | —.60 | " | —.60 |
| Mozambique Esc. | 1.— | " | —.60 | " | —.60 |
| Manchurian Cent | 15.— | " | —.50 | " | 7.50 |
| China Dollars | 1.— | " | 1.50 | " | 1.50 |
| | | | | RM | 4,521,244.10 |

<u>Foreign Currencies in Coins:</u>

| | | | | | | |
|---|---|---|---|---|---|---|
| USA Dollars | 249,771.50 | | @ RM | 4.20 | RM | 1,049,040.30 |
| Engl. Pounds | 610.— | | " | 20.40 | " | 12,444.— |
| Roubles | 198,053.— | | " | 2.15 | " | 425,813.95 |
| Austr. Crowns | 73,230.— | | " | —.85 | " | 62,245.— |
| French Frs. | 38,870.— | | " | 1.62 | " | 62,969.40 |
| Reichsmarks | 23,485.— | | " | 1.— | " | 23,485.— |
| Port. Reis | 20,000.— | 200 Esc | " | 1.— | " | 200.— |
| Swiss Frs. | 6,970.— | | " | 16.50 | (f. 20 Frs) | 23,001.— |
| Ducats | 6,614.— | | " | 10.— | RM | 66,140.— |
| Lira | 3,740.— | | " | —.50 | " | 1,870.— |
| Aust. Shillings | 2,925.— | | " | 2:3 | " | 1,950.— |
| Turk. Pounds | 417.75 | | " | 3.50 | " | 1,462.12 |
| Belga | 1,740.— | | " | —.50 | " | 870.— |
| Leva | 30.— | | " | —.50 | " | 15.— |
| Lei | 1,177.50 | | " | —.50 | " | 588.75 |
| South Afr. £ | 4.— | | " | 20.40 | " | 81.60 |
| Dutch Guilders | 905.— | | " | 17— | (f. 10 fl) | 1,538.50 |
| Austral. Pounds | 7.— | | " | 20.40 | RM | 142.80 |
| Dinar | 41.— | | " | —.50 | " | 20.50 |
| Swed. Krona | 30.— | | " | 11.20 | (f. 10 Kr) | 33.60 |
| Norw. Kr. | 55.— | | " | 11.20 | (f. 10 Kr) | 61.60 |
| Pesetas | 50.— | | " | 1.50 | RM | 75.— |
| Finn. Mk. | 80.— | | " | 1.— | " | 80.— |
| Zlotys | 2,060.— | | " | —.50 | " | 1,030.— |
| Dan. Kr. | 360.— | | " | 11.20 | (f. 10 Kr) | 403.20 |
| Czech Ducats | 17.— | | " | 10.— | RM | 170.— |

| | | | | | |
|---|---|---|---|---|---|
| Yen | 2.— | " | —.50 | " | 1.— |
| Cuban Pesos | 10.— | " | 4.20 | " | 42.— |
| Mex. Pesos | 111.50 | " | 4.20 | " | 468.— |
| Alb. Frs. | 20.— | " | —.50 | " | 10.— |
| Yugosl. Ducats | 1.— | " | 5.— | " | 5.— |
| Tunis. Frs. | 180.— | " | 1.62 | " | 291.60 |
| Peru Libra | 1.— | " | 1.— | " | 1.— |
| Chile Dollars | 1.— | " | 4.20 | " | 4.20 |
| | | | | | RM 1,736,554.12 |

Jewelry and Other Valuables:

| | | | on average @ RM | RM |
|---|---|---|---|---|
| 15,883 | pieces | rings of gold with prec. stones and diamonds | 1,500.— | 23,824,500.— |
| 9,019 | " | women's golden wristwatches | 250.— | 2,254,750.— |
| 3,681 | " | men's golden pocket watches | 500.— | 1,840,500.— |
| 353 | " | bracelets with prec. stones and diamonds | 3,500.— | 1,232,000.— |
| 1,716 | pairs | gold earrings with prec. stones and diamonds | 250.— | 429,000.— |
| 2,497 | pieces | gold brooches " " " " " | 2,000.— | 4,994,000.— |
| 130 | pieces | separate large precious stones | 1,000.— | 130,000.— |
| 2511.37 | carats | separate pieces of precious stones | 100.— | 251,137.— |
| 13458.62 | " | separate pieces of diamonds | 50.— | 672,931.— |
| 291 | pieces | pins with precious stones | 100.— | 29,100.— |
| 660 | " | men's wristwatches golden | 100.— | 66,000.— |
| 458 | " | women's pendant watches with precious stones | 500.— | 229,000.— |
| 273 | " | women's platinum watches with precious stones | 1,200.— | 327,600.— |
| 349 | " | women's pendant watches golden | 250.— | 87,250.— |
| 362 | " | women's gold watches with prec. stones, diam. | 600.— | 217,200.— |
| 27 | " | arm circlets with prec. stones and diamonds | 250.— | 6,750.— |
| 40 | " | gold brooches | 350.— | 14,000.— |
| 18 | " | cuff-links with prec. stones and diamonds | 150.— | 2,700.— |
| 114.20 | kg | pearls | | 6,000,000.— |

| | | | | |
|---|---|---|---|---|
| 63 | pieces | platinum watch cases with precious stones | 1,000.— | 63,000.— |
| 4 | " | women's platinum watches | 300.— | 1,200.— |
| 5 | " | men's pocket watches with prec. stones | 600.— | 3,000.— |
| 4 | " | necklaces with prec. stones and diamonds | 1,500.— | 6,000.— |
| 8 | " | women's ring watches golden | 150.— | 1,200.— |
| 4 | " | women's pendant watches with pearls | 200.— | 800.— |
| 18 | " | gold fountain pens | 20.— | 360.— |
| 5 | " | golden mechanical pencils | 15.— | 75.— |
| 1 | " | golden cigarette case | 400.— | 400.— |
| 60,125 | " | watches, various types | 10.— | 611,250.— |
| 7.80 | kg | corals | | 600.— |
| 3 | pieces | gold powder boxes | 50.— | 150.— |
| 103,614 | " | watches needing repair | 2.— | 207,228.— |
| 29,391 | " | eye-glasses | 3.— | 88,173.— |
| 350 | " | razors | 2.— | 700.— |
| 800 | " | pocket knives | 1.— | 800.— |
| 3,240 | " | money purses | 1.50 | 4,860.— |
| 1,315 | " | wallets | 2.50 | 3,287.50 |
| 1,500 | " | scissors | —.50 | 750.— |
| 230 | " | flashlights | —.50 | 115.— |
| 6,943 | " | alarm clocks for repair | 1.— | 6,943.— |
| 2,343 | " | working alarm clocks | 4.— | 9,372.— |
| 627 | " | sunglasses | —.50 | 313.50 |
| 41 | " | silver cigarette boxes | 15.— | 615.— |
| 230 | " | fever thermometers | 3.— | 690.— |
| | | | | 43,662,450.00 |

Textiles:

| | | |
|---|---|---|
| 1901 boxcars with clothing, underwear, feather beds and rags with average value of | RM | 26,000,000.— |
| warehouse inventory with average value of | " | 20,000,000.— |
| | RM | 46,000,000.— |

Summary Table:

| | | |
|---|---|---|
| surrendered funds in Zloty and RM notes | RM | 73,852,080.74 |
| precious metals | " | 8,973,651.60 |
| foreign currencies in notes | " | 4,521,224.13 |
| foreign currencies in coins | " | 1,736,554.12 |
| jewelry and other valuables | " | 43,662,450.— |
| textiles | " | 46,000,000.— |
| | RM | 178,745,960.59 |

signed R z e p a
SS-Oberscharführer
and Treasurer

signed W i p p e r n
SS-Sturmbannführer
and Director of Administration

[signature] Globocnik

This long document preserves a remarkable aspect of the carefully planned Holocaust, the use of money and valuables confiscated from the Jewish victims to pay the costs of their murder. At the end of the *Aktion Reinhardt*, Globocnik wrote this self-congratulatory report for Himmler. In a letter to Himmler in November 1943, Globocnik asked that some Iron Crosses be awarded for his unit's achievements.[1]

Globocnik was proud of the enormous scale of this enterprise. In two years between late 1941 and late 1943, over 1.5 million Jews were killed at Treblinka, Sobibor, and Belzec. The list of 'assets' represents pure profit from the *Aktion Reinhardt*. Between April 1942 and December 1943, 86 million RM in cash were taken from these people. Expenses for deportation and murder totalled only about 12 million RM, leaving the nearly 74 million RM in cash listed in the Summary Table, as one element of the profit of this gigantic business. As Globocnik makes clear, the deportation paid for itself: Jews supplied the cash, food, clothing, and other items which were used in their own destruction.[2]

The detailed tables here show exactly what was taken from them on their way to the gas chambers: nearly 2000 boxcars of textiles, almost 200,000 watches, roughly 3000 kilograms of gold, much of it extracted from teeth. While 2000 people were killed per day, the details of economic accounting were not neglected. Although only one golden cigarette case was found, 103,614 watches in need of repair were separated from 75,003 working watches in twelve precise categories of value. The precision here was meant to hide from Globocnik's superiors the inevitable corruption which these valuables brought to camp life. That corruption entailed both personal enrichment for some SS guards and possibilities of survival for certain prisoners.

The proper distribution of the valuable pieces of jewelry was given considerable attention by Nazi leaders. Oswald Pohl, head of the Economic and Administrative Main Office, sent the most valuable watches directly to Himmler for distribution to SS commanders.[3] This was merely the final stage of economic dispossession of Jews, since most of their possessions had already been taken from them before deportation.

This report lists only the goods stolen from Jews who were sent to the three *Aktion Reinhardt* camps. Over 1 million Jews who were sent to Auschwitz were also systematically robbed of everything of value, and the proceeds were similarly accounted for and distributed. The best items were used to help ethnic German settlers and to finance SS enterprises. A preliminary report from February 1943 lists 825 boxcars of various textiles delivered to various offices for reuse by settlers, Hitler Youth, I. G. Farben at Auschwitz, soldiers, and other concentration camp inmates. One boxcar was filled with 3000 kilograms of women's hair.[4]

Odilo Globocnik committed suicide on 31 May 1945, after being taken prisoner by the British. Oswald Pohl was tried in Nuremberg and executed in 1951.

## Notes

1 This letter, as well as the documents shown here, and other documents prepared at the end of Aktion Reinhardt, are all collected as Nuremberg document PS-4024.

2 Many other financial documents were created during this period, showing the collection of valuables. The balance of expenses and receipts is shown in Nuremberg document NO-063, translated in *Trials of War Criminals before the Nuernberg Military Tribunals under Control Council Law No. 10, Nuernberg, October 1946 – April 1949* (Washington, DC: US Government Printing Office, 1950), Vol. 5, pp. 544–5. A preliminary listing of the goods taken from Jews up to 3 February 1943 can be found in 4024-PS, also numbered NO-061. Other documents pertaining to the financial aspects of *Aktion Reinhardt* are NO-057, 060, 064, 726, 3034.

3 Nuremberg document NO-2756, *Trials of War Criminals under Control Council Law No. 10* (1950), Vol. 5, p. 721.

4 Nuremberg document NO-1257, translated in Mendelsohn (ed.), *The Holocaust: Selected Documents in Eighteen Volumes*, Vol. 12, *The "Final Solution" in the Extermination Camps and the Aftermath*, pp. 198–9.

Section VII

# 'Arbeit Macht Frei': Work and Death in Concentration Camps and Ghettos

The documents in the previous section, mainly official German sources, displayed policy. This section and the next present many sources from Jewish eyewitnesses, and portray experience.

Unlike the Nazis, who were trying to avoid leaving a clear paper record of their actions by employing obscure language, the victims try their best to explain exactly what happened. Yet they despaired of their ability to use words to convey what they had seen and felt, what had been done to them and to others. Because their experiences were so unimaginable, normal language rooted in everyday usage is inadequate. No set of words on paper can transport the reader to the alien world of the concentration camp or ghetto.

We must nevertheless attempt to use these documents to help us understand what the Nazis and their helpers were really doing, behind their euphemisms and camouflage. The reader's task is somewhat different here than in the previous section: there we must imagine what the Nazis wouldn't say, here we try to visualize what these victims can't say. The short pieces in this collection, however, can only begin the process of communicating truth about daily life and death in the Holocaust as experienced by its targets. The rich and voluminous eyewitness literature of diaries, memoirs, and interviews from which they were chosen is much more appropriate to that task.

The final 3 documents from camps deep within the Third Reich show the last stages of the Holocaust, in which prisoners of all types were killed by disease and bullet. Even with the entry of Allied soldiers into Germany and the liberation of the first camps, the killing continued. Two days after American soldiers found 21,000 inmates still alive in Buchenwald on 11 April, SS guards and local police in Gardelegen, 100 miles to the north, herded over 1000 death marchers into a barn which had been prepared with gasoline-soaked straw, and burned them alive.[1]

## Note

1 Daniel Goldhagen cites the extreme cruelty during the many death marches as support for his controversial contention that most Germans wanted Jews to be killed: *Hitler's Willing Executioners: Ordinary Germans and the Holocaust* (New York: Alfred A. Knopf, 1996), pp. 364–71. He reproduces two photographs of the victims of this mass burning.

# 55. Normal murders at Buchenwald in 1941

## The Murder of the Brothers H a m b e r

In spring 1941 an event occurred that at the time took place almost daily. In the garrison garage work detail (a Jewish work detail) a Jew, namely, the Viennese Hamber, was fatally abused by Technical Sergeant A b r a h a m, one of the worst sadists of Buchenwald. Abraham struck the comrade down and then threw him into a pool of water. There he kicked him in the head so long, until the comrade had miserably drowned. As has been said, this was an everyday occurrence; not an everyday event, however, was the aftermath.

Hamber's brother lodged a complaint with the deputy commandant over the murder of his brother. The surviving Jew Hamber was then locked into the cellblock; after 3 days, he, too, was dead. – Beaten to death by Sommer.

After this witness was silenced, the SS band of murderers wanted to be on the safe side. The entire work detail – 35 Jews – was called to the gate and there they were interrogated about the murder by Deputy Commandant R ö d l, Roll Call Officer S t r i p p e l, and the camp doctor, E y s e l e. The SS men assured the prisoners that nothing would happen to them. They should just tell the whole truth. But the prisoners were familiar with SS practices and unanimously declared that they knew nothing about any murder. Nevertheless, 3 days later 5 comrades of the work detail were called to the gate and sent to the cellblock. Within 6 days not one of them was alive any more. Two days later the next 5 victims followed the same path.

I will never forget the looks of death candidates, who waited for the call to the gate, and knew precisely that their fate was unavoidable. I myself had a cousin among them, Jacob P e l z of Emden. He, too, was called one day and left the cellblock only as a corpse. Within 3 weeks the entire work detail of 35 inconvenient witnesses was liquidated in this terrible manner. But we survivors can provide witnesses for these horrible crimes.

Herbert M i n d u s, Hamburg.

---

This brief narrative comes from a unique enterprise, the 'Report on the Concentration Camp Buchenwald near Weimar'. This report was compiled by an intelligence group from the Psychological Warfare Division of the US Army during April and May 1945, with the active assistance of many surviving prisoners. Survivors were interviewed upon liberation, while still in the camp. Much of the report was written by Eugen Kogon, who published *The SS-State*, the first scholarly analysis of concentration camps, the next year. The many personal reports of survivors have the great advantage of immediacy.

The statement by Herbert Mindus of Hamburg appears as an appendix to the 'Report'. Its details are corroborated in a report by another prisoner. SS Sergeants Hubert Abraham and Martin Sommer appear in numerous places in these reports as unusually sadistic killers.

The Hamber brothers were film producers in their native Austria. Although the murder of Philipp Hamber was itself part of the normal camp routine, the complaint by Eduard Hamber obviously caused consternation throughout the SS camp leadership. This was apparently the first case in Buchenwald of open resistance to an SS murder. The completely hopeless situation of camp prisoners is demonstrated by the choiceless choice presented to the other members of the work detail, who believed they could save themselves only by pretending not to have seen the initial murder.

Although the US Army had already stumbled across an abandoned concentration camp in Natzweiler, France at the end of 1944, they were not prepared for the realities of the Nazi concentration camp system which they discovered in April 1945. First at Ohrdruf, then a week later at the huge camp at Buchenwald, the sights and smells of mass death shocked the American soldiers. A couple of days later, British soldiers arrived at Bergen-Belsen, where epidemics of typhus and typhoid were killing the starving survivors.

# 56. Speech by Chaim Rumkowski, Chairman of Łódź Jewish Council, 17 January 1942

"ONLY WORK CAN SAVE US"

Brothers and sisters. Today, in a corner of the ghetto, we celebrate an anniversary which, under present circumstances, is quite an achievement. A certain analogy comes to mind, concerning religious holidays. Every year we celebrate the holiday of Succoth. However, the joy of those days depends entirely on the weather. When the weather is good, the religious Jew occupies his *succah* with pleasure, but during cold and inclement days he is forced to abandon this time-honored tradition. It's the same with today's celebration. We rejoice at our accomplishments of the year, at our having successfully traversed twelve months. But clouding our joy is the fact that the present moment coincides with yet another affliction.

We live today beneath the specter of deportation. Only recently, at tremendous sacrifice, we accepted into our population of 140,000 an additional 23,000 exiles. I am proud to say that these exiles can consider themselves lucky, for the merciless fate which befell them nevertheless extended them some good fortune in bringing them here to our ghetto. It is good fortune in misfortune. However, I cannot remain silent on the subject of the 10,000 people we are now deporting. Unfortunately, I received a most uncompromising order, one I had to carry out so as to prevent others from doing it. Within the bounds of my ability, in this case as in other sad predicaments, I've tried to mitigate the severity as much as possible.

I did so as follows: I assigned for deportation that element of our ghetto which was a festering boil. And so the list of exiles includes members of the underworld and other individuals harmful to the ghetto. I've been criticized many times that smuggling into the ghetto continues. This was irrefutable, and I couldn't deny it. Now, when I am deporting all kinds of connivers and cheats, I do it fully convinced that they asked for this fate.

A commission of my trusted aides determines the list of deportees. This commission guarantees, basically, that it will only designate people for deportation if they deserve it. I realize, of course, that in acting with all deliberate speed the commission might make errors, but the fact remains that there is absolutely no malice on the part of those who decide.

Some people ask others to intervene on their behalf and don't care what crooked means are used. These interventions are to no avail. My expectation, based on authoritative information, is that the deportees' fate will not be as tragic as is expected in the ghetto. They will not be behind wire, and they will work on farms.

A gossip hydra has sprung up on the margins of the deportation procedure. I must condemn, in the strongest terms, the act of disturbing the common peace. I've stated many times that you can build your peace only on work, and the influence of gossip can only undermine this iron foundation which work represents.

Every ghetto citizen should identify himself by means of his work identification card, and that identification card should be without blemish. A work identification card with court remarks on it is worse than no card at all.

We are now on the threshold of very bad times, and everyone needs to be aware of this.

Only work can save us from the worst calamity.

---

This speech was delivered at the opening of an exhibit of dresses and undergarments at 'Glazer's' factory, located at 14 Dworska Street. The audience consisted of invited guests from Rumkowski's administration and the workers of the factory. The speech raises all the issues which have caused the institution of Jewish Councils in Nazi-created ghettos to be so controversial. Members of Jewish Councils who cooperated with Nazi demands offered the same two justifications made by Rumkowski here: cooperation could save some lives and the severity of persecution could be lessened. Rumkowski's logic was of little help to those he selected for deportation.

By forcing Jews to participate in the process of their own destruction, the Nazis relieved themselves of many burdens and divided the victims against each other. To starving ghetto inmates, those who risked their lives to smuggle in food offered heroic resistance to Nazi persecution. But smugglers made Rumkowski's efforts to cooperate with his overlords more difficult, so he portrayed them as deserving deportation. Most dangerous were those (the 'gossip hydra') who whispered that deportation did not mean resettlement in the East, but certain death in the gas chambers of Chelmno. They subverted Rumkowski's claim that his cooperation was a service to the Lódź Jews.

Eight months later, Rumkowski appeared again in public to plead with ghetto survivors to give up their children for deportation in order to save the remnant of adult workers.[1] His tone had changed from the confident and authoritative critique of all who opposed him to pleading that he was taking the only possible path. By the end of 1942, most of the Lódź Jews had been murdered in Chelmno. A remnant labored for the German war effort until 1944, when they were all transported to Auschwitz, including Rumkowski and his family.

Rumkowski's short career as a Jewish leader brings up the central problem of how much Jews contributed to bringing themselves and their communities to the sites of murder, which is exactly what he did in September. This question applies more widely to all victims who cooperated in some way with the process of genocide, from ghetto policemen to death camp *Sonderkommandos* who pulled the bodies out of the gas chambers for cremation. Primo Levi, who survived Auschwitz, addresses this dilemma with uncommon authority and sensitivity in the chapter 'The Gray Zone' in his book, *The Drowned and the Saved*.[2] The constant threat of arbitrary German brutality must be considered in any assessment of people like Rumkowski: less than one month after he appointed a 30-person Jewish Council, 22 members were arrested and killed.

## Notes

1 This speech is also translated in *Łódź Ghetto: Inside a Community under Siege*, compiled and edited by Alan Adelson and Robert Lapides (New York: Viking Penguin, 1989) pp. 328–31.

2 Primo Levi, *The Drowned and the Saved*, trans. Raymond Rosenthal (New York: Vintage Books, 1989).

# 57. Call for resistance in the Vilna Ghetto, January 1942

Let us not be led like sheep to the slaughter!

Jewish youth!

In a time of unparalleled national misfortune we appeal to you!

We do not yet have the words to express the whole tragic struggle which transpires before our eyes. Our language has no words to probe the depths to which our life has fallen nor to voice the anguish which strangles us.

It is still too hard to find the proper definition for the state in which we find ourselves, for the extraordinary cruelty with which the annihilation of the local Jewish population has been carried out.

The community of the Jerusalem of Lithuania numbered 75,000. On entering the ghetto, 25,000 were already missing, and today only 12,000 remain. All the others have been killed! Death strolls in our streets; in our tents—powerlessness. But the anguish at this huge misfortune is much greater in the light of the ignoble conduct of the Jews at the present time. Never in its long history of martyrdom has the Jewish people shown such abjectness, such a lack of human dignity, national pride, and unity, such communal inertia and submissiveness to the murderers.

The heart aches even more at the conduct of the Jewish youth, reared for twenty years in the ideals of upbuilding and halutz defense, which now is apathetic, lost, and does not respond to the tragic struggle.

There are, however, occasions in the life of a people, of a collective, as in the life of an individual, which seize you by the hair of your head, shake you up, and force you to gird up all your strength to keep alive. We are now experiencing such an occasion.

With what can we defend ourselves? We are helpless, we have no possibilities of organizing any defense of our existence. Even if we are deprived of the possibility of an armed defense in this unequal contest of strength, we nevertheless can still defend ourselves. Defend ourselves with all means—and moral defense above all—is the command of the hour.

Jewish youth!

On none but you rests the national duty to be the pillar of the communal defense of the Jewish collective which stands on the brink of annihilation!

I Let us defend ourselves during a deportation!

For several months now, day and night, thousands and tens of thousands have been torn away from our midst, men, the aged, women, and children, led away like cattle—and we, the remainder, are numbed. The illusion still lives within us that they are still alive somewhere, in an undisclosed concentration camp, in a ghetto.

You believe and hope to see your mother, your father, your brother who was seized and has disappeared.

In the face of the next day which arrives with the horrors of deportation and murder, the hour has struck to dispel the illusion: There is no way out of the ghetto, except the way to death!

No illusion greater than that our dear ones are alive.

No illusion more harmful than that. It deadens our feelings, shatters our national unity in the moments before death.

Before our eyes they led away our mother, our father, our sisters,enough!

We will not go!

Comrades! Uphold this awareness and impart to your families, to the remnants of the Jerusalem of Lithuania.

—Do not surrender into the hands of the kidnappers!

—Do not hand over any other Jews!

—If you are caught, you have nothing to lose!

—Let us defend ourselves, and not go!

Better to fall with honor in the ghetto than to be led like sheep to Ponary!

II On guard over national honor and dignity

We work for Germans and Lithuanians. Everyday we come face to face with our employers, the murderers of our brothers. Great the shame and pain, observing the conduct of Jews, stripped of the awareness of human dignity.

Comrades!

—Don't give the foe the chance to ridicule you!

—When a German ridicules a Jew—don't help him laugh!

—Don't play up to your murderers!

—Denounce the bootlickers at work!

—Denounce the girls who flirt with Gestapo men!

—Work slowly, don't speed!

—Show solidarity! If misfortune befalls one of you—don't be vile egoists—all of you help him. Be united in work and misfortunes!

—Jewish agents of the Gestapo and informers of all sorts walk the streets. If you get hold of one such, sentence him—to be beaten until death!

III In the presence of the German soldier

Instead of submissiveness and repulsive bootlicking, you are given the possibility in daily encounters with German soldiers to perform an important national deed. Not every German soldier is a sworn enemy of the Jews, not every German soldier is a sworn Hitlerite. But many have false ideas about Jews. We, the youth, by our conduct, in word and deed, can create in the mind of the German soldier another image of a Jew, a productive one, a Jew who has national and human dignity.

Comrades, show the Jews with whom you work and live together that this is the approach to the German soldier.

IV To the Jewish police

Most tragic is the role of the Jewish police—to be a blind tool in the hands of our murderers. But you, Jewish policemen, have at least a chance to demonstrate your personal integrity and national responsibility!

—Any act which threatens Jewish life should not be performed!

—No actions of mass deportation should be carried out!

—Refuse to carry out the orders which bring death to Jews and their families! ...

—Do not let service in the police be turned into national disgrace for you!

—Jewish policemen, sooner risk your own life than dozens of Jewish lives!

Comrades!

Convey your hatred of the foe in every place you are working for your murderers!

Better to fall in the fight for human dignity than to live at the mercy of the murderer!

Let us defend ourselves! Defend ourselves until the last minute!

---

This summons was read by Abba Kovner on 31 December 1941, to several Jewish youth groups who had organized to fight the Germans in Vilna, Lithuania. It represents an understanding of the broader intentions of the Nazis going beyond the murders of Vilna Jews. Kovner represents the opposite end of the spectrum of Jewish responses to the developing Holocaust from Rumkowski.

Vilna was called the Jerusalem of Lithuania, because of its importance as a center of Jewish culture. The Jewish population of Vilna before the war was nearly 60,000, which grew to nearly 70,000 as Jewish refugees from Poland fled from the Nazis. A few thousand were able to escape before the German army occupied the city on 24 June 1941. The Einsatzgruppen began actions in September, killing about 20,000 Jews before the Vilna ghetto was established.

Further actions during 1941 claimed the lives of another 20,000. Ponary forest, just outside of Vilna, was the site of these mass shootings.

This cry for resistance was thus formulated after the killing of Jews from Vilna was nearly completed. Many of the resistance movements in ghettos and camps developed at points of crisis, in the face of imminent death. With some exceptions, such as in the ghetto of Minsk, Jewish leaders, who did not yet know what the Nazis planned, attempted to isolate those who called for armed resistance. In the face of uncertainty, resistance meant a certain death, while cooperation might prolong survival. Such disparate efforts at resistance as the revolt in the Warsaw Ghetto in April 1943 and the uprising of the *Sonderkommando* in Auschwitz in October 1944 both erupted when cooperation could no longer offer the possibility of survival, although much planning had preceded them.

Kovner and about 200 ghetto fighters from Vilna escaped into the surrounding forests in September 1943, just as the ghetto was being finally liquidated, and established a partisan battalion. Kovner survived and testified at Adolf Eichmann's trial in Israel in 1961.

# 58. Letter about feeding Soviet POWs working for German industry, 21 February 1942

The German Labor Front
Area Headquarters Essen
District Headquarters Essen
to the files, Lehmann 6 July 1942
The District Chief,
Department: Labor Allocation

Essen, 21 February 1942
Steubenstrasse 61
Telephone 5 12 51

To the Workers' Council of the Firm Fried. Krupp A.G.
Essen Bu
Lehm

24 February
Labor Allocation A
Received 24 February, Diary No. 897
Replied:

Subject: *Feeding of Soviet Russian prisoners of war*

On 1 October 1941 the Reich Minister of Food and Agriculture issued special instructions concerning the rations for Soviet Russian prisoners of war. These instructions will also be adhered to by the camp kitchen Weidkamp which is responsible for the additional rations.

It is beyond comprehension that German employees should criticize these rations and state that they are insufficient and that the hot meals are not served until the evening. Repeated efforts have been made to induce Miss Bloch, who is in charge of the kitchen, to issue larger portions. Party member Fritz Soelling in particular has intervened on behalf of the Soviet Russian prisoners of war. In order to avoid that this conception spreads to larger circles, we have informed S. in our office that the rations issued in camp Weidkamp are in conformance with the regulation and that the kitchen manageress was not authorized to increase these rations in compliance with his request. The Dutch workers also receive higher rations; however, the food is not issued at the place of work.

It is necessary to take energetic steps to combat all unjustified criticism.

Heil Hitler!
By Instruction:
[Signature illegible]

---

The ability of the Nazis to carry out their genocidal intentions has often been attributed to the secrecy surrounding their actions and the inability of ordinary people to offer any effective opposition. After the war, many Germans used these twin defenses: 'We didn't know' and 'Anyone who refused to cooperate was killed.' This letter about a minor controversy far from the front offers an alternative view.

Soviet POWs and other prisoners, who were worked and starved to death in industrial plants throughout Germany, were visible to many Germans on a daily basis. Nazi Party member Fritz Söhling (spelled incorrectly in the letter), the office manager of a locomotive factory in Essen, tried to get more food for the 23 Soviet POWs who had been assigned to work for Krupp, one of the largest metal and armaments producers in the world. Some had collapsed within a week of arrival. Söhling's intervention caused a local uproar, and he was accused of supporting Bolsheviks. Eventually, however, the rations for the Soviets were increased by the addition of a hot midday meal.[1] There is no record of any punishment for Söhling.

The actions of those who observed the Holocaust, from passing a starving prisoner a piece of bread to offering refuge to a Jew on the run, could prolong survival or save lives. The difference between rescuers and bystanders lay in the willingness to do something about the scenes played out in public view.

## Note

1 Details of this incident beyond the letter printed here are taken from a subsequent letter, Nuremberg document D-164, translated in *Trials of War Criminals under Control Council Law No. 10,* Vol. 9, p. 1213–15.

# 59. Order to Warsaw Jewish Council to organize deportation 'to the East', 22 July 1942

Notifications and Instructions for the Jewish Council

The Jewish Council is notified of the following:

1. All Jewish persons, no matter what age or sex, who live in Warsaw will be resettled to the East.

2. Excepted from the resettlement are:

(a) all Jewish persons who are employed by the German authorities or enterprises and can furnish proof of this;

(b) all Jewish persons who belong to the Jewish Council and are employees of the Jewish Council (qualifying date is the date of publication of the order);

(c) all Jewish persons who are employed by German firms and can furnish proof of this;

(d) all Jews capable of work who have hitherto not been enlisted in the work process, they are to be quartered in the Jewish residential district;

(e) all Jewish persons who are members of the personnel of the Jewish hospitals. Similarly, the members of the Jewish disinfection troops;

(f) all Jewish persons who are members of the Jewish Order Service;

(g) all Jewish persons who are close relatives of the persons listed in a) through f). Relatives are exclusively wives and children;

(h) all Jewish persons who on the first day of the resettlement are in one of the Jewish hospitals and are not capable of being released. Fitness for release will be ascertained by a doctor to be designated by the Jewish Council.

3. Every Jewish resettler may take 15 kg. of his property as luggage. All valuables, gold, jewelry, money, etc., may be taken. Food for three days is to be taken.

4. The resettlement begins on 22 July 1942 at 11 o'clock.

I. In the course of the resettlement, the following instructions will be imposed on the Jewish Council, for whose exact compliance the members of the Jewish Council are held responsible with their lives:
The Jewish Council takes orders only from the Commissioner for the Resettlement or his representatives, who are connected with the resettlement. For the period of the resettlement the Jewish Council can choose a special resettlement committee, whose chairman must be the head of the Jewish Council and his representative, the commander of the Jewish Order Service.

II. The Jewish Council is responsible for supplying the Jews who come daily for shipping. To carry out this task, the Jewish Council will use the Jewish Order Service (100 men). The Jewish Council ensures that daily from 22 July 1942, by 4 PM at the latest, 6000 Jews are supplied at the collecting point. The collecting point for the entire period of the evacuation is the Jewish hospital in Stawki Street. On 22 July, the 6000 Jews will be supplied directly on the loading platform at the transfer office. To start with, the Jewish Council can take the daily quotas of Jews to be supplied from the whole population. Later, the Jewish Council will receive a special instruction, according to which particular streets or blocks of houses are to be cleared....

IV. The Jewish Council furthermore ensures that the objects and valuables left behind by the resettled Jews, insofar as they are not infected, are gathered and registered at collection points still to be determined. For this purpose the Jewish Council draws in the Jewish Order Service and sufficient Jewish workers. This function will be overseen by the Security Police, who give the Jewish Council special instructions about it. Illegal appropriations of objects and valuables during this function will be punished by death.

V. The Jewish Council furthermore ensures that during the period of resettlement, the Jews who work in German enterprises or in the German interest attend to their work....

VI. The Jewish Council is further responsible that the Jews who die during the period of resettlement are buried on the same day....

VIII. Punishments:

(a) every Jewish person who leaves the ghetto at the start of the resettlement without belonging to the categories of persons listed under numbers 2a and c, and insofar as they were not hitherto entitled to do so, will be shot;

(b) every Jewish person who undertakes an action which is intended to evade or disturb the resettlement measures will be shot;

(c) every Jewish person who assists in an action which is intended to evade or disturb the resettlement measures will be shot;

(d) all Jews who are encountered in Warsaw after completion of the resettlement, without belonging to the categories of persons listed under 2a to h, will be shot.

The Jewish Council is informed that, in case the orders and instructions given to it are not carried out 100%, an appropriate number of hostages, who in the meantime have been taken, will be shot.

Dictated by the Commissioner for the Resettlement.

---

On 19 July 1942 Himmler wrote Friedrich Wilhelm Krüger, Higher SS and Police Leader of the General Gouvernement, ordering that its whole Jewish population had to be 'resettled' by end of 1942, except those working in a few ghettos. That communication began a frenzy of deportations. This order of 3 days later was delivered to Adam Czerniakow, Chairman of the Warsaw Jewish Council, by Hermann Höfle, one of Globocnik's deputies, who was responsible for organizing the transportation of Jews from ghettos to death camps as part of Operation Reinhardt. The use of haste as a tactic is apparent: at 10 a.m. on 22 July, Höfle ordered that 6000 Jews must be ready for resettlement by 4 p.m. on that day and every day thereafter. Jews could bring whatever possessions they wanted, as long as they observed the 15 kilogram limit.

At first the Jewish ghetto police delivered the victims to the collection point (*Umschlagplatz*). When these policemen began to disappear, the SS took over the operation. In 53 days, about 250,000 Jews from Warsaw were put on trains to Treblinka, where they were killed immediately.

Czerniakow's wife was taken hostage and he wrote in his diary that 'Höfle informed me that if the deportation were impeded in any way, she would be the first to be shot.'[1] He committed suicide the next day.

## Note

1 His diary is an excellent source for the early history of the Warsaw ghetto: Adam Czerniakow, *The Warsaw Diary of Adam Czerniakow: Prelude to Doom* (New York: Stein and Day, 1978).

# 60. Diary of Oskar Singer in Lódź Ghetto, 27 July 1942

LITZMANNSTADT DEATH

Litzmannstadt Death has been unknown in Europe. Perhaps our early ancestors experienced similar events, but human beings have not known death like this. In a very brief span of time, life has veered off its usual course, and death has changed its face. This has taken place with a speed not even the wildest imagination could have predicted. Life has become strange, and death, therefore, has also. The surviving world will have only the barest idea of what it was like here. Repeatedly, one hears the muted question: Will there be anyone able to tell the world how we lived and died here?

This is, indeed, a horror that challenges the creative hands of the poets. I do not know if among those living here there is a poet who could master the task, and if so, whether he will survive. Not everything that happens here can be explained by war. We have witnessed war and know that life takes on a different face when cannons speak. The basic forms, though,the elements of daily life,stay the same. Morality cracks, but ethics remain. The rules of social life are not abolished; at most, they are altered. The family, the pillar of domestic life—does not collapse. There is an evolution of thought during war, which we see among the young.

It is different here in the ghetto. Everything is upside-down, and yet we are far removed from the war itself. The ghetto developed without a period of transition, which created an unbridgeable gulf between us and the rest of the world. This cannot be explained entirely by the strict separation. For us Jews, the ghetto is a basic catastrophe.

We can no longer die as other people do. We no longer have the possibility of a noble end. Litzmannstadt Death is an alien, ugly death. I will draw it as it is—with no fictitious stories. He shall parade past us unadorned by literary device.

Mordche K. works in the carpentry workshop. Skilled furniture-maker that he is, he once had a good shop in Lodz, lived in a four-room apartment, and ran a respectable bourgeois household. A good, hard-working wife stood by his side, and they had two good-looking, well-built young lads. Naturally, the world changed for him in the ghetto. Now he lives in a small house very near the barbed wire at the edge of the ghetto. His wife, 19-year-old Icek, and 13-year-old Chajmek work in different factories.

Mordche K. is a sincerely good man who works honestly. But winter was rough and early spring cruel. He complains of being tired, of general weakness. His feet, especially his feet, do not want to do their duty. They have become very heavy, and the knee joints have become strangely stiff. But that will pass.

It looks very desperate in his apartment. But who should make it neat? The most his wife can do is make the beds; to dust or scrub the floor is impossible. Her strength does not extend that far. It must be accepted this way. One cannot afford to waste the slightest amount of energy not directed at acquiring food. Only now does she understand what she could never grasp before: the hopeless dirt in the apartments of the very poor. All her thoughts circle around only one thing: the dinner soup.

Where does one get some vegetables, carrots, a spoonful of flour for a soup? To hell with cleanliness. Dirt does not kill as fast as hunger.

Mordche feels his feet getting even heavier. Is this because of his worn-out shoes with the holes in the soles and the slanting heels? Does one walk with so much difficulty because of that? He must freshen up his feet; a hot bath might help. He just does not want to think about the swelling in his joints. It is not necessarily caused by hunger. Feet also swell for other reasons. You stand at the machines too long, and the long walk to work ... no, it can't be hunger, as it is with so many ghetto people.

Mordche tries to ignore the water in his feet. He can only drag himself about, for this is no longer walking. Suddenly he realizes that his tools no longer rest as securely in his grip as they once did. His hands tremble. Very often, the hammer or the screwdriver falls. What the hell is this? Such weakness at only 45 years of age? He studies his hands. They are not that skinny. On the contrary, the right one has grown heavier. The fingers have heavy padding. This is strange: a hand like this should be able to work. Mordche would like to ignore the water in his hands. He knows that his hands are swollen, really swollen. But hands can also swell up for other reasons. For example, from being overworked. From being injured. The last injury caused an inflammation that has probably gone into the fingers. You must bathe the hands warmly; that helps with inflammations. But water is water! It will not be driven from the flesh by warm water.

Mordche explains to his frightened wife that he has burnt his hands with acid and now they're swollen. His wife knows better. Also his feet are not swollen from exhaustion. She knows that what's going on is hunger. She does not say anything. Why should she frighten him? And if he does know, why should she unmask his fiction?

Now when she handles the little weights—28 decagrams per day, 14 in the morning, 14 in the evening—she must cheat slightly. Her husband must not notice that his slice has become thicker. Naturally, it is not the children who can be deprived. Women need less, she has often heard, they can take it more easily. A few deca will not be a great loss to her, and they might help him.

And, in fact, it does go better. A few deca of bread make a difference. And he notices how it is happening. But should he do anything about it? Scared, he watches his wife, in case the same symptoms now show up in her. It is not from egoism but for his family's sake that he wants to live. Better times are bound to come. One day this war must end, and then he'll be able to give the boys a good start and his wife an easier life. One day. Till then one must sustain oneself.

This goes on for two weeks. The slice of bread is still as thick, and now the margarine is spread more heavily. Why the margarine? Mordche is not blind. The bundle in the shopping bag did not escape his eyes. His heart stopped at this discovery. Mother sells a quarter loaf to get the margarine on his slice. He doesn't say a word. Isn't that horrible? The few deca for me already equal more than a quarter. What is left for her, then? This is going too far. At night Mordche tells her he will not put up with it. He tells her he feels much better, it is not necessary any more. But she denies it. Not a trace of bread has been sold; he is making a mistake. Mordche likes so much to be put at ease.

But the swelling returns. He goes to a hard-working doctor he knows from the old days in town. The doctor shrugs his shoulders, cannot prescribe anything. No injection, no medication. Perhaps K. can get a few ampoules of Campellon in some clandestine way—that would help. It can be had, but it costs a fortune. That much money doesn't even exist—100 marks for four ampoules, and there would be no sense in getting less. He cannot tell his wife. God only knows what she would sell of her ration to get these ampoules. The doctor also prescribes yeast. But where does one get yeast? The drugstore does not distribute it anymore. From private hands, one can get some at three marks a deca. How often can one buy that, if one only earns three marks a day? Even so, he will have to buy yeast. He buys, and the swelling goes down a bit again. Or is it just his imagination? It doesn't matter. Objectively or subjectively, better is better.

After two weeks he can stop the yeast. But Mordche is out of luck. A boil on his hand hinders his work. But he cannot call in sick. Anxiety about [missing] the designated day for rations forces him to keep struggling. The hand gets worse. Off to the emergency room. The doctor can do nothing. To cut is a possibility, but in the ghetto boils are not lanced, because then they never heal. The body lacks immunity. Take yeast! All right, he takes yeast again. He must tell his wife: his last few pfennigs are used up. Mrs. K. gets yeast. We don't even want to ask what she has sold, our heart would break. That her feet are swelling, we already know, but we are not concerned with her at the moment. She is one of the many unknown soldiers of the ghetto. Her heroism belongs on a different page.

The boil gets larger. Mordche is in terrible pain. Finally, it opens, and he is relieved. But immediately another appears. The next day a third, and soon his entire body is covered. A very bad case, the doctor reports. Only yeast, over and over again yeast. Now, thank God, getting it is not such a problem. Large amounts of it have come into the ghetto for therapeutic needs, and each week 5 deca can be had. That is affordable. Mordche eats yeast, raw and prepared. He is sick of it, but it's rich in vitamins. The boils heal, but his body is swollen even more. The sleepless nights have ravaged his strength. The money spent on yeast has not been spent on food.

Mrs. K. wears down her tired feet trying to get food for her husband, and finally, Mordche eats well for a couple of days. He is really satisfied, but his stomach and bowels are not used to it, and they rebel. He becomes sick with diarrhea. The doctor cannot prescribe the usual diet in these cases, as the organism cannot afford to go without food even for a day. Not in the ghetto. Eat, eat at all costs. The patient forces himself to take nutrition, and every hour his bowels force him to leave his bed. He falls down like a stick. His feet are merely bones covered with skin.

The swelling in his face has gone, but the skin on his forehead is now like tough leather. The intervals become shorter and shorter; soon he must go out every 15 minutes. A European normally has everything at his disposal in such a case, but here there is only a pail in the middle of the room, one pail for four people. In the past, K. carried the pail out himself. Now he has to leave this to his wife. He is too weak.

She wants to force into him what she can come up with that is edible. K., in fact, does want to eat. He knows too well that this is the only way to keep himself strong. But an alarming loss of appetite settles in. Perhaps a delicacy—fried potatoes—could still taste good. But potatoes are not to be had.

He would like to rest for just one hour without interruption, but his body refuses to obey. Every ten minutes he must get up. Mother K. finally gets a bowl. At first he rejects this convenience. A man cannot expect his wife to do this. Finally, she teaches him, and he permits her.

He asks for sleeping pills. Perhaps sleep will calm the body; that could be the answer. The pharmacy no longer has sleeping powders. She tracks down acquaintances who have brought some with them from Berlin. He takes the medication with the hope of a believer.

No, the illness stubbornly remains, but now K. lies in semiconsciousness during the small breaks his suffering permits him. Now, he cannot be made to eat anything. Here and there, a sip of coffee, that's all. Incomprehensible, where his body gets all the fluid from, since nothing goes into his stomach anymore.

Mrs. K. checks anxiously: perhaps this is dysentery. No, there is no blood to be seen. The doctor finally comes to the house again. He comes, knowing he is superfluous. He cannot prescribe anything. There are medications that might help, strong opiates, for example. But such things do not come into the ghetto. What for?—we are supposed to die.

Mordche can hardly speak anymore. He can only give tired signs with his finger. He wants to tell the doctor something but can't. Yet one must be careful. He hears everything. Outside, the doctor says it could take hours, perhaps a day.

Mordche's strength makes it for two days. Then he dozes off.

People die this way in great numbers, a result of the so-called Ghetto Disease, diarrhea. The doctor fills out the death certificate. "Cause of death: heart failure!" Nobody in the ghetto is allowed to die of hunger.

—27 July 1942

---

Oskar Singer was born in 1883, earned a doctorate, and made a literary career in Prague before being deported to Łódź (renamed Litzmannstadt by the Germans) in 1941. He continued writing in the ghetto, surviving until 1944. Like many writers after him, he chose to abandon fictional devices in his attempt to tell the world about the inexplicable nature of ghetto life and ghetto death.[1]

The Nazi authorities who ruled the ghettos deliberately created living conditions which struck 20th-century Europeans as primitive. Horse-drawn carriages replaced tramways, industrial goods disappeared, food consumption fell catastrophically, toilets vanished, disease spread. The huge ghettos in Poland were cleared by disease and starvation as well as by deportation. In Warsaw, during the year before the deportations of summer 1942, over 4000 people died every month. As the ghetto inhabitants were pushed into misery, the Nazi overlords could confirm their ideological prejudices. Propaganda Minister Goebbels used ghetto scenes to create a perverse image of racial inferiors in the pseudo-documentary film 'The Eternal Jew', shown in Germany starting in 1940.

Ghetto conditions created special burdens for women, whose traditional tasks of taking physical care of their families became impossible to accomplish. Children who could slip through tiny cracks in ghetto walls might become the sole support of their families through smuggling. Although ghetto inmates knew well whose actions determined their fate, feelings of guilt still pervaded the ghetto. Here Mordche, his wife, and the doctor all display a sense of responsibility for conditions created by forces entirely outside of their control.

## Note

1 Daily life in the Łódź ghetto is recorded by another resident who died of the 'ghetto disease' in 1943: *The Diary of Dawid Sierakowiak: Five Notebooks from the Łódź Ghetto*, ed. Alan Adelson, trans. Kamil Turowski (New York: Oxford University Press, 1996).

# 61. Diary of Emanuel Ringelblum in Warsaw Ghetto, 14 December 1942

Dec. 14

HIDING PLACES

Now, in December, 1942, hiding places are very popular. Everyone is making them. Everywhere, in all the shops and elsewhere in the Ghetto, hiding places are being built. Their construction has actually become a flourishing specialized craft. Skilled workers, engineers, etc., are making a living out of it. Hiding places go back many years. People began to hide out when the Germans entered Warsaw, in October, 1939. People hid themselves, hid their goods. On Franciszkanska and Nalewki Streets, cellars were walled up, attics, special rooms, stores of merchandise — because the Germans used to confiscate everything, removing complete truck-loads of goods. Even then there were scoundrels who made it their business to knock down the walls of these hiding places. These were the professional informers, who recruited themselves for the job. The majority were porters. They used to uncover stores of goods which the Germans would otherwise never have found. The details of the removal of whole wagons full of leather worth millions from Franciszkanska Street have stuck in my memory. Days on end large military trucks removed this merchandise from the hiding places.

And then people used to hide themselves. In those days, during 1939, 1940, and part of 1941, people would be seized for forced labor almost every day — so the men hid out in the shops, under bench beds, in mezzanines, cubbies, cellars, garrets, etc. Some of the apartments were so arranged that a room could be set off for the men to hide in — usually behind a shop, credenza, or the like. The Germans knew the location of such hideouts, thanks to their Jewish informers, who accompanied them and pointed out the hiding places. Pious Jews, wearing beards and ear locks, used to hide out, too — showing yourself bearded was perilous, because there were often Gestapo agents, or just mean Germans, who couldn't bear the sight of an "uncivilized" bearded Jew. They would shave off the offending beard, or just rip it off, skin and all.

During the time when there were blockades, the resettlement period, hideouts assumed a new importance. People took special pains to build good hiding places, because they had become a matter of life and death. Old folks, children, and women hid out there. The men were not afraid to go to all kinds of selections, because they had a chance to get various work certificates and exemption papers.

In those days the hideouts were more refined, better concealed. My family, for example, used to hide out in a subroom in an old house, on the third floor. It consisted of the few steps of another house. Entry was through a trap door in the floor, which the wife of a policeman, who was not afraid of any blockade — policemen were safe at the time — used to cover with a rug and a table on top of it. In another place, they used a secret tannery, specially built into a cellar, for a hideout. A third place used a clandestine grain mill, marvelously disguised. Air-raid shelters were also used as hideouts. In one courtyard the air-raid shelter was underground. Entry was through a trap door, which the men used to cover with boards. In many apartments, people set aside special rooms, masking the entry a number of ways, for example, the entry would be through the next-door kitchen. They used to lift out the tiles to enter. Entry to the sealed-off room would be through the water closet, a trap door in the next room, or in the room above, which would be connected to the hideout by a ladder. In some places the entry would be masked by a movable block of tiles, so that, in case the walls were tapped, there would be no empty hollow spaces. If the hideout was in a cellar, people made sure that it was very far away, in some distant corner, where there were no windows.

These hideouts were given away by accident, very often by a child's crying. I know of a case on Nowolipie Street were several dozen people were hiding in two walled-up rooms. The Ukrainians blockading the house threw a party in the next room. They were about to leave when they heard a child crying. They chopped down the wall and found one of the rooms, with twenty-six people in it. They shot six of them on the spot; the rest bought the Ukrainians off and went to the Umschlagplatz. The second sealed room was not discovered.

In 90 per cent of the cases it was the Jewish police who uncovered the hideouts. First they found out where the hideouts were; then they passed the information along to the Ukrainians and Germans. Hundreds and thousands of people are on those scoundrels' conscience.

After the selection — for deportation or forced work — when things calmed down a bit in the Ghetto, a new chapter in the story of hideouts began. The populace had by this time learned to distrust the Germans. It was obvious that so long as the present system continued, there would be a new operation against the Jews sooner or later, and in the end the Ghetto would be liquidated. Two events contributed to the popular refusal to accept the mollifying statements of the Germans at their face value: first, the continuing massacre of Jews in Treblinki and other camps; and second, the fact that 800 people were seized in the shops and deported toward Lublin. Nothing has since been heard of them.

Consequently, the populace has begun to plan how to secure their lives in case of danger. The richer people have begun to cross over to the Other Side. Others, less fortunate, are planning hiding places. During November and December, there was a feverish activity in the construction of new hideouts, differing completely from those built during the summer, during the time of the "operation." In the first place, they had to be usable in cold weather; secondly, they had to be furnished for people to be able to live there months on end. The reasoning was that if all the Jews of Warsaw were to be liquidated, those who had hideouts would go into them and stay there until they were rescued. The new hideouts were built in one of three places: cellars, underground, or on the floor of an apartment. The present hideouts are ... equipped with gas, electricity, water, and toilets. Some of them cost tens of thousands of zlotys. They contain food supplies sufficient to last for months (preserves, sugar, and the like). Since there is the fear that the Germans might stop the water passage, as they did in a number of the houses where the "wild people" are living, people have stocked up on supplies of distilled water, buried in barrels in the hideouts. Or else, special artesian wells are dug. Of course, only the well-to-do can afford such luxuries. I know of one case where for 3,000 zlotys a water-works man connected the water pipes of a hideout with the water pipes of an Aryan factory, so that the people in the hideout would continue to have water, even if the water was shut off in the house.

The Jewish brains that are working on problems of this kind have worked out a brilliant scheme to insure against the shutting off of water. They'll creep out of their hideout at night and set fire to the next house. They say the firemen will have to open the water connections then, and those in the know will take advantage of this to put in a fresh supply of water to last for a time.

Jewish craftsmen have also thought up a way of seeing to it that there is no shortage of gas and electricity — the plan is known supposedly only to them. The idea is to steal gas and electric current from the next house. Naturally, this is only possible when the gas or electricity is cut off in one house, not in the whole street.

Some hideouts are built into apartments. They locate an alcove or room corner and wall it in so that it can't be noticed. The chief trouble with such a hideout is that windows always betray its existence. A few weeks ago, a special police division of the Property Collection Agency came to Warsaw and used this technique: they counted the number of windows on each floor, and then sent that many policemen up to each floor and ordered them to stick out their heads. It was easy to find out whether there were any disguised rooms, and where they were.

As a general rule, walling up windows is the hardest problem. In one courtyard, the tenants concealed the walled-up window of the basement by placing a garbage can in front of it; elsewhere, the window was concealed by steps.

As everyone knows, modern apartment houses are so constructed that all the apartments in the same line have the same layout. Walling up an alcove in one apartment does not provide an adequate hiding place, because it is quite easy to find the same alcove on a higher or lower floor in the same line of apartments. The way out of this dilemma was for all the persons living in the same line to wall up their alcoves. In one house, the residents all walled up one corner of a room, built an entry through a bakery oven, and put in a passageway from one floor to the next through a chain of ladders pushed through holes cut into the floors. An impressive hideout like that accommodates up to sixty persons.

The most important problem in any hideout is masking the entry. Every day sees the invention of new solutions, each cleverer than the previous one. What is involved is seeing to it that when the German detective taps the walls, he doesn't find any empty space. On the other side of one walled-up room, tiles were pasted into a frame, and the whole thing was pushed aside when people wanted to enter the hideout. In another place, the entry was through a water closet, in a third through a bakery oven.

Communication with the outside world is another basic problem. Arrangements are made in advance with a Christian, who looks after the needs of the Jews in the hideout on the days when they go into hiding. A few shops have hideouts so built that they have an underground connection with the Other Side. This is only possible where the shops border on the Aryan Side. Building that kind of a tunnel is one of the hardest things to do. A good deal of earth has to be dug up and removed surreptitiously. This is far from easy; consequently, the diggers make it a rule that only those who have worked on the tunnel may use the hideout.

It is said that Germans have used hounds to search houses from which Jews have been driven out, to ferret out the hidden survivors. Thus far, no way has been found to put the hounds off the trace. Lysol is said to be effective. But there is danger that, smelling lysol, the Germans will know that Jews are in hiding in that particular house.

Besides supplying Jewish craftsmen with a source of livelihood, the hideouts have become a business for gangs that sell places in them for thousands of zlotys. This includes food supply.

There is altogether too much talk about hideouts — more talk than action. The Jewish Gestapo agents know about them, so, inevitably, the Germans do, too. There was even an informer in Hallman's shop who informed on a large hideout there. The argument runs that if the Germans know about Ghetto hideouts, they have lost their value. So, a few people maintain, the best thing to do is to build a hideout on the Other Side. Find a Christian family willing to rent a large apartment, wall up a room where Jews can be concealed, and, naturally, give the Christian family proper financial satisfaction. But the populace is afraid that at the crucial terrifying moment the Germans will discover some clever way of turning to nought all our efforts at self-rescue. Whether this is true or not, only the future will tell.

---

Emanuel Ringelblum was a Jewish historian in Warsaw when the Germans invaded Poland. He had taught history in high school, written four books on Jews in recent Polish history, lectured to adults in night classes, organized sport clubs and music circles, and was active in leftist Jewish politics.

Within a couple of weeks, Ringelblum began to collect materials about the Nazi persecution of Polish Jews. Soon he had organized a staff to create an archive documenting Jewish life in Warsaw, and he began to make his own daily notes. After Warsaw's Jews were locked into the Ghetto in November, 1940, Ringelblum's historical work expanded; he named it simply 'O.S.', for Oneg Shabbat. Preserving the history of the Warsaw Ghetto was a major enterprise, involving representatives of various political and cultural groups, including the youth movements. Anyone connected with the Jewish Council was excluded.

This was the final entry in Emanuel Ringelblum's notes. It demonstrates Ringelblum's historical approach, his effort to summarize ghetto experience for future readers. The description of the development of hideouts offers insight into the collective efforts of Warsaw's Jews to resist increasingly brutal German treatment.

Ringelblum's notes break off as the final crisis of the Warsaw Ghetto began. Mass deportations to Treblinka since July 1942 had decimated the Ghetto population. The clandestine fighting organizations made their first attempt at an uprising in January 1943. The efforts of the Germans to empty the Ghetto led to the final revolt of April 1943, when the hideouts Ringelblum described became a central element of military strategy. Ringelblum was smuggled out of the Ghetto, but captured by the Germans; he then escaped and hid on the 'Aryan Side' of Warsaw. In 1944 he was captured again and executed with his wife and son.

The Oneg Shabbat archive outlasted its organizer. The papers were buried under the ruins of the Ghetto and discovered after the war. Ringelblum's notes had been hidden in rubberized milk cans. Now the Oneg Shabbat papers are preserved in Yad Vashem.

# 62. Report of SS Concentration Camp Office on mortality of prisoners, 28 December 1942

SS Economic and Administrative Main Office
Section D Concentration Camps
DIII/Az.14 h(KL) 82.42.Lg/Wy
Secret Diary No. 66/42. 21st Copy

Oranienburg, 28 December 1942

signed Pister
Schobert

Regarding: Medical Duties in the Conc. Camps
Reference: None
Enclosures: 1

To the Camp Doctors of the Conc. Camps

Da., Sh., Bu., Neu., Bu., Rav., Flo., Lu., Stu., Gr.-Ro., Nied., Natz., Hinz., Mor., Herzog., Mau.
Copy to the Camp Commandants.

In the enclosure a table of current arrivals and departures in all concentration camps is transmitted for your information. It shows that of 136,000 arrivals, around 70,000 have dropped out through death. With such a high death toll, the number of prisoners can never be brought to the level that the Reichsführer-SS has ordered. The chief camp doctors must do their utmost with all means at their disposal to substantially lower mortality figures in the individual camps. The best doctor in a concentration camp is not the one who believes that he must stand out through unexcelled hardness, but the one who keeps work capacity at the highest possible level through supervision and exchange at the individual work sites.

The camp doctors must supervise the feeding of prisoners more than previously and, in agreement with the administrations, submit suggestions for improvement to the camp commandant. These must not only exist simply on paper, but are to be regularly supervised by the camp doctors. The camp doctors must further see to it that work conditions at individual work sites are improved, if possible. For this purpose, it is necessary that the camp doctors personally confirm working conditions at the work sites.

The Reichsführer-SS has ordered that mortality must be reduced unconditionally. For this reason, the above is ordered, and reports on what has been achieved are to be made monthly to the chief of Section D III. First time on 1 February 1943.

signed [illegible]
SS-Brigadeführer and Major General of the Waffen SS

Table overleaf

Summary
<u>of the Months June – November 1942</u>

| Month | Arrivals | | | Departures | | | | |
|---|---|---|---|---|---|---|---|---|
| | Deliveries | Transfers | Total | Releases | Transfers | Death | E | Total |
| June | 10,322 | 2,575 | 11,897 | 673 | 2,903 | 4,080 | 243 | 6,899 |
| July | 25,716 | 6,254 | 31,970 | 907 | 4,340 | 8,536 | 477 | 14,260 |
| August | 25,407 | 2,742 | 28,149 | 581 | 2,950 | 12,733 | 99 | 16,363 |
| Septemb. | 16,763 | 6,438 | 23,201 | 652 | 6,805 | 22,598 | 144 | 30,199 |
| October | 13,873 | 5,345 | 19,218 | 1,089 | 6,334 | 11,858 | 5,954 | 25,235 |
| Novemb. | 17,780 | 4,565 | 22,345 | 809 | 5,514 | 10,805 | 2,350 | 19,478 |
| total | 109,861 | 26,919 | 136,780 | 4,711 | 27,846 | 70,610 | 9,267 | 112,434 |

This letter was sent to the major forced labor camps in Germany, Austria, France, and Poland, including Buchenwald (where this copy was found), Dachau, Sachsenhausen, Neuengamme, Ravensbrück, Flossenbürg, Lublin, Stutthof, Gross-Rosen, Niederhagen, Natzweiler, Hinzert, Moringen, Herzogenbusch, and Mauthausen. The names of the mass murder camps in Poland do not appear on the list. The document is part of the report on Buchenwald which also included the earlier statement of Herbert Mindus.

The report demonstrates the peculiar combination of fanatical statistical accuracy about mass murder, sloppy arithmetic, and bureaucratic formality that characterized the SS. Over the course of 6 months, deaths in concentration camps totalled 51% of 'new admissions'. Although the letter attributes all these deaths to the new 'arrivals', some of the inmates who died had probably arrived earlier. Six of the figures in the table are in error due to mistakes in addition. The heading 'E' is unexplained; it might mean 'executed'.[1] This report shows that the usual distinction between death camps and slave labor camps can be misleading. On average, half of the new prisoners died within three months.

The conflict within the SS between the desire to maintain a useful work force and the urge to murder the regime's enemies is apparent. The letter is addressed to camp doctors, as if the main issue concerns health conditions rather than ubiquitous killing, as seen in previous documents. The remarkable vision of SS doctors as men who desire to display 'unexcelled hardness' precisely matches the more general SS ideal. The idea that camp doctors might improve conditions at camp work sites displays a view of the camp system which does not match the grim realities of daily life in the SS state.

According to another Nuremberg document, NO-1010, between January and August 1943, about 60,000 inmates in the labor camp system died, perhaps representing a very slight improvement over the conditions shown here for 1942. Of the 239,000 prisoners who arrived at Buchenwald, about 60,000 died there.

This copy was signed by the camp commandant, SS Colonel Hermann Pister, and the deputy commandant, SS Major Max Schobert. They were both convicted at the trial of the Buchenwald camp guards in 1946–47 and sentenced to hang.

## Note

1 This document is discussed by Eugen Kogon, *Der SS Staat: Das System der deutschen Konzentrationslager* (Munich: Wilhelm Heyne Verlag, 1974), pp. 170–3.

# 63. SS report on revolt in Warsaw Ghetto, 13 May 1943

Copy Teletype message
Sender: The SS and Police Leader in the District of Warsaw

Warsaw, 13 May 1943

Ref. No.: I ab -St/Gr- 16 07–Diary No. 641/43 secret.
Re: Large Ghetto Operation

To the Higher SS and Police Leader East,
SS-Obergruppenführer and Police General
Krüger – or deputy

Cracow

Progress of large operation on 13 May 1943, start: 10 a.m.:

In today's combing of the large and small Ghettos (Prosta), 234 Jews were hunted down. In battle 155 Jews were shot. Today it became clear that the Jews and bandits whom we are catching now belong to the so-called battle groups. All of them are young fellows and females between 18–25 years of age. At the capture of one bunker, a real skirmish took place, in which Jews not only fired from .08 pistols and Polish Vis pistols, but also threw Polish "pineapple" hand grenades at the Waffen-SS men. After a portion of the bunker crew had been caught and were about to be searched, one of the females, as so often before, as quick as lightning put her hand under her skirt, and pulled from her bloomers a "pineapple" hand grenade, drew the safety-catch, threw it among the men who were searching her, and jumped quick as lightning to cover. It is only thanks to the presence of mind of the men that no casualties ensued.

The few Jews and criminals still staying in the Ghetto have for the last 2 days used the hideouts offered by the ruins, in order to return at night into the bunkers known to them, to eat and get provisions for the next day. Lately it is not possible to extract a statement about further bunkers known to them from the captured Jews. The remainder of the crew where the skirmish took place were destroyed by stronger explosive charges. From a Wehrmacht concern 327 Jews were seized today. The Jews seized are sent to T.II.

The total number of Jews caught has risen to 55,179.

Our strength:

| Used in operation | | |
|---|---|---|
| | German police | 4/182 |
| | Engineering Em. Service | 1/6 |
| | Security Police | 2/14 |
| | Engineers | 4/74 |
| | Waffen SS | 12/517 |

| Cordoning forces | by day | by night |
|---|---|---|
| German police | 2/137 | 1/87 |
| Waffen SS | — | 1/300 |
| Trawniki | 270 | — |
| Polish Police | 1/160 | 1/160 |

Our losses: 2 Waffen SS dead
3 Waffen SS wounded
1 Policeman wounded.

The 2 fallen men of the Waffen SS lost their lives during the air attack against the Ghetto.

33 bunkers were discovered and destroyed. Booty: 6 pistols, 2 hand grenades, and explosive charges.

End of today's operation: 9 p.m., continuation on 14 May 1943, 10 a.m.

I intend to terminate the large operation on 16 May 1943 and to turn all further measures over to Police Battalion III/23. Unless ordered otherwise, I will submit to the conference of SS and Police Leaders a detailed report, with photo appendix.

The SS and Police Leader
in the District of Warsaw
signed Stroop
SS-Brigadeführer and Major General of Police.

Certified copy:
SS-Sturmbannführer.

---

This report is part of the much larger so-called Stroop report, which consists of an introduction providing an overview of the history of the Warsaw Ghetto, and then reports issued daily, sometimes twice daily, by Jürgen Stroop and sent by SS teletype to Stroop's superior officer, Friedrich Krüger, in Cracow.[1]

The uprising began in response to the German intention to wipe out the remnants of the Ghetto, beginning, as the Nazis often did, on the eve of Passover, 19 April. By the time of this report, most ghetto inmates had been killed or removed. Each day Stroop specified exactly the number of Jews, referred to here as bandits and criminals, who were captured, and then added up the total who had been caught during the entire operation.

The massive forces assembled by the Germans are indicated in Stroop's report: for example, 517 Waffen SS soldiers, led by 12 officers, combined with regular and security police, engineers, Polish police, and Trawniki, who were non-German volunteer units, such as Ukrainians or Latvians. The mismatch in weaponry is clear from the report that only pistols and hand-made grenades were used by the ghetto fighters against the massive armaments of the Nazis, including tanks, cannons, flame-throwers, and even the air strikes mentioned here. Given the information that the day's booty was only 6 pistols, it seems unlikely that the 155 Jews who were shot were all engaged in battle.

Stroop did end the operation on 16 May. His elegantly bound report was entitled 'The Jewish Residential Quarter in Warsaw is No More'. One copy was discovered by Allied troops in his villa in Wiesbaden and became evidence for the Nuremberg trial. Yet the Jewish resistance continued beyond 16 May. SS soldiers fought with Jews until the beginning of June, and a small number of survivors were able to slip into the Polish part of Warsaw as late as September.

Stroop was tried in Poland and hanged in Warsaw on 8 September 1951. Krüger committed suicide in May 1945.

## Note

1 The whole report is reprinted in *Nazi Conspiracy and Aggression*, Vol. 3 (Washington, DC: US Government Printing Office, 1946), pp. 718–75.

# 64. Diary of Hanna Lévy-Hass in Bergen-Belsen, March 1945

BB. March 1945. Everything that one sees here, and everything that happens before our eyes, causes one to begin to doubt the human qualities of one's being. Slowly a gloomy and heavy mistrust grows – the mistrust of people. And one begins to put extraordinary questions to oneself. Yesterday for the first time I had a long conversation with Professor K. He is in the "Revier", completely exhausted. Limbs and face completely swollen from freezing and edema, wounds on his whole body, which do not heal. And in addition, dysentery and all other possible ailments torment him. I visit him regularly, to help him and to relieve his suffering at least a bit. And we talk about the great misfortune that has befallen us. We are perplexed, we ask ourselves, after everything that we have experienced here, whether a normal life is still possible. Almost impossible ... It seems it is our end, a shameful, terribly shameful *Finale* of our existence.

We analyze the attitude of some people. Each "helps" himself, as he can. The question forces itself on us: Is this all just a great test? In order to determine how much ability to find one's way one or another possesses. Or "fitness for life"? Is that it? Fitness for life? The struggle against death, the instinct for self-preservation? Does the test of individual strength and vitality lie there? Must the human being become brutal, become a wild animal, to stay alive?

Then would it mean that we others, who cannot "struggle" this way and who do not seize on animal methods, are unfit for life and doomed to destruction? I don't know any more. Should that be the highest law of nature, the law of all creatures. One could say: Yes, it is so. Good. But what then? And human reason, doesn't that count? The human mind has created many ethical laws and concepts, which stand in contrast to animal laws dictated completely by instinct. What has become of them, of these ethical laws and concepts? Do they mean nothing here?

No, I am firmly and deeply convinced that those people do not die, will not go to ruin, for whom ethical principles represent fundamental laws, which have become second nature for them, become their "human instinct", I would say, which replaces their animal instinct ... In this bestial struggle, which rages around them here, they are not doomed to finally disappear. I am also convinced, that I will finally succeed in mastering my situation, in upholding my principles, in helping humanity to break through – provided that my health remains as it is. Thus health, the physical power of resistance! That is thus still the decisive factor, this objective fact, which is responsible that I can maintain myself on a certain moral level, in human dignity. Thus it is not a personal achievement. I can't get beyond that ...

We continue the discussion. Who is right, who is wrong? How should one behave? We analyze a bit. J. and his morality, L. and his reflections, Li. and his tactics, R. and his logic, the family K. and their readiness to compromise, and thereby we also touch upon the theme: "the art of giving" and from where comes the right of one to distribute charity and of the other to receive it. It is also the place to investigate the sources of the truly fantastic commercial abilities which I. possesses and which in the current circumstances are expressed especially repulsively.

Professor K. believes that ethics, as we understand them, do not belong in these concentration camps, that they exclude themselves. According to his opinion, ethics are not even necessary, and that one cannot help renouncing them, if one wants to survive in spite of everything, in order to contribute to the building of a new world in which these ethics will prevail. Mind is subordinated to matter, it is only its outward form, the sublimation of matter, the superstructure. Consequently it is fateful and unavoidable, that matter expels mind, from where it does not belong and is an anomaly.

I don't know, that doesn't go into my head ... Concretely in the cases which interest us here, what does the victory of matter really mean? It means simply: to make a compromise with the enemy to betray one's own principles, to deny the soul, in order to maintain the body. And if one wants to follow this argument further with concrete examples, that means: to flirt with the hangman, to prostitute oneself and like a coward to close one's eyes before misery and mass murder, to eat what one has stolen from another, and to dance around the piles of bodies. That means: to sell one's human reason, human dignity, and principles, that means finally to save one's skin at the cost of the skin of another ... But should then this human life possess such a great value, that for its preservation all this atrocity is allowed?

---

The rarest form of victim testimony is the diary written in a concentration camp. Hanna Lévy-Hass was a Jewish Yugoslav teacher, active in the resistance after 1941 as a communist. She began her diary while in a Gestapo prison in Montenegro, and was transferred to Bergen-Belsen in summer 1944. After liberation, she returned to Yugoslavia to begin the process of building the new world that she mentions in this excerpt. Most of her family had been murdered, along with about 80% of Yugoslavia's 75,000 Jews. In 1948 she went to Israel to help in the construction of a socialist Jewish homeland.

The diary was written in Serbo-Croatian. Lévy-Hass quickly reproduced about a dozen copies for people who knew her at home, translated her diary into French, and also produced a few private copies. The Eichmann trial spurred publication in French and German in 1961. This 1979 version was the first publication in German of a larger edition.[1]

The camp between the towns of Bergen and Belsen in northern Germany was established in 1943 as a prisoner transit camp for 10,000 Jews who might be ransomed to the Allies. Although only 358 Jews obtained their freedom this way, Belsen eventually became a dumping ground for sick prisoners from other camps. At the end of the war, Belsen received enormous transports of prisoners from camps to the East and South. Starving, sick, and exhausted prisoners were simply allowed to die in Belsen in the final months of the war. As Lévy-Hass wrote this entry, nearly 20,000 prisoners died in March 1945. Among them was Anne Frank, author of the famous diary, who was deported from Holland to Auschwitz in September 1944, then sent to Belsen in October. In an earlier entry, Lévy-Hass compared Belsen with Auschwitz: 'There a fast cynical process, mass murder by gas – and here, the slow, vile, calculated destruction by hunger, violence, terror, and deliberately sustained epidemics.' Even after liberation in April by the British army, another 13,000 of the 60,000 prisoners present could not be saved.

In one of the first postwar Holocaust trials, 33 SS guards and 11 Kapos who were still at Belsen were tried between September and November 1945 by a British military tribunal. Eleven SS men were condemned to death.

## Note

1 Information about the diary and Lévy-Hass taken from Jane Caplan, 'Introduction', in Hanna Lévy-Hass, *Inside Belsen*, trans. Ronald Taylor (Brighton, UK: Harvester Press, 1982), pp. vii–xv, and from the 1978 interview with Lévy-Hass by Eike Geisel in Lévy-Hass, *Vielleicht war das alles erst der Anfang: Tagebuch aus dem KZ Bergen-Belsen 1944–1945*, ed. Eike Geisel (Berlin: Rotbuch Verlag, 1979), pp. 61–100.

# 65. Mauthausen death list, 19 March 1945

| 568 Cont No | Prisoner's Type | Prisoner's No | Camp | Last and First Name | Birth- Day | Birth- Place | Cause of Death | Day of Death | Hour of Death | 569 |
|---|---|---|---|---|---|---|---|---|---|---|
| 8390 | Pole | 134737 | SL | Smigielski Kazimierz | 24. 2. 10 | Warschau | circulatory weakness – general wasting away | 21. 3. 1945 | $7^{30}$ | |
| 1 | Hun | 135245 | ″ | Bazso Sandor | 12. 5. 20 | Budapest | ac. heart weakness – collapse | “ | $7^{35}$ | |
| 2 | Jew Pol | 135411 | Solvay | Ajzenberg Mojzes | 1. 9. 17 | Lodz | ac. heart weakness | 19. 3. 1945 | $1^{20}$ | |
| 3 | ″ ″ | 135410 | ″ | Ajnenbaum Abram | 16. 6. 11 | ″ | “ | “ | $1^{15}$ | |
| 4 | ″ Hun | 135405 | ″ | Ackermann Miklos | 10. 4. 25 | Munkasc | ″ | “ | $1^{15}$ | |
| 5 | ″ ″ | 135409 | ″ | Adler Mozes | 12. 9. 26 | Szeklene | “ | “ | $1^{15}$ | |
| 6 | ″ ″ | 135417 | ″ | Apfel Josef | 14. 4. 01 | Ramoli | heart a. circ. weakness – heart muscle inf. | “ | $1^{20}$ | |
| 7 | ″ Pol | 135424 | ″ | Baharjer Josef | 17. 7. 05 | Lodz | “ “ “ “ “ “ | “ | $1^{20}$ | |
| 8 | ″ Hun | 135433 | ″ | Beckmann Zoltan | 25. 2. 25 | Ermihalyfalva | ac. heart weakness | “ | $1^{20}$ | |
| 9 | ″ Pol | 135441 | ″ | Berkenwald Hersch | 6. 3. 19 | Czarkow | “ | “ | $1^{25}$ | |
| 8400 | ″ Hun | 135444 | ″ | Berkovics Paul | 28. 9. 98 | Brzevice | ″ | “ | $1^{25}$ | |
| 1 | ″ Czech | 135454 | ″ | Bienenfeld Ervin | 1. 3. 06 | Oceschnitz | heart a. circ. weakness – heart muscle inf. | “ | $1^{25}$ | |
| 2 | ″ Hun | 135458 | ″ | Birn Jenö | 17. 3. 95 | Sohol | “ “ “ “ “ “ | “ | $1^{25}$ | |
| 3 | ″ ″ | 135459 | ″ | Biro Albert | 12. 7. 97 | Nagy Karoly | “ “ “ “ “ “ | “ | $1^{30}$ | |
| 4 | ″ ″ | 135471 | ″ | Bleier Ignac | 21. 7. 95 | Nyir Gebe | “ “ “ “ “ “ | “ | $1^{30}$ | |
| 5 | ″ ″ | 135473 | ″ | Blonder Ludwig | 23. 1. 92 | Bojan | ac. heart weakness | “ | $1^{30}$ | |
| 6 | ″ Pol | 135477 | ″ | Bochmann Haim | 10.11.24 | Lodz | “ | “ | $1^{30}$ | |
| 7 | ″ Hun | 135480 | ″ | Borsadi Istvan | 5. 5. 89 | Ormos Pusata | “ | “ | $1^{30}$ | |
| 8 | ″ ″ | 135486 | ″ | Braun Endre | 10. 9. 11 | Rismaszombat | “ | “ | $1^{35}$ | |
| 9 | ″ Pol | 135499 | ″ | Broder Menachem | 24. 4. 23 | Lodz | “ | “ | $1^{35}$ | |
| 8410 | ″ Hun | 135501 | ″ | Broder Leopold | 13. 5. 85 | Sobotka | “ | “ | $1^{40}$ | |
| 1 | ″ ″ | 135505 | ″ | Buchhalter Julius | 7. 4. 92 | Ozel | “ | “ | $1^{40}$ | |
| 2 | ″ ″ | 135507 | ″ | Burger Zoltan | 6. 1. 92 | Marmarosziget | “ | “ | $1^{40}$ | |
| 3 | ″ ″ | 135509 | ″ | Chaimovics Bernat | 16. 5. 99 | Köresliget | heart a. circ. weakness – heart muscle inf. | “ | $1^{40}$ | |
| 4 | ″ ″ | 135510 | ″ | Chaimovics Majer | 10.10.96 | Köresliget | ac. heart weakness | “ | $1^{40}$ | |
| 5 | ″ Pol | 135513 | ″ | Cynamon Maks | 6. 3. 06 | Pnicwo | “ | “ | $1^{40}$ | |
| 6 | ″ Hun | 135522 | ″ | Davidovics Miklos | 3. 3. 25 | Nagyvarad | “ | “ | $1^{45}$ | |
| 7 | ″ ″ | 135537 | ″ | Dub Oskar | 16. 3. 26 | Marmarosziget | “ | “ | $1^{45}$ | |
| 8 | ″ Pol | 135540 | ″ | Dudelczyk Motek | 5.10.23 | Lodz | “ | “ | $1^{45}$ | |

| 570 Cont No | Prisoner's Type | Prisoner's No | Camp | Last and First Name | Birth- Day | Birth- Place | Cause of Death | Day of Death | Hour of Death | 571 |
|---|---|---|---|---|---|---|---|---|---|---|
| 8419 | Jew Hun | 135549 | Solvay | Edelmann Georg | 30. 3. 19 | Pelgar | ac. heart weakness | 19. 3. 1945 | $1^{45}$ | |
| 8420 | " Pol | 135554 | " | Eisenberg Max | 17. 4. 97 | Lodz | " | " | $1^{45}$ | |
| 1 | " Hun | 135559 | " | Engländer Lajos | 1. 2. 05 | Munkacs | " | " | $1^{50}$ | |
| 2 | " " | 135565 | " | Farkas Aron | 15.10.06 | Mesaszenygel | " | " | $1^{50}$ | |
| 3 | " Pol | 135575 | " | Felbe Simon | ? 1891 | Luslavice | " | " | $1^{50}$ | |
| 4 | " Hun | 135577 | " | Felbermann Mozes | 14.10.27 | Ungvar | " | " | $1^{50}$ | |
| 5 | " " | 135579 | " | Fendrich Simon | 3. 2. 94 | Satoraljaujhely | heart a. circ. weakness – heart muscle inf. | " | $1^{50}$ | |
| 6 | " " | 135580 | " | Fenner Emil | 14. 6. 27 | Szilagysomlya | " " " " " " | " | $1^{50}$ | |
| 7 | " " | 135587 | " | Fischer Leon | 21. 5. 92 | Mozsor | " " " " " " | " | $1^{55}$ | |
| 8 | " " | 135586 | " | Fischer Josef | 25. 6. 96 | Pelsöe | " " " " " " | " | $1^{55}$ | |
| 9 | " Pol | 135596 | " | Fogel Icek | 14. 8. 21 | Turek | ac. heart weakness | " | 2 | |
| 8430 | " Hun | 135597 | " | Forkovits Mandel | 15. 5. 94 | Marmarosziget | " | " | 2 | |
| 1 | " Pol | 135598 | " | Forma Jakob | 13. 9. 17 | Lodz | " | " | 2 | |
| 2 | " Hun | 135601 | " | Fränkel Samuel | 21. 8. 01 | Nagy Linoska | " | " | 2 | |
| 3 | " " | 135602 | " | Frenkel Jakub | 1. 5. 10 | Lask | " | " | 2 | |
| 4 | " " | 135606 | " | Fried Imre | 17.11.00 | Ura | " | " | 2 | |
| 5 | " " | 135607 | " | Fried Jakob | 10. 6. 96 | Keresfelek | " | " | $2^{10}$ | |
| 6 | " " | 135608 | " | Fried Jakub | 2. 8. 00 | Iluszt | " | " | $2^{10}$ | |
| 7 | " " | 135613 | " | Friedländer Jenö | 4. 1. 02 | Farolosin | heart a. circ. weakness – heart muscle inf. | " | $2^{15}$ | |
| 8 | " " | 135618 | " | Friedman Ernö | 6. 1. 24 | Mikala | " " " " " " | " | $2^{15}$ | |
| 9 | " " | 135621 | " | Friedmann Iszak | 22. 6. 27 | Bergszasz | " " " " " " | " | $2^{15}$ | |
| 8440 | " " | 135634 | " | Fuchs Deszö | 30.10.02 | " | ac. heart weakness | " | $2^{15}$ | |
| 1 | " " | 135638 | " | Fuchs Simon | 10.12.98 | Auschandor | " | " | $2^{15}$ | |
| 2 | " Pol | 135640 | " | Fuks Bencjou | 20. 7. 09 | Lodz | " | " | $2^{15}$ | |
| 3 | " " | 135647 | " | Gabrelewics Mojzes | 28.12.11 | " | " | " | $2^{20}$ | |
| 4 | " " | 135652 | " | Gasior Moritz | 10.10.04 | " | " | " | $2^{20}$ | |
| 5 | " Hun | 135654 | " | Gelber Moric | 1. 6. 27 | Nyirmegyes | " | " | $2^{20}$ | |
| 6 | " Pol | 135661 | " | German Abraham | 28.12.07 | Lodz | heart a. circ. weakness – heart muscle inf. | " | $2^{20}$ | |
| 7 | " " | 135662 | " | Gerszi Bincen | 18. 9. 05 | " | " " " " " " | " | $2^{25}$ | |

At the Mauthausen concentration camp in Austria, the camp officials produced a 'death book' by entering precise handwritten personal information about prisoners who died. Four pages are reproduced here, the first of 20 pages which list deaths for 19 March 1945. These entries exemplify both the Nazi passion for maintaining records of their murderous accomplishments and the systematic falsification which characterizes these records.

For 19 March there are 280 entries. All but the last two are labelled 'Jew'. The entries provide precise times of death, which are entered in chronological order, beginning at 1.15 in the morning, continuing usually at 5- or 10-minute intervals until 4.30 in the afternoon. The Jewish fatalities happen to be in alphabetical order. The prisoner numbers are also in order, including on average every seventh person in a span of about 2000 numbers. Only two causes of death are mentioned: 'acute heart weakness' and 'heart and circulatory weakness – heart muscle infection'. The two non-Jewish prisoners who are listed at the top of the first page, although their deaths supposedly occurred two days later on 21 March, show the only variation in the cause of death. A great deal of bureaucratic effort went into the creation of the death book. Dead Jews were identified, alphabetized, and their birth information gathered. It is reasonable to assume that the names listed here represent only a portion of those who actually died on 19 March.

The conditions in Mauthausen deteriorated in late 1944 and early 1945, when the camp was enlarged to hold the newly deported Hungarian Jews. During 1944 the average daily death toll was about 40, before the flow of Hungarian Jews reached its peak. Other camps were being evacuated in the East as the Soviet armies advanced, and many of these prisoners were sent by train and on foot to Mauthausen. Hundreds arrived already dead, and many others died before they could be recorded. The total population of Mauthausen in late 1944 reached over 110,000. Hundreds of pages of the Mauthausen death list are contained in Nuremberg document PS-493. Between 18 March and 25 April, over 6600 names are listed, nearly 200 per day.

The camp was located near the village of the same name, 14 miles from Linz. Local citizens provided food, drink and skilled labor to the camp, arranged for the cremation of some of the bodies of prisoners, bartered goods and services for the valuables taken from inmates, and smelled the smoke from burning bodies. They also volunteered for a massive hunting party, when a few hundred Soviet POWs escaped in February 1945, just before war's end.[1]

American armed forces entered Mauthausen on 5 May. Another 3000 inmates died in the days after liberation. After the six extermination camps in Poland, Mauthausen was the deadliest camp: about 120,000 people met their deaths there.

## Note

1 In a unique study, Gordon J. Horwitz interviewed local residents who remember the camp, to find out how such camps extended into the surrounding communities: *In the Shadow of Death: Living Outside the Gates of Mauthausen* (New York: Free Press, 1990).

# 66. Report of SS doctor on health conditions in Neuengamme, 29 March 1945

SS Garrison Doctor Hamburg-Neuengamme, 29 March 45
C.C. Hmb.-Neuengamme

Az.: 14h (KL) 3.45/Tr./Mue
Re: Quarterly report on medical condition of prisoners in Con.Camp Hmb.-Neuengamme

Reference: Letter of 27 Dec. 1944 Nr. 242/Az. 14h (KL) 12.44/Dr.Lg.-/Wy.-
Attached: 2 graphs
Deadline: 1 April 45

To the
Director of Medical Service
in SS Economic and Administrative Main Office
and Manager of Bureau D III,
Oranienburg

I. Conc. Camp

1.) the average population in the concentration camp Hmb.-Neuengamme during the quarter under review numbered 40,393 prisoners (including the satellite work camps). In addition are an average of 11,768 female prisoners.

2.) 6,224 deaths occurred during the quarter under review (from 26 December 1944 to 25 March 1945), including 95 female prisoners....

3.) The average population in the infirmaries 1, 2, 3, 4, 5 during the quarter under review numbered 1,711 prisoners daily.

4.) An average of 815 prisoners were treated daily as out-patients during the time under review.

5.) During the period under review one prisoner was castrated in the infirmary C.C. Hmb.-Neuengamme....

6.) 51 prisoners with open tuberculosis and 190 prisoners with closed tuberculosis are presently being treated as in-patients.

Despite the raw, damp weather in the past quarter under review, stomach and intestinal illnesses in C.C. Hmb.-Neuengamme could be held to an acceptable level.

At present, 71 prisoners with stomach and intestinal illnesses are being treated as in-patients.

89 prisoners with edema are presently being treated. Those with stomach and intestinal illnesses continue to receive special diet with white bread. In the aseptic department, the following were reported in the past quarter under review:

7 cases of scarlet fever
254 cases of open TB
292 cases of closed TB
34 cases of erysipelas
17 cases of diphtheria
2 cases of gonorrhea
1 case of syphilis
6 cases of paratyphus
8 cases of abdominal typhus

7.) The hygienic conditions in the barracks in C.C. Hmb.-Neuengamme provide no reason for objection. The provision of water is in equally unobjectionable condition.

All the camps and infirmaries are regularly disinfected with chloride of lime or cresol by a special squad. A further special squad inspects all camps and infirmaries for the presence of vermin and scabies. Those carrying lice are appropriately deloused. In cases of stronger infestations the whole barracks is disinfected.

It should be mentioned that "Zyklon B" is no longer available, and that a noticeable shortage of "Lauseto" exists.

The camp inmates are bathed once per week. As far as available, clean clothing is distributed.

During the period under review larger transports were again conveyed to the satellite work camps for work purposes. Many sick transports were needed during the time under review. The majority of the returned patients had to be taken into the infirmaries.

The satellite work camps were inspected repeatedly during the period under review by the SS garrison doctor and the SS camp doctors. Existing problems were remedied and improvements made....

SS Troops

1.) The average strength of the SS troops (including commander, staff, SS troops) numbered 2211 SS members during the month or quarter under review (including the satellite work camps).

2.) 7 SS members died during the time under review....

IV. Other ...

4.) The provisioning of the SS troops remains good and sufficient. The provisioning of the prisoners is constantly checked by the camp doctor and is also sufficient.

In order to determine if the prisoners receive the amount of foodstuffs to which they are entitled, it was ordered by the garrison doctor of C.C. Hmb.-Neuengamme, that the entire prisoner ration for eight days, including full portions for normal and heavy workers, be tested for calorie content in the chemical laboratory of Army District X Wandsbeck.

The results were satisfactory. In general, the portions given to the prisoners correspond to the amounts in the menu....

It follows, though, that the diet due to the prisoners, and according to the results of the investigation, that they actually receive, when the work demanded of the prisoners is considered, is sufficient to keep them barely above water, that from this food extra reserves for work cannot be stored, and thus a slow but constant sinking of strength of each prisoner must be counted on....

No further special features are to be reported.

SS Garrison Doctor
C.C. Hmb.-Neuengamme

---

The dry factual tone of this report obscures the remarkable information it contains and the callous attitudes it demonstrates. The irrationality and internal contradictions of SS medicine are apparent throughout the report.

The SS doctor reported that 12% of the 52,000 total prisoners at Neuengamme had died within the past three months, a yearly mortality rate of about 50%. He then described the treatment of sick prisoners and hygienic measures, as if such efforts might mitigate this appalling human catastrophe. In contrast, the yearly death rate of the SS soldiers was about 1%. Neuengamme's prisoners were mainly Poles and Soviet POWs. Over 40 satellite work camps used Neuengamme prisoners as slave labor for varied tasks in the armaments industry. From this report, it appears that mortality was many times higher for men than for women. Hospital facilities were maintained, and thousands of prisoners received some medical treatment, however inadequate.

The diet of the prisoners was tested carefully to insure that they received exactly the calories that were prescribed by the detailed instructions from the administration of the camps. These results were 'satisfactory'. Yet the doctor freely accepted that the prisoner diet was so deficient that they would all gradually lose strength and die. The extraordinary death rate is, to him, not a 'special feature'.

Although the SS doctor offers no indication that the war is nearly over, the evacuation of Neuengamme began a few weeks after this report was written. Thousands of prisoners were marched out of Neuengamme, including nearly 10,000 Jews who were marched 60km to Lübeck, loaded onto two ships in the harbor, and put to sea, where British planes were bombing all vessels. Very few survived.

One month after this report, on 29 April 1945, British troops entered Neuengamme, but few inmates were still alive. About 55,000 people died there, just 15km from the center of Hamburg, Germany's second-largest city.

Section VIII

# Assembly Lines of Death: Extermination Camps

The death camps were the most remarkable, inventive, unprecedented aspect of the Holocaust. Even finding a set of words to label them has proved elusive: I first heard the phrase 'assembly line of death' ('Fliessband des Todes') from the mouth of Franz Suchomel, an SS guard at Treblinka who was filmed secretly by Claude Lanzmann in his astonishing film 'Shoah'. On these 6 spots of earth, over 3 million people were murdered in 3 years using the most highly developed industrial methods of transportation, killing, and disposal. The vast riches that Globocnik tallied up in the table shown previously (document 54) were carefully separated from the new arrivals, individually made destitute by previous persecution, but collectively a source of the resources needed to run the whole operation. At Treblinka the SS boasted 'from door to door in 45 minutes'.

The Germans dismantled these camps as much as possible before the advancing Soviet armies and destroyed much of the documentation they had created. After the war, camp guards told lies in countless trials. So this section relies on the words of victims, mainly but not all survivors, to describe the industrialization of genocide. The one exception is the testimony of Kurt Gerstein in the next document, a Nazi participant who tried to tell what he had seen.

# 67. Postwar deposition about the use of gas chambers in Belzec in August 1942

... On 10 March 1941 I joined the SS.... In January 1942 I became the department head of the Department of Health Technology ... I took over in this capacity the whole technical disinfection service, including disinfection with highly poisonous gases.

In this capacity I received a visit on 8 June 1942 from SS-Sturmführer Günther from the Reich Security Main Office, at that point unknown to me .... He gave me the order, immediately for an extremely secret Reich mission to obtain 100 kg. of hydrocyanic acid and with it to travel to an unknown place by car, which was known only to the driver of the car. We drove then a few weeks later to Prague. I could figure out approximately the type of mission, and took it, however, because this gave me by chance a long desired opportunity to look into these things....

We drove then by car to Lublin, where SS-Gruppenführer Globocnek[1] expected us.... Globocnek said: "This entire matter is one of the most secret things, which exist at the moment, one can say the most secret. Whoever speaks about it, will be shot on the spot. Just yesterday two chatterboxes were shot." Then he explained to us:

At the moment – this was on 17 August 1942 – we have three installations in operation, namely

1. Belcec, on the road and train route Lublin-Lemberg, on the intersection with the demarcation line with Russia. Top capacity per day 15,000 persons.

2. Treblinca, 120 kilometers northeast of Warsaw. Top capacity 25,000 persons per day.

3. Sobibor, also in Poland, I don't know exactly where. 20,000 persons top capacity per day.

4. – Then in preparation – Maidanek near Lublin....

The next day we drove to Belcec. A small special train station had been built for this purpose on a hill just north of the Lublin-Lemberg road .... Close to the little two-track station was a large barracks, the so-called changing room, with a large valuables counter. Then followed a room with about 100 chairs, the hair-cutting room. Then a small path outside under birch trees, right and left surrounded by double barbed wire, with the signs: "To the

Inhalation and Bathing Rooms!" In front of us a kind of bathhouse with geraniums, then some steps, and then right and left 3 rooms each 5 by 5 meters, 1.90 meters high, with wooden doors like garages. On the back wall, in the darkness not easily visible, large wooden loading doors. On the roof as a "clever little joke" the star of David!! – In front of the building a sign: Heckenholt Foundation! – I was not able to see more on that afternoon.

On the next morning just before seven o'clock I was told: in ten minutes the first transport arrives! – In a few minutes the first train from Lemberg did actually arrive. 45 boxcars with 6700 people, of which 1450 were already dead on their arrival. Behind the barred windows, dreadfully pale and fearful children looked out, eyes full of mortal fear, further men and women. The train pulls in: 200 Ukrainians rip open the doors and whip the people with their leather whips out of the cars. A large loudspeaker gives the next instructions: "Completely undress, including prostheses, glasses, etc. Turn in valuables at the window, without receipt. Tie shoes carefully together" (for the textile collection), since in the pile at least 25 meters high nobody would be able to find the shoes that went together. Then the women and girls to the hairdresser, who with two or three swipes of the scissors cuts off all the hair and it disappears into potato sacks. "That is intended for some special purpose for submarines, for sealing or the like!" says the SS-Unterscharführer who is on duty there.

Then the column moves off. At front a pretty young girl, they go down the path, all naked, men, women, children, without prostheses. I myself stand with Captain Wirth up on the ramp between the chambers. Mothers with their babies at the breast, they come up, hesitate, step into the death chambers! – At the corner stands a strong SS-man, who says to these poor people with a pastoral voice: "Nothing in the least will happen to you! You must only breathe deeply in the chambers, that expands the lungs, this inhalation is necessary against sicknesses and epidemics." To the question what would happen to them, he answers: "Yes, naturally the men must work, building houses and roads, but the women don't need to work. Only if they want, they can help in the household or in the kitchen." – For some of these poor people a small glimmer of hope, which is enough that they go without opposition the few steps to the chambers – the majority knows what is happening, the smell announces their fate! – So they climb up the steps and then they see everything. Mothers with children at the breast, little naked children, adults, men and women, all naked – they hesitate, but they step into the death chamber, pushed by others behind them or driven by the leather whips of the SS. The majority without saying a word. A Jewess of about 40 years with burning eyes calls the blood which will be spilled here onto the murderers. She gets 5 or 6 blows with the whip in the face, from Captain Wirth personally, then she too disappears into the chamber. – Many people pray. I pray with them, I press myself into a corner and cry loudly to my and their

God. How much I would like to go with them into the chambers, how I would like to die with them. Then they would find a uniformed SS officer in their chambers – the incident would be understood and treated as an accident, and unceremoniously forgotten. So I may not yet, I must still make known what I experience here! – The chambers are filled. "Pack them full" – so commanded Captain Wirth. The people stand on each others' feet. 700–800 on 25 square meters, in 45 cubic meters! The SS forces them together, as much as possible. – The doors close. Meanwhile the rest wait outside, naked. Someone says to me: "In winter, too, the same thing!" "Yes, they could catch their death of cold," I say. "Yeah, that's just what they're here for!" says an SS-man in his dialect. – Now I finally understand also, why the whole plant is called the Heckenholt Foundation. Heckenholt is the driver of the diesel engine, a little engineer, also the builder of the facility. With the diesel exhaust gases the people are supposed to be killed. But the diesel engine doesn't work! Captain Wirth comes. One sees how painful it is for him, that this happens today, when I am here. Yes, I see everything! And I wait. My stopwatch faithfully records it all. 50 minutes, 70 minutes – the diesel doesn't start! The people wait in their gas chamber. Futilely. One hears them crying, sobbing.... Captain Wirth hits the Ukrainian, who should help Unterscharführer Heckenholt with the engine, with his whip, 12, 13 times in the face. After 2 hours, 49 minutes – the stopwatch has recorded everything – the engine starts. Up to this moment, the people are living in these 4 chambers, four times 750 people in four times 45 cubic meters! – Another 25 minutes pass. Right, many are now dead. One sees that through the little window, as the electric light illuminates the chambers for a moment. After 28 minutes only a few still live. Finally, after 32 minutes everything is dead!—

From the other side men from the work detail open the wooden doors. One had promised them – Jews – freedom and a certain percentage of all found valuables for their terrible service. Like basalt pillars, the dead stand upright, pressed against each other in the chamber. There had been no place to fall over or even to lean forward. Even in death one can recognize the families. They hold each other's hands, stiffened in death, so that one has difficulty tearing them apart, in order to clear the chamber for the next load. One throws the bodies out – wet from sweat and urine, smeared with excrement, menstrual blood on the legs. Children's bodies fly through the air. There is no time, the whips of the Ukrainians whistle down on the work detail. Two dozen dentists open the mouths with hooks and look for gold. Gold left, without gold right. Other dentists break the gold teeth and crowns out of the jaws with pliers and hammers....

We drove then in the car to Warsaw. There in the train, as I tried in vain to get a bed in the sleeping car, I met the Secretary of the Swedish Embassy in Berlin, Baron von Otter. Still under the immediate impression of the horrible experiences, I told him everything, with the request to report this immediately to his government and to the Allies, since every day's delay could cost further thousands and ten thousands their lives.... I met then Mr. von Otter again two times in the Swedish Embassy. He had meanwhile reported to Stockholm and told me that this report had had considerable influence on Swedish-German relations. I tried similarly to make a report to the Papal Nuncio in Berlin. There I was asked if I were a soldier. Thereupon any further conversation with me was refused, and I was ordered to leave the Embassy of His Holiness....

All of my information is literally true. I am fully aware of the extraordinary importance of these notes before God and all of humanity, and swear an oath that nothing of what I have recorded was invented or made up, but that everything was exactly so....

---

Kurt Gerstein made this deposition on 4 May 1945. Although he had been a Nazi since 1933, he spent time in a concentration camp for his religious activities. When he found out that his sister-in-law had been killed in the euthanasia action, he determined to see the deadly machinery for himself. Gerstein was able to get into the SS and use his medical and engineering knowledge to become an acknowledged expert on the use of poison gases for disinfection, and later for the gas chambers. He was the middleman between the producers of hydrocyanic acid, or Zyklon B, and the concentration camps. But he also said he encouraged opposition to the Nazis. He committed suicide in a French prison on 25 July 1945.

As in the cases above of Dr Möller's complaint about the murders of Polish civilians and Carl's report of Einsatzgruppen shootings in Sluzk, Gerstein's will to describe in detail how murder was done was connected with his opposition to the genocidal project. He might be labelled as an 'unwilling executioner', for he participated in the operation of the gas chambers at the extermination camps, while also trying to alert various foreign officials.

Captain Christian Wirth first appeared at the experimental gassing of the handicapped. After Belzec was dismantled, he moved to the Italian concentration camp La Risiera di San Sabba, where he organized deportations to Auschwitz. Wirth was assassinated by Yugoslav partisans in 1944.

## Note

1 Gerstein misspells a number of names and places in his deposition.

# 68. Memoir by Filip Müller on use of gas chambers at Auschwitz in 1942

It was dawn, a few hours before roll-call, when we entered the crematorium yard. The prisoners in the camp were still asleep. But the SS men with their machine-guns in their watch-towers were particularly vigilant at that hour, for it was at break of day that prisoners would decide upon the only way of escape: across the prohibited area into the high-tension barbed-wire fence.

Oberscharführer Quackernack turned up with several young SS-Unterführers. Today we noticed, they did not carry any truncheons. Once more we had to stand by the wall beneath the window of the cremation room. For a few minutes there was tense silence. Then we heard the noise of trucks approaching. They stopped outside the crematorium yard, the engines were switched off and all was silent once more until the two halves of the wooden gate were opened. A procession of a few hundred middle-aged men and women entered the yard. Once again there was also a sprinkling of old people and children. Peaceably they came in, showing none of the signs of utter exhaustion we had observed in the people of a few days earlier. Their SS escorts, too behaved differently: there was no shouting, no goading, guns were carefully tucked away in their pockets, and not a word of abuse passed their lips. The guards at the gate were becoming impatient. They thought the prisoners could smell a rat; the column was walking far too slowly, and before they could close the gate they had to wait until the very last person, a little one-legged man limping on crutches, had reached the yard.

We, too, thought the surprisingly gentle demeanor of the SS men very odd indeed. They looked amiable, they behaved affably, directing people like traffic policemen to get them distributed right across the yard. Some of the arrivals looked around curiously but also somehow alarmed before putting down their small suitcases, rucksacks and parcels. They spoke Polish and Yiddish. I was able to catch a few words and learned that these people had been working in a factory. From there they were deported quite suddenly, supposedly for important work using their special skills. Although the behavior of the SS men gave them no cause for alarm, the locked yard made them suspicious and afraid. The main subject of their conversation was work, for they were all skilled workers, and death, for they were fully aware of their situation and were anxiously looking for some glimmer of hope. Would they be given an opportunity of doing something useful? For life in the ghetto – and their yellow Stars of David indicated that it was thence they had come – had taught them that only the useful had a chance of survival.

And how were we to act in this situation? Was there anything at all we could do? For we knew only too well what was going to happen to these people within the next hour. We stood rooted against the wall, paralyzed by a feeling of impotence and the certainty of their and our inexorable fate. Alas, there was no power on earth which could have saved these poor innocent wretches. They had been condemned to death by a megalomaniac dictator who had set himself up to be judge and jury. Hitler and his henchmen had never made a secret of their attitude to the Jews nor of their avowed intention to exterminate them like vermin. The whole world knew it, and knowing it remained silent; was not this silence equivalent to consent? It was considerations like these which led my companions and me to the conviction that the world consented to what was happening here before our eyes.

Would anything have been changed in the course of events if any of us had stepped out and, facing the crowd, had shouted: "Do not be deceived, men and women, you are taking your last walk, a terrible death in the gas chamber awaits you!" The majority would not have believed us because it was too terrible to be believed. On the other hand a warning like this would have led to a panic, ending in a bloody massacre and our certain death. Did we have the right to take such a risk and, in taking it, to gamble away our chance to go on living for the time being? What, at that moment, was more important: a few hundred men and women, still alive but facing imminent death from which there was no saving them, or a handful of eyewitnesses, one or two of whom might, at the price of suffering and denial of self, survive to bear witness against the murderers some day?

All at once the crowd fell silent. The gaze of several hundred pairs of eyes turned upwards to the flat roof of the crematorium. Up there, immediately above the entrance to the crematorium, stood Aumeier, flanked by Grabner, and by Hössler who later was put in charge of the women's camp. Aumeier spoke first. His voice thick with booze, he talked persuasively to these frightened, alarmed and doubt-racked people. "You have come here," he began, "to work in the same way as our soldiers who are fighting at the front. Anybody who is able and willing to work will be all right." After Aumeier it was Grabner's turn. He asked the people to get undressed because, in their own interest, they had to be disinfected. "First and foremost we shall have to see that you are healthy," he said.

"Therefore everyone will have to take a shower. Now, when you've had your showers, there'll be a bowl of soup waiting for you all." Life flooded back into the upturned faces of the men and women listening eagerly to every word. The desired effect had been achieved: initial suspicion gave way to hope, perhaps even to the belief that everything might still end happily. Hössler sensing the change of mood quickly began to speak. In order to invest this large-scale deception with the semblance of complete honesty, he put on a perfect act to delude these unsuspecting people. "You over there in the corner," he cried, pointing at a little man, "what's your trade?" "I'm a tailor," came the prompt reply. "Ladies' or gents'?" inquired Hössler. "Both," the little man replied confidently. "Excellent!" Hössler was delighted. "That's precisely the sort of people we need in our workrooms. When you've had your shower, report to me at once. And you over there, what can you do?" He turned to a good-looking middle-aged woman who as standing right in front. "I am a trained nurse, sir," she replied. "Good for you, we urgently need nurses in our hospital, and if there are any more trained nurses among you, please report to me immediately after your shower."

Now it was Grabner's turn again. "We need craftsmen of all kinds, fitters, electricians, motor mechanics, welders, bricklayers and cement mixers; you must all report. But we'll also need unskilled helpers. Everybody is going to get well-paid work here." and he finished with the words: "Now get undressed quickly, otherwise your soup will get cold."

All the people's fears and anxieties had vanished as if by magic. Quiet as lambs they undressed without having to be shouted at or beaten. Each tried his or her best to hurry up with their undressing so that they might be among the first to get under the shower. After a very short time the yard was empty but for shoes, clothing, underwear, suitcases and boxes which were strewn all over the ground. Cozened and deceived, hundreds of men, women and children had walked, innocently and without a struggle, into the large windowless chamber of the crematorium. When the last one had crossed the threshold, two SS men slammed shut the heavy iron-studded door which was fitted with a rubber seal, and bolted it.

Meanwhile, the Unterführers on duty had gone onto the crematorium roof, from where the three SS leaders had addressed the crowd. They removed the covers from the six camouflaged openings. Then, protected by gas-masks, they poured the green-blue crystals of the deadly gas into the gas chamber.

At Grabner's command the engines of the trucks still standing near by were turned on. Their noise was to prevent anyone in the camp from hearing the shouting and the banging on the doors of the dying in the gas chamber. We, however, were spared nothing, but had to witness everything in close proximity. It was as though Judgement Day had come. We could clearly hear heart-rending weeping, cries for help, fervent prayers, violent banging and knocking and, drowning everything, the noise of the truck engines running at top speed. Aumeier, Grabner and Hössler were checking by their watches the time it took for the noise inside the gas chamber to cease, cracking macabre jokes while they were waiting, like "The water in the showers must be very hot to make them scream so loudly." Their triumphant faces showed clearly that they were delighted with the easy victory they had today scored over the declared arch-enemy of the Third Reich. When the groans and death-rattles had stopped the engines were switched off. One more mission in the campaign called *Sonderbehandlung* (Special Treatment) had been successfully completed.

Shortly afterward camp life awoke to a new day. Ration carriers were lugging vats of tea into the barracks, senior prisoners were busy getting ready for counting roll-call, Kapos were assigning prisoners to working parties, and from the camp we could hear the rousing music of the camp orchestra sending the prisoners off to work.

Aumeier and his underlings had climbed down from the roof. With some considerable pride he turned to Stark and Quackernack who were walking by his side and remarked like a master addressing his apprentices: "Well, you two, have you got it now? That's the way to do it!"

Afterwards this technique was used as a reliable method for the mass extermination of human beings without bloodshed, and it began to assume monstrous proportions. From the end of May 1942 one transport after another vanished in this way into the crematorium of Auschwitz.

---

Filip Müller arrived at Auschwitz from Slovakia in April 1942, where he soon was made part of the Sonderkommando, the special detail of Jews who cleared the corpses out of the gas chambers and burned them. Remarkably he survived to liberation, although the *Sonderkommando* was constantly subjected to selections. His memoir brings the reader to the center of the Auschwitz death factory, the gas chambers and crematoria. Even at this final stage of the Holocaust operation, the perpetrators invented and taught others procedures which allowed for efficient processing of thousands of unsuspecting arrivals.

Müller alludes to the feeling within the camps of being abandoned by the outside world, how this contributed to passivity and a sense of hopelessness. Yet even the most degraded prisoners of the *Sonderkommando* preserved the hope to survive as an eyewitness; was this an *ex post facto* justification of his participation in the process of industrial death? or a reason to try to last one more day?

Of the SS guards mentioned by Müller, Hans Aumeier and Maximilian Grabner were sentenced to death by a Polish court in 1947, in a larger trial of Auschwitz guards; Franz Hössler was executed in 1945 by the British for his activities in Bergen-Belsen; Hans Stark was a defendant in the 1963–1965 Frankfurt trial of the Auschwitz SS, found guilty, but dealt with leniently because he was under 21 during the Holocaust.

Filip Müller's question continues to reverberate in contemporary discussions of the Holocaust and the behavior of western governments, of the Pope, of the bystanders: was silence equivalent to consent?

# 69. Memoir by Irene Schwarz of Gestapo office work at Birkenau

... I worked the night shift in the Revier of the women's camp in Birkenau, along with twenty other Jewish secretaries. Our chief was Frinke, a German communist prisoner. She was a bespectacled women, a typical clerk. As Blockälteste, or chief of both the hospital and the office, she controlled the entire roll call of the hospital. Her supervisor, the German physician-in-chief, Dr. Vetter, came to the office every day on his motorcycle to sign various documents prepared for him in advance....

The night shift started at seven o'clock in the evening and finished at six in the morning, precisely when roll call was held. Every night we had to type death certificates. For each dead prisoner there was a card to be processed according to specific regulations. The hour of death had to be indicated; for the directive permitted only one death every two minutes and the morning and evening roll calls were the points of departure in our time schedule. The notations were as mechanical as those of an army payroll. "After evening roll call at 7:02 P.M. the Dutch Jewish prisoner X died of pneumonia. At 7:04 P.M. the Polish Jewish prisoner Y died of tuberculosis at Lagerstrasse," etc., etc. The typists could choose any time and any of the thirty-four prescribed diseases for the victim's death. They usually preferred heart failure, because the short word in German (*Herzschwäche*) facilitated the fulfilment of quotas. The card had to be filled in accurately although the information was utterly false, since the cause of death was always the gas chamber. These documents were completed with the signature of an SS physician, and then telegrams were sent announcing the demise of the prisoner.

Shortly after I started to work at the Revier, an epidemic of typhus and spotted fever broke out which caused between four and five hundred deaths daily in Birkenau. It had been an extremely hot summer. There was no water. The barracks had been built on swamps under which, according to rumor, the corpses of fourteen thousand Russian prisoners had been buried. It was said that they had constructed the barracks of Birkenau and this was why they were called "Russian barracks". Conditions there were horrible. There were no facilities whatsoever, and the crumbs of food were vile. When the prisoners returned from hard labor in the *Aussenkommandos*, they rushed to the rain puddles and fought for every drop of this muddy, contaminated water. No wonder there was an epidemic of spotted fever.

"We have about four hundred and fifty reports of death today," Frinke shouted. "You must finish the records by five o'clock in the morning. Any of you who misspells a name or makes a mistake in the numbers may prepare for Block 25." Each of us knew the meaning. Block 25 faced our office and it contained those destined for the gas chamber. The women in it lay in rags, mud and excrement. Some of them grasped the iron gates of the windows, moaning and yelling. They knew that soon SS men, together with SS Arbeitsführerin Dreschler and three or four of her assistants, would throw them onto a truck headed for the gas chamber and then the crematorium.

Every night I would look out of the office. Punctually at half-past eight, a truck would arrive with the SS guard. Shortly after I would hear the cries of the victims, who, beaten with guns and truncheons, were pulled by their hair and limbs and flung onto the truck. I would also hear the callous laughter of the SS who were usually given a supplementary ration of two or three liters of brandy to carry out this job. Through the square window of the office, one could see the beams of huge searchlights illuminating the entire camp, the electrical wires with their white poles and the guard-house with the SS-sentinels. Truck after truck would leave with its cargo, until Block 25 was empty. In the morning, immediately after roll call and before the prisoners' details left for work, the block would again be crammed with fuel for the chimneys, which operated day and night. There were five such chimneys in Auschwitz. They consumed their innocent victims, transforming them to ashes, which, in conformity with practical Nazi economy, were utilized as fertilizer.

The look in my eyes and the expression on my face were frozen. I was called a mummy because I rarely spoke and never laughed, although laughter had once been one of my trademarks. I was always exhausted by the constant pressure of work and the eternal threat of Block 25. Mountains of files stared me in the face and had to be in perfect order by morning. Each night I yearned to write the truth just once, to let it be known. Frinke would hand me a card and say, "Make this one 10:56 P.M. Body found on Kasernenstrasse. Heart failure." Couldn't I just write that this was a lie, an invention of the devil? That this life was snuffed out deliberately to fill the quota of the chimney? My heart bled for the mothers whose little ones were destroyed before they saw the light of day and who were then themselves assigned to heavy labor so that they would perish quickly. That is how I lost my best friend. She made the mistake of admitting that she was four months pregnant and was systematically added to the transports, depending upon the number of available places in the gas chambers. The chief of this block was an eighteen-year-old girl in high black boots who ran about her living cemetery, laughing every time a truck arrived. What made a young girl so abnormal? I recalled the words which were written above the

Holy Ark: "Keep the Lord always before thee!" In Birkenau, I always saw Block 25 before me.

---

Irene Schwarz describes the remarkable efforts by the organizers of mass death to keep meticulous records of their prisoners. Most of those deported to Auschwitz died almost immediately in the gas chambers of Birkenau, and their names disappeared with them. But the small percentage selected for slave labor were carefully entered into a card file kept by the Politische Abteilung (Political Section) of Auschwitz, run by Maximilian Grabner. The records combined fanatical attention to accuracy (no erasures were permitted on the cards) with deliberate falsification of information, in order to keep the nature of Auschwitz a secret from the outside world. SS physicians oversaw the process of death. Victims were deliberately implicated in the death process through jobs which gave them the privilege of temporary survival.

Like Filip Müller, Irene Schwarz represented the Jewish labor which performed all the work of the camps, allowing a small number of SS personnel to oversee their city of death. In the camp hierarchy, Jews typically did the meanest labor under the supervision of Aryan prisoners, who often adopted the manner of the SS in order to keep their privileged positions. But Schwarz, too, was privileged: able to work indoors at a job with less physical demands, she was more likely to survive.

It was very unusual for Jewish prisoners to be given positions with as much security as these secretaries. They were selected for their high levels of education and for particular skills with languages and typing. Despite their knowledge of the actual methods of the SS at Auschwitz and the constant deceptions practiced in the record-keeping, they were not constantly selected. Some could use these positions to participate in careful resistance activities, such as saving the lives of resistance organizers who happened to be selected for death. A number of these secretaries testified in postwar trials.

# 70. Memoir by Shalom Kohn of the revolt in Treblinka on 2 August 1943

Even before I arrived at Treblinka, i.e., before October 1, 1942, cases of individual revenge on the part of Jews had been reported. Thus, for example, a Jewish man from Warsaw who worked in one of the death details and had seen his wife and child taken away to the gas chambers, attacked the SS man Max Biel[as] with a knife and killed him on the spot. From that day on, the SS barracks bore the name of this Hitlerite "martyr." But neither the plaque on the wall of the barracks nor the massacre of Jews that followed this attack deterred us. On the contrary: this episode encouraged us to fight and take our revenge. The young man from Warsaw became our ideal.

As we witnessed Hitler's horrible methods of extermination, a desire for revenge burned within us and grew each day, starting to concretize into something precise, particularly from the moment when the 50-year-old doctor, Chorazycki of Warsaw, began to be active. This doctor worked in the camp as a "medical counsellor," a position invented by the Germans to mock the hapless victims even more cruelly before dispatching them to the gas chamber. He was a calm, prudent man who on the surface, appeared rather cold. He went around in his white apron with the Red Cross emblem on his arm as he had in the old days at his Warsaw office, and he seemed completely detached from what was going on around him. But beneath his apron beat a warm Jewish heart, aflame with a desire for revenge.

After the gruesome experiences of the day, the four plotters of the revolt met by night around his plank bed and discussed the plans. Their first problem was how to get hold of the weapons and explosives which were needed. These four men were the above-mentioned Dr. Chorazycki, the Czech army officer Zelo – a Jew, of course – Kurland from Warsaw and Lubling from Silesia. After a short time, when it was considered necessary to enlarge the organization committee, we were joined by Leon Haberman, an artisan from Warsaw; Salzberg, a furrier from Kielce; a 22-year-old youth from Warsaw named Marcus, and the Warsaw agronomist Sudowicz. We could procure arms either from the outside or else we could steal them from the Germans and Ukrainians inside the camp itself. We tried both ways. We began to make a study of the camp arsenal and the headquarters barrack.

But they were guarded by Germans and there was no way for us to get in. At first, we thought of digging a subterranean passage, but we felt this would be difficult, because of the constant danger of discovery. Then we decided at all costs to manufacture a duplicate key to the arsenal. This could only be done, however, if one of us could somehow gain access to the iron door of the arsenal. We had no alternative but to wait for a propitious moment.

An opportunity soon presented itself. Somehow the lock of the arsenal got jammed and the Germans had to call in one of the Jewish mechanics to fix it.

The Germans were extremely cautious. They had the door taken off its hinges and taken to the workshop. However, the mechanic managed to distract the attention of the German guard for just one moment, and managed to make an impression of the key in cobbler's wax. A few days later, our group received a key to the arsenal. We guarded it like a precious relic, waiting for the proper opportunity to use it. Dr. Chorazycki himself assumed the task of acquiring weapons from outside the camp. He managed to get in touch with a Ukrainian guard who agreed, for a large sum of money, of course, to buy some light weapons for us. A few of our purchases were safely smuggled in, but then something happened which put an end to our equipment and cost the life of Dr. Chorazycki. One day, while the doctor had with him a large amount of money intended for the guard, the camp's vice-commandant, SS Untersturmführer Franz, a bloody murderer notorious for his sadist methods, entered the room, accompanied by his dog, Barry. By pure chance, Franz spotted the packet of banknotes peeping out of the doctor's apron pocket.

"Give me that money!" the SS man roared. He suspected that the doctor was planning to escape from the camp. Chorazycki attacked him with a surgical lancet, stabbing him in the neck. Franz was able to jump out of the window and call for help. Well aware of the tortures which would await him, and realizing the threat to the entire conspiracy, Chorazycki swiftly swallowed a large dose of poison which the conspirators always carried on their persons. The SS men rushed up and tried to revive him in order to take their revenge, but to no avail.

In this way the initiator of the revolt died, but his death did not put an end to the matter. On the contrary, it encouraged the others to continue.

If Dr. Chorazycki was the initiator and the leader of the of the Treblinka revolt, then the title of chief of staff must be given to Captain Zelo. The participation of this military expert greatly facilitated the fulfilment of a mission which was both difficult and complicated. At difficult moments, when many of us fell prey to resignation and abandoned all hope of a revolt, Captain Zelo continued to encourage us to carry on. When he was transferred to another part of the camp, all the plans and decisions were submitted to him for his approval despite the danger involved in such contacts.

The engineer Galewski of Lodz was chosen to replace Dr. Chorazycki. He, too, dedicated himself to the cause with all his heart. He was a very cautious, reserved man, and this proved useful to our cause.

The date of the revolt was postponed several times for various reasons. The first date was fixed in April, 1943, while Dr. Chorazycki was still alive. And then the last transports of Jews from the Warsaw ghetto were brought to Treblinka. From them we first learned about the Warsaw ghetto revolt. The Germans treated them with particular savagery; most of the railroad cars were full of the corpses of ghetto fighters who had refused to leave the ghetto alive. Those who now arrived were no longer resigned and indifferent creatures like those who had come before them.

The leaders decided that the hour for the revolt had arrived. In the camp there were a number of so-called "Court Jews," boys who rendered personal services to the Germans, like cleaning their quarters, etc. These individuals enjoyed a certain freedom of movement within the camp. At times they even able to get close to the arsenal. The leadership decided to entrust to these boys the task of expropriating 100 hand grenades from the arsenal on the day of the revolt.

They proved to be equal to the task. Haberman, who worked in the German laundry, the shoeblack Marcus, and Jacek, a Hungarian boy of 17, managed to get his hands on a certain number of hand grenades. Exceptionally lithe and skilful, the boy Salzberg, age 14, son of the leader we have already mentioned, took a huge pile of SS uniforms as though he were taking them to the tailor's for pressing, but in fact the pockets of these uniforms were filled with hand grenades. Unfortunately these hand grenades lacked detonators, and for this reason the revolt had to be postponed at the very last moment.

Meanwhile, we were joined by other activists. Dr. Leichert, of Wengrow, whom the Nazis had selected from a new transport to replace Dr. Chorazycki, soon became a member of the committee. We were also joined by a Czech, Rudolf Masaryk, a relative of the late President of Czechoslovakia.[1] He had refused to leave his Jewish wife and had accompanied her to Treblinka. Here, he became one of the privileged characters and was attached to a labor detail. With his own eyes he had seen his pregnant wife being taken to the gas chamber. Masaryk became one of the most active members of the committee. We must also mention Rudek, the driver-mechanic from Plotzk, who worked in the garage. His job was very important for our operation because it was there that we stored our weapons.

Months of waiting and tension passed in this way. Every day we looked death in the face and witnessed German atrocities. Every day hundreds of thousands of men and women, stark naked, arrived in long lines at the "Jewish State" — this was the name the Germans had cynically given to the building that housed 12 gas chambers. Untersturmführer Franz kept giving us speeches: "The gas chambers will continue to operate as long as so much as one Jew is left in the world."

The desire for revenge increased all the time. The terror-stricken eyes of the Jews who were led to their death and were thrust into the gas chambers cried out for revenge.

At last the leader, Galewski, gave the signal for the revolt. The date had been set for Monday, August 2, 1943, at 5 p.m. This was the plan of action: to lay an ambush for the chief murderers and to liquidate them; to disarm the guards; to cut the telephone wires; to burn and destroy all the extermination plants so that they would never function again; to free the Poles from the Treblinka detention camp a mile away, and, together with them, flee into the woods to organize a partisan unit.

An atmosphere of great tension lay upon the camp that Monday morning. The leaders needed all their energies to calm the people down. Finally, special inspectors came to see that the normal quota of work was carried out as usual in order not to arouse suspicion. All the details of the plan were known only to the 60 people who constituted the nucleus of the fighting organization. The activists were divided into three groups and, as soon as the signal would be given, each group was to occupy the position assigned to it.

At one o'clock in the afternoon we lined up as we had been doing every day, for the roll call, the last roll call in this camp because there was never to be another. But when Galewski, the head of a group of workers, told us that work that day would end an hour earlier than usual because Scharführer Rotner was going to Malkinia to bathe in the river Bug, he gave us a little wink as though alluding to the "bath" we had prepared for the Nazis.

At two o'clock in the afternoon the distribution of weapons began. Young Salzberg and the other looked for weapons in their masters' barracks. They managed to steal about a score of rifles and one machine gun and took them to the garage. It was very difficult to steal the hand grenades from the arsenal. That day a pile of garbage was being removed from near the arsenal. This was very convenient but it disturbed the camp administrator, SS man Miller, who had just arrived and wanted to sleep. The agronomist, Sudowicz, who was in charge of the garden, called on him with the excuse of wanting to talk over some problems relating to the plants. At the same time Marcus and Salzberg picked up the rugs and beat them in front of the arsenal, so that the guards had to move out of the way for a while. At that moment the door of the arsenal was opened with our key and Jacek, the Hungarian boy, slipped inside, climbed onto the window sill at the end of the room, used a diamond to cut a small square in the glass and handed the bombs and other weapons to Jacob Miller from Wlodzimierz-Wolynski, who was waiting outside and put them on his garbage cart. The arms were taken to the garage. This time the hand grenades had their detonators all right and acted as a spur to flagging spirits.

Spirits grew agitated and it seemed that no one would be able to keep the secret. The leaders therefore decided to start the revolt an hour before the time originally agreed upon.

At four o'clock sharp that afternoon, messages were sent to all the groups with orders to assemble immediately at the garage to pick up their weapons. Rudek from Plotzk was responsible for the distribution. Anyone who came to fetch weapons had to give the password "Death!" to which the proper reply was "Life!" "Death! Life! Death! Life!" Cries of enthusiasm arose as the long-awaited rifles, revolvers and hand grenades were handed out. At the same time the chief murderers of the camp were attacked. Telephone wires were cut and the watchtowers were set on fire with gasoline. Captain Zelo attacked two SS guards with an ax and joined us to take over the command.

Near the garage stood a German armored car, but Rudek swiftly put the motor out of commission. Now the car served as an ambush from which to fire at the Germans. Our gunfire felled Sturmführer Kurt Seidler and other Nazi dogs. The arsenal was taken by assault and the captured weapons handed out to the insurgents. We already had 200 armed men. The others attacked the Germans with axes and spades.

We set fire to the gas chambers, to the "bathhouse," burned the simulated railroad station with all the fake signs: "Bialystok-Wolkowysk," "Office," "Tickets," "Waiting Room," etc. The barracks who bore the name of the Nazi hangman Max Biel[as] were ablaze too.

Captain Zelo gave commands and encouraged the men to fight. Nobody cared about his own life. A fiery spirit of revenge had taken hold of us. We had acquired more weapons; we even had a machine gun now. Rudolf Masaryk took care of it. He stationed himself on the roof of the pigeon coop and poured fire on the confused Germans. Through the exchange of fire we can hear his voice shouting, "Take that for my wife, and take that for my child who did not even have a chance to come into the world! And take that, you murderers, for the humanity which you have insulted and degraded!"

Roused to action by the flames and the firing, the Germans began to arrive from all sides. SS and police arrived from Kosów, soldiers from the nearby airfield and finally a special squad of the Warsaw SS. A full-scale battle developed. Captain Zelo was darting in and out among the flames, giving us courage and urging us to fight on. He gave orders, concise, warlike — until a Nazi bullet put an end to his life.

Night fell. The battle had already been going on for six hours. The Germans were getting reinforcements, and our ranks had become thinner. Our ammunition was running out.

We had been ordered to make for the nearby woods. Most of our fighters fell but there were many German casualties. Very few of us survived.

---

Shalom Kohn (Stanislaw Kon) worked as a building contractor in Łódź. He served in the Polish army for 18 months in 1932–1933. At the outbreak of World War II, he was called to active duty. His outfit held out for 20 days before being overrun by German tank troops. After Poland's surrender, he made his way home. On 1 October 1942, Kohn and his family were deported to Treblinka. His wife and mother-in-law went to the gas chambers, but since Kohn himself was young and strong, the Germans put him to work as a slave laborer, carrying corpses and sorting the clothes of new arrivals. He frequently received beatings from the SS men and the Ukrainian guards.

Of the 1000 prisoners in Treblinka at the time of the revolt, about 600 reached nearby forests. When the Red Army arrived about a year later, only 40 still survived. The rest had died or been killed by German army patrols or Polish partisans. Soon after the revolt, the camp at Treblinka was destroyed and the land plowed over, in an attempt to hide the existence of the camp. There is little documentation left about Treblinka, so the history of that camp must be written from the memories of the few survivors.[2]

Inmates also revolted at Sobibor and Birkenau, and in many concentration camps and ghettos. Under conditions which appeared to make even the slightest resistance impossible or suicidal, Jews and other prisoners built organizations, procured weapons, made escapes, and fought their murderers.[3]

Kurt Franz and Franz Stangl, the commandant of Treblinka, were sentenced to life in prison in Germany.

## Notes

1 The man's name was actually Masarek, but the misspelling gave rise to the legend that he was related to Masaryk.

2 Based on survivor testimony, the revolt is described by Jean-François Steiner, *Treblinka* (New York: Penguin Books USA, 1979), employing some novelistic techniques; interviews with Franz Stangl produced an equally fascinating work: Gitta Sereny, *Into That Darkness: An Examination* of Conscience (London: Andre Deutsch, 1974).

3 The great variety of resistance actions is described in Hermann Langbein, *Against All Hope: Resistance in the Nazi Concentration Camps 1938–1945*, trans. Harry Zohn (New York: Paragon House, 1994). This book was originally written in German, under a title which directly addresses the erroneous charge leveled primarily at Jews: 'not like sheep to the slaughter'.

# 71. Postwar statement by Arnest Tauber about slave labor at Auschwitz between 1942 and 1944

Declaration under Oath

I, Arnest Tauber
civil servant in the Czechoslovakian Foreign Office, after I have been made aware that I am liable to punishment by making false statements, hereby declare the following under oath voluntarily and without coercion:

1. I was arrested twice. The first time in May 1939 for the distribution of illegal leaflets. I was imprisoned for 77 days. In September 1939 I was arrested for the second time in the course of the hostage actions and brought to Dachau by way of the Pankratz Prison, and from there to Buchenwald. From Buchenwald I arrived in the main camp at Auschwitz /October 1942/ and from there after a week with the first transport to Monowitz. I was in Monowitz until 4 August 1944, then I was transferred to Treblinka.

2. In Monowitz usually four hundred prisoners slept in one block. The block was furnished for 162 prisoners. In 1943, up to 3 men slept in one bed.

At that time two tents for approximately 800 to 1000 prisoners were also erected. Each of these tents had a large exit and a small hatch-window. If a fire had broken out, and the danger of fire existed constantly, since straw was in the tents, not many people could have saved themselves. I. G. Farben was responsible for the housing.

3. At the beginning of 1943, I. G. Farben took over the provisioning of the Camp Monowitz. The food was somewhat better only in the first days after the takeover. In general, it was insufficient and had no fat at all. It consisted of 1 liter of water soup, boiled from unpeeled potatoes and other things which were not beneficial for health, so that abdominal typhus appeared in Camp Monowitz as a result of the food. In the morning there was only coffee, in the evening 375 grams of bread and an allowance of 8 grams of margarine. On many days there was a double portion of margarine.

This food was completely insufficient for our existence with the work demanded of us at the IG Buna plant. Many prisoners died as the result of undernourishment and bad clothing.

The weight of some of my fellow prisoners at I. G. Auschwitz dropped to 35-44 kilograms. The average weight was 55 kilograms.

Duerfeld, the manager of I. G. Farben Auschwitz, was completely informed about the bad food. He tasted the soup once in the spring of 1943 in my presence. He praised the soup and I asked him whether he was serious about it, to which he said: Well, it is capable of improvement.

4./ The IG Buna camp registered 30,000 deaths in the 3 years of its existence from a labor force of at most 10,000 men. I obtained this information from prisoners who were employed in the office in Monowitz and who had to know it exactly, as for example, Stefan Hymann.

5./ The hardest work that I had to do in Buna was carrying 100-pound cement sacks on the double. This work forced by the kapos was carried out on the initiative of the foreman and was general practice. I myself had to carry two cement sacks at once on the double.

If a prisoner collapsed at work, he was kicked and beaten in order to determine if he still lived. If he was dead, the body-carriers would either come right away or otherwise he would be carried into the camp in the evening on the shoulders of his comrades.

A large percentage of the deaths is also explained by accidents, insufficient protective clothing, and insufficient safety measures from I. G. Farben Auschwitz.

6./ It lay in the power of the foreman of I. G. Farben or the building firms to evaluate the productivity of the prisoners according to their own judgment. When the prisoner reached a 75% productivity, nothing happened to him. If the prisoner repeatedly achieved under 75% work and the foreman noted it on the worksheet, the prisoner would be punished with blows from a rod. There were foremen who sometimes wrote only 20% productivity. The foremen were completely informed about the consequences of a bad work evaluation. The foremen also frequently threatened that the prisoners would go to the gas because of insufficient productivity. /Here I particularly remember foreman Wittig/.

7./ In winter there was hardly a detail where cases of freezing to death did not occur daily. On a severe winter day, 30 deaths were nothing out of the ordinary. The dead had to be carried past the buildings of the I. G. management. It was impossible that Duerfeld did not see this. Duerfeld furthermore inspected the details and had to therefore know about the frequent changes in personnel.

8./ I. G. Farben not only knew about the atrocities which took place, but it also took an active part in them. I personally saw how Chief Engineer Faust beat several prisoners with a club, because the driving of loaded wagons during road construction did not function as he desired. I know that it was Chief Engineer Faust, because I inquired after his name.

Master Carpenter Wittig of detail 19 and foreman Richter frequently beat the prisoners.

9./ On the suggestion of the management of I. G., the excavation of unexploded bombs was carried out only by prisoner details under the direction of a fireman. Prisoners were used because they were worthless material. Sometimes the easiest available detail was used for this work, but there were also special details for it. Fatal accidents occurred as a result.

10./ Hygienic conditions in Monowitz were bad. The sewage system was insufficient, the garbage pits overflowed, the water was contaminated so that official warnings against drinking the water were issued.

11./ Up to 1944, one was not allowed to be sick longer than two weeks. After 1944, up to 6 weeks. That was based on the fact that I. G. Farben would pay only 14 days, or 6 weeks, for the sick prisoners. For this reason selections were carried out by the camp doctor regularly every 14 days.

Furthermore, not more than 5 % of the labor force of I. G. Auschwitz were allowed to be in the infirmary. If this number was surpassed, a selection took place, and those selected went to Birkenau to be gassed. A sickness report went to the plant management of I. G. Farben. Furthermore one discussed the gassings with the foremen at the shop-unit....

13. In July 1944, I spoke in the name of the so-called Beskide Liberation Committee, where I stressed that, due to the advance of the Soviet Army, one could soon count on being occupied by them. We urged Duerfeld to surrender the plant and the camp without a battle.... The sole result of this letter was the search for the writer.

I have carefully read and personally signed each of the 3 pages of this declaration under oath, have made the necessary corrections in my own handwriting and countersigned them with my initials, and hereby declare under oath, that I have said the whole truth in this declaration according to my best knowledge and belief.

[signature] Arnest Tauber

Sworn to and signed before me this 3rd day of March 1947 at Prag by Arnest Tauber known to me to be the person making the above affidavit.

[signature] Benvenuto von Halle
US Civilian AGO D 432532
Office of Chief of Counsel for
War Crimes U.S. War Department

Arnest Tauber gave this affidavit about his two years at Auschwitz, and then testified at the trial of I. G. Farben directors in 1947–48. Tauber participated in the national economic cooperation between the SS concentration camp empire and German industry. The chemical manufacturer I. G. Farben was the largest corporation in Europe and one of the major economic beneficiaries of the vast pool of prisoner labor in concentration camps. Representatives of the company, like the general supervisor Walter Dürrfeld (Tauber spells his name incorrectly) and Max Faust, planned the construction of an enormous facility near Auschwitz with SS architects. The camp at Monowitz was called Buna, because I. G. Farben wanted to produce synthetic rubber, called buna. I. G. Farben and other companies bought prisoners from the SS for a few Marks a day, and the SS profited from the difference between that figure and the tiny amount it spent to maintain a prisoner. The companies used up the labor power of thousands of prisoners and then returned them to the SS to be gassed.

Most of the work at Buna was the construction of an enormous industrial complex. Over 20,000 of I. G. Farben's prisoner laborers died at Auschwitz. The synthetic rubber plant was never finished. The company still profited from its relationship to Auschwitz-Birkenau: its subsidiary Degesch manufactured the Zyklon B used in the gas chambers.

At the trial, Dürrfeld stressed his own suffering and claimed that 'not one single soul, due to anything I did, lost life or health.' Of the 23 I. G. Farben executives who were tried, 13 were found guilty. Dürrfeld was convicted of slave labor, for which he received a sentence of 8 years. By 1951 all the executives had been released.[1]

## Note

1 The trial records can be found in *Trials of War Criminals under Control Council Law No. 10,* Vols. 7–8; the quotation from Dürrfeld is on p. 1078. Two books detail the role of the company at Auschwitz: Peter Hayes, *Industry and Ideology: IG Farben in the Nazi Era* (Cambridge: Cambridge University Press, 1987), and Joseph Borkin, *The Crime and Punishment of I. G. Farben* (New York: The Free Press, 1978).

# 72. Letter by British Foreign Secretary Anthony Eden about bombing Auschwitz, 7 July 1944

My dear Archie,

You will remember that I referred in the House last Wednesday to the appalling persecution of Jews in Hungary. On July 6th Weizmann, of the Jewish Agency for Palestine, came to see me with further information about it which had reached the Agency's representatives in Istanbul, Geneva and Lisbon, the main point of which was that, according to these reports 400,000 Hungarian Jews had already been deported to what he called "death camps" at Birkenau in Upper Silesia, where there are four crematoriums with a gassing and burning capacity of 60,000 a day and where, incidentally, in the course of the last year, over one and a half million Jews from all over Europe are reported to have been killed.

Dr. Weizmann admitted that there seemed to be little enough that we could do to stop these horrors, but he suggested that something might be done to stop the operation of the death camps by

(1) bombing the railway lines leading to Birkenau (and to any other similar camps if we get to hear of them); and

(2) bombing the camps themselves with the object of destroying the plant used for gassing and burning.

I should add that I told Weizmann that, as you may know, we had already considered suggestion (1) above but that I would re-examine it and also the further suggestion of bombing the camps themselves.

Could you let me know how the Air Ministry view the feasibility of these proposals? I very much hope that it will be possible to do something. I have the authority of the Prime Minister to say that he agrees.

Sincerely,
Anthony Eden

---

This letter was written to Sir Archibald Sinclair, the Secretary of State for Ai He replied a week later that British planes could not help, but that the Americans should be asked.

One of the most controversial topics in discussions of the Holocaust over the past decades has been whether the Western Allies should have taken more aggressive steps to try to stop the killing, especially by using air power to bomb Auschwitz or the rail lines to Auschwitz. Both the British and American governments and military leaders rejected suggestions for such action in 1944, prompting many commentators to accuse them of callous inaction.

The idea of using bombing to disrupt mass murder was first raised in spring 1944 in connection with the massive deportations from Hungary to Auschwitz. By that time the British and Americans were systematically bombing targets in Eastern Europe, and the function of Auschwitz as a killing center was widely known. But the lack of specific and convincing knowledge about the Holocaust prevented forceful action. Eden himself does not take responsibility for the accuracy of 'reports' about Birkenau. His hesitancy about his information was characteristic of top military and civilian policymakers in 1944.

In fact, the Hungarian deportations had already ended by the date of this letter. The final transport left on 5 July, after which the Hungarian government under Miklós Horthy, fearing eventual retaliation from the victorious Allies, forced the Germans to stop deportations out of Budapest. But many thousands more were gassed after this date.

British and American military leaders universally rejected the idea of using bombing to disrupt the Holocaust. John J. McCloy, the US Assistant Secretary of War, expressed the main justification in a letter of 18 November 1944: 'The positive solution to this problem is the earliest possible victory over Germany, to which end we should exert our entire means.'[1] Behind this operational perspective lay a general reluctance to divert significant military resources to save Jewish 'refugees'. In fact, the neighboring industrial facility at Monowitz was bombed on 20 August.

The impassioned discussions about bombing Auschwitz, both in 1944 and since, reveal the confusing nature of information about the Holocaust among Western governments, the difficulties of understanding the Nazi drive to murder millions of people, the competing interests and interpretations of decision-makers, and the underlying indifference to the anguish of the Nazis' victims.

## Note

1 This letter is reprinted, along with many other documents, in Michael J. Neufeld and Michael Berenbaum (eds), *The Bombing of Auschwitz: Should the Allies Have Attempted It?* (New York: St. Martin's Press, 2000), pp. 279–80.

# ıoir by Judith Isaacson on selection of ıen in Auschwitz, July 1944

**STAY TOGETHER!**

Auschwitz-Birkenau, Poland • July 1944

The sun was in the west when the kapo, Yellow Blouse, finished the head count. But she wouldn't let us disperse. "Single file!" she roared in her Slavic German, "Single file, you swine! Single file!" We milled about, confused. In three weeks at Auschwitz-Birkenau, we had never stood *Zähl Appell* except by fives. Red Kerchief, the assistant kapo, danced her own whip above the heads of the crowd. "C'mon, girls!" she coaxed in Hungarian, "Forget the fives!"

A telling froth bubbled from Yellow Blouse's mouth. She swooped at her young assistant. "Whip them, you devil," she croaked, "or I'll whip you to a pulp!"

I watched, hypnotized. The events of a few days ago flashed through my mind. Suppose I had not resigned as a kapo? I'd be wearing that red kerchief now. My successor raised her whip and shut her eyes. "Don't!" I wanted to shriek. But Red Kerchief struck. Once. Twice. Then again. "Damn it all," swore a comrade, "We've got another rotten kapo now."

Both kapos lashed until all of us—the entire Lager B III b—queued up into a long, twisting line. "Attention, swine!" Yellow Blouse bellowed. "Off with the rags! Medical exam."

Medical exam? My hands flew to the front of my dress. Where is the doctor? The mob buzzed, a frantic beehive. Buzzed, but hardly moved.

"Off with those rags!" echoed Red Kerchief, whipping at bare shoulders and scalps. I pulled off my dress quickly.

Mother shed her blanket and stood nude and frail in front of me. Both kapos have gone raving mad," she whispered. "I'd die if you were one of them."

But I am not — I boasted silently to Socrates and Dr. Biczó.

Magda leaned forward to whisper: "Another selection? What d'you think, Jutka?"

Red Kerchief rushed by, whipping with closed eyes: "Line up, you scum!" she shrieked, striking out at random. I winced, mortified.

"March!" barked the kapos in two languages and one voice. And we marched in a gigantic curve around and around, naked.

I was nauseated by all the nudity, the breasts, the buttocks, the pathetic pubic slits, so visible on the shaven parts. I stretched my neck to see beyond our own compound: grey earth, pale sky, thousands upon thousands of bald women swirling in the nude. Twenty-first-century Europe? The Brave New World is dwarfed by comparison — the same mad discipline, the same infernal crowding, but our world beastly, Huxley's overrefined.

A sharp whistle brought me back to the moment. Yellow Blouse yelled: "Up with the arms! March, left!"

Left? Which way was my left now? The kapos herded us with shouts and lashes. We filed out of our own compound and started, naked, down the main road between the barracks.

Glancing around, I tried to estimate the size of the crowd. Thirty or more barracks ... each barrack now down to three or four hundred: some ten to fourteen thousand nude women! Who would believe it? After the war, they would have to make a movie, a Hollywood epic — Budapest wouldn't have the props. I gazed at the scene to record every detail, more like a spectator than a participant.

My arms ached from holding the dress up high, and the tender skin around the nipples blistered in the sun. But amazement muted all pain. I was still bewildered by all the nudity, especially my own, and I blushed hotly when a male figure came into view. It was an SS officer, in full military attire, complete with hat, jacket, white gloves, and tie. Surrounded by thousands of nude women, he looked bored as he fingered his pistol.

I shall call him Dr. Mengele, because of what I've read of his role, and because several of my former comrades recognized him later from his photo. But personally, I did not think to study his features and I cannot be sure.

My attention was completely absorbed by a hound and a tall kapo who held it fast at Mengele's side. Of the group of three, man, woman, and beast, I, naively, dreaded the beast. As the nude women filed past, the hound was tugging at the leash, trying to lick the bleeding parts.

Mengele put away his pistol and began brandishing his cane. The swish of his staff parted the row of nude women into three distinct herds. He sent the majority straight ahead, toward the freight train. The sick and worn wobbled left, toward a waiting truck. A select group of young girls steered right and marched off nude, in rows of fives.

Mother glanced back, pale under her white-fuzzed scalp. "Don't worry, Jutka. We'll be off to work camps."

I whispered to Magda with lips rather than sound: "Mother is optimistic."

"Isn't she always?" Magda replied.

Ahead of us, the mob was reassembling along the railroad banking. Some of the women were still naked, others were pulling their rags back on.

"See, Magda," I pointed, "no kapos. They're staying behind. Just lucky, I resigned."

"Lucky? Have you looked left and right?"

To my right, the block of young girls was marching off in the nude. A girls' transport for the Russian front? My uncle Imre's warnings came again: "Risk your life to avoid a girls' transport."

I searched for familiar figures among my would-be comrades. I thought I recognized two: a girl from our barrack and my former classmate, Ági Salgó. Frantically I signalled to Ági, but she did not turn around; her tight twin buttocks floated away on the sea of the naked. Imre's dread image rose again—the pregnant girls, the ditch, the shots.

Magda touched my arm, pointing to the left. The discarded wobbled along, stooped and skeletal. Mechanically, a couple of striped attendants heaved the nude wretches on a waiting truck. The women on the bottom, could they breathe? Could they breathe at all? The scene on arrival came again: Sári, Dr. Nemes, the pile; I shuddered with a sudden insight into our options. Straight ahead — slave labor. To the left — death. To the right — mass rape at the Russian front.

"Magda," my voice broke, pleading. "We'll go straight ahead, won't we, Magda?"

"Can't you see?" she whispered, pointing to the right: "It's the girls' transport for us."

"Magda! But you're married!"

"It won't matter to the soldiers."

"And mother?"

Magda whispered close into my ear: "I'm terrified. Your mother is five years beyond the Nazi deadline. And her new hair has come in so white."

"Mama," I anguished, leaning forward, "let me ..." I pulled down the blanket to cover her white scalp.

"Quick!" hissed Magda, "Tell her not to walk so stooped."

"Mama," I whispered, "pull back your shoulders."

"I will, I will."

Mengele swung his staff, randomly but rhythmically, as he let the majority of the mob stream ahead, toward the freight train. But he shoved every fourth or fifth woman left or right. Five more women remained in front of us now. Selfishly, I hoped the SS would send at least one of them left or right, but Mengele's cane swept all five toward the freight train. God, my God! Mother'll go left!

Mengele's gaze fell on my nude torso, while his cane whisked mother routinely ahead. I did not have a moment to rejoice. "*Rechts!*" snapped Mengele, his cane at my breasts, "*Rechts!*"

Was it the terror of rape that emboldened me, or was it the hope of staying with my mother? Perhaps it was only a surge of adrenalin. I forgot I was naked. I forgot Mengele's gun. Ignoring his command, I started after mother. The hound growled, the SS pushed me to the right with a tone of well-meant advice: "Go with the young ones. Run!"

"I'm going with my mother!" I said, and turned back again.

"Bitch," she yelled, roughly now. "He'll shoot you down!"

"Let him," I said, suddenly calm. "I don't care." Once more I turned and followed mother, this time slowly, with deliberate steps. How easy it is to face death, I thought. In the middle of my back, a tiny spot began to tingle, expecting the bullet. The spot seared into my flesh. I glanced over my shoulder: Magda was sprinting after me, her nude thighs leaping high.

"She's my mother too!" Magda lied in fright. How beautiful she is, I thought, strangely detached.

The Kapo yelled: "Fools! He'll shoot you both!"

Mengele lifted his pistol. My eyes shut themselves. Was the gun pointed at my aunt's naked back? "Magda, run!" I cried, and we fled until we reached the thick of the crowd. I glanced back over my shoulder. Mengele's right hand was on his pistol, the left one swung the cane — ahead, ahead, fast. A statuesque blonde was next in line; Mengele's cane swept her — right. That luckless girl, I mourned, and Ági Salgó too. But my racing heart beat its own triumph: all those others, but not Magda ... A whole transport, but not I!

In the west, a red sun was sinking fast. Mother caught up with us, panting hard. "You're here! Both here, with me!" She let the blanket drop on the ground and sank on it, naked. Knees clasped in tight-knit fingers, she rocked herself, slowly, rhythmically, like a cradle. "I'm so happy! So happy! I've never been so happy in my whole life!"

---

Resistance, survival, and family are prominent themes in this excerpt from Judith Isaacson's memoir about her journey from Hungary to Auschwitz to the United States in 1944–1945. From the moment of their arrival in Auschwitz, multiple acts of individual resistance by Isaacson, her mother Rose and her aunt Magda enabled their survival. The significance of their determination to remain together echoes the stories of other survivors, such as Elie Wiesel's *Night.*

Although both women and men have written memoirs about survival since the camps were liberated, the issue of gender has only recently become prominent.[1] Isaacson's narrative of her experiences in Hungary, during 3 weeks in Auschwitz, and in the slave labor camp of Hessisch-Lichtenau deliberately highlights experiences particular to women. She reveals the Nazi tactics designed to sexually humiliate women, as well as the gendered concepts which women brought to their camp experiences, such as the fear of rape.

Historians approach memoirs written decades after traumatic experiences with caution. A handful of purported survivor memoirs have proven to be hoaxes, such as the book *Fragments* by Binjamin Wilkomirski, who was never in a concentration camp.[2] But the larger issue concerns the multiple meanings of memory, as recorded in memoirs, interviews, letters, or diaries. The normal historical practice of source criticism must also be applied to the published forms of survivors' memories, even though this may feel disrespectful to their ordeal.

This excerpt provides a revealing example of how the process of writing and remembering is related to quality and reliability of memory. After Isaacson began to write her memoirs in 1976, the details returned gradually to her consciousness. Determined to be as accurate as possible, she travelled to Hungary, Auschwitz, and Israel to gather information and check her memories with those of other survivors. Early in this process, a version of this excerpt was published in *The Yale Review* in 1984. Isaacson continued her research, corresponded with Hungarian comrades, and thought more about her memories. By the time *Seed of Sarah* was published in 1990, the wording had barely changed, but certain details were corrected. For example, right and left were reversed in the revised version, and the name of her classmate who was sent to the right with other young women was changed.[3] Isaacson's compulsion to be as accurate as possible is characteristic of the writings of Holocaust victims.

## Notes

1. Recent overviews of the significance of gender in the persecution and responses of Jews are Marion A. Kaplan, *Between Dignity and Despair: Jewish Life in Nazi Germany* (New York: Oxford University Press, 1998); Dalia Ofer and Lenore J. Weitzman (eds), *Women in the Holocaust* (New Haven, CT: Yale University Press, 1998); Elizabeth R, Baer and Myrna Goldberg (eds), *Experience and Expression: Women, the Nazis, and the Holocaust* (Detroit, MI: Wayne State University Press, 2003).
2. *Fragments: Memories of a Wartime Childhood*, translated by Carol Brown Janeway (New York: Schocken Books, 1996), originally published in German as *Bruchstücke : aus einer Kindheit 1939–1948* (Frankfurt am Main: Jüdischer Verlag, 1995).
3. This information comes from a conversation with Isaacson on 5 January 2002.

# 74. List of transports to Birkenau gas chambers during October 1944

| | | | | |
|---|---|---|---|---|
| 9/10 | 2000 | men | German camp | Cr 1 |
| 9/10 | 2000 | families | Terezin | " 1 |
| 9/10 | 2000 | women | Camp "C" | " 4 |
| 10/10 | 800 | children | Gypsies | " 4 |
| 11/10 | 2000 | families | Slovakia | " 2 |
| 12/10 | 3000 | women | Camp "C" | " 1 |
| 13/10 | 3000 | women | Camp "C" | " 2 |
| 13/10 | 2000 | families | Terezin | " 1 |
| 14/10 | 3000 | families | Terezin | " 2 |
| 15/10 | 3000 | women | Camp "C" | " 1 |
| 16/10 | 800 | men | German camp | " 2 |
| 16/10 | 600 | men | Infirmary camp | " 2 |
| 17/10 | 2000 | men | Buna | " 1 |
| 18/10 | 3000 | families | Slovakia | " 1 |
| 18/10 | 2000 | families | Terezin | " 2 |
| 18/10 | 300 | families | miscellaneous | " 2 |
| 18/10 | 22 | political, men | Bunker | " 2 |
| 18/10 | 13 | political, women | Prison | " 2 |
| 19/10 | 2000 | families | Slovakia | " 1 |
| 20/10 | 2500 | families | Terezin | " 2 |
| 20/10 | 2500 | families | Terezin | " 1 |
| 20/10 | 1000 | men, children | Dy village | " 2 |
| 20/10 | 200 | women | Camp "C" | " 2 |
| 20/10 | 1000 | families | Terezin | " 1 |
| 21/10 | 1000 | women | Camp "C" | " 4 |
| 23/10 | 400 | men | Gliwice | " 2 |
| 24/10 | 2000 | families | Terezin | " 1 |

[along right side of paper]

| | | | | |
|---|---|---|---|---|
| 7/10 | 460 | men | Sonderkommando | shot to death |

Despite unbelievably difficult circumstances, members of the *Sonderkommando* managed to write diaries and notes and bury them near the crematoria of Birkenau. The Soviet army found the first fragments within two months of liberation, and other pieces turned up gradually in the ruins. In 1952 a search party found a diary near crematorium 3, whose author was eventually identified as Leib Langfuss, a local religious leader from Poland. Langfuss arrived in Auschwitz in December 1942, at which time his wife and son were killed in the gas chambers. He became a worker in the *Sonderkommando,* whose task it was to disinfect and prepare women's hair for shipment to Germany. Langfuss was part of the *Sonderkommando* revolt of October 1944. He was probably killed at the end of November.

This list was scribbled in Polish in the immediate aftermath of the *Sonderkommando* uprising in Birkenau, which destroyed crematorium 4. The listing of 460 men shot on 7 October represents the reprisal for that rebellion. Thereafter only three crematoria could be used to gas and burn the bodies of prisoners on these incoming transports. Langfuss could only estimate the numbers of people handled by the *Sonderkommando,* yet his figures are confirmed by other documents relating to these transports.

In this period of 16 days, over 44,000 Jews and Gypsies were gassed. They were among the last victims of the Holocaust, just before the crematoria were dismantled as the Soviet army approached Auschwitz. German Jews from Berlin ('German camp'), the so-called privileged Jews who had been interned as families in Terezin outside of Prague, and a final group of Gypsy children were murdered. 'Camp C' refers to Camp B-II C: its inmates were all Jewish women from various countries. Several selections each day were held in this camp. 'Bunker' refers to the bunker prison in Auschwitz, Block 11. 'Dy village' is Dyherrnfurth, an auxiliary camp of Gross-Rosen. Gliwice housed one of the many auxiliary camps of Auschwitz complex. In November and December these crematoria were dismantled by Jewish prisoners under the direction of the SS, and then dynamited, in order to hide evidence of mass murder.

Although Langfuss numbers the crematoria 1, 2, and 4, historians usually number them 2, 3, and 5, according to the numbering in German documents describing the layout of Birkenau. Crematorium 1 was a facility in Auschwitz.

Section IX

# The Aftermath

The Holocaust was unbelievable. Despite accurate reports by eyewitnesses to all aspects of this genocide, those outside could not and would not grasp what they were being told. American and British leaders hearing Jan Karski describe the Warsaw ghetto or reading the report on Auschwitz made by two escapees, Western newspaper readers confronted with vivid stories, even Jews with relatives in Europe could not understand what they could not imagine.[1]

It has taken decades for the reality of the Holocaust to be accepted, understood, and finally acted upon. The meticulous planning, the huge bureaucratic structure, the industrial assembly lines of death in Poland, have all been revealed gradually through a combination of voluminous eyewitness testimony, scholarly research, and important trials, such as the Frankfurt Auschwitz trial (1963–65) and the Eichmann trial in 1961. Only gradually have the meanings of the Holocaust for conventional assumptions about immigration policy, racial prejudice, religious doctrine, and political structure been assimilated and acted upon.

The documents in this section display attempts by the most varied people to act appropriately in the post-Holocaust world. Some, like the Nazi witnesses at Nuremberg, began a lifetime of denial. West German law-makers struggled to define the responsibility of their new democracy to the victims of the Nazi state which preceded them. Others, such as Lutherans across the world and East German politicians newly freed from Soviet domination, admitted error only after decades of delay, finally accepting responsibility for their beliefs and actions. Those who argued that it was time to put all the unpleasantness into the past usually demonstrated that they had never understood it.

Public reactions to the Holocaust since 1945 have usually been closely tied to politics, in the broad sense. Discussions of memorialization and compensation, reevaluations of the actions of significant people, and decisions about bringing perpetrators to trial all involve political authority and political judgment. As soon as it ended, the negotiations among the victorious Allies brought politics into the center of the public understanding of the Holocaust, where it has remained.

## Note

1 Jan Karski, a Polish Catholic, who risked his life to slip into the Warsaw ghetto and then carry the news as far as Washington DC, found it difficult to convince government officials that what he had seen was 'fact'. Supreme Court Justice Felix Frankfurter responded to Karski's stories by saying: 'I know that what you have to say is true, but I don't believe it'. His remarkable efforts to tell the world about the Holocaust while it happened can be found in E. Thomas Wood and Stanislaw M. Jankowski, Karski: *How One Man Tried to Stop the Holocaust* (New York: Wiley and Sons, 1994).

# 75. London Agreement among Allies about nature of war crimes trial, 8 August 1945

LONDON AGREEMENT OF 8 AUGUST 1945

*Agreement by the Government of the United States of America, the Provisional Government of the French Republic, the Government of the United Kingdom of Great Britain and Northern Ireland, and the Government of the Union of Soviet Socialist Republics for the Prosecution and Punishment of the Major War Criminals of the European Axis.*

WHEREAS the United Nations have from time to time made declarations of their intention that war criminals shall be brought to justice;

AND WHEREAS the Moscow Declaration of 30 October 1943 on German atrocities in Occupied Europe stated that those German officers and men and members of the Nazi Party who have been responsible for or have taken a consenting part in atrocities and crimes will be sent back to the countries in which their abominable deeds were done in order that they may be judged and punished according to the laws of these liberated countries and of the free Governments that will be created therein;

AND WHEREAS this Declaration was stated to be without prejudice to the case of major criminals whose offenses have no particular geographic location and who will be punished by the joint decision of the Governments of the Allies;

NOW THEREFORE the Government of the United States of America, the Provisional Government of the French Republic, the Government of the United Kingdom of Great Britain and Northern Ireland, and the Government of the Union of Soviet Socialist Republics (hereinafter called "the Signatories") acting in the interests of all the United Nations and by their representatives duly authorized thereto have concluded this Agreement.

Article 1. There shall be established after consultation with the Control Council for Germany an International Military Tribunal for the trial of war criminals whose offenses have no particular geographical location whether they be accused individually or in their capacity as members of organizations or groups or in both capacities.

Article 2. The constitution, jurisdiction, and functions of the International Military Tribunal shall be those set out in the Charter annexed to this Agreement, which Charter shall form an integral part of this Agreement.

Article 3. Each of the Signatories shall take the necessary steps to make available for the investigation of the charges and trial the major war criminals detained by them who are to be tried by the International Military Tribunal. The Signatories shall also use their best endeavors to make available for investigation of the charges against and the trial before the International Military Tribunal such of the major war criminals as are not in the territories of any of the Signatories.

Article 4. Nothing in this Agreement shall prejudice the provisions established by the Moscow Declaration concerning the return of war criminals to the countries where they committed their crimes.

Article 5. Any Government of the United Nations may adhere to this Agreement by notice given through the diplomatic channel to the Government of the United Kingdom, who shall inform the other signatory and adhering Governments of each such adherence.

Article 6. Nothing in this Agreement shall prejudice the jurisdiction or the powers of any national or occupation court established or to be established in any Allied territory or in Germany for the trial of war criminals.

Article 7. This Agreement shall come into force on the day of signature and shall remain in force for the period of one year and shall continue thereafter, subject to the right of any Signatory to give, through the diplomatic channel, one month's notice of intention to terminate it. Such termination shall not prejudice any proceedings already taken or any findings already made in pursuance of this Agreement.

IN WITNESS WHEREOF the Undersigned have signed the present Agreement.

DONE in quadruplicate in London this 8th day of August 1945 each in English, French, and Russian, and each text to have equal authenticity.

For the Government of the United States of America
[signature] ROBERT H. JACKSON
For the Provisional Government of the French Republic
[signature] ROBERT FALCO

For the Government of the United Kingdom of Great Britain and Northern Ireland
[signature] JOWITT
For the Government of the Union of Soviet Socialist Republics
[signature] I. NIKITCHENKO
[signature] A. TRAININ

---

While the Western Allies refrained from military action to save Jews from the Holocaust, they focused on threatening public language as a tool to persuade the Nazis to abandon their genocidal projects. Their most serious threat was that those who took part in mass murder would face a legal reckoning for these crimes. On 8 September 1942, after reports about death camps had filtered out of Eastern Europe, British Prime Minister Winston Churchill declared that Nazi criminals would have to stand trial. Similar statements from US President Franklin Roosevelt and Soviet Foreign Minister Vyacheslav Molotov followed. By 1943 the seeds of postwar distrust were germinating, and these three Allies had difficulty agreeing about how to proceed with such trials.

Finally on 1 November 1943 in Moscow, the British, American and Soviet foreign ministers signed a broadly worded statement of their intent to try those German leaders, soldiers, and Nazi Party members who took part in 'atrocities, massacres and executions'. During the next two years, political figures in all three countries weighed the alternatives of public trials versus summary execution for Nazi leaders. While the advocates of war crimes trials won Roosevelt over, Churchill continued to favor immediately silencing Nazi leaders, worrying that Hitler might be able to turn a public trial into an opportunity for propaganda.

At the conference in San Francisco in April 1945 which founded the United Nations, American diplomats presented the case for postwar trials, with the strong support of the new President, Harry Truman. Once Germany had surrendered in May, this argument won over the rest of the Allied nations, who signed the London Agreement in August 1945. Nazi leaders whose crimes could not be attached to a particular 'geographical location' would be tried by an International Military Tribunal. Lesser perpetrators would be tried where they had committed their crimes. A Charter of the International Military Tribunal was appended to the London Agreement, which spelled out the kinds of crimes which would be tried. The category 'crimes against humanity' included 'murder, extermination, enslavement, deportation, and other inhumane acts committed against any civilian population'. As in all the documents pertaining to the preparation for the Nuremberg trial, there is no mention of gas chambers or particular groups of victims.

The cases at Nuremberg were not intended to explain, display, or even try the Holocaust. The dimensions of mass murder in Eastern Europe had brushed but not yet been absorbed into the public consciousness of the Western Allies. The leaders of the Soviet Union had been faced with the worst genocidal excesses for four years, from the experimental gassing of Soviet prisoners-of-war to the liberation of Majdanek and Auschwitz. But Josef Stalin and his supporters had no interest in drawing attention to the main victims of the camps, European Jews, nor to the vast destruction of Soviet territories.

The signatories here played major roles at Nuremberg. Iola Nikitchenko, vice president of the Soviet Supreme Court, served as senior Soviet judge; Robert Falco was the French alternate judge. US Supreme Court Justice Robert H. Jackson was appointed chief prosecutor. The preparation for the trials involved the largest collection of documentary evidence ever undertaken. Despite the subsidiary role played by the Holocaust at Nuremberg, these documents still represent the most significant source of information about the Holocaust.[1]

## Note

1 Michael R. Marrus has put together a fine selection of documents about the background to and course of the Nuremberg Trial: *The Nuremberg War Crimes Trial 1945–46: A Documentary History* (Boston, MA: Bedford Books, 1997).

# 76. Summary of evidence from defense witnesses at Nuremberg Trial, August 1946

TO: THE INTERNATIONAL MILITARY TRIBUNAL

I have the honour to submit a final report on the hearing of witnesses for Organizations alleged to be criminal in accordance with Paragraph 4 of the Tribunal's Order of March 13th, under which I was appointed Commissioner....

A. M. S. NEAVE
Lt. Colonel, A.A.G.
NURNBERG, GERMANY AUGUST 1946 ...

THE CORPS OF POLITICAL LEADERS

... According to Gauleiter WAHL concentration camps were established by the SS who provided supplies for the prisoners interned. The POLITICAL LEADERS had no part in their administration and as a general practice were not allowed to visit them except by special permission of HIMMLER. This witness claimed to have opposed the maintenance of concentration camps and expressed this view to HITLER himself.

The witnesses, including the Ortsgruppenleiters, denied receiving directives regarding the detention of political opponents. There were cases, however, in which POLITICAL LEADERS obtained the release of prisoners from the camps....

Questioned with respect to Point 4 of the Party Program dealing with Jews and anti-semitism, under which no one could be part of the German Volk who was not entirely of Aryan blood, HIRT admitted that this was unfair discrimination against the Jews. He claimed that the decent elements among the German people did not want any part in such discrimination. However, after HITLER came into power no individual had any power to resist this policy. Such resistance would have meant they would have been thrown into a concentration camp.

He denied that Gauleiters participated in the measures against the Jews or carried out instructions that they should wear yellow badges and have their property confiscated. KUEHL said that Political Leaders in his district did not know of any of the intentions of the Reich Leaders with respect to the solution of the Jewish problem. On the basis of the Party program they believed this problem could be solved legally by emigration. He had never heard of the term "final solution". The Party Leaders were in no sense responsible for the deportation of Jews....

## THE GESTAPO

... All the witnesses denied that the GESTAPO had anything to do with atrocities committed in concentration camps. The witness ALBATH in cross-examination denied that the GESTAPO carried out any mass executions....

All the witnesses deny that at any time were they given orders for the extermination of the Jews although local branches received orders to take into protective custody Jews within certain age groups. This was after the middle of 1941....

In regard to the knowledge of conditions in concentration camps, ALBATH stated that sometimes inmates released from concentration camps had to report to GESTAPO officials and in this way the GESTAPO were able to get some information. He said that his subordinates who received such information did not give him the impression that atrocities were being committed. He admitted that the GESTAPO officials knew people arrested under orders of the RSHA were to be sent to concentration camps.

## THE SS

... The Defense alleged that the WAFFEN-SS had no direct relation to the police work of HIMMLER, especially the GESTAPO and concentration camps. As previously stated, HIMMLER deliberately deceived the public by calling the concentration camp guards members of the WAFFEN-SS although they were really only ordinary troops under the SS administration. There was no exchange of personnel between the WAFFEN-SS, GESTAPO, Security Police or SD....

In answer to the statement that the "whole world" knew what was going on, VON THADDEN observed that the SS and the foreign office had no access to the foreign press or radio. He alleged that the sole purpose of his department working in liaison with EICHMANN was to prepare propaganda for the "comprehension" amongst other nations of the executive measures against the Jews.

Cross-examined as to what he meant by "executive measures" and why he had made a speech on EICHMANN'S behalf, the minutes of which were not published, he said the executive measures only referred to deportation. He thought only two or three officials of the foreign office could have known about the proposed liquidation. Even the Foreign Secretary knew only of the deportation.

He said that he was prevented by EICHMANN from going to the extermination camp at Auschwitz for security reasons. EICHMANN said that secret weapons were being made there. EICHMANN thought that reports in the foreign press of exterminations in this camp were of an advantage since the camp might not be attacked by enemy bombers. EICHMANN assured the foreign office that these reports were untrue and that the Jews were properly cared for.

During a discussion as to the relevancy of the evidence of this witness, the Defense claimed that the fact that a very high official of the foreign office and an honorary member of the SS such as VON THADDEN did not know of the exterminations, implied that the SS as a whole did not know of them either....

The relation of the SS personnel to concentration camps has already been described. The purpose of the defense was to show that the details of administration of concentration camps were not widely known and that the guards, particularly towards the end of the war, were drawn from persons who were only nominally members of the SS....

Cross-examined REINECKE said that he had no knowledge of the order of the Reichsfuehrer-SS that certain anti-social elements such as Jews and gypsies with more than three year sentences were to be "worked to death". It was suggested to him that it was odd that the highest SS and judicial authorities were informed of this and he knew nothing about it. He answered that such things could only have taken place within the sphere of administration of concentration camps and as he had testified it was impossible to penetrate the secrecy surrounding them.

He admitted that the men who were guarding concentration camps belonged to the SS. He never heard any of the guards mention atrocities and said that the reports received by the SS and police courts were carefully and expertly drawn up....

## THE SD

... The witnesses who covered this subject were EHLICH and KNOCHEN. EHLICH said that the SD did not deal with Jewish problems or carry out the extermination of Jews. They reported, however, on all sections of the population who were liable to be hostile to the regime. Asked by the Prosecution whether, since his Section (III B of the SD) was concerned with racial problems, this did not involve the Jewish question, the witness answered that the problem was only dealt with in the general sense of reporting intelligence....

All the witnesses denied that the SD had any control over concentration camps or any executive powers with regard to the carrying out of the "bullet decree," the Nacht und Nebel decree or the suppression of political and racial undesirables....

## THE GENERAL STAFF AND HIGH COMMAND

... In describing the war in Russia, von MANSTEIN said that it was a war fought with great bitterness on both sides. The Russians fought for every inch of their country and committed atrocities themselves. HITLER ordered that the troops should not be punished for action they took against the population and this greatly complicated the position of higher commanders in maintaining discipline.

Questioned concerning the activities of Einsatzgruppen, von MANSTEIN said that he had been informed that it was their function to report on the population and that they carried out their activities in the rear of the Army. He never saw any Einsatzgruppen or SD in his area, though he occasionally saw some of their reports which mentioned the black market and the political attitude of the population....

Most of the witnesses testified that it was their policy to keep on good terms with the civilian population in Russia....

REINHARDT denied the statement of Ohlendorf that SD groups were subordinate to Army Commanders. As an Army Commander, he was unacquainted with any orders received by Einsatzgruppen. He adopted a policy of living in amicable relations with the civilian population. He arranged that the Army should assist the civilian population in every way and punished any violation of this order....

With regard to the extermination of Jews, very little evidence was given on this subject, except to the effect that the High Command were in no sense concerned with the activities of EICHMANN.

MANSTEIN reiterated that he had only once heard of the shooting of Jews. On the night before he moved his headquarters from Nikolaew an officer had told him that the SS had recently shot some Jews in a town to the rear. MANSTEIN left a message for the Commander to the effect that he would not tolerate such activities. His observation on the statement of Ohlendorf that Einsatzgruppe D had killed 90,000 Jews in one year within the area of the 11th Army was as follows: The Army area was from Chernovitz to Rostov about 1200 kilometers long and 400 kilometers wide. Three or four German armies operated in this area. There were very few Jews in the sector as they had already taken refuge elsewhere. If the SD did in fact shoot Jews, it would have been done in a very lonely spot. At any rate, he never heard of it....

THE SA

... Questioned concerning the policy of the SA towards the Jews, JUETTNER said that the SA were against the immigration of Jews from the East into German territory. This was the limit of their anti-Semitism and they were strongly opposed to the use of brute force in dealing with the problem. JUETTNER claimed that the same attitude with regard to the immigration of Jews from the East was adopted by Jewish associations in Germany. He denied that the leadership of the SA made speeches inciting excesses against the Jews. He agreed that a number of members of the SA disobeyed orders and committed crimes against people of Jewish faith. Whenever the leaders of the SA heard of such crimes they always took steps to stop them.

---

'We didn't kill Jews. If it was done, someone else did it. I didn't know about it. When I did act, it was to help Jews. Lots of reports were made. Conditions weren't so bad. Hitler, Himmler, Heydrich and Eichmann were the guilty ones.' The major planners and perpetrators of 12 years of violent attacks on civilians and 6 years of mass murder defended themselves by denying the obvious and diverting attention to those who were dead or vanished. Col. Airey Neave, a war hero, acted as the judges' assistant in putting together this summary of the defendants' arguments to help the tribunal reach a judgment.[1]

It was not easy to prove how false these defenses were. The immense labor of assembling documentary evidence was decisive in showing precisely what the defendants had done. The final verdicts were that 12 defendants should be hanged, 3 received life in prison (although 2 were released in the 1950s for health reasons), 4 had to spend 10 to 20 years in prison, and 3 were acquitted.

Some of the witnesses cited here knew much more than they said. Juettner, an SA Obergruppenführer in Munich, was involved in organizing Kristallnacht and its aftermath. SS-Obersturmführer Helmut Knochen was chief of the SD and Security Police in France 1942–44, and was responsible for rounding up French Jews and deporting them to the death camps in Poland. He was jailed from 1946 to 1962. Eberhard von Thadden worked in the Foreign Office in charge of Jewish affairs and as liaison with the SS from 1943 to 1945. He was involved in deportations of Jews throughout Europe, especially the massive 1944 Hungarian deportations to Auschwitz. General von Manstein had ordered his soldiers to kill Jews.

## Note

1 Neave wrote a memoir of the trial: *Nuremberg: A Personal Record of the Major Nazi War Criminals* (London: Hodder and Stoughton, 1978).

# st German law to compensate victims ersecution, 29 June 1956

Federal Law
for Restitution for Victims of National Socialist Persecution
(Federal Restitution Law – BEG – )

In recognition of the fact,

that people were wronged, who on grounds of political opposition against National Socialism or on grounds of race, belief, or philosophy were persecuted under National Socialist tyranny,

that the resistance against National Socialist tyranny out of conviction or for the sake of belief or conscience was a service to the welfare of the German people and state and

that democratic, religious and economic organizations were also illegally injured by National Socialist tyranny,

the Bundestag with the agreement of the Bundesrat has passed the following law: ...

§ 1

(1) A victim of National Socialist persecution is whoever on grounds of political opposition against National Socialism or on grounds of race, belief, or philosophy were persecuted by National Socialist measures of violence, and thereby suffered injury to life, body, health, freedom, property, fortune, in his occupational or in his financial livelihood (persecutee)....

§ 2

... (2) The assumption of National Socialist measures of violence is not precluded, even if they were directed against the persecutee based on legal regulations or in improper application of legal regulations.

§ 3

The persecutee has claim to restitution under this law.

§ 4

(1) Claim to restitution is valid,

1. if the persecutee

a) on 31 December 1952 had his residence or permanent domicile in territory within the jurisdiction of this law;
b) died before 31 December 1952 and had his last residence or permanent domicile in territory within the jurisdiction of this law;
c) before 31 December 1952 emigrated, was deported or expelled, and had his last residence or permanent domicile in a territory, which belonged to the German Reich on 31 December 1937, unless at the moment of the decision he had his residence or permanent domicile in territories with whose governments the Federal Republic of Germany has no diplomatic relations;
d) as returnee in the sense of the Law on Relief Measures for Returnees (Returnee Law) took or takes his residence or permanent domicile in territory within the jurisdiction of this law;
e) is an expellee in the sense of § 1 of the Law on the Situation of Expellees and Refugees (Federal Expellee Law) and took or takes residence or permanent domicile in territory within the jurisdiction of this law;
f) is recognized as a refugee from the Soviet Zone in the sense of § 3 of the Federal Expellee Law ... and took or takes residence or permanent domicile in territory within the jurisdiction of this law ...

§ 13

(1) The claim to restitution is inheritable....

§ 15

(1) Claim to restitution for injury to life is valid if the persecutee intentionally or carelessly was killed or driven to death. It is sufficient that the causal connection between death and persecution is probable.

(2) If the persecutee died during the deportation or during a deprivation of freedom in the sense of this law or immediately following, it will be assumed that he intentionally or carelessly was killed or driven to death by National Socialist measures of violence....

§ 28

(1) The persecutee has claim to restitution, if he suffered not insignificant injury to his body or to his health. It is sufficient that the causal connection between the injury to body or health and the persecution is probable....

§ 51

(1) The persecutee has claim to restitution for injury to property, if a thing which belonged to him at the moment of injury was destroyed, defaced, or exposed to plundering in Reich territory as of 31 December 1937....

§ 56

(1) The persecutee has claim to restitution, if he suffered injury to his fortune in Reich territory as of 31 December 1937. An injury to fortune also exists if the persecutee was impaired in the use of his property or fortune. The claim is valid also if the injury was caused by boycott. For injuries up to the sum of 500 Reichsmark, no restitution will be provided....

§ 64

(1) The persecutee has claim to restitution for injury in occupational or in financial livelihood, if in the course of a persecution begun in Reich territory as of 31 December 1937 he was substantially disadvantaged in occupational or in financial livelihood. If the persecutee is an expellee in the sense of § 1 of the Federal Expellee Law, then he has claim also if the persecution began in the territory of expulsion.

---

The first law on restitution in Germany was adopted by the US occupation authorities in November 1947, offering compensation to Jews whose property had been 'aryanized'. It was immediately denounced by an organization of the aryanizers, the 'Union for Honest Restitution', which found sympathizers in the ranks of the conservative Christian Democratic Party. The partial nature of restitution offered, the powerful opposition by the political right, and the hostility towards survivors expressed in the public discussion all characterized West German debates on restitution for decades. The demands of victims that the crimes of the Holocaust be acknowledged were always countered by demands from former supporters of the Nazi state that they, too, deserved special consideration.

This Federal Restitution Law of 1956 demonstrates the compromises necessary to get restitution for Holocaust victims through the German political system. Every clause which offered restitution also excluded groups of people whose claims were not considered valid. The Cold War politics of divided Europe were expressed in the unwillingness to compensate victims still living in Eastern Europe and the juxtaposition of refugees from East Germany with Holocaust victims. The willingness to extend economic benefits to ethnic Germans from Eastern Europe, who had been the proposed benefactors of Nazi resettlement schemes, reflects German political realities of the 1950s. These so-called expellees could claim restitution for persecution by communist states, while the victims of the much deadlier German persecution on the Eastern Front were excluded.

Restitution debates exhibited the continuing influence of discriminatory ideology in Germany. Opponents of restitution complained of Jewish greed and financial corruption. Gypsies were systematically excluded from compensation. Homosexuals were not only prevented from filing claims, but they continued to be prosecuted under the laws carried over from the Third Reich.

Constant pressure from victims, often working through the US judicial system, forced West Germany to keep expanding the offer of restitution through new laws in 1957, 1965, and 1969. The reunification of Germany and the end of the Cold War extended the scope of German payments into Eastern Europe. Over 100 billion German marks have been paid out to individuals, organizations, and nations as compensation for Nazi crimes. In recent years, restitution debates have expanded beyond Germany to all European nations where governments collaborated in the Holocaust (document 81 on Norway). Some African Americans refer to this model in their demands for compensation for the injustices of slavery.

# 78. Statement of Lutherans about Christians and Jews, July 1983

We Lutherans take our name and much of our understanding of Christianity from Martin Luther. But we cannot accept or condone the violent verbal attacks that the Reformer made against the Jews. Lutherans and Jews interpret the Hebrew Bible differently. But we believe that a christological reading of the Scriptures does not lead to anti-Judaism, let alone anti-Semitism.

We hold that an honest, historical treatment of Luther's attacks on the Jews takes away from modern anti-Semites the assumption that they may legitimately call on the authority of Luther's name to bless their anti-Semitism. We insist that Luther does not support racial anti-Semitism, nationalistic anti-Semitism, or political anti-Semitism. Even the deplorable religious anti-Semitism of the 16th century, to which Luther's attacks made an important contribution, is a horrible anachronism when translated to the conditions of the modern world. We recognize with deep regret however, that Luther has been used to justify such anti-Semitism in the period of national socialism and that his writings lent themselves to such abuse. Although there remain conflicting assumptions, built into the beliefs of Judaism and Christianity, they need not and should not lead to the animosity and the violence of Luther's treatment of the Jews. Martin Luther opened up our eyes to a deeper understanding of the Old Testament and showed us the depth of our common inheritance and the roots of our faith.

Many of the anti-Jewish utterances of Luther have to be explained in the light of his polemic against what he regarded as misinterpretations of the Scriptures. He attacked these interpretations, since for him everything now depended on a right understanding of the Word of God. The sins of Luther's anti-Jewish remarks, the violence of his attacks on the Jews, must be acknowledged with deep distress. And all occasions for similar sin in the present or the future must be removed from our churches.

A frank examination also forces Lutherans and other Christians to confront the anti-Jewish attitudes of their past and present. Hostility toward the Jews began long before Luther and has been a continuing evil after him. The history of the centuries following the Reformation saw in Europe the gradual acceptance of religious pluralism. The church was not always the first to accept this development; yet there have also been examples of leadership by the church in the movement to accept Jews as full fellow citizens and members of society.

Beginning in the last half of the 19th century, anti-Semitism increased in Central Europe, and at the same time Jewish people were being integrated in society. This brought to the churches, particularly in Germany, an unwanted challenge. Paradoxically, the churches honored the people of Israel of the Bible but rejected the descendants of those people; myths were perpetuated about the Jews and deprecatory references appeared in Lutheran liturgical and educational material. Luther's doctrine of the Two Kingdoms was used to justify passivity in the face of totalitarian claims. These and other less theological factors contributed to the failures, which have been regretted and repeatedly confessed since 1945.

To their credit, it is to be said that there were individuals and groups among Lutherans who in defiance of totalitarian power defended their Jewish neighbors, both in Germany and elsewhere.

Lutherans of today refuse to be bound by all of Luther's utterances on the Jews. We hope we have learned from the tragedies of the recent past. We are responsible for seeing that we do not now nor in the future leave any doubt about our position on racial and religious prejudice and that we afford to all the human dignity, freedom, and friendship that are the right of all the Father's children.

---

On the 500th anniversary of Luther's birth, Jewish and Lutheran representatives met in Stockholm for an official dialogue. The Lutherans produced this statement, which was subsequently affirmed and recommended to all Lutheran member churches by the Assembly of the Lutheran World Federation in 1984.

While acknowledging Luther's diatribes against Jews, this statement labels them 'religious antisemitism', to distinguish Luther's beliefs from the presumably more modern forms of antisemitism which motivated the Nazis. Apologists for centuries of Catholic preaching against Jews also use this distinction to deny causal links between Christian teachings and Nazi deeds. Luther's own words quoted at the beginning of this book (document 3) do not lend themselves so easily to such distinctions.

The Evangelical Lutheran Church in America and the Evangelical Lutheran Church in Canada adopted notably stronger statements in 1984 and 1985. They made no distinctions between forms of antisemitism, nor did they offer explanations for Luther's beliefs about Jews. Acknowledging the violence of Luther's language, they recognized the 'complicity of our own tradition' for attacks on Jews in Germany, where Lutheranism was especially powerful. In 1997, the Lutheran Church of Bavaria admitted its partial responsibility for the Holocaust. The United Evangelical Lutheran Church of Argentina and Uruguay formally apologized to Jews in those countries in 2002. Other Protestant denominations have recently made similar statements. The General Assembly of the Presbyterians Church (USA) noted its contribution to persecution of Jews in 1987. In 1995 the Alliance of Baptists confessed their sins of complicity and silence.[1]

It has taken a long time for Christian leaders to concede the role of their religious beliefs in creating the context for genocide. Christian-Jewish dialogue is now a staple of religious life in the Western world. Much remains to be done, attested to by the continuing controversy over Catholic theology and Papal practice during the Holocaust.

## Note

1 These statements and further discussions of relationships between Christians and Jews are all available on the websites of these denominations.

# 79. Speech by Elie Wiesel about President Ronald Reagan's planned visit to Bitburg cemetery, 19 April 1985

Mr. President, Mr. Vice President, Secretary Bennett, Mr. Agresto, Mr. Regan, very distinguished members of the Senate, my friends, and of the House.

Mr. President ... It was good talking to you and I'm grateful to you for the medal. But this medal is not mine alone. It belongs to all those who remember what SS killers have done to their victims. It was given to me by the American people for my writings, teaching, and for my testimony.

When I write, I feel my invisible teachers standing over my shoulders, reading my words, and judging their veracity. And while I feel responsible for the living, I feel equally responsible to the dead. Their memory dwells in my memory.

Forty years ago, a young man awoke and he found himself an orphan in an orphaned world. What have I learned in the last 40 years? Small things. I learned the perils of language and those of silence. I learned that in extreme situations when human lives and dignity are at stake, neutrality is a sin. It helps the killers, not the victims.

I learned the meaning of solitude, Mr. President. We were alone, desperately alone. Today is April 19th, and April 19, 1943, the Warsaw Ghetto rose in arms against the onslaught of the Nazis. They were so few and so young and so helpless. And nobody came to their help. And they had to fight what was then the mightiest legion in Europe.

Every Underground received help, except the Jewish Underground. And yet, they managed to fight and resist and push back those Nazis and their accomplices for six weeks.

And yet, the leaders of the free world, Mr. President, knew everything and did so little, or nothing, or at least nothing specifically to save Jewish children from death.

You spoke of Jewish children, Mr. President. One million Jewish children perished. If I spent my entire life reciting their names, I would die before finishing the task.

Mr. President, I have seen children — I have seen them being thrown in the flames alive. Words — they die on my lips....

I have learned that the Holocaust was a unique, a uniquely Jewish event, albeit with universal implications. Not all victims were Jews, but all Jews were victims. I have learned the danger of indifference, the crime of indifference. For the opposite of love, I have learned, is not hate, but indifference. Jews were killed by the enemy, but betrayed by their so-called allies who found political reasons to justify their indifference or passivity.

But I've also learned that suffering confers no privileges. It all depends what one does with it. And this is why survivors of whom you spoke, Mr. President, have tried to teach their contemporaries how to build on ruins, how to invent hope in a world that offers none, how to proclaim faith to a generation that has seen it shamed and mutilated. And I believe, we believe, that memory is the answer — perhaps the only answer....

But, Mr. President, I wouldn't be the person I am, and you wouldn't respect me for what I am, if I were not to tell you also of the sadness that is in my heart for what happened during the last week. And I am sure that you, too, are sad for the same reasons. What can I do? I belong to a traumatized generation. And to us, as to you, symbols are important. And furthermore, following our ancient tradition — and we are speaking about Jewish heritage — our tradition commands us "speak truth to power."

So may I speak to you, Mr. President, with respect and admiration of the events that happened. We have met four or five times. And each time I came away enriched, for I know of your commitment to humanity. And, therefore, I am convinced, as you have told us earlier when we spoke that you were not aware of the presence of SS graves in the Bitburg cemetery. Of course, you didn't know. But now we all are aware. May I, Mr. President, if it's possible at all, implore you to do something else, to find a way — to find another way, another site. That place, Mr. President, is not your place. Your place is with the victims of the SS.

Oh, we know there are political and strategic reasons. But this issue, as all issues related to that awesome event, transcends politics and diplomacy. The issue here is not politics, but good and evil. And we must never confuse them, for I have seen the SS at work, and I have seen their victims. They were my friends. They were my parents. Mr. President, there was a degree of suffering and loneliness in the concentration camps that defies imagination. Cut off from the world with no refuge anywhere, sons watched helplessly their fathers being beaten to death. Mothers watched their children die of hunger. And then there was Mengele and his selections, terror, fear, isolation, torture, gas chambers, flames, flames rising to the heavens.

But, Mr. President, I know and I understand, we all do, that you seek reconciliation. So do I. So do we. And I, too, wish to attain true reconciliation with the German people. I do not believe in collective guilt, nor in collective responsibility, only the killers were guilty. Their sons and daughters are not. And I believe, Mr. President, that we can and we must work together with them and with all people. And we must work to bring peace and understanding to a tormented world that, as you know, is still awaiting redemption.

I thank you, Mr. President.

---

Elie Wiesel made this speech at the White House, where he was given the Congressional Gold Medal. By this time, Wiesel had become the most publicly prominent concentration camp survivor through his unceasing public efforts to maintain the memory of the victims against forgetting. *Night*, his brief memoir of his year in Auschwitz and Buchenwald, is perhaps the most widely read camp memoir. In 1986, he was awarded the Nobel Peace Prize. Wiesel offers a Jewish survivor's view of the Holocaust as a 'uniquely Jewish event', stressing the argument often used in discussions of what was specifically Jewish about the Holocaust: 'Not all victims were Jews, but all Jews were victims.'

Forty years after the end of World War II, the graves of German soldiers became the focal point of political controversy. Weeks before President Reagan's visit to Germany in May 1985, it was revealed that he planned to visit a cemetery in Bitburg, Germany, that housed graves of SS soldiers. His itinerary became the subject of international media attention and political debate. Religious leaders of all denominations pleaded with Reagan to alter his plans. After publicly refusing to include a visit to a concentration camp, Reagan said at a press conference that the German soldiers buried at Bitburg were 'victims of Nazism ... just as surely as the victims in the concentration camps'. On the day that Wiesel delivered this speech, the White House announced that Reagan would, after all, visit Bergen-Belsen. Both major parties in the German Bundestag voted against a resolution that the German government not attend the visit to Bitburg. Within a few days, both the US Senate and House of Representatives overwhelmingly passed resolutions asking Reagan to change his itinerary.

Three days after the Bitburg visit, German President Richard von Weizsäcker, whose father was a Nazi diplomat, made an extraordinary speech to the Bundestag. Despite the efforts of the Nazis to hide the Holocaust from public view, he said, 'every German was able to experience what his Jewish compatriots had to suffer, ranging from plain apathy and hidden intolerance to outright hatred.... Whoever opened his eyes and ears and sought information could not fail to notice that Jews were being deported.'[1]

Wiesel served as chair of the US Holocaust Memorial Council, established by the Congress in 1980 to raise funds for the building of a Holocaust Memorial Museum in Washington. Wiesel has consistently been critical of the lack of Allied efforts to save Jews from the Nazis. He has written more than 20 books and teaches at Boston University.

## Note

1 Weizsäcker's speech is translated in its entirety in Geoffrey H. Hartman (ed.), *Bitburg in Moral and Political Perspective* (Bloomington, IN: Indiana University Press, 1986), pp. 262–73.

# 80. Resolution of the East German Parliament on the Holocaust, 12 April 1990

We, the first freely elected parliamentarians of the DDR, acknowledge the responsibility of the Germans in the DDR for their history and their future, and declare unanimously before the world:

During the time of National Socialism immeasurable suffering was inflicted by Germans on the peoples of the world. Nationalism and racist madness led to genocide, especially against the Jews from all European nations, against the peoples of the Soviet Union, against the Polish people and against the Sinti and Roma people.

This guilt may never be forgotten. From it we wish to derive our responsibility for the future.

1. The first freely elected Parliament of the DDR acknowledges in the name of the citizens of this nation the responsibility for humiliation, expulsion and murder of Jewish women, men and children. We feel sadness and shame, and acknowledge this burden of German history.

We ask the Jews of the whole world for forgiveness. We ask the people of Israel for forgiveness for the hypocrisy and hostility of the official politics of the DDR towards the state of Israel and for the persecution and degradation of Jewish citizens in our nation also after 1945.

We declare that we wish to contribute everything possible towards the healing of the spiritual and physical injuries of the survivors and to advocate for a just compensation for material losses.

We understand ourselves to be obligated especially to support and protect the Jewish religion, culture and tradition in Germany, and perman- ently to care for and maintain Jewish cemeteries, synagogues and memorial sites.

We recognize a special duty to educate the youth of our nation to respect the Jewish people and to transmit knowledge of the Jewish religion, tradition and culture.

We advocate offering asylum in the DDR to persecuted Jews.

We declare that we wish to strive for the establishment of diplomatic relations and manifold contacts with the state of Israel.

2. It is for us, the delegates of the first freely elected Parliament of the DDR, a profound need to turn to the citizens of the Soviet Union with the following declaration:

We have not forgotten the terrible harm that Germans inflicted on the people in the Soviet Union in the Second World War. This violence emanating from Germany finally struck also our own people. We wish to continue intensively the process of reconciliation of our peoples....
3. The Parliament of the DDR acknowledges the complicity of the DDR in the suppression of the "Prague Spring" in 1968 through troops of the Warsaw Pact....
The first freely elected Parliament of the DDR asks the peoples of Czechoslovakia to excuse this injustice.
4. The population of the DDR abolished through its peaceful revolution in fall 1989 the divisive effects of the inhuman internal German border. Now both parts of Germany should grow together and thereby support the development of a peaceful European system within the scope of the KSZE-process. We recognize a special responsibility to contribute our historically developed relationships with the peoples of eastern Europe to the European process of unification.
In this connection, we declare solemnly that we recognize without conditions the German borders with all neighboring states that emerged as a result of the Second World War.
Especially the Polish people should know that its right to live in secure borders will not be questioned through territorial demands by us Germans either now or in the future.
We confirm the invulnerability of the Oder-Neisse border with the Republic of Poland as the basis of the peaceful coexistence of our peoples in a common European house.
This should be contractually ratified by a future unified German parliament.
Berlin, 12 April 1990

The Party Delegations of the Parliament
of the German Democratic Republic

---

This declaration was read by the President of the DDR Parliament (Volkskammer), Sabine Bergmann-Pohl, to the newly elected delegates at their second meeting. The voting on the resolution was 379 to 0, with 21 abstentions.[1]

This statement reverses 40 years of official East German policy towards the Holocaust, Jews, and Israel. Unlike the gradual West German recognition of historical responsibility and willingness to make amends through compensation, the government of the DDR had consistently refused to see itself or its citizens as linked to Nazi crimes. Closely following Soviet Cold War policy, the East German government participated in the wave of political antisemitism in the early 1950s, which resulted in arrests, loss of jobs, and expulsions from the Communist Party of prominent Jews. Official Communist antifascism downplayed the suffering of Holocaust victims who had been targeted by racial criteria, while raising political opponents of the Nazis to the status of heroes. Shunning Israel as a capitalist state allied with the imperialist West, the DDR courted the Arab states of the Middle East. The East German government supported Yasser Arafat and the Palestine Liberation Organization with arms and training. This entire history is admitted and regretted here.

The declaration goes beyond accepting a share of German responsibility for the Holocaust. The Volkskammer addressed all the major issues of World War II which had been evaded in the intervening decades of Cold War. While stressing the genocidal attack on Jews, the Nazi program of mass murder in Poland and the Soviet Union was also acknowledged as a result of German racism.

Since the revolutions of 1989, the newly democratic nations of Eastern Europe have begun a belated process of coming to terms with the Holocaust, which occurred on their soil and involved their citizens on both sides of the killing. History and politics have mixed with practical economic considerations, brought up by the double burden of claims for the return of confiscated assets by Jews and by those whose property was taken by communist governments.

## Note

1 A comprehensive study of East and West German reactions to the Holocaust is Jeffrey Herf, *Divided Memory: The Nazi Past in the Two Germanys* (Cambridge, MA: Harvard University Press, 1997).

Section X

# The Holocaust in Contemporary Life

The Holocaust demands a response. The fact that a powerful 20$^{th}$-century nation organized the killing of millions as a state project has forced people in Europe and across the world to acknowledge an ugly abscess under the skin of modern society. As the previous section displayed, it has been difficult for groups of people to find the social courage to make appropriate responses. Every response bears political, intellectual, and emotional weight, and each effort has been controversial. Powerful voices urge an end to dealing with the past, while others insist that more needs to be done.

The attempts to ignore the Holocaust have not succeeded. Those groups of survivors who feel slighted by the partial efforts at compensation have won a hearing in the court of world opinion. Gypsies and forced laborers are closer than ever to receiving some form of monetary restitution. Countries like Norway, which tried to evade the truth about their role, are now offering plans for making amends, as documented below. These decisions can provoke wrenching reexaminations of history, as in the case of Switzerland. Insurance companies which profited from the disappearance of policy-holders, firms which produced the machinery of death, even American corporations whose German subsidiaries played a role in the Holocaust, such as IBM, have recently been forced to come to a reckoning with their past.

The Holocaust is part of contemporary life. The following documents display the power of this event to move people and governments in the 21$^{st}$ century.

# 81. Recommendation of Norwegian government to compensate Jews, 26 June 1998

**White Paper No. 82 to the Storting**
**(1997-98)**
**Historical and moral settlement for the treatment in Norway of the economic liquidation of the Jewish minority during World War II**

## 1 Main contents of the White Paper

The Ministry of Justice hereby submits a White Paper to the Storting on historical and moral settlement for the treatment in Norway of the economic liquidation of the Jewish minority during World War II. The economic liquidation of the group as a whole was unique, and the organized arrest, deportation and physical destruction of the Jews was genocide. Since the aim was to completely destroy the Jewish group in Norway, the economic and physical liquidation must be regarded as two parts of the same crime....

In the White Paper the Ministry of Justice proposes that the historic and moral settlement is given economic expression by making collective and individual settlements. The collective settlement is proposed to consist of three parts. The first is the allocation of a sum to ensure the preservation of Jewish culture and the future of the Jewish community in Norway. Secondly, it is proposed to support efforts outside Norway to commemorate and develop the traditions and culture that the Nazis sought to eradicate. Finally, it is proposed to set up a resource center on the Holocaust and on religious minorities' position and history in general. It is proposed that the individual compensation should take the form of an *ex gratia* payment to persons in Norway who were affected by the anti-Jewish measures during the war.

This White Paper has been drawn up in close collaboration with representatives of the Jewish community in Norway.

The Ministry of Justice wishes by these means to make a worthy final settlement.

## 2 Background

A number of individuals had their property seized by the Nazi occupation authorities and the Quisling regime during World War II, but of these it was the Jews who were by far the most seriously affected as a group. The seizure of property belonging to the Jewish community was an integral part of the Nazis' attempt to eradicate the entire Jewish community in Norway.

The first measures against the Jewish population in Norway were initiated in May 1940, when radios belonging to Jews were confiscated. This was followed by the registration of real estate owned by Jews, special stamps on Jewish identity documents, economic liquidation and arrests, culminating in the period of November 1942 to March 1943 in the deportation of Jews from Norway to Auschwitz....

It is estimated that the number of Jews in Norway before the war and up to the arrests in 1942 amounted to about 2200. Seven hundred and sixty-seven Jews were deported from Norway, mainly to Auschwitz, and of these only 30 survived. Two hundred and thirty families were completely eradicated. Those who were not deported fled the country, mainly to Sweden. There were also about 50 Jews imprisoned in Norway and about 10 who remained in the country in hiding. Every person who was defined as a Jew by the Nazi authorities had his or her property seized....

What characterized the Jewish group after the war was that so many of its members had been killed. Thus they were in a different situation, especially emotionally, from other Norwegian refugees who returned home after fleeing the country because of their resistance to the Nazi regime. The leaders and heads of families in the Jewish group had in many cases been killed, which weakened the ability of these families to safeguard their interests. In some cases whole families had been wiped out, and because of the close family ties within the group, all of the survivors had lost relations, either close or distant.

In section 16, subsection 5, Provisional Act No. 3 of 25 April 1947 relating to war damage to moveable property laid down a general provision that the amount of compensation could be reduced or in the case of partial damage completely rejected "when this is found to be reasonable with regard to the claimant's financial status and needs ". This had direct economic consequences in cases where many members of a family had been killed. Reduced compensation was paid because, as it was put, the heirs could otherwise have profited from the war, since under normal circumstances they would not have inherited from so many people at once. In addition the payments were regulated by establishing an order of inheritance. On account of the differentiated inheritance tax, which was lower for direct heirs than for more distant relatives, the percentage paid out varied according to whether the heir was direct or indirect. The order of inheritance was established on the basis of assumptions of who had died first in a family that entered the gas chamber together. There are examples in the available evidence where the result of this supposed order of inheritance was very unfavorable for the survivors...

Since death certificates were not issued in Auschwitz, those who died there were classified as missing persons, not as dead. The survivors were not given assets from their estates since the assets were transferred to the public guardian's office. This applied to half of the group of survivors. From the public guardian's office the assets were transferred to the probate and bankruptcy court to be dealt with there. This process took many years, during which new orders of inheritance were also established. During the administration of estate proceedings, amounts charged to the estates included mortgage debt, taxes and inheritance tax. It is probable that such deductions in connection with public and private administration of estates were almost equivalent to the total payments to the Jewish group from the reparations agencies.... It was also difficult for the survivors to find out what their rights were, partly because no separate office was set up for Jewish matters, in contrast to the situation for other groups with a common fate...

It is proposed that the collective compensation should amount to NOK 250 million....

### 5.1.3 Establishment of a resource center for studies of the Holocaust and religious minorities in Norway

One of the most important lessons learned from World War II and the Holocaust was how vulnerable minorities are to prejudice, hatred and persecution, which taken to extremes led to the most systematic and gruesome genocide in history. The best means of combating prejudice is through unbiased information, which relies on knowledge of the minorities in our society. Thus the sum of NOK 40 million is proposed for the establishment and operation of a documentation and resource center for promoting expertise in Norway on the Holocaust in general and more specifically on the Norwegian chapter of the history of the Holocaust....

### 5.2 Individual compensation

The Government proposes a compensation in the form of a standard amount of NOK 200,000 to those persons in Norway who suffered from the anti-Jewish measures, for example who had their property and assets confiscated by the occupation authorities during the war. Many of these are now dead, and spouses and direct heirs will take their place and inherit according to the provisions concerning distribution laid down in the Inheritance Act. It is difficult to estimate the total cost of the individual compensation, since the amount will vary according to the number of applicants. The amount is expected to be in the region of NOK 100 to 200 million in addition to the collective compensation. If the individual payments should amount to substantially less than NOK 200 million, the Government will consider increasing the collective compensation. The Government will decide on how this should be used in collaboration with the Jewish communities in Norway....

The Ministry of Justice and the Police hereby recommends:
that Your Majesty approves and signs the submitted proposal for a White Paper to the Storting...

We Harald, King of Norway, hereby confirm:
that the Storting is requested to make a decision on the historical and moral settlement for the treatment in Norway of the economic liquidation of the Jewish minority during the Second World War in accordance with the submitted proposal.

---

During the 1990s many European institutions and states reconsidered their responses to the Holocaust and to the linked issues of responsibility and compensation. This document from the Norwegian government demonstrates many of the difficulties typically involved in this process.

As the recommendation makes clear, the Norwegian government's methods of resolving restitution questions right after the war were particularly difficult for Jewish victims. Continuing antisemitism was manifested at every turn in the process of dealing with Jews who had been persecuted by the wartime Norwegian state. Confiscated assets of Jewish families were underestimated, payments were delayed for years as the assets were passed from one government agency to another, and fees were deducted from the assets. It took two years to convince the Norwegian government to return the synagogue in Trondheim to the Jewish community. Such difficulties were encountered across Europe by Jews attempting to get back their property.

For nearly 50 years nothing more was done to offer recompense to Jewish Norwegians victimized by the Quisling government. In 1995 Bjarte Bruland wrote his Master's thesis on the destruction of the Norwegian Jews; his chapter on the confiscation of Jewish property was the first serious study of that issue. In May 1995, Bjorn Westlie wrote an article for his newspaper *Dagens Naeringsliv* on the confiscation of Jewish property in Norway. Questions were raised in the Parliament about postwar restitution, which the Department of Justice tried to quash. Meanwhile the Oslo Jewish community asked Bruland to help them investigate the issue themselves. In January 1996 the government decided to appoint a commission to investigate. Bruland and the psychologist Berit Reisel were asked to participate as nominees of the Jewish community. Bruland's archival research finally provided a complete picture of what had happened to Norway's Jews during and after the war.

The committee submitted a report in June 1997, in which Reisel and Bruland dissented from the majority about the damage done to Jews through Norwegian antisemitism and the incomplete nature of postwar restitution. Their minority report, the so-called Reisel/Bruland Report, offers considerable historical detail about what happened to Jews during the Holocaust and in their postwar efforts to get restitution. Bruland's documentation of the injustices done to survivors and families of victims convinced the government to disregard the majority's recommendation. The White Paper accepts the Reisel/Bruland Report, quoting some of its language and evidence. All political parties in the Norwegian Parliament, the Storting, adopted the White Paper on 11 March 1999. The next month, Prime Minister Kjell Magne Bondevik was awarded the Raoul Wallenberg Prize.

# 82. Article 'In Defense of Hitler' in Egyptian government newspaper, 27 May 2001

... I do not know what would have happened to Churchill, de Gaulle and Roosevelt, had Hitler won. Perhaps the crimes for which they deserve the death sentence would have been much worse than all that Hitler has done.

But all of Hitler's crimes and infractions were forgotten by the world, except for one crime that was exaggerated and blown completely out of proportion, thanks to the insistence of world Zionism to continue to stoke the fire. The reason for this was the emotional need of the Sons of Jacob to extort Germany and to eat away at its resources. It is hard to believe that the Europeans and Americans, who are entitled to thinking, confirming or denying anything — including the prophets and God himself — cannot address the 'Jewish Question', or more precisely, the false Holocaust, whose numbers and scope they have exaggerated until it has reached the level of the merciless destruction of six million Jews, only because Hitler saw them as an inferior race unworthy of living next to the Germanic race, which must rule the world.

Anyone who knocks on this door encounters the most horrible accusations and is tried in all of the European countries and in the US for anti-Semitism, for two reasons:

The first is Zionism's control over thinking in the West. This control testifies to the degree of oppression of thought by the Zionist propaganda apparatus in those nations. No one can oppose this oppression, for fear of being tried and sent to prison, or having his livelihood and his reputation threatened....

The second reason is, without a doubt, the great fear that the lies of Zionism will be exposed if the subject is investigated by facts and if logical conclusions are made.

The first dubious fact is the number of six million Jews who were burnt in the gas chambers. Did they have families, children, who demanded compensation, or did Zionism see itself as their only heir? If we assume that every person had an average of five family members, this would bring the number of Jews affected to thirty million. It is certain that many Jews escaped before the ship sunk, that many of them therefore, survived, despite the so-called extermination and burning. This would mean that the number of Jews in Germany was sixty million, although the total number of Germans has never reached this number.

Even if we cross off one zero from the six million and are left with a tenth of this number, it would still seem exaggerated and would have to be investigated.

No one can ask why Hitler punished the Jews. The reason had nothing to do with that broken record known as anti-Semitism. If Hitler was an anti-Semite, why was this anti-Semitism mentioned only after the World War was declared? Hitler could have expelled — in the period in which he built Germany up and prepared it for the War in order to recover what it lost in WWI — this undesirable race from Germany and planted it in South Africa or anywhere else in the world. Did Hitler attack the Jews or did their crime deserve even more? ...

The Zionists were a fifth column in Germany, and they betrayed the country that hosted them, in order to realize their aspirations. This had to be exposed, Hitler discovered that the Zionists were spies for the Allied Powers. Inevitably, he was enraged and took revenge on them for this great betrayal.

Both the Zionist movement and the Allied Powers had an interest in keeping this matter a secret, so that people would not know that the Zionists were punished for helping the Allied Powers, for betraying, and for stabbing Hitler in the back.

Even Germany and the government set up by the Allied Powers could not tell the truth, although they knew it, because it was under the influence of the Allied Powers, and because defeated nations must pay. Thus, the Zionist movement took control over the subject from Europe and the US and has easily made laws with which they try anyone who wants to raise the subject. Even historians can research any subject except for this forbidden one....

We denounce racial discrimination and the persecution of any person on the basis of religion, race or color, anywhere in the world. Those who yell about false persecutions that allegedly occurred half a century ago, must not ignore the persecution of others, their expulsion from their houses and their land, and the confiscation of their property. They should not commit those crimes that they claim were committed against them.

Likewise, Germany should pay compensations to the victims of mines that were planted in the Western desert [in Egypt], and compensations for the land that lay untouched for half a century, before it pays compensations for false crimes that have no proof except for false and misleading claims.

---

This article was written by Mahmoud Muhammad Khadhr, a cleric from Al-Azhar University, an Islamic institution in Cairo. The content exemplifies the way denial of the Holocaust is currently used as a rhetorical weapon against Israel. The references at the end to expulsion and confiscation bring this discussion of the Holocaust into the Arab-Israeli territorial conflict.

This piece displays features which are common to Holocaust denial in many countries. The staple claims of antisemitism, that Jews control the media or collectively betray their host countries, are placed into an argument about how lies about the Holocaust became so prevalent. As in other forms of denial, nonsensical historical and mathematical claims are presented as fact. Unlike denial in Western countries, which often tries to persuade a skeptical audience by raising doubts about the Holocaust, such claims can be made more openly in many countries of the Middle East, because they enjoy official support and operate within a context of public antisemitism. Thus here the Nazi attack on Jews is both denied and justified. Denials of the Holocaust can be found in the words of Ayatollah Ali Khameini, leader of Iran, Sheikh Ikrima Sabri, mufti of Jerusalem, and in leading newspapers in Syria and Jordan. Holocaust denial and comparisons of Zionism with Nazism are frequent in the writings and speeches of Palestinian intellectuals and politicians.[1]

The appearance of this translation on the website of the Middle East Media Research Institute is not only a public service, but part of that group's efforts to display the most extreme examples of antisemitism in various Arab media. The depth of Arab hatred of Jews is revealed in the open use of the most outrageous devices of antisemitism. In 2002, the Egyptian government's support for a television series based on the early 20th-century forgery, the so-called Protocols of the Elders of Zion, created further international controversy.

## Note

1 Robert Wistrich, *Muslim Anti-Semitism: A Clear and Present Danger* (New York: American Jewish Committee, 2002), pp. 37–43.

# 83. International Tribunal judgement against Radislav Krstić for Srebrenica massacre, 2 August 2001

UNITED NATIONS

| | | |
|---|---|---|
| International Tribunal for the Prosecution of Persons | Case No. | IT-98-33-T |
| Responsible for Serious Violations of International Humanitarian Law Committed in the Territory of | Date: | 02 August 2001 |
| Former Yugoslavia since 1991 | Original: | English |

IN THE TRIAL CHAMBER

Before: Judge Almiro Rodrigues, Presiding
Judge Fouad Riad
Judge Patricia Wald

Registrar: Mr. Hans Holthuis

PROSECUTOR
v.
RADISLAV KRSTIC

JUDGEMENT

... 1. The events surrounding the Bosnian Serb take-over of the United Nations ("UN") "safe area" of Srebrenica in Bosnia and Herzegovina, in July 1995, have become well known to the world. Despite a UN Security Council resolution declaring that the enclave was to be "free from armed attack or any other hostile act", units of the Bosnian Serb Army ("VRS") launched an attack and captured the town. Within a few days, approximately 25,000 Bosnian Muslims, most of them women, children and elderly people who were living in the area, were uprooted and, in an atmosphere of terror, loaded onto overcrowded buses by the Bosnian Serb forces and transported across the confrontation lines into Bosnian Muslim-held territory. The military-aged Bosnian Muslim men of Srebrenica, however, were consigned to a separate fate. As thousands of them attempted to flee the area, they were taken prisoner, detained in brutal conditions and then executed. More than 7,000 people were never seen again....

539. General Krstić is principally charged with genocide and, in the alternative, with complicity in genocide in relation to the mass executions of the Bosnian Muslim men in Srebrenica between 11 July and 1 November 1995....
552. United Nations General Assembly resolution 96 (I) defined genocide as "a denial of the right of existence of entire human groups".... In 1951, following the adoption of the Genocide Convention, the International Court of Justice observed that the Convention looked "to safeguard the very existence of certain human groups and ... to confirm and endorse the most elementary principles of morality"....
594. The Trial Chamber concludes from the evidence that the VRS forces sought to eliminate all of the Bosnian Muslims in Srebrenica as a community. Within a period of no more than seven days, as many as 7,000 – 8,000 men of military age were systematically massacred while the remainder of the Bosnian Muslim population present at Srebrenica, some 25,000 people, were forcibly transferred to Kladanj....
598. The Chamber concludes that the intent to kill all the Bosnian Muslim men of military age in Srebrenica constitutes an intent to destroy in part the Bosnian Muslim group within the meaning of Article 4 and therefore must be qualified as a genocide....
633. The Trial Chamber concludes beyond reasonable doubt that General Krstić participated in a joint criminal enterprise to kill the Bosnian Muslim military-aged men from Srebrenica from the evening of 13 July onwards. General Krstić may not have devised the killing plan, or participated in the initial decision to escalate the objective of the criminal enterprise from forcible transfer to destruction of Srebrenica's Bosnian Muslim military-aged male community, but there can be no doubt that, from the point he learned of the widespread and systematic killings and became clearly involved in their perpetration, he shared the genocidal intent to kill the men....
727. Based upon the facts and the legal findings as determined by the Trial Chamber and for the foregoing reasons, the Trial Chamber:

**FINDS** Radislav Krstić **GUILTY** of:

g) Genocide;
h) Persecution for murders, cruel and inhumane treatment, terrorizing the civilian population, forcible transfer and destruction of personal property of Bosnian Muslim civilians;
i) Murder as a violation of the Laws and Customs of War;

**SENTENCES** Radislav KRSTIĆ to Fourty six years of imprisonment and **STATES** that the full amount of time spent in custody of the Tribunal will be deducted from the time to be served.

Done on second of August 2001 in English and French, the English text being authoritative.

At the Hague, The Netherlands

[signatures] Judge Fouad Riad Judge Almiro Rodrigues Judge Patricia Wald Presiding

---

The concept of an international court which could try cases of genocide developed as a result of the Nuremberg trials and the creation of the United Nations. In December 1948, the UN General Assembly adopted the Convention on the Prevention and Punishment of the Crime of Genocide. Despite many instances of genocidal murder across the world since the end of World War II, the first use of the International Court in the Hague for prosecuting genocide came out of the wars in the former Yugoslavia in the 1990s. Vast civilian casualties resulted from horrific practices on all sides of the war in Bosnia Herzegovina. Between 1992 and 1995, over 200,000 people died, mainly Muslims, and nearly 3 million became refugees. Serbian forces were responsible for most of the deaths, as well as for the mass rapes of an estimated 20,000 to 50,000 Bosnian Muslim women.[1]

As an international response to the civilian deaths in the Balkans, the UN Security Council established the International Criminal Tribunal for the former Yugoslavia (ICTY) in the Hague in May 1993. As soon as peace terms were negotiated to end the war in Bosnia in November 1995, preparations for the trial of war criminals began. Mass graves with thousands of Muslim corpses were unearthed at Srebrenica by UN workers. In 1996 the ICTY began to process cases, and the scope of these proceedings rivals the Nuremberg trials. By the end of 2002, 5 defendants had been found not guilty, 29 found guilty and sentenced, 3 were awaiting judgment, 8 were on trial, 26 were in the pre-trial stage, 42 were in custody, and 24 arrest warrants were still outstanding. General Krstić is the only defendant who has been found guilty of genocide.

The most significant defendant is Slobodan Milosevic, former President of Serbia and Yugoslavia, whose trial includes crimes committed in Serbian wars in Bosnia Herzegovina, Croatia, and Kosovo since 1987. His trial, which began in February 2002, brings the highest political authority to answer to the international community of nations for crimes committed by the armed forces of his state, including genocide.

## Note

1 Sabrina Petra Ramet, *Balkan Babel: The Disintegration of Yugoslavia from the Death of Tito to the War for Kosovo* (Boulder, CO: Westview Press, 1999), p. 239.

# 84. Joint resolution of Maine legislature on Holocaust remembrance, 13 March 2002

## State of Maine

In the Year of Our Lord Two Thousand and Two

**JOINT RESOLUTION COMMEMORATING THE HOLOCAUST HUMAN RIGHTS CENTER'S LEGISLATIVE AWARENESS DAY AND YOM HASHOAH, THE DAY OF REMEMBRANCE OF THOSE WHO SUFFERED AS VICTIMS OF THE HOLOCAUST**

**WHEREAS,** from 1933 to 1945, 6,000,000 Jews were murdered in the Nazi Holocaust as part of a systematic program of genocide, and millions of other people suffered as victims of Nazism; and

**WHEREAS,** the people of the State of Maine should always remember the atrocities committed by the Nazis so that such horrors are never repeated; and

**WHEREAS,** the people of the State of Maine should always remember those who liberated the Nazi concentration camps, some at the cost of their lives and others with lifelong emotional suffering, as holding an honored place in our history; and

**WHEREAS,** the people of the State of Maine should continually rededicate themselves to the principle of equal justice for all people, remain eternally vigilant against all tyranny and recognize that bigotry provides a breeding ground for tyranny to flourish; and

**WHEREAS,** March 13, 2002 has been designated internationally as the Holocaust Human Rights Center's Legislative Awareness Day; and

**WHEREAS,** April 9, 2002 has been designated internationally as a Day of Remembrance of the Victims of the Nazi Holocaust, and is known as Yom HaShoah; and

**WHEREAS,** the national community, pursuant to an Act of Congress, will be commemorating the week of April 7th to April 14th as the Days of Remembrance of the Victims of the Nazi Holocaust, with the theme of "Memories of Courage"; and

**WHEREAS,** it is appropriate for the people of the State of Maine to join in this international commemoration; now, therefore, be it

**RESOLVED:** That, We, the Members of the One Hundred and Twentieth Legislature, now assembled in the Second Regular Session, on behalf of the people we represent, pause in solemn memory of the victims of the Nazi Holocaust, urge one and all to recommit themselves to the lessons of the Nazi Holocaust through the Holocaust Human Rights Center's Legislative Awareness Day and the international week of commemoration and express our common desire to continually strive to overcome prejudice and inhumanity through education, vigilance and resistance; and be it further

**RESOLVED:** That suitable copies of this resolution, duly authenticated by the Secretary of State, be transmitted to the United States Holocaust Memorial Council in Washington, D.C., on behalf of the people of the State of Maine.

| House of Representatives | | In Senate Chamber |
|---|---|---|
| Read and Adopted | | Under Suspension of the Rules |
| March 13, 2002 | | Read and Adopted |
| Sent for Concurrence | | March 13, 2002 |
| Ordered Sent Forthwith | | In Concurrence |
| MILLICENT M. MacFARLAND | [signatures] | PAMELA L. CAHILL |
| Clerk of the House | | Secretary of the Senate |

**H.P. 1668**

**ATTEST:** MICHAEL V. SAXL [signatures] **ATTEST:** RICHARD A. BENNETT
Speaker of the House of Representatives President of the Senate

---

Every year the Maine legislature passes this resolution recognizing the significance of the Holocaust and its remembrance. In 2002, the 5 Jewish members of the Maine House of Representatives co-sponsored the resolution. This official political act indicates the extent to which the Holocaust has become part of American political life at all levels. It refers to the yearly action of the US Congress which recognizes Yom HaShoah, creates a week of remembrance, and selects a theme for educational activities involving government and military personnel. Maine has a tiny Jewish population.

In Maine, as in other states, a privately funded statewide organization, the Holocaust Human Rights Center, develops educational materials, organizes events including memorial services on Yom HaShoah, and generally raises the level of awareness of the Holocaust. The explicit linking of the Holocaust with more general issues of prejudice, tolerance, and equal rights, both in the name of the Center and in the Joint Resolution, is sometimes seen as an Americanization of the Holocaust. In a number of American states with significant Jewish populations, the teaching of the Holocaust in public schools has been mandated by the state legislature.

This attention to the Holocaust is a sign that the acceptance of social discrimination against Jews, part of American culture since colonial days, was finally broken after the Holocaust. Although hatred of Jews remains in isolated pockets, in all classes and subcultures in America the issue of religious affiliation has diminished in relationships between Christians and Jews. As a measure of religious parity, probably as many Jewish voices are raised against marrying out of the faith as Christian.

Section XI

# Conclusion

A document alone, seen apart from its context, reveals little. Numerous documents must be read together to understand the meanings of any one. Viktor Brack's suggestion that 7 to 8 million Jews be killed or Goebbels' claim that Jews started World War II could be taken for the ravings of the insane. Placed next to repeated tabulations of how many people the Nazis planned to kill or had already killed, their words radiate much more ominous meanings. Only when read together with detailed descriptions of killing operations, can their historical significance be fully understood.

The juxtaposition of the words of perpetrators and victims is especially import- ant. By this point, readers of these documents have experienced the simplifying and distancing effects produced by the language and form of Nazi writing. The reduction of human victims to numbered objects was a technique mutually understood by the writers and recipients of the unending reports which accompanied the murder and disposal of millions of people. Falsification took place at every level, because it was systematically embedded in the process. One of the aspects of Jewish behavior that the Nazis most wished to hide from everyone was resistance; their documents thus offer a deliberately falsified picture of Jewish responses to persecution.

In the years after 1945, it was extraordinarily difficult for the few living victims to express what they had survived. Even Jews did not welcome their mournful voices.[1] Historians, trained to rely upon official written sources, depended upon Nazi documentation to understand the Holocaust. They were therefore unable to perceive Jewish responses, specifically Jewish resistance, accurately. For decades after 1945, Jewish behavior in Europe lay buried under the flood of Nazi documents, which portrayed Jews at best as stoically going to their deaths and at worst as accomplices in the process. Through the Nazi portrayal of the quantity and quality of Jewish resistance, the legend of sheep to the slaughter was born.

If we wish to understand the actual human interactions which had been refracted through Nazi perceptions and language, we must listen to the voices of those who survived. What they say, as the most natural part of their narratives, is how persistently they tried to thwart the Nazis' intentions for themselves, for their families, for their neighbors. From Ella Czecher's attempt to keep her business, to Eduard Hamber's official complaint about his brother's murder at Buchenwald, to the burial of the Oneg Shabbat archives by Emanuel Ringelblum, to the refusal by Judith Isaacson to obey Mengele, to Shalom Kohn's escape from Treblinka, ordinary Jews resisted their extraordinary circumstances.

Survivors also universally spoke of luck, not their own actions or decisions, as the reason for their survival. Only by reading, hearing, and seeing survivors' accounts, which have continued to multiply in their uniqueness and variety, can we recognize what survivors mean by this talk of luck. The people around them, in unfathomable numbers, were killed suddenly and arbitrarily, with the ultimate intention of killing them all. It was not resistance which made the survivors unique, but the fact that out of all those who resisted in countless ways, they lived to tell the tale. Communicating about their experiences to later generations has required a struggle with the most complex emotional and linguistic obstacles. Usually the survivor is the only one who can tell us about their entire social network; their stories are unique and thus usually unverifiable.

The unofficial and highly personal sources which survivors have produced continue to be discounted, or even disdained. Raul Hilberg's manual on Holocaust sources unfavorably compares the value of victim testimony to the voluminous Nazi documents that he used in such a masterly way in his path-breaking study of the process of annihilation.[2] Peter Novick, who has argued that Americans pay too much attention to the Holocaust, claims that survivors' memories 'are not a very useful historical source'.[3] In fact, the determined efforts of survivors to tell the truth in all European languages must be scrutinized for the necessary insights they provide about what the Holocaust really was. The history of the Holocaust cannot be written without the memories of those who want above all to tell what they saw, what they felt, what they thought, and what they did.

I use the word Holocaust here to include the whole range of destructive forces that the Nazis unleashed against unarmed men, women, and children across Europe. I do not mean by that usage to diminish the differences among the separately developed and ideologically distinct Nazi designs for Jews, Gypsies, Poles, or the handicapped. The documents display clearly, both in content and tone, how the Nazis distinguished one set of victims from another, precisely whom they wanted to eliminate, and what reasons they offered for killing them. Methods varied in the extreme: the architects of genocide dreamed of a world free of Jews, including those converted to Christianity, but also attempted to convert 'Aryan' homosexuals and Jehovah's Witnesses to proper Germanic thought and behavior.

A major strand of intellectual contention winds around the particular question of whether the Nazi murder of Jews was so different from the other components of Nazi genocide that it should be uniquely labelled and analyzed. The differences are obvious even from this small selection of documents. The Nazi genocide of the Jews was so unlike the pogroms of the previous thousand years that it requires a particular understanding and analysis. The attempt to kill all the Jews listed in the minutes of the Wannsee Conference was qualitatively distinct from the plans to kill some kinds of Gypsies and a substantial number of Poles. The Nazis took pains to humiliate Jewish victims as they murdered them; for example, attacks on Jews in ghettos and camps were regularly timed to fall on Yom Kippur and Rosh Hashana. Even at the end, the SS made distinctions between Jews and other prisoners. On 8 April, just 3 days before American soldiers arrived, most of the remaining Jews were marched out of Buchenwald and walked to Flossenbürg camp, 100 miles southeast, many dying along the way. Over 20,000 other prisoners were left to be liberated.

All of the genocidal projects perpetrated by the Nazis were conceived as necessary parts of enormous plans of social engineering to create their perfect Aryan space across Central and Eastern Europe. An ideological compound of cultural superiority, social Darwinism, racial hatred, and disregard for human life, each pushed to an insane extreme, linked the ambitions and the methods of these projects. I do not agree, therefore, that we should reserve the word Holocaust for the murder of Jews. Holocaust seems uniquely suitable as a single label charged with evoking the slaughter and destruction, often through fire, which tore across European life. Like a tornado it touched down sporadically in Western Europe; like a tidal wave it obliterated everything in its path in Eastern Europe. Each region and each people suffered uniquely, while all suffered in unprecedented dimensions.

I have included evidence here about the most significant groups of victims of the Nazis. There were yet other victims. On 10 June 1944, four days after D-Day, the men of Oradour-sur-Glane were machine-gunned and the women and children were burned alive in their church, in retaliation for the killing of one SS officer by the French resistance.[4] Among the 642 victims, there were 7 Jewish refugees who had escaped deportation. These Jews were Holocaust victims even before they were murdered. While ignoring the different paths these two kinds of victims took to their deaths would misrepresent history, claiming that the non-Jewish French victims were not killed in the Holocaust does not increase our comprehension.

While the projects of genocide were different, I do not see the sense in exaggerating their separateness, as opposed to explicating their distinctiveness.

The SS coordinated plans for deporting Catholic and Jewish Poles and Gypsies out of conquered territory; Gypsies and Jews were shot together in Yugoslavia; Soviet soldiers, Gypsies, and Jewish civilians were killed by gas in Auschwitz; the bodies of Orthodox and Jewish citizens filled mass graves in the Ukraine; Jews, Polish priests, and Soviet POWs were exhumed and burned together; the final transports to the gas chambers of Birkenau carried German Jews and Gypsy children to their deaths. The men who invented the technological process of killing Germany's handicapped then applied their expertise to Europe's Jews. It does not help our understanding to say that the Jews died in the Holocaust, but the others died in a genocide which should carry a different name.[5]

The dispute about naming, as well as the documents in the final section, shows that there has been no conclusion to the Holocaust. It certainly did not close with the first liberations of the concentration camps. Decades later many American camp liberators are still brought to tears when describing the piles of corpses they saw scattered all over Germany.[6] Even after the end of fighting in Germany in May 1945, the dying continued. Thousands of released prisoners died after the liberation of Bergen-Belsen, Mauthausen, and other camps.

The Jews who survived and recovered enough to return to their homes were not welcomed back. Viennese expressed surprise at the appearance of returning survivors and refugees, but offered little regret or willingness to part with the property they had aryanized. The violence continued in Poland. After a few isolated incidents where Catholic Poles killed returning Jewish Poles, the myth of Jewish ritual murder of Christian children once again aroused violent hatred. A pogrom broke out in Kielce against the 200 Jews who had survived from the original community of 15,000. A crowd which included police and a priest killed 42 of them.[7]

Most remaining Jews fled Europe to the large Jewish communities in American cities and in Palestine. For decades the Holocaust was ignored, despite the revelation of all its evils in Nuremberg. Eventually the lonely work of historians like Hilberg and the testimony of survivors broke through walls of disbelief and denial. Articulate survivors eventually regained their power of expression and have produced an extraordinary literature. That literature has expanded into new media, trying to meet the continuously expanding demand for authentic experience.

I applaud the understanding throughout English-speaking countries that the Holocaust is also part of our culture, even though it did not take place on our soil. As the documents in the final section show, the process of facing the Holocaust will continue for some time. For the dwindling number of survivors, it has never stopped. Psychologists have demonstrated the existence of traumatic effects in survivor families into the third generation. Not only they should be affected. We can all continue to be shocked. According to today's use of the word genocide, the Nazis committed genocide on Jewish Poles every day during *Aktion Reinhardt,* then congratulated themselves, and tried to finish off Jews in Western Europe.

I see in my classes a generation of students from across the world. Most have read Wiesel's *Night,* one of the most memorable literary productions of the 20th century. They are seeking to know more, because they are stunned at what they have learned. The more they know, the more distressed, frustrated, angry and sad they become. They would like truth, but they find death. They get closer to answering 'why?', but further from believing that it can be answered. A few say much later that by reading and talking and thinking about what these documents show, their lives were changed in profound ways. I believe in Holocaust education. No other piece of our history has the capacity of the Holocaust to force us to reconsider our deepest assumptions about the human race and ourselves.

One of Western civilization's most comfortable assumptions has been the cultural superiority of that civilization. Open expressions of that superiority accompanied the worldwide thrusts of European imperialism, many times genocidal in their results. After the tragic events of the 20th century, cultural superiority no longer so thoroughly pervades our language, but still runs beneath the surface of Western contacts with the rest of humanity. The Western sense of self has depended on a willingness to accept the frequently repeated assertion of the so-called bystanders that they knew little about the Holocaust. I think these few documents tell a different story. Explicit knowledge travelled widely throughout European society and across the Atlantic Ocean. Goebbels' pronouncements of state policy could not have received more publicity. From the beginning, the Nazis as high as Hitler and as low as the average SA man talked about killing millions, and then did it. Filip Müller returned from the alien planet of Auschwitz with an understanding created out of trauma: 'Hitler and his henchmen had never made a secret of their attitude to the Jews nor of their avowed intention to exterminate them like vermin. The whole world knew it, and knowing it remained silent; was not this silence equivalent to consent?'

To assert Western superiority, one needs a better answer to that question than I can give.

## Notes

1 Tom Segev showed how unsympathetic Israeli responses to survivors obstructed an understanding of their experiences until after the Eichmann trial in 1961: *The Seventh Million: The Israelis and the Holocaust,* trans. Haim Watzman (New York: Hill and Wang, 1993).

2 For Hilberg's comments on the limitations of victims' accounts, see *Sources of Holocaust Research*, pp. 44–9, 153. His major work in 3 volumes is *The Destruction of the European Jews*, Second ed. (New York: Holmes & Meier, 1985).

3 Peter Novick, *The Holocaust in American Life* (Boston, MA: Houghton Mifflin, 1999), p. 275. Novick's scorn for survivors as unreliable witnesses is polite compared to the malicious derision offered by some recent authors who have attracted attention by ridiculing everyone who writes about the Holocaust; examples are Norman Finkelstein, *The Holocaust Industry: Reflections on the Exploitation of Jewish Suffering* (London: Verso, 2000), or Tim Cole, *Selling the Holocaust: From Auschwitz to Schindler: How History is Bought, Packaged, and Sold* (New York: Routledge, 1999).

4 Sarah Farmer, *Martyred Village: Commemorating the 1944 Massacre at Oradour-sur-Glane* (Berkeley, CA: University of California Press, 1999) describes this event.

5 The argument for reserving the word 'Holocaust' for the killing of Jews is made most cogently by Yehuda Bauer, *Rethinking the Holocaust* (New Haven, CA: Yale University Press, 2001). Works published in Germany generally assume that Holocaust means only the murder of Jews: for example, the reference work edited by Wolfgang Benz, *Lexikon des Holocaust* (Munich: Verlag C.H. Beck, 2002).

6 Videotaped interviews with camp liberators have been preserved by many local Holocaust organizations. The interview collection of the Holocaust Human Rights Center of Maine includes the memories of 5 American Army veterans. An equivalent effort to record the experiences of Soviet liberators, who stumbled upon Auschwitz and the other centers of destruction in Poland, would yield remarkable results for historians and society.

7 The Polish historian Jan Gross is currently embarked on a remarkable research effort to uncover evidence of the murders of Jews by Poles, both during and after the Holocaust. His first book on this subject, *Neighbors: The Destruction of the Jewish Community in Jedwabne, Poland* (Princeton, NJ: Princeton University Press, 2001) set off a storm of controversy in Poland. Like all historians trying to tell histories not welcomed by their countrymen, he faces tremendous obstacles in pursuing this work.

# Sources

## The Context of Christian Antisemitism

1. *The Holy Bible Containing the Old and the New Testaments*, Authorized King James Version, ed. Rev. C.I. Scofield (New York: Oxford University Press, 1945), pp. 1041, 1127, 1332–4.
2. Translated from the Hebrew by Robert Chazan, *European Jewry and the First Crusade* (Berkeley, CA: University of California Press, 1987), pp. 225, 232–4. Chazan and other scholars attribute this chronicle to an anonymous Mainz Jew writing about events that he did not personally witness. A different translation is provided in Shlomo Eidelberg, *The Jews and the Crusaders: The Hebrew Chronicles of the First and Second Crusades* (Madison, WI: University of Wisconsin Press, 1977), pp. 99–115.
3. Martin Luther, 'On the Jews and Their Lies', 1543, trans. Martin H. Bertram, in *Luther's Works*, Vol. 47, ed. Franklin Sherman (Philadelphia, PA: Fortress Press, 1971), pp. 121–306, excerpts from pp. 137, 217, 266–75, 292, 305–6.
4. Based on the translation in Kenneth R. Stow, *Catholic Thought and Papal Jewry Policy 1555–1593* (New York: Jewish Theological Seminary of America, 1977), pp. 294–8; some changes to this translation were made.
5. Excerpts from Father Saverio Rondina, 'La morale giudaica', *Civiltà cattolica*, 10 January 1893, I, pp. 145–53, 160, provided by David Kertzer, translated by Francesco Duina.

## The Creation of Monsters in Germany: Jews and Others

6. Translated from original in Bayerisches Hauptstaatsarchiv, Munich, Kammer der Reichsräte 2658, partly based on translation in James F. Harris, *The People Speak! Anti-Semitism and Emancipation in Nineteenth-Century Bavaria* (Ann Arbor, MI: University of Michigan Press, 1994), pp. 252–3.
7. Translated from Heinrich von Treitschke, 'Unsere Aussichten', *Preussische Jahrbücher*, 44 (1879), pp. 572–5.
8. Translated from Professor Dr Karl Binding and Professor Dr Alfred Hoche, *Die Freigabe der Vernichtung lebensunwerten Lebens: Ihr Maß und ihre Form* (Leipzig: Verlag von Felix Meiner, 1920), pp. 27, 32, 54–5.
9. Translated from reprint of court verdict in *Vierteljahrshefte für Zeitgeschichte*, 5 (1957), pp. 286–97, excerpts 286–7, 289–91, 296–7.

## The Nazi Attack on Jews and Other Undesirables in the Third Reich, 1933–1938

10. Translated from original in Bayerisches Hauptstaatsarchiv, Munich, Akt StK Nr. 6672. This incident is referred to by Saul Friedländer, who quotes extensively

from this report in *Nazi Germany and the Jews: Volume 1: The Years of Persecution, 1933–1939* (New York: HarperCollins, 1997), p. 18.

11. Translated from manuscript by Paula Tobias, Houghton Library, Harvard University (bMS Ger 91 (235)/Tobias, Paula), pp. 178–9, 185.
12. Translated from a reprinted version, *Deutschland-Bericht der Sopade, 1935*, Vol. 2 (Salzhausen: Verlag Petra Nettelbeck, 1980), pp. 893, 920–2.
13. Translated from *Reichsgesetzblatt*, Part I, 1935, No. 100, pp. 1146–7. A different translation is published in Yitzhak Arad, Yisrael Gutman, and Abraham Margaliot (eds), *Documents on the Holocaust: Selected Sources on the Destruction of the Jews of Germany and Austria, Poland, and the Soviet Union* (Jerusalem: Yad Vashem, 1981), pp. 78–9.
14. Translated from copy of German original archived in Florida Holocaust Museum in Tampa.
15. Translated from speech printed in *Heinrich Himmler: Geheimreden 1933 bis 1945 und andere Ansprachen*, ed. Bradley F. Smith and Agnes F. Peterson (Frankfurt a.M.: Verlag Ullstein, 1974), pp. 93–104, excerpts pp. 93, 94, 97–8; a different translation of excerpts of this speech is in Michael Burleigh and Wolfgang Wippermann, *The Racial State: Germany 1933–1945* (Cambridge: Cambridge University Press, 1991), pp. 192–3.
16. Translated from Ernst Hiemer, *Der Giftpilz: Ein Stürmerbuch für Jung und Alt* (Nuremberg: Verlag Der Stürmer, 1938), pp. 33–6. Nuremberg document PS-1778 contains a photocopy of *Der Giftpilz*, and extracts are translated in *Nazi Conspiracy and Aggression*, Vol. 4 (Washington, DC: United States Government Printing Office, 1946), pp. 358–60.

## The Physical Assault on Jews in Germany, 1938–1939

17. Translated from Walter Grab, 'Die Juden sind Ungeziefer, ausgenommen mein jüdischer Schulkamerad Grab', in Jörg Wollenberg (ed.), *"Niemand war dabei und keiner hat's gewußt": Die deutsche Öffentlichkeit und die Judenverfolgung 1933–1945* (Munich: Piper, 1989), pp. 45–50, excerpt on pp. 47–50.
18. Translated from a reprinted version in Hans Witek and Hans Safrian (eds), *Und keiner war dabei: Dokumente des alltäglichen Antisemitismus in Wien 1938* (Vienna: Picus Verlag, 1988), pp. 63–4. The original is archived in Dokumentationsarchiv des Österreichischen Widerstands, Vienna, Akt 5305.
19. Translated from a reprinted version in Witek and Safrian, *Und keiner war dabei*, pp. 108–9. The original is archived in Allgemeines Verwaltungsarchiv, Vienna, Vermögensverkehrsstelle, Karton 905, R.A. 32.
20. Translation of letter issued by the office of Feng Shan Ho in Vienna, now in possession of Serge Bluds, nephew of Paul Lagstein. Manli Ho, daughter of Feng Shan Ho, alerted me to the existence of this document.
21. Facsimiles of the memo from the British Embassy and a German reply are printed in John Mendelsohn (ed.), *The Holocaust: Selected Documents in Eighteen Volumes*, Vol. 5, *Jewish Emigration from 1933 to the Evian Conference of 1938* (New York: Garland Publishing, 1982), pp. 141–8.
22. Translated from Nuremberg document PS-1721, United States National Archives (USNA), Record Group (RG) 238, microfilm publication T988, roll 17. A different translation is reprinted in *The Crystal Night Pogrom*, pp. 281–2; also in *Nazi Conspiracy and Aggression*, Vol. 4, pp. 215–19. The document PS-1721 includes similar reports from many places in Southwest Germany.

23. Translated from copy in United States Holocaust Memorial Museum, Record Group-14.006*03; original letter archived in Zentrales Staatsarchiv Potsdam, 75 C Hil HICEM, Prag, Nr. 7, Bl. 1–3. Mrs. Schmolkova's reply is archived in the same places.
24. Translated from reprinted version in Joachim Meynert and Friedhelm Schäffer, *'Die Juden in der Stadt Bielefeld während der Zeit des Nationalsozialismus'*, Bielefelder Beiträge zur Stadt- und Regionalgeschichte, Vol. 3 (Bielefeld: 1983), pp. 159–60. Original is archived in Staatsarchiv Detmold, Regierung Minden, M 1 I P (Polizei), Bd. 1, Nr. 1714.
25. Translated from Nuremberg document NG-1793, reprinted in *The Crystal Night Pogrom*, pp. 211–15. A different translation is presented on pp. 216–22.
26. Cordell Hull's instruction to US Embassy in Berlin, as amended by Theodore C. Achilles, archived in USNA, file number 893.55J/4, microfilm publication LM63, roll 143. I am grateful to David S. Wyman for alerting me to this document.

## The Perfection of Genocide as National Policy, 1939–1943

27. Translated from Nuremberg document PS-3363, USNA, RG 238. Different translations are reprinted in *Nazi Conspiracy and Aggression*, Vol. 6 (Washington, DC: United States Government Printing Office, 1946), pp. 97–101, and in Lucy S. Dawidowicz (ed.), *A Holocaust Reader* (New York: Behrman House, Inc., 1976), pp. 59–64.
28. Translated from a microfilm copy of Groscurth's diary, archived at Bundesarchiv Ludwigsburg, Ordner USA, film 4, pp. 346–7.
29. Translated from facsimile of German original reprinted in *Faschismus – Getto – Massenmord: Dokumentation über Ausrottung und Widerstand der Juden in Polen während des zweiten Weltkrieges* (Berlin: Rütten und Loening, 1960), p. 69; original archived in Archive of the Jewish Historical Institute in Warsaw, poster No. 166.
30. Translated from report of interrogation of Dr August Becker on 4 April 1960, pp. 4–5, archived in Bundesarchiv Ludwigsburg, B 162 ARZ 6000018a/ Vol. 1; reprinted in E. Klee, *"Euthanasie" im NS-Staat: Die Vernichtung "lebensunwerten Lebens"* (Frankfurt: 1983), pp. 110–12; a different translation appears in J. Noakes and G. Pridham (eds), *Nazism 1919–1945: A History in Documents and Eyewitness Accounts*, Vol. 2, *Foreign Policy, War and Racial Extermination* (New York: Schocken Books, 1990), pp. 1019–20.
31. Translated from Nuremberg document NO-5322, USNA, RG 238; a different translation is reprinted in *Trials of War Criminals before the Nuernberg Military Tribunals under Control Council Law No. 10, Nuernberg October 1946 – April 1949*, Vol. 4, pp. 855–61.
32. Translated from reprinted version in Götz Aly, *Aktion T4 1939–1945: Die "Euthanasie"-Zentrale in der Tiergartenstraße 4* (Berlin: Edition Hentrich, 1987), pp. 50–2; a different translation is reprinted in Götz Aly, 'Medicine against the Useless', in Götz Aly, Peter Chroust, and Christian Pross, *Cleansing the Fatherland: Nazi Medicine and Racial Hygiene*, trans. Belinda Cooper (Baltimore, MD: Johns Hopkins University Press, 1994), pp. 48–50.
33. Archived in Library of Congress, Breckinridge Long to Adolf A. Berle, Jr., and James C. Dunn, June 26, 1940, Breckinridge Long Papers, Box 211, Visa Division, General, 1940.
34. Translated from p. 29 of brochure of statistics on the economic value of the 'euthanasia' program, found by liberating British troops in a locked safe in

Hartheim Castle, reprinted in Johannes Tuchel (ed.), *"Kein Recht auf Leben": Beiträge und Dokumente zur Entrechtung und Vernichtung "lebensunwerten Lebens" im Nationalsozialismus* (Berlin: Wissenschaftlicher Autoren-Verlag, 1984), pp. 92–3; archived in Bundesarchiv Koblenz, All. Proz 7., FC 1813, Bild 91ff.

35. Translated from Nuremberg document NO-3137, USNA, RG 238; a facsimile of the original is reprinted in *The Holocaust*, Vol. 10, *The Einsatzgruppen or Murder Commandos* (New York: Garland Publishing, Inc., 1982), pp. 45–8.
36. Translated from Nuremberg document NOKW-309, USNA, RG 238; a facsimile of the original is reprinted in *The Holocaust*, Vol. 10, *The Einsatzgruppen or Murder Commandos*, pp. 8–9, with a different English translation from 1948 on pp. 11–12. The document is also reprinted in *Trial of the Major War Criminals before the International Military Tribunal, Nuremberg, 14 November 1945 – 1 October 1946* (Nuremberg, 1949), Vol. 35, pp. 84–6. This document also appears as Nuremberg document D-411.
37. Translated from Nuremberg document NO-365, USNA, RG 238. A different translation appears in *Trials of War Criminals before the Nuernberg Military Tribunals under Control Council Law No. 10*, Vol. 1, pp. 870–1. A different translation appears in Gerald Fleming, *Hitler and the Final Solution* (Berkeley, CA: University of California Press, 1984), pp. 70–1.
38. English translation printed in *Documents on German Foreign Policy 1918–1945, Series D 1937–1945, Volume 13, The War Years, June 23 – December 11, 1941* (Washington, DC: US Government Printing Office, 1949), pp. 697–9.
39. Translated from Nuremberg document NOKW-905, USNA, RG 238. A facsimile is reprinted in *Trials of War Criminals before the Nuernberg Military Tribunals under Control Council Law No. 10*, Vol. 11, pp. 1139–40; a different translation is given on pp. 996–7.
40. Translated from Nuremberg document PS-1104, USNA, RG 238; a facsimile in reprinted in *The Holocaust*, Vol. 10, *The Einsatzgruppen or Murder Commandos*, pp. 240–4, with a different English translation on pp. 248–50. PS-1104 also contains a letter of Kube to Lohse transmitting Carl's report, and a further letter of transmittal to Rosenberg.
41. Translated from *Das Reich*, No. 46, 16 November 1941, pp. 1–2, as reproduced in facsimile in Hans Dieter Müller (ed.), *Facsimile Querschnitt durch Das Reich* (Munich: Scherz Verlag, 1964), pp. 98–101; a different translation is printed in Joachim Remak (ed.), *The Nazi Years: A Documentary History* (New York: Simon and Schuster, 1969), pp. 155–7.
42. Translated from Nuremberg document NG-2586, USNA, RG 238; a facsimile is printed in John Mendelsohn (ed.), *The Holocaust: Selected Documents in Eighteen Volumes*, Vol. 11, *The Wannsee Protocol and a 1944 Report on Auschwitz by the Office of Strategic Services* (New York: Garland Publishing, 1982), pp. 3–17; a different translation is reprinted on pp. 18–32.
43. Translated from Nuremberg document PS-501, USNA, RG 238; also reprinted in *Trial of the Major War Criminals before the International Military Tribunal*, Vol. 26, pp. 102–5. Excerpts from this letter were used in the Nuremberg trial of Einsatzgruppen officers and are reprinted in a different translation in *Trials of War Criminals before the Nuernberg Military Tribunals under Control Council Law No. 10*, Vol. 4, pp. 198–9.
44. Translated from Nuremberg document NO-205, USNA, RG 238; reprinted in Ernst Klee (ed.), *Dokumente zur "Euthanasie"* (Frankfurt am Main: Fischer Verlag, 1985), pp. 274–5, and in Tuchel, *"Kein Recht auf Leben": Beiträge und Dokumente zur Entrechtung und Vernichtung "lebensunwerten Lebens" in Nationalsozialismus*, pp. 96–7.

45. Translated from copy in US Holocaust Memorial Museum, Record Group-14.006*1; original is archived in Stadtarchiv Rostock, 1.1.8. Nr. 646.
46. Translated from copy in Archives du Centre de Documentation Juive Contemporaine, Paris, XXVb-55; also reprinted in Serge Klarsfeld, *Vichy-Auschwitz: Die Zusammenarbeit der deutschen und französischen Behörden bei der "Endlösung der Judenfrage" in Frankreich*, trans. Ahlrich Meyer (Nördlingen: DELPHI Politik, 1989), pp. 400–2.
47. Translated from the French in Serge Klarsfeld, *Vichy-Auschwitz: le rôle de Vichy dans la solution finale de la question juive en France – 1942* (Paris: Librairie Arthème Fayard, 1983), p. 364; original in Archives du Centre de Documentation Juive Contemporaine, Paris, AN-AGII 492.
48. Translated from Nuremberg document NO-3392; a facsimile is reprinted in Gerald Fleming, *Hitler and the Final Solution* (Berkeley, CA: University of California Press, 1984), plate 6, between pp. 92 and 93.
49. Translated from copy in Archives du Centre de Documentation Juive Contemporaine, Paris, XXVc-214; reprinted in Serge Klarsfeld, *Vichy-Auschwitz: Die Zusammenarbeit der deutschen und französischen Behörden*, pp. 501–2.
50. English translation printed in Tsvetan Todorov, *The Fragility of Goodness: Why Bulgaria's Jews Survived the Holocaust*, trans. Arthur Denner (Princeton, NJ: Princeton University Press, 2001), pp. 78–80.
51. Translated from Nuremberg document NO-007, USNA, RG 238; a facsimile is reprinted in *Archives of the Holocaust*, Vol. 2, pt. 2, p. 182; copy also printed in *Trial of the Major War Criminals before the International Military Tribunal*, Vol. 38, p. 210.
52. Translated from Nuremberg document PS-1919, reprinted in *Trial of the Major War Criminals before the International Military Tribunal*, Vol. 29, pp. 110–73, excerpts from pp. 121–3, 145–6, 172–3; this entire speech is on audiotape in USNA, RG 242. A different translation of a portion can be found in Noakes and Pridham, *Nazism 1919–1945: A History in Documents and Eyewitness Accounts*, Vol. 2, pp. 1199–1200.
53. Translated from Nuremberg document D-964, USNA, RG 238; also reprinted in *Trial of the Major War Criminals before the International Military Tribunal*, Vol. 36, pp. 94–7.
54. Translation of one item from Nuremberg document PS-4024, USNA, RG 238; also reprinted in *Trial of the Major War Criminals before the International Military Tribunal*, Vol. 34, pp. 82–9. This document is also labelled NO-059 (text) and NO-062 (list) as part of prosecution of Pohl, and a different translation appears in *Trials of War Criminals before the Nuernberg Military Tribunals under Control Council Law No. 10*, Vol. 5, pp. 725–31.

## 'Arbeit Macht Frei': Work and Death in Concentration Camps and Ghettos

55. Translated from copy in US Holocaust Memorial Museum, Record Group-04.015*01. A different translation appears in David A. Hackett (ed. and trans.), *The Buchenwald Report* (Boulder, CO: Westview Press, 1995), pp. 171–2; I am indebted to him for information about this document.
56. Reprinted in *Łódź Ghetto: Inside a Community under Siege*, compiled and edited by Alan Adelson and Robert Lapides (New York: Viking Penguin, 1989), pp. 206–7; Rumkowski's speeches were given in Yiddish.
57. Reprinted in Dawidowicz, *A Holocaust Reader*, pp. 334–6.

58. English translation printed in *Trials of War Criminals before the Nuernberg Military Tribunals under Control Council Law No. 10*, Vol. 9, p. 1218–19.
59. Translated from reprinted version in *Faschismus – Getto – Massenmord*, pp. 305–7; original in Archive of the Jewish Historical Institute in Warsaw, Ring II, Nr. 192. A different, edited translation is printed in Noakes and Pridham, *Nazism 1919–1945: A History in Documents and Eyewitness Accounts*, Vol. 2, pp. 1157–8.
60. English translation printed in *Łódź Ghetto: Inside a Community under Siege*, pp. 298–303.
61. English translation printed in *Notes from the Warsaw Ghetto: The Journal of Emmanuel Ringelblum*, trans. Jacob Sloan (New York: Schocken Books, 1974), pp. 338–44.
62. Translated from a copy, provided by David A. Hackett, of the original page in *Bericht über das Konzentrationslager Buchenwald bei Weimar*, prepared after liberation of the camp, in April–May, 1945, by an intelligence team led by Albert G. Rosenberg from Psychological Warfare Division, SHAEF, with the collaboration of a committee of Buchenwald survivors. A different translation is in Hackett, *The Buchenwald Report*, pp. 226–7.
63. Translated from portion of Nuremberg document PS-1061, USNA, RG 238; a different translation is printed in *Nazi Conspiracy and Aggression*, Vol. 3 (Washington, DC: United States Government Printing Office, 1946), pp. 767–8.
64. Translated from Hanna Lévy-Hass, *Vielleicht war das alles erst der Anfang: Tagebuch aus dem KZ Bergen-Belsen 1944–1945*, ed. Eike Geisel (Berlin: Rotbuch Verlag, 1979), pp. 54–6. A different translation, which does not closely follow the German text, can be found in Hanna Lévy-Hass, *Inside Belsen*, trans. Ronald Taylor (Brighton, UK: Harvester Press, 1982).
65. Translated from Nuremberg document PS-493 (also numbered D-964), USNA, RG 238; this portion is reprinted in *Trial of the Major War Criminals before the International Military Tribunal*, Vol. 26, pp. 65–85.
66. Translated from reprinted version in Erich Kosthorst and Bernd Walter, *Konzentrations- und Strafgefangenenlager im Dritten Reich: Beispiel Emsland; Zusatzteil: Kriegsgefangenenlager* (Düsseldorf: Droste Verlag, 1983), Vol. 1, pp. 442–7.

## Assembly Lines of Death: Extermination Camps

67. Translated from the German deposition by Kurt Gerstein, first given in French on 26 April 1945, and then in German on 4 May 1945, printed as 'Augenzeugenbericht zu den Massenvergasungen', *Vierteljahrshefte für Zeitgeschichte*, 1 (1953), pp. 185–94, excerpt pp. 187–93. The French statement is part of Nuremberg document PS-1553; a translated extract was published in *Trials of War Criminals before the Nuernberg Military Tribunals under Control Council Law No. 10*, Vol. 1, pp. 865–70. The two statements differ only in wording.
68. Excerpt from Filip Müller, *Eyewitness Auschwitz: Three Years in the Gas Chambers*, trans. Susanne Flatauer (New York: Stein and Day, 1979), pp. 35–9.
69. Excerpt from the account of Irene Schwarz (née Irka Anis), in Lore Shelley (ed.), *Secretaries of Death: Accounts by Former Prisoners who worked in the Gestapo of Auschwitz* (New York: Shengold Publishers, 1986), pp. 12–15.
70. English Translation printed in Alexander Donat (ed.), *The Death Camp Treblinka: A Documentary* (New York: Holocaust Library, 1979), pp. 224–30; originally translated from *Dos Naye Lebn*, Warsaw, 10 May 1945.

71. Translated from Nuremberg document NI-4829, USNA, RG 238. A different translation is reprinted in *Trials of War Criminals before the Nuernberg Military Tribunals under Control Council Law No. 10*, Vol. 8, pp. 575–8. The published record in this volume, including the reproduction of Tauber's testimony before the court, cites his first name as Arnost. The original document signed by Tauber shows his first name as Arnest.
72. Reprinted in Michael J. Neufeld and Michael Berenbaum (eds), *The Bombing of Auschwitz: Should the Allies Have Attempted It?* (New York: St. Martin's Press, 2000), pp. 267; original archived in Public Record Office, Kew, AIR 19/218, 46–7.
73. Excerpt from Judith Magyar Isaacson, *Seed of Sarah: Memoirs of a Survivor*, Second edition (Urbana, IL: University of Illinois Press, 1991), pp. 83–6; this chapter appeared in an earlier version as 'Seed of Sarah: A Memoir', *The Yale Review*, 73 (1984), pp. 349–53.
74. English translation printed in Ber Mark, *The Scrolls of Auschwitz*, trans. Sharon Neemani (Tel Aviv: Am Oved Publishers, 1985), p. 215; a copy of the Polish original on p. 285.

## The Aftermath

75. Reprinted in *Trial of the Major War Criminals before the International Military Tribunal*, Vol. 1, pp. 8–9.
76. Excerpted from 'Colonel Neave Report', *Trial of the Major War Criminals before the International Military Tribunal*, Vol. 42, pp. 1–153.
77. Translated from *Bundesgesetzblatt*, Teil I, Nr. 31, 29 June 1956, pp. 562–96, excerpts on pp. 562–72.
78. Reprinted in *LWF Report*, No. 19–20, February 1985, pp. 256–8.
79. Reprinted in Geoffrey H. Hartman (ed.), *Bitburg in Moral and Political Perspective* (Bloomington, IN: Indiana University Press, 1986), pp. 241–4.
80. Translated from reprinted version in *Deutschland Archiv*, 23, May 1990, pp. 794–5.

## The Holocaust in Contemporary Life

81. The entire White Paper has been reprinted on the website of the Norwegian Ministry of Justice and the Police since June 1998: http://odin.dep.no/jd/engelsk/publ/stprp/012005-030013
82. Excerpts from a translation from Arabic published by the Middle East Media Research Institute on its website as Special Dispatch No. 231, 20 June 2001: http://memri.org/bin/articles.cgi?Page=archives&Area=sd&ID=SP23101
83. Excerpts from the full judgment, which is printed on the website of the International Criminal Tribunal for the former Yugoslavia: http://www.un.org /icty/judgement.htm
84. Reprinted from a document in the author's possession.

# Bibliography


## Document Collections from the Nuremberg Trials

*Nazi Conspiracy and Aggression*, 11 vols. (Washington, DC: US Government Printing Office, 1946–1948); documentary evidence in English for Nuremberg Trial of 1945–1946.

*Trial of the Major War Criminals before the International Military Tribunal, Nuremberg, 14 November 1945 – 1 October 1946*, 42 vols. (Nuremberg, 1947–1949); trial proceedings and documents, many in German, for the Nuremberg Trial 1945–1946.

*Trials of War Criminals before the Nuernberg Military Tribunals under Control Council Law No. 10, Nuernberg October 1946 – April 1949*, 15 vols. (Washington, DC: US Government Printing Office, 1949); documentary evidence for trials conducted by US Military Court from 1946–1949.

## Other Document Collections in English

Arad, Yitzhak, Yisrael Gutman, and Abraham Margaliot (eds), *Documents on the Holocaust: Selected Sources on the Destruction of the Jews of Germany and Austria, Poland, and the Soviet Union* (Jerusalem: Yad Vashem, 1981).

*Archives of the Holocaust: An International Collection of Selected Documents*, Henry Friedlander and Sybil Milton, general editors (New York: Garland Publishing, Inc., 1989–1995); at least 25 volumes of reproductions of original documents held by important archives in Germany, Austria, Israel, Canada, and the US.

Dawidowicz, Lucy S (ed.), *A Holocaust Reader* (New York: Behrman House, Inc., 1976).

Donat, Alexander (ed.), *The Death Camp Treblinka: A Documentary* (New York: Holocaust Library, 1979).

Gurewitsch, Brana (ed.), *Mothers, Sisters, Resisters: Oral Histories of Women who Survived the Holocaust* (Tuscaloosa, AL : University of Alabama Press, 1998).

Hackett, David A. (ed. and trans.), *The Buchenwald Report* (Boulder, CO: Westview Press, 1995).

Hilberg, Raul (ed.), *Documents of Destruction: Germany and Jewry 1933–1945* (Chicago: Quadrangle Books, 1971).

Łódź *Ghetto: Inside a Community under Siege*, compiled and edited by Alan Adelson and Robert Lapides (New York: Viking Penguin, 1989).

Marrus, Michael R., *The Nuremberg War Crimes Trial 1945–46: A Documentary History* (Boston, MA: Bedford Books, 1997).

Mendelsohn, John, and Donald Detweiler (eds), *The Holocaust: Selected Documents in Eighteen Volumes* (New York: Garland Publishing, 1982).

Mendes-Flohr, Paul R., and Jehuda Reinharz (eds), *The Jew in the Modern World: A Documentary History* (New York: Oxford University Press, 1980).

Noakes, J., and G. Pridham (eds), *Nazism: A History in Documents and Eyewitness Accounts, 1919–1945*, 3 vols. (New York: Schocken Books, 1988).

Remak, Joachim (ed.), *The Nazi Years: A Documentary History* (New York: Simon and Schuster, 1969).

Shelley, Lore (ed.), *Secretaries of Death: Accounts by Former Prisoners who worked in the Gestapo of Auschwitz* (New York: Shengold Publishers, 1986).

Wyman, David A. (ed.), *America and the Holocaust* (New York: Garland, 1990); 13 volumes of documents related to the editor's book, *The Abandonment of the Jews.*

## Other Works Used

Aly, Götz, *Aktion T4 1939-1945: Die "Euthanasie"-Zentrale in der Tiergartenstraße 4* (Berlin: Edition Hentrich, 1987).

Aly, Götz, Peter Chroust and Christian Pross, *Cleansing the Fatherland: Nazi Medicine and Racial Hygiene,* trans. Belinda Cooper (Baltimore, MD: Johns Hopkins University Press, 1994).

Barber, John, and Mark Harrison, *The Soviet Home Front 1941–1945: A Social and Economic History of the USSR in World War II* (London: Longman, 1991).

Bartov, Omer, *Hitler's Army: Soldiers, Nazis and War in the Third Reich* (New York and Oxford: Oxford University Press, 1991).

Bauer, Yehuda, *A History of the Holocaust* (New York: Franklin Watts, 1982).

Bauer, Yehuda, *Rethinking the Holocaust* (New Haven, CT: Yale University Press, 2001).

Benz, Wolfgang, *Lexicon des Holocaust* (Munich: Verlag C. H. Beck, 2002).

Berenbaum, Michael, and Abraham J. Peck (eds), *The Holocaust and History: The Known, the Unknown, the Disputed, and the Reexamined* (Bloomington, IN: Indiana University Press, 1998).

Bessel, Richard, *Political Violence and the Rise of Nazism: The Storm Troopers in Eastern Germany 1925–1934* (New Haven, CT: Yale University Press, 1984).

Bessel, Richard, 'The Potempa Murder', *Central European History,* 10 (1977), pp. 241–54.

Binding, Professor Dr Karl, and Professor Dr Alfred Hoche, *Die Freigabe der Vernichtung lebensunwerten Lebens: Ihr Maß und ihre Form* (Leipzig: Verlag von Felix Meiner, 1920).

Borkin, Joseph, *The Crime and Punishment of I. G. Farben* (New York: The Free Press, 1978).

Breitman, Richard, *Official Secrets: What the Nazis Planned, What the British and Americans Knew* (New York: Hill and Wang, 1998).

Brennecke, Fritz, *Vom deutschen Volk und seinem Lebensraum: Handbuch für die Schulungsarbeit in der HJ* (Munich: Zentralverlag der NSDAP, 1937).

Broszat, Martin, Elke Fröhlich, and Falk Wiesemann (eds), *Bayern in der NS-Zeit: Soziale Lage und politisches Verhalten der Bevölkerung im Spiegel vertraulicher Berichte* (Munich: R. Oldenbourg Verlag, 1977).

Browning, Christopher R., *Ordinary Men: Reserve Police Battalion 101 and the Final Solution in Poland* (New York: HarperCollins, 1992).

Chazan, Robert, *European Jewry and the First Crusade* (Berkeley, CA: University of California Press, 1987).

Cooper, Matthew, *The Phantom War: The German Struggle against Soviet Partisans 1941–1944* (London: Macdonald & Jane's, 1979).

Czerniakow, Adam, *The Warsaw Diary of Adam Czerniakow: Prelude to Doom* (New York: Stein and Day, 1978).

Eisner, Jack, *The Survivor of the Holocaust* (New York: Kensington Books, 1980).

Evans, Richard, *Lying about Hitler: History, Holocaust, and the David Irving Trial* (New York: Basic Books, 2001).

*Faschismus – Getto – Massenmord: Dokumentation über Ausrottung und Widerstand der Juden in Polen während des zweiten Weltkrieges* (Berlin: Rütten und Loening, 1960).

Fleming, Gerald, *Hitler and the Final Solution* (Berkeley, CA: University of California Press, 1984).

Friedländer, Saul, *Nazi Germany and the Jews: Volume 1: The Years of Persecution, 1933–1939* (New York: HarperCollins, 1997).

Garbe, Detlef, *Zwischen Widerstand und Martyrium: Die Zeugen Jehovas im "Dritten Reich"*, Second edition (Munich: R. Oldenbourg Verlag, 1994).

Garz, Detlef, 'Nachwort', in Käthe Vordtriede, *"Es gibt Zeiten, in denen men welkt": Mein Leben in Deutschland vor und nach 1933* (Lengwil, Switzerland: Libelle Verlag, 1999), pp. 243–65.

Gilbert, Martin, *Atlas of the Holocaust* (Oxford and New York: Pergamon Press, 1988).

Goldhagen, Daniel Jonah, *Hitler's Willing Executioners: Ordinary Germans and the Holocaust* (New York: Alfred A. Knopf, 1996).

Gutman, Yisrael, *The Jews of Warsaw, 1939–1943: Ghetto, Underground, Revolt*, trans. Ina Friedman (Bloomington, IN: Indiana University Press, 1989).

Harris, James F., *The People Speak! Anti-Semitism and Emancipation in Nineteenth-Century Bavaria* (Ann Arbor, MI: University of Michigan Press, 1994).

Hartman, Geoffrey H. (ed.), *Bitburg in Moral and Political Perspective* (Bloomington, IN: Indiana University Press, 1986).

Hayes, Peter, *Industry and Ideology: IG Farben in the Nazi Era* (Cambridge: Cambridge University Press, 1987).

Herf, Jeffrey, *Divided Memory: The Nazi Past in the Two Germanys* (Cambridge, MA: Harvard University Press, 1997).

Hilberg, Raul, *The Destruction of the European Jews*, Second edition, 3 vols. (New York: Holmes & Meier, 1985).

Hilberg, Raul, *Sources of Holocaust Research: An Analysis* (Chicago: Ivan R. Dee, 2001).

Hitler, Adolf, *Mein Kampf*, trans. Ralph Manheim (Boston, MA: Houghton Mifflin, 1971).

Hochstadt, Steve, 'Review of Tim Cole, *Selling the Holocaust: From Auschwitz to Schindler: How History is Bought, Packaged, and Sold* (New York: Routledge, 1999)', *Journal of Holocaust Education*, 10, 2002.

Hochstadt, Steve, 'Review of Peter Novick, *The Holocaust in American Life* (New York: Houghton Mifflin Co., 1999)', *Modern Judaism*, 21, May 2001, pp. 184–92.

*The Holocaust Chronicle* (Lincolnwood, IL: Publications International, 2001).

Horwitz, Gordon J., *In the Shadow of Death: Living Outside the Gates of Mauthausen* (New York: Free Press, 1990).

Hubatsch, Walther, *Hindenburg und der Staat: Aus den Papieren des Generalfeldmarschalls und Reichspräsidenten von 1878 bis 1934* (Göttingen: Musterschmidt-Verlag, 1966).

Isaacson, Judith Magyar, *Seed of Sarah: Memoirs of a Survivor*, Second edition (Urbana, IL: University of Illinois Press, 1991).

Jansen, Christian, and Arno Weckbecker, *Der "Volksdeutsche Selbstschutz" in Polen 1939/40* (Munich: R. Oldenbourg Verlag, 1992).

Johnson, Eric A., *Nazi Terror: The Gestapo, Jews, and Ordinary Germans* (New York: Basic Books, 1999).

Kaplan, Marion A., *Between Dignity and Despair: Jewish Life in Nazi Germany* (New York: Oxford University Press, 1998).

Katz, Steven T., *The Holocaust in Historical Context*, Vol. 1 (New York: Oxford University Press, 1994).

Kershaw, Ian, *Hitler 1936–45: Nemesis* (New York: W.W. Norton and Company, 2000).

Kertzer, David I., *The Popes Against the Jews: The Vatican's Role in the Rise of Modern Anti-Semitism* (New York: Alfred A. Knopf, 2001).

Kogon, Eugen, *Der SS Staat: Das System der deutschen Konzentrationslager* (Munich: Wilhelm Heyne Verlag, 1974).

Langbein, Hermann, *Against All Hope: Resistance in the Nazi Concentration Camps 1938–1945*, trans. Harry Zohn (New York: Paragon House, 1994).

Laqueur, Walter (ed.), *The Holocaust Encyclopedia* (New Haven, CT: Yale University Press, 2001).

Levi, Primo, *The Drowned and the Saved*, trans. Raymond Rosenthal (New York: Vintage Books, 1989).

Lévy-Hass, Hanna, *Inside Belsen*, trans. Ronald Taylor (Brighton, UK: Harvester Press, 1982).

Lévy-Hass, Hanna, *Vielleicht war das alles erst der Anfang: Tagebuch aus dem KZ Bergen-Belsen 1944–1945*, ed. Eike Geisel (Berlin: Rotbuch Verlag, 1979).

Lewy, Guenter, *The Nazi Persecution of the Gypsies* (New York: Oxford University Press, 2000).

Lohfeld, Wiebke, *Im Dazwischen: Porträt der jüdischen und deutschen Ärztin Paula Tobias (1886–1970)* (Opladen: Leske und Budrich, 2003).

London, Louise, *Whitehall and the Jews, 1933–1948: British Immigration Policy, Jewish Refugees, and the Holocaust* (Cambridge: Cambridge University Press, 2000).

Luther, Martin, *Luther's Works*, Vol. 47, ed. Franklin Sherman (Philadelphia, PA: Fortress Press, 1971).

Mark, Ber, *The Scrolls of Auschwitz*, translated by Sharon Neemani (Tel Aviv: Am Oved Publishers, 1985).

Meynert, Joachim, and Friedhelm Schäffer, '*Die Juden in der Stadt Bielefeld während der Zeit des Nationalsozialismus*', *Bielefelder Beiträge zur Stadt- und Regionalgeschichte*, Vol. 3 (Bielefeld: 1983).

Michael, Robert, and Karin Doerr, *Nazi-Deutsch / Nazi German: An English Lexicon of the Language of the Third Reich* (Westport, CT: Greenwood Press, 2002).

Neufeld, Michael J., and Michael Berenbaum (eds), *The Bombing of Auschwitz: Should the Allies Have Attempted It?* (New York: St. Martin's Press, 2000).

Novick, Peter, *The Holocaust in American Life* (Boston, MA: Houghton Mifflin, 1999).

Ofer, Dalia, and Lenore J. Weitzman (eds), *Women in the Holocaust* (New Haven, CT: Yale University Press, 1998).

Plant, Richard, *The Pink Triangle: The Nazi War Against Homosexuals* (New York: Henry Holt and Co., 1986).

Pross, Christian, *Paying for the Past: The Struggle over Reparations for Surviving Victims of the Nazi Terror*, trans. Belinda Cooper (Baltimore, MD: Johns Hopkins University Press, 1998).

Ramet, Sabrina Petra, *Balkan Babel: The Disintegration of Yugoslavia from the Death of Tito to the War for Kosovo* (Boulder, CO: Westview Press, 1999).

Ringelblum, Emanuel, *Notes from the Warsaw Ghetto: The Journal of Emmanuel Ringelblum*, trans. Jacob Sloan (New York: Schocken Books, 1974).

Schweitzer, Arthur, *Big Business in the Third Reich* (Bloomington, IN: Indiana University Press, 1977).

Segev, Tom, *The Seventh Million: The Israelis and the Holocaust*, trans. Haim Watzman (New York: Hill and Wang, 1993).

Sereny, Gitta, *Into That Darkness: An Examination of Conscience* (London: André Deutsch, 1974).

Sierakowiak, Dawid, *The Diary of Dawid Sierakowiak: Five Notebooks from the Łódź Ghetto*, ed. Alan Adelson, trans. Kamil Turowski (New York: Oxford University Press, 1996).

Steiner, Jean-François, *Treblinka* (New York: Penguin Books USA, 1979).

Stow, Kenneth R., *Catholic Thought and Papal Jewry Policy 1555–1593* (New York: Jewish Theological Seminary of America, 1977).

Todorov, Tsvetan, *The Fragility of Goodness: Why Bulgaria's Jews Survived the Holocaust*, trans. Arthur Denner (Princeton, NJ: Princeton University Press, 2001).

Tuchel, Johannes (ed.), *"Kein Recht auf Leben": Beiträge und Dokumente zur Entrechtung und Vernichtung "lebensunwerten Lebens" im Nationalsozialismus* (Berlin: Wissenschaftlicher Autoren-Verlag, 1984).

Wilhelm, Hans-Heinrich, 'Wie geheim war die "Endlösung?' in Wolfgang Benz (ed.), *Miscellanea: Festschrift für Helmut Krausnick zum 75. Geburtstag* (Stuttgart: Deutsche Verlags-Anstalt, 1980).

Wistrich, Robert, *Muslim Anti-Semitism: A Clear and Present Danger* (New York: American Jewish Committee, 2002).

Witek, Hans, and Hans Safrian (eds), *Und keiner war dabei: Dokumente des alltäglichen Antisemitismus in Wien 1938* (Vienna: Picus Verlag, 1988).

Wood, E. Thomas and Stanislaw M. Jankowski, *Karski: How One Man Tried to Stop the Holocaust* (New York: Wiley and Sons, 1994).

Wyman, David S., *The Abandonment of the Jews: America and the Holocaust 1941–1945* (New York: Pantheon Books, 1984).

Yahil, Leni, *The Holocaust: The Fate of European Jewry, 1932–1945*, trans. Ina Friedman and Haya Galai (New York: Oxford University Press, 1990).

Zuccotti, Susan, *The Holocaust, the French and the Jews* (New York: Basic Books, 1993).

Zuccotti, Susan, *The Italians and the Holocaust: Persecution, Rescue, and Survival* (New York: Basic Books, 1987).

# Index


Abraham, SS Sergeant Hubert, 182
*Aktion Reinhardt* (Operation Reinhardt), 141, 170–8, 194, 223, 298
*Anschluss*, *see* Austria
antisemitism
  Arab, 285–7
  Austrian, 28, 58–62
  Christian, 7–21
  French, 159
  German, 22–8, 54–5, 261, 268, 270–1, 277–8
  Hungarian, 159
  Polish, 300
  in the United States, 271–2, 293
  *see also* Jews; Nazis
Arabs, 285–7
Arafat, Yasser, 278
archives, 2, 204
Argentina, 272
aryanization, 63–4, 69, 79–82, 268
Aumeier, Hans, 228–31
Auschwitz-Birkenau complex (camps), 117, 136, 145, 148–9, 157, 159, 178, 185, 213, 226, 227–31, 232–4, 242–5, 248–52, 253–4, 263, 265, 275, 281–2, 296–8
  bombing of, 246–7
  escapees from, 255
  liberation of, 260
  resistance in, 189, 240, 248–52, 254
  *Sonderkommandos*, 189, 253–4
  women's camp, 232–4, 248–52, 254
Austria, 181–2
  German annexation of (*Anschluss*), 56, 58–60, 62, 64, 74, 84
  popular support for persecution of Jews, 60–2, 63–4

Babi Yar massacre, 85, 110–11
Bartov, Omer, 115 n.1
Bauer, Yehuda, 299 n.5
Bavaria, 23–5, 37–8, 78 n.1, 272
Beaune-la-Rolande (camp), 147
Becker, Dr August, 95–7, 137–9
Belgrade, 118–19, 121–2, 139
Belorussia, 111, 117, 124–8, 162
Belzec (camp), 96–7, 141, 177, 223–6
Bergen-Belsen (camp), 182, 211–13, 231, 275, 297
Bergmann-Pohl, Sabina, 277
Berle, Adolf A., Jr, 106–7
Berlin, 28, 35, 38, 40, 43, 68–9, 75, 79, 83–4, 87, 95–6, 98, 103, 105, 110–11, 116, 118, 123, 137–8, 140, 149, 153, 198, 254, 277
Bialystok, Poland, 134, 152
Bielefeld, 75–7
Binding, Dr Karl, 29–31, 105
Birkenau, *see* Auschwitz
Bitburg, Germany, 273–5
Blobel, Paul, 111, 168–9
Böhme, Gen. Franz, 119, 122–3
Bohemia, *see* Czechoslovakia
Boris, King of Bulgaria, 160

Bouhler, Philipp, 140–1
Bosnia, 288–90
Brack, Viktor, 3, 95–7, 103–5, 116–17, 140–1, 294
Brandt, Dr Eduard, 108–9
Brandt, Dr Karl, 95–6, 141
Britain
  armed forces of, 168, 178, 182, 213, 221, 246–7
  immigration to, 67–9, 73–4, 83–4
  policies of government, 57, 67–9, 83–4, 246–7, 257–60
Browning, Christopher, xii, 128
Bruland, Bjarte, 284
Buchenwald (camp), 72, 76, 78, 179, 181–2, 206–7, 242, 275, 296
  resistance in, 181–2, 295
Budapest, 247
Bulgaria, 3, 136, 158–60
Buna (camp), 242–5, 253
*Bund deutscher Mädel* (BDM), 52–5
bystanders, 191, 231, 273, 298

camps, 56, 69, 72, 179, 261–4
  death marches from, 216, 221
  escapes from, 216, 235–40, 255
  forced labor in, 205–7, 218–20
  liberation of, 179, 182, 212–13, 260, 291, 297
  mortality in, 205–7
  resistance in, 48, 181–2, 234, 235–40, 248–52, 254, 295
  *Sonderkommandos*, 185, 189, 225, 253–4
  types of, 222
  women in, 211–13, 218–220, 227–9, 232–4, 248–52, 253–4
  *see also* killing, *and under specific camps*
Canada, 66, 272
Catholic Church
  opposes Nazis, 37–8, 76, 104–5, 109, 150–1, 156
  policies toward Jews, 16–21, 150–1, 156, 226, 231, 272
  *see also* Christianity
Central Office for Jewish Emigration, 132
Chamberlain, Neville, 74
Chelmno (camp), 136, 168, 184–5
children, *see* killing, of children
China, 5, 66, 83–4
Christian Democratic Party of West Germany, 268
Christianity
  antisemitism and, 7–21, 271–3, 293
  *see also* Catholic Church; Jehovah's Witnesses; Lutherans
Chrysostom, Saint John, 10
Churchill, Winston, 259, 285
Clement VIII, Pope, 18
compensation, 266–9, 278, 279, 280–4
Compiègne (camp), 147
Constantine I, Emperor, 10
Councils of Jewish Elders, *see* Jewish Councils
cremation, *see* killing, cremation and
Crimea, 114
Croatia, 136, 157, 290
Crusades, 8, 11–12
Czecher, Ella, 63–4, 295
Czechoslovakia, 73–4, 135, 242, 277
Czerniakow, Adam, 192–4

Dachau (camp), 41, 72, 206, 242
Dannecker, Theodor, 101, 146–9, 156, 159–60
Degesch, 117, 245
Denmark, 160
Dickmann, August, 48
Drancy (camp), 147
Dürrfeld, Walter, 243–5
Dunn, James C., 106–7

East Germany, *see* German Democratic Republic
Eden, Anthony, 246–7
Egypt, 285–7
Ethnic German Self-Defense (*Volksdeutsche Selbstschutz*), 91–2
Eichmann, Adolf, 62, 101, 116–17, 120, 136, 156, 189, 213, 255, 262–5
Einsatzgruppen, *see* Nazis, SS
emigration, *see* Jews; *Kindertransport*
England, *see* Britain
epidemics, *see* killing, by disease or epidemic
escapes from camps, 216, 235–40, 255
Essen, 190–1
Estonia, 102
'Eternal Jew, The', 199
eugenics, 22, 29–31, 44–6, 50–1, 55
'euthanasia' program, 22, 29–31, 95–7, 103–5, 108–9, 226
  *see* killing, of handicapped
evacuation, *see* Jews, expulsions and deportations of

Evans, Richard, 1
Evian conference (1938), 66, 67–9, 82
experimentation, medical, 140–1

Falco, Robert, 258, 260
Farben, I. G., 178, 242–5
Federal Republic of Germany, 101, 266–9, 273–5, 277
'final solution', 51, 119–20, 153, 262–3
  plans for, 87–9, 94, 116–17
  Wannsee Conference, 132–6, 296
  *see also* genocide; Holocaust; killing
flight tax (*Reichsfluchtsteuer*), 133
Flossenbürg (camp), 206, 296
France, 20, 66
  antisemitism in, 159
  camps in, 147, 182
  German occupation of, 148
  Nazis in, 265, 296
  rescue operations in, 65
  resistance in, 150–1, 156–7, 296
  Vichy government Jewish policies, 146–9, 150–1, 154–7
Frank, Anne, 213
Frank, Hans, 89, 94
Frankfurt, 231, 255
Franz, Kurt, 236–40
Frick, Wilhelm, 45

Gardelegen, 179
gas chambers, *see* killing, by gas
gender, 251–2
General Gouvernement, Poland, 89, 94, 98–100, 135, 170, 194
genocide, 289, 290, 297
  *see also* 'final solution'; Holocaust; killing
Germans
  Baltic, 98–102
  ethnic, 102, 170, 172, 178, 268
  Volhynian, 98–102
German Democratic Republic, 268, 276–8
Germany, 2–4, 20, 30, 48
  antisemitism in, 22–8, 54–5, 261, 268, 270–1, 277–8
  armed forces of, 90–2, 111, 112–14, 119–20, 121–3, 162, 188
    High Command of Army, 92, 112–14, 264
  eugenics in, 29–31
  Foreign Office, 69, 79–82, 118–20, 135, 136, 155–6, 262–5
  Labor Front, 190–1
  Poland and, 22
  popular support for persecution of Jews, 38, 39–41, 43, 57, 76–8, 85–6, 261
  resistance to Nazis, 91–2, 190–1, 225–6, 261–3, 266, 271
  reunification of, 269
  Weimar Republic of, 32–5, 43
Gerstein, Kurt, 222, 223–6
Gestapo, *see* Nazis
ghettos, 199
  earliest, in Italy, 16–18
  formation of, 87–9
  Jewish Councils of, *see* Jewish Councils
  Jewish police, 185, 188, 192–4, 201, 203
  in Poland, 87–9, 93–4, 199
  resistance in, 185–8, 199, 200–4
  in Serbia, 119
  in the Soviet Union, 125
  *see also specific cities*
Gineste, Marie-Rose, 151
Globocnik, Odilo, 3, 101, 140–2, 170–8, 194, 222
Goebbels, Josef, 129–31, 199, 294, 298
Göring, Hermann, 35, 132
Goldhagen, Daniel, 180 n.1
Grab, Walter, 56–7, 58–60, 69
Grabner, Maximilian, 228–31, 234
Great Britain, *see* Britain
Greece, 119, 157, 159
Gregory XIII, Pope, 18
Gross, Jan, 299 n.7
Gross-Rosen (camp), 206, 254
Gypsies, 5, 36, 46, 98–101, 118–20, 121–3, 253–4, 263, 269, 276, 279, 295–6

Hackett, David, xii
Hamber, Eduard and Philipp, 181–2, 295
Hamburg, 218–21
handicapped, 5, 29–31, 36, 95–7, 103–5, 108–9, 226, 295
Harris, James F., 25
Hebrews, *see* Jews
Hess, Rudolf, 45
Hessisch-Lichtenau (camp), 251
Heydrich, Reinhard, 62, 87–9, 98–100, 127, 132–6, 265
Hiemer, Ernst, 52–5
Hilberg, Raul, 4, 295, 297, 299 n.2
Himmler, Heinrich, 3, 41, 48, 49–51, 62, 89, 98–101, 127, 132, 136, 140–1,

152–3, 161–2, 163–5, 168, 170, 172, 177–8, 194, 205–6, 261–2, 265
Hinzert (camp), 206
Hitler, Adolf, 6, 45, 77, 101, 165, 228, 261, 264–5, 285–7, 298
  and Holocaust, 2, 3, 90–1, 96, 109, 114, 141, 152–3
  *Mein Kampf*, 2
  Reichstag speech of 30 January 1939, 129, 131
  rise to power, 35, 36
Hitler Youth (*Hitlerjugend*, HJ), 55, 178
Ho, Dr Feng Shan, 65–6
Hoche, Dr Alfred, 30–1, 105
Höfle, Hermann, 194
Hössler, Franz, 228–31
Holland, *see* Netherlands
Holocaust
  causes of, 3
  compensation for, 266–9, 278, 279, 280–4
  denial, 1, 85, 285–7
  industrial participation in, 85, 96, 137–9, 170–3, 178, 190–1, 220, 242–5, 247, 279
  knowledge of, 85, 129–31, 139, 190–1, 216, 262–3, 275, 298
  memorialization of, 291–3
  popular participation in, 61–2, 85–6, 103–5, 117, 216
  psychological explanations of, 2
  secrecy of, 85–6, 87, 92, 104–5, 114, 121, 124, 131, 132, 137–9, 161, 164, 168, 191, 222, 223, 240
  teaching about, xiii, 1, 292, 298
  as term, 5, 273, 295–7
homosexuals, 5, 36, 49–51, 56, 269, 296
Horthy, Miklós, 247
Hull, Cordell, 83–4
Hungary
  antisemitism in, 159
  deportations from, 136, 216, 246–7, 265

IBM, 279
Inter-Governmental Committee on Refugees, 67–9, 83
International Criminal Tribunal for the former Yugoslavia, 288–90
Iran, 287
Irving, David, 1
Isaacson, Judith Magyar, 248–52, 295
Israel, 60, 136, 189, 213, 252, 276–8, 287
  *see also* Palestine
Italy, 18, 20, 66, 154–7, 160, 226

Jackson, Robert H., 258, 260
Jehovah's Witnesses, 5, 36, 47–8, 56, 296
Jerusalem, 2, 11–12, 13, 60, 287
Jewish Agency in Palestine, 246
Jewish Councils, 88–9, 183–5
  resistance to, 183
  *see also specific cities*
Jews
  compensation to, 266–9, 278, 280–4
  cooperation in Holocaust, 183–5, 186–9, 192–4, 200, 294
  diaries of, 212–13, 252, 254
    *see also under individual documents*
  economic sanctions against, 38–45, 56, 61–2, 63–4, 79–82, 261, 280–4
  emancipation of, 23–5
  emigration of, 38, 40, 60, 62, 65–6, 67–9, 72, 74, 76, 83–4, 106–7, 132–3, 262, 267
  expulsions and deportations of, 12, 87–9, 98–101, 143–5, 146–9, 150–1, 154–7, 158–60, 183–5, 186, 192–4, 199, 227, 240, 247, 262, 265, 267, 280–1
  as forced laborers, 117, 135, 140–1, 145, 166–8, 181, 183–5, 192–4, 200, 232–4, 240, 242–5, 251, 279
  marking of, 17–18, 93–4, 129–31, 148, 261
  memoirs of, 41, 179, 251, 275
    *see also under individual documents*
  as partisans, 189, 273
  physical attacks on, 11–12, 37–8, 55, 56, 58–60, 69, 70–2, 75–8
  plunder of property of, 63–4, 79–82, 102, 122, 126–7, 143–5, 170–8, 193, 200, 222, 225, 261, 267–9
  resistance to persecution, 63–4, 145, 186–9, 199, 200–4, 208–10, 234, 235–40, 242, 248–52, 253–4, 273, 294–5
  as *Sonderkommandos*, 185, 189, 225, 253–4
  as witnesses, 228, 254, 273–5, 295, 297
  women, 5, 11–12, 17, 39–41, 63–4, 65, 72, 74, 76–8, 112, 117, 119–20, 140–1, 147, 195–9, 201, 224–5, 227–9, 232–4, 248–52, 253–4
  *see also* antisemitism; final solution; genocide; Holocaust; killing

Jordan, 287
*Judenräte, see* Jewish Councils
Juettner, 265

Kaltenbrunner, Ernst, 61
Karski, Jan, 255–6
Kaunas, *see* Kovno, Lithuania
Kertzer, David I., xii, 20
Kielce, Poland, pogrom, 297
Kiev, Ukraine, 111
  Babi Yar massacre, 85, 110–11, 168
killing
  by beating, 181
  by burning, 179–80, 296
  of children, 11–12, 85, 96, 109, 120, 122–3, 149, 165, 184, 224–5, 253–4
  cremation and, 104–5, 166–8, 230, 232, 296
  in Crusades, 11–12
  by disease or epidemic, 182, 195–9, 213, 218–21, 232–3
  by freezing, 243
  by gas, 95–7, 108–9, 116–17, 123, 136, 137–9, 145, 184–5, 194, 223–6, 227–31, 232–4, 240, 243–5, 247, 253–4, 285–6, 297
  of Gypsies, 5, 118–20, 121–3, 253–4, 263, 296–7
  of handicapped, 5, 29–31, 95–7, 103–5, 108–9, 111, 117, 141, 226, 297
  of homosexuals, 5, 49–51
  of Jews, 5, 11–12, 37–8, 72, 75–8, 92, 101, 110–11, 116–17, 118–20, 121–3, 124–8, 137–9, 140–1, 145, 152–3, 166–9, 170–8, 181–2, 183–5, 186–9, 194, 195–9, 216, 221, 223–6, 227–31, 243–5, 253–4, 261–4, 294–8
  of Jehovah's Witnesses, 5, 48
  of Polish civilians, 5, 86, 90–2, 101, 111, 166–8, 220, 296–8
  of Serbian communists, 118
  by shooting, 37–8, 90–2, 110–11, 118–20, 121–3, 124–8, 136, 152–3, 188–9, 201, 264, 296
  of Soviet citizens, 5, 110–11, 112–14, 117, 152–3, 162, 166–8, 190–1, 216, 220, 232, 260, 297
  by starvation, 191, 195–9, 213, 220, 242
  Wannsee Conference and, 132–6
  *see also* final solution; genocide; Holocaust; *specific camps and cities*
*Kindertransport*, 74
Klemperer, Victor, 6 n.7
Knochen, Helmut, 263, 265
Kogon, Eugen, 182
Kohn, Shalom, 235–40, 295
Korherr, Richard, 153
Kosovo, 290
Kovner, Abba, 186–9
Kovno (Kaunas), Lithuania, 66, 124
*Kristallnacht* pogrom, 56–7, 65–6, 70–2, 74, 75–8, 84, 265
KrstiD, Radislav, 288–90
Krüger, Friedrich Wilhelm, 98–100, 194, 208–10
Krupp, 190–1
Kube, Wilhelm, 127
Kursk, Soviet Union, 162

Lagstein, Dr Paul, 65–6
Langfuss, Leib, 253–4
language
  of Nazis, 4, 6 n.7, 36, 56–7, 78, 85–6, 109, 120, 138, 145, 153, 179, 210, 294–5
  of victims, 86, 179, 186, 199, 294–5
Lanzmann, Claude, 222
Latin America, 66, 272
Latvia, 102
Latvians as perpetrators, 209–10
Laval, Pierre, 156
League of German Girls, 52–5
Lemberg, *see* Lvov
Leningrad, 162
Levi, Primo, 185
Lévy-Hass, Hanna, 211–13
Linz, Austria, 217
Lithuania, 102, 123, 185–8
{ódΠ, Poland, 89, 93–4, 117, 240
Lohse, Hinrich, 117, 127
London Agreement (1945), 257–60
Long, Breckinridge, 106–7
Lublin, Poland, 171, 202, 206, 223
Lübeck, 221
Lueger, Karl, 28
Luther, Martin, 13–15, 270–1
Luther, Martin (Foreign Office), 120, 136
Lutherans, 255, 270–2
Lvov, Ukraine, 223–4

McCloy, John J., 247
Maine, US, 291–3
Majdanek (camp), 223, 260
Manstein, Gen. Erich von, 114, 264–5
Marr, Wilhelm, 28
Marrus, Michael R., 260 n.1
Mauthausen (camp), 206, 214–17, 297

medicine, *see* Nazis, SS doctors
*Mein Kampf* (Hitler), 2
Mengele, Dr Josef, 249–51, 274, 295
Milgram, Stanley, 6 n.2
Milosevic, Slobodan, 290
Mindus, Herbert, 181–2, 206
Minsk, Belorussia, 116–17, 124, 127, 188
Möller, Dr Wilhelm, 90–2, 226
Molotov, Vyacheslav, 259
Monowitz (camp), 242–5, 247
Moravia, *see* Czechoslovakia
Moscow Declaration (1943), 257, 259
Moslems, 114, 288–90
Müller, Filip, 227–31, 234, 298
Munich, 38, 55, 74, 265
Mussolini, Benito, 156

National Socialist German Workers' Party, *see* Nazis
Natzweiler (camp), 182, 206
Nazis
  attacks on political opponents, 35–8, 56, 62
  boycott of Jews, 38–41, 56
  falsification of records, 77–8, 104–5, 153, 214–16, 232–4, 294
  Gestapo, 50, 66, 75–8, 118–19, 143–5, 146–9, 154–6, 187, 200, 232–4, 262
  ideology of, 45–6, 49–51, 55, 101, 112–14, 129–31, 163–5, 199
  propaganda of, 4, 15, 53–5, 77–8, 114, 129–31
  rise to power, 36, 40
  SA (Sturmabteilung), 32–5, 37–41, 50, 56, 58–60, 70–2, 75, 166–8, 265, 298
  SS (Schutzstaffel or Defense Corps), 48, 49–50, 77, 90, 94, 98–101, 121, 161–2, 163–5, 167, 170–3, 177–8, 179, 194, 206–7, 208–10, 242–5, 254, 261–4, 273–5, 296
    camp guards, 181–2, 213, 219, 222, 223–6, 227–31, 232–4, 235–40, 263
    doctors, 51, 95–7, 109, 181, 205–7, 218–21, 232, 244
    Economic and Administrative Main Office, 170–2, 178, 205
    Einsatzgruppen, 87–9, 101, 110–11, 114, 117, 127–8, 162, 168–9, 188, 226, 264
    Higher SS and Police Leaders, 116, 161–2, 194, 208
    Order Police, 124–8, 161
    Reich Security Main Office (RHSA), 62, 111, 116–17, 136, 139, 156, 223, 262
    SD (Sicherheitsdienst), 76, 100, 110, 132–6, 161, 167, 262–5
    Security Police, 87–9, 100, 110, 132–6, 161, 262, 265
  trials of, *see* trials of perpetrators
Neave, Col. Airey, 261–5
Nebe, Arthur, 96
Netherlands, 190
Neuengamme (camp), 206, 218–21
New Testament, 7–10, 25
Nikitchenko, Iola, 259–60
Norway, 269, 279, 280–4
Novick, Peter, 295
Nuremberg, 55
  documents, 3, 4, 166–9, 207, 210, 216, 259–60, 265
  laws, 3, 44–6, 56, 61
  Party Congress, 43, 45
  trials, 3, 4, 55, 62, 141, 169, 178, 210, 244–5, 255, 257–60, 261–5, 290, 297

*On the Jews and Their Lies* (Luther), 13–15
Ohlendorf, Otto, 169, 264
Ohrdruf (camp), 182
Oradour-sur-Glane, France, 296
Oranienburg (Sachsenhausen, camp), 48, 72, 205–6, 218
Oreglia, Father Guiseppe, 20–1
Oslo, 284

Palestine, 66, 297
  *see also* Israel
Palestine Liberation Organization (PLO), 278
Paris, 146, 150, 157
partisans, 112–13, 152–3, 189, 273
Paul IV, Pope, 16–18, 45
Pellepoix, Darquier de, 146–8
Peshev, Dimitâr, 158–60
Pétain, Marshal Philippe, 148, 155–6
Pietzuch, Konrad, 32–5
Pister, SS Colonel Hermann, 207
Pithiviers (camp), 147
Pius V, Pope, 18
pogroms, *see* killing; *Kristallnacht*
Pohl, Oswald, 164, 178
Poland
  antisemitism in, 297
  deportations in, 87–9, 98–101

Germany and, 35, 277–8
Jews of, 26–7, 66, 87–9, 93–4, 98–101, 297
invasion of, 240
rescue in, 66
*see also specific camps and cities*
Ponary, Lithuania, 187, 189
Posen, 163–5, 168
Prague, 12, 73, 199, 223, 244, 254
Property Transfer Office (*Vermögensverkehrsstelle*), 64
'Protocols of the Elders of Zion', 287
Prützmann, Hans-Adolf, 161–2

quotas, *see* United States, immigration to

Rademacher, Franz, 118–20
Rauff, Walther, 137–9
Ravensbrück (camp), 206
Reagan, Ronald, 273–5
*'Das Reich'*, 129–31
Reich Representation of Jews in Germany (*Reichsvertretung*), 46
Reich Security Main Office (RSHA), *see* Nazis, SS
Reichenau, Field Marshall Walter von, 112–14
Reichsbank, 170, 171
Reichsführer-SS, *see* Himmler
Reichswehr, *see* Germany, armed forces of
Reisel, Beril, 284
resistance
in Auschwitz-Birkenau, 189, 240, 248–52, 254
in Buchenwald, 181–2, 295
in camps, 48, 181–2, 234, 235–40, 248–52, 254, 295
in France, 150–1, 156–7, 296
in Germany, 91–2, 190–1, 225–6, 261–3, 266, 271
in ghettos, 186–9, 199, 200–4
to Jewish Councils, 183
by Jews, 63–4, 186–9, 199, 200–4, 208–10, 234, 235–40, 242, 248–52, 273, 294–5
in Warsaw, 189, 200–4, 208–10, 237, 273, 295
by women, 63–4, 201, 212, 224, 234, 248–51
restitution, 266–9, 278, 279, 280–4
Riga, Latvia, 116–17, 138
Ringelblum, Emanuel, 200–4
La Riseria di San Sabba (camp), 226
Röhm, Ernst, 35, 50
Röthke, Heinz, 154–7
Romania, 118, 136, 154
Rome, 18, 157
Rondina, Father Saverio, 19–21
Roosevelt, Franklin D., 69, 84, 259, 285
Rosenberg, Alfred, 117, 127
Rostock, Germany, 143–5
Rublee, George, 68
Rumkowski, Mordechai Chaim, 183–5, 188
Rundstedt, Field Marshall Gerd von, 114
Rupprecht, Philip, 54

SA (*Sturmabteilung* or Storm Troops), *see* Nazis
Sachsenhausen (Oranienburg, camp), 48, 72, 205–6, 218
Saliège, Archbishop Jules-Gérard, 150–1
Schobert, SS Major Max, 207
Schwarz, Irene, 232–4
Schwerin (Mecklenburg), 143–5, 149
SD (Sicherheitsdienst), *see* Nazis, SS
Security Police, *see* Nazis, SS
Serbia, 97, 118–20, 121–3, 136, 290
Seyss-Inquart, Artur, 98–100
Shanghai, 5, 66, 83–4
'Shoah', 222
Sinclair, Sir Archibald, 246–7
Singer Oskar, 195–9
slavery, 269
Slovakia, 74, 136, 230
Sluzk, Belorussia, 86, 124–8, 226
Sobibor (camp), 97, 141, 177, 223, 240
Social Democratic Party of Germany, 42–3
Söhling, Fritz, 190–1
Sommer, SS Sergeant Martin, 182
*Sonderkommandos*, 185, 189, 225, 227–30
Soviet Union, 66, 161–2
armed forces of, 162, 216, 222, 240, 244, 254
citizens as slave laborers, 190–1
invasion of, 114, 119, 188, 260
killing in, 110–11, 112–14, 152–3, 278
partisans, 112–13, 152–3
policies of government, 257–60, 277
Spain, 20
Srebrenica, 288–90
SS (*Schutzstaffel* or Defense Corps), *see* Nazis
Stalin, Joseph, 163, 260
Stalingrad, 92, 156, 160, 162
Stangl, Franz, 141, 240
Stark, Hans, 231

sterilization, 30–1, 140–1
Stoecker, Adolf, 28
Streicher, Julius, 54–5
Stroop, Jürgen, 208–10
*'Der Stürmer'*, 54–5
Stutthof (camp), 206
Suchomel, Franz, 222
Sudetenland, 74
Sugihara, Chiune, 66
Sweden, 281
Switzerland, 279
Syria, 287
Szloma, Gol, 86, 166–8

T4, *see* 'euthanasia'
Talmud, 14, 18, 19–20, 54
Tauber, Arnest, 242–5
Terezin (Theresienstadt, camp), 253–4
Testa, 117
Thadden, Eberhard von, 262–5
Théas, Bishop Pierre-Marie, 150–1
Tobias, Dr Paula, 39–40
Torah, 10
Treblinka (camp), 97, 141, 160, 177, 194, 201, 204, 222, 223, 235–40, 242, 295
Treitschke, Heinrich von, 26–8, 54
trials of perpetrators, 3, 4, 55, 62, 98, 141, 168–9, 178, 207, 210, 213, 222, 231, 234, 244–5, 255–6, 257–60, 261–5, 290, 297
Turner, Harald, 118–20, 123

Uebelhoer, Friedrich, 93–4
Ukraine, 101, 114, 138, 152, 161–2, 296
Ukrainians as perpetrators, 201, 209–10, 224–5, 235–6, 240
Union General of Israelites of France, 147, 149
United Nations, 288–90
United States, 269
  antisemitism in, 272, 29
  armed forces of, 142, 160, 179, 182, 216, 247, 268, 296
  Holocaust Memorial Museum, 2, 275, 292
  immigration to, 40, 66, 67–9, 83–4, 106–7
  policies of government, 30, 57, 66, 67–9, 83–4, 106–7, 247, 257–60, 273–5, 292
Uruguay, 272
USSR, *see* Soviet Union

Vatican, *see* Catholic Church
Vélodrome d'Hiver, 147
Vichy, *see* France
Vienna, 58–60, 61–2, 63–4, 65–6, 181
Vilna, Lithuania, 117, 166–7, 186–9
  resistance in, 186–9

Wagner, Gen. Eduard, 114
Wagner, Richard, 22
Wannsee Conference, 132–6, 296
Warren, Avra, 107
Warsaw, Poland, 89, 199, 210, 223, 225, 237, 255
  Jewish Council of, 192–4, 204
  Oneg Shabbat archive, 200–4, 295
  resistance in, 189, 200–4, 208–10, 237, 273, 295
Wehrmacht, *see* Germany, armed forces of
Weimar Republic, 32–5, 43
Weizäcker, Richard von, 275
West Germany, *see* Federal Republic of Germany
Westlie, Bjorn, 284
Wetzel, Erhard, 116–17
White Russia, *see* Belorussia
Widmann, Dr Albert, 95–7
Wiesel, Elie, 251, 273–5, 297
Wilkomirski, Binjamin, 252
Winterton, Lord, 68
Wirth, Christian, 95–7, 141, 224–6
women
  Christian, and Jews, 17, 44–6
  as kapos, 232–3, 248–51
  as resisters, *see* resistance, by women
  as victims, 5, 11–12, 17, 39–40, 63–4, 65, 72, 74, 76–8, 112, 117, 119–20, 121–3, 140–1, 143, 147, 150, 165, 166, 187, 195–9, 201, 211–13, 218–20, 224–5, 226, 227–9, 232–4, 248–52, 253–4, 290, 296
Women's International Zionist Organization (WIZO), 74
Wyman, David, 107

Yad Vashem Memorial, 2, 66, 204
Yiddish, 8, 227
Yom HaShoah, 291–2
Yugoslavia, 111, 118–20, 121–3, 159, 212–13, 288–90, 296

Zionism, 74, 285–7
Zwartendijk, Jan, 66
Zyklon-B, 117, 219, 226, 245
  *see also* killing, by gas

CPSIA information can be obtained at www.ICGtesting.com
Printed in the USA
BVOW010409030812

296911BV00002B/2/A

9 780333 963456